DATE DUE

"Traitors to the Masculine Cause"

Men's Federation for Women's Suffrage.

II.

OBJECT.

To secure for Women the Parliamentary Vote as it is, or may be, secured for Men.

METHODS.

The Object of the Federation shall be promoted by the following methods, or any of them :

1. Action entirely independent of all political parties.
2. Opposition to whatever Government is in power until such time as the Franchise is secured for Women.
3. Participation in Parliamentary Elections in opposition to the Government Candidate, and independently of all other Candidates.
4. Vigorous agitation, such as is rendered necessary by the present outlawed position of Women.
5. The organising of Men all over the country to enable them to give adequate expression to their desire for the political freedom of Women.
6. Education of public opinion by all the usual methods, such as public meetings, demonstrations, debates, distribution of literature, newspaper correspondence, and deputations to public representatives.

MEMBERSHIP.

Men of all shades of political opinion, who endorse the Object and Methods of the Federation, and are prepared to sign the Membership Pledge, are eligible for membership.

There is an entrance fee of 1/-. No definite subscription is fixed, as it is known that all members will give to the full extent of their ability to further the campaign funds of the Federation.

[EXTRACT FROM RULES.—"A General Meeting of the Federation shall be held annually in March for the election of Officers and a Committee, and the transaction of other necessary business."]

MEMBERSHIP PLEDGE.

I hereby apply for Membership of the Men's Federation for Women's Suffrage, of which I endorse the constitution and rules as herein set forth. I pledge myself to work in every possible way for the fulfilment of the Object of the Federation.

Signature ....

Full Permanent Address ....

....
(Add name of Town)

Date.........................191...

This Form to be posted, with the Entrance Fee of 1/-, to the Hon. Secretary, Men's Federation for Women's Suffrage, 23, St. Paul's Chambers, Ludgate Hill, E.C.

N.B.—Please write distinctly.

Plate 1. Membership Application for Men's Federation for Women's Suffrage. Used with the permission of the London Museum, London.

"Traitors to the Masculine Cause"

The Men's Campaigns for Women's Rights

Sylvia Strauss

Contributions in Women's Studies, Number 35

GREENWOOD PRESS

WESTPORT, CONNECTICUT · LONDON, ENGLAND

‡ 8110468
DLC

10-26-83 A+

Library of Congress Cataloging in Publication Data

Strauss, Sylvia.
  Traitors to the masculine cause.

  (Contributions in Women's Studies, ISSN 0147-104X ;
no. 35)
  Bibliography: p.
  Includes index.
  1. Feminists—History—19th century. 2. Suffrage—
History—19th century. 3. Humanism—History—19th
century. I. Title. II. Title: Men's campaigns for
women's rights. III. Series.
HQ1154.S69   305.4′2   81-20299
ISBN 0-313-22238-X (lib. bdg.)   AACR2

Library of Congress Catalog Card Number: 81-20299
ISBN: 0-313-22238-X
ISSN: 0147-104X

First published in 1982

Greenwood Press
A division of Congressional Information Service, Inc.
88 Post Road West
Westport, Connecticut 06881

Printed in the United States of America

10 9 8 7 6 5 4 3 2 1

TO MY MOTHER, FOR HER UNFAILING SUPPORT
OF ALL MY ENDEAVORS

CONTENTS

ILLUSTRATIONS

PREFACE

When one studies a subject that has been neglected in the past, writing about it provides its own justification but presents other problems. One desires to be comprehensive and inevitably questions arise. Why include this person and not that one? Why a chapter on literary figures? Criteria had to be established; I realized that to include everyone who was absorbed by the woman's question in the nineteenth century would result in a tome of unmanageable proportions. My criteria were first, that each man I included had to not only comment or make observations on women's status, but had to think of himself as a feminist; and second, that each had to be in some sense an activist—in putting forth a program and/or supporting women's rights. Thus, the literary figures included all sought to shape one facet—the intellectual one—of the new woman. All were conscious reformers, and all supported women's rights in some concrete way, for example, the vote. In that they were "campaigners" as well as interested observers or sympathizers, the same can be said for all the men discussed. Frequently their treason is measured by the outcry it produced from established authority.

In tracing a tradition over the course of more than one hundred years, one is likely to come across schisms and shifts of emphasis, both ideological and programmatic. The major shift I came across occurred toward the end of the nineteenth century and involved those men who have come to be called domestic feminists—social scientists who saw women primarily as sexual beings whose biology was their destiny. They believed that women could improve their status and enhance their value to society by performing more expertly in their traditional sphere.

Those men I refer to as philosophical feminists prized women's intellect and those qualities of mind and temperament which they believed inhered in women's nature and comprised a female culture. They gave these traits an overriding social import and considered women to be more democratic, more moral, more sensitive to those in distress, and respectful of human life than men. Women were thus regarded as civilizers. Philosophical feminism was broad enough to include secular rationalists, religious believers, and men from all shades of the political spectrum. It emerged as the mainstream of male feminism and its exponents remained remarkably consistent and tenacious in their treason to masculinity well into the twentieth century. The endurance of the male feminist tradition was the result of the adoption of a feminist perspective by such influential intellectual circles as the Owenites and the Millites. These groups surely deserve further study.

The philosophical feminists' theory that biological gender differences have psychological consequences has become highly politicized. Their conclusions were based on reason and empirical evidence. The philosophical feminists did not discount conditioning as significant in sex role definitions since the ability to reason was considered inherent in all humankind. However, they believed that conditioning accounted for the more superficial personality traits, often gender-connected, such as submissiveness and dependence in women. The characterological traits which had wide-ranging social and political ramifications were thought to be related to women's reproductive functions, and, while subject to modifications, were viewed as innate.

The theory of innateness was abandoned by American feminists who staked their political future on the assumption that gender traits, even including the motherhood instinct, are acquired through cultural influences. As the American feminist movement goes into the second stage—somewhat chastened by recent events—the innateness conditioning controversy is sure to be the subject of intense debate. It is my hope that this work will provide some necessary background for the debate.

ACKNOWLEDGMENTS

I would like to extend my appreciation to the Librarians of the Museum of London for the indispensable help they gave in providing material on the male suffragettes. My gratitude also to the Research Groups of the Institute for Research in History for the exchange of ideas that acted as a constant stimulus, and for the consistent support of the institute's Executive Director, Marjorie Lightman. For helping me fill in gaps on the men involved in the Contagious Diseases Repeal campaign, my thanks to Judith Walkowitz, Professor of History at Rutgers University. The insights of Helene Mann, Librarian in the Upper Darby, Pennsylvania, school system proved to be very valuable, and I wish to acknowledge my debt. For their cooperation, I am very appreciative of the students in my Spring, 1981 class in Women in the Modern Age.

INTRODUCTION

Where are the men in women's history? Are women historians perpetuating the same kinds of distortions perpetrated by those historians who wrote histories devoid of women? The field of women's studies has produced a considerable body of writing in the past fifteen years. In general, the majority of men are depicted as dyed-in-the-wool patriarchs determined to hold on to their historic prerogatives at all costs. This perception will not be challenged as a result of this study. It is the tendency to portray those men who did support women's rights as, in the main, devoted husbands loyally falling in step behind their strong-minded wives that is the issue here. Examination reveals that this was often not the case; reform-minded men promoted, organized, and financed many of the campaigns for women's rights that were fought in the nineteenth and early twentieth century.

To say the foregoing is not in any way to diminish the women honored by contemporary feminists as their founding mothers. It is merely to acknowledge in a palpable way the enormous handicaps that legal disabilities and lack of educational opportunities imposed on women. Indeed, many of the early female reformers, bound by their own limited horizons, could hardly conceive of any woman stepping beyond her sphere, and sought only to widen that sphere in their efforts at reform.

The male campaigns for women's rights were part of a humanitarian movement that embraced all oppressed groups. The male feminists gave priority to women's liberation because women constituted at least half the population; women's disabilities were universal and of the longest duration. It was women who shaped men in their cradles, and it was with women that men were expected to form their most intimate and profound relationships.

Men's activism on women's behalf was coterminous with a protest against various manifestations of the masculine cause. It was one of the male feminists who labelled his breed "traitors to the masculine cause" and saw their ranks growing as male pretensions to dominance were exposed. These traitors to the masculine cause were bound together by a conviction that the extension of rights to women was the test a civilization had to meet to be worthy of the name, and they made women's rights a criterion for judging mankind's progress.

In a larger context, the traitors were dissidents against patriarchal authority in government, religion, the economic world, and the family itself. They were iconoclasts who expressed democratic ideals in an age of privilege; they were rationalists, atheists, and nonconformists who often went to prison for their defiance of established authority; they were socialists who believed that human nature was cooperative when individualistic capitalism was being touted as the vehicle to progress. Their feminism was a function of their belief that women's values were needed to balance the masculine culture which inhered in all the institutions they challenged, and which they identified as the masculine cause.

Treason to masculinity had its roots in the eighteenth-century Enlightenment. It was a middle-class phenomenon and had its most devoted adherents in England and the United States. In the wake of the English Revolution of 1689, the middle class, reacting against the manners and morals of a privileged aristocracy they held in contempt, evolved an ethic more suited to their newly acquired economic importance—one which extolled morality, sobriety, thrift, and reason. They were somewhat disconcerted that their wives aped the behavior and attitudes of the aristocracy in their superficiality and their trivial interests. Women's education was the first reform to which they addressed themselves, on the rationalist's assumption that character was not innate but was a product of conditioning. Mary Wollstonecraft's *Vindication of the Rights of Women* was unique in that it was written by a woman. The campaign urging women to cultivate their intellects and submerge their sexuality, however, was launched much earlier by male reformers.

The masculine cause against which the traitors first revolted in the French and American revolutions was authoritarian government, its allies a hierarchical church and an effete, parasitical aristocracy whose privileges were acquired by birth. Along with the English radicals, the eighteenth-century revolutionaries articulated the case against despotism and for equal rights. In their search for justice, the radicals eventually "turned their searchlights upon their own homes and a long struggle began—the struggle for women's legal and political rights."[1] They saw the domestic tyranny of the husband in the family as a microcosm of the absolute authority exercised by kings in the larger society. The feminist reformers concluded that despotism could never be abolished if it were condoned in every household through the vows a woman made when she married.

Enlightenment philosophes laid the basis for a feminist philosophy when they examined male and female nature and found them to be fundamentally different, with the female's traits being determined by her reproductive functions and the male's characteristics by his sexual drives. A longstanding theory of innateness, that maintained that women's nature was primarily sexual and therefore inferior, was cast into doubt when Edmund Burke and Thomas Malthus insisted that it was men who were driven by their sexual passions and that these predominated over their reasonable faculties. The theory of female inferiority was left an inadvertent casualty of irrefutable evidence of the intensity of male sexual drives.

The male feminists came full circle when they suggested that women were potentially the more reasonable sex. Since reason was considered a prerequisite for morality they were also thought to be the more moral sex.

As the male feminists elaborated on male-female differences, they saw men as primarily aggressive, authoritarian, egoistic, and materialistic, while women were relatively more cooperative, pacific, democratic, and idealistic. Convinced that the difference between male and female culture had social and political significance and that male traits were responsible for the ills (for example, wars) that hindered progress, they wanted to see women, who possessed the civilizing and humanizing characteristics, gain power and influence. Sigmund Freud accomplished a profound intellectual revolution no less than a sexual revolution when he succeeded in reversing the valuation the male feminists placed on male and female traits, putting a positive stamp on the male traits they considered destructive and a negative one on female characteristics that they valued.

Treason to masculinity flourished during the nineteenth century, and its various manifestations are an unexplored aspect of the Victorian age. The Victorian period is one of the most compelling for study precisely because it was so rich in ideas. It is perhaps not surprising that some of these ideas which challenge the Victorian stereotype have been neglected. The Victorians at once attract and repel individuals of the twentieth century, who are still haunted by the moral dogmas propounded by the Victorians and are still reacting against them. Viewed through the Marxist-Freudian prism that people in the twentieth century use to look at the past, the middle-class Victorians emerge as smugly secure in their financial and political predominance, putting forth a hypocritical and self-serving morality that enabled them to exploit the working classes economically, and women sexually as well as economica   They established and used their power to enforce a sex code repressive in the extreme and productive of a variety of physical and emotional disorders in women. For Marxists, revolution was the proper and inevitable response to the depredations of the middle class, and one which in any case they brought on themselves. For Freudians, the sexual revolution which is viewed as having freed men and women from a dark age of ignorance and repression is in and of itself enough to justify their faith in modernism.

It is a central thesis of this work that the Marxist-Freudian perspective does not do justice to the diversity and complexity of the moral idealism of the Victorians. An examination of the traitors to masculinity lends another dimension to the period. The traitor to masculinity felt that, far from living in a stable society, the center of a world empire, he was sitting on a powder keg. He was keenly aware that all the promising developments that, according to the Enlightenment philosophes, foreshadowed unending progress, could backfire, and as easily cause disaster. To the extent that the masculine cause became identified with individualistic capitalism and its ethos of unlimited profits, he saw the widening disparity between rich and poor as ominous as well as unjust—a phenomenon which could only lead to revolutionary violence. The Owenites proposed cooperative socialism as a solution and made feminism an integral part of their program. Their propagation of the use of moral force, or nonviolence, to attain their ends was virtually synonymous with woman's power.

The optimism of the Enlightenment philosophes was predicated on the availability of unlimited natural resources that need only be tapped, and on a theory of human nature that elevated reason as the preeminent faculty of the human species. When the feminist reformers became aware that at least one resource—land—was in limited supply, and that the male sex drive—more powerful than reason and associated with the masculine cause—might precipitate a population explosion intolerably straining resources, their feminism found a new outlet in the advocacy of a woman's right to control her body.

The disparate elements of male feminism came together in the person of John Stuart Mill, who was involved in all the campaigns for women's rights. A conviction that women must have voting rights, not only in their own interests but in society's, led Mill to spearhead the drive. His efforts, which included establishing the historical validity of the cause, recruiting men and women, and organizing pressure groups, were fundamental to eventual success. Both feminists and antifeminists have sought to attribute Mill's feminism and his feminist activities to the influence of his wife, Harriet Taylor Mill; the former to give the feminist movement a distinctively female parentage; the latter to taint Mill's entire liberal philosophy with feminism as a means of discrediting it. Indeed, feminism did suffuse the entire corpus of Mill's work, but it antedated his acquaintance with Harriet Mill and was part of his utilitarian background. Feminism was the basis of the radicalism with which he tried to infuse the Liberal party, and made him the acknowledged leader of a group of parliamentarians who would not violate their feminist principles even for party loyalty. The fact that Mill failed in his aim had significant repercussions for the Liberal party and for the politics of the late nineteenth and early twentieth centuries.

The social histories that are the current vogue have increased awareness of the common people and made them a central focus of historical study. But in large measure they have followed the anti-ideological tendencies of the present period by positing impersonal forces, for example, modernization, to account for far-reaching changes. The individual and the power of ideas thus get lost in the shuffle. The male feminists were unabashed ideologues who believed that ideas could change the world more effectively and enduringly than force. The feminist ideas they espoused were compelling enough to crisscross the Atlantic Ocean and be enriched and amplified by Englishmen and Americans.

Whether they considered themselves secular rationalists or religious believers, the traitors to masculinity were implacable moralists who made no distinction between public and private morality. The "sensualist" who exploited women to satisfy his lust was as reprehensible as the capitalist or the politician who betrayed the public interest to satisfy his greed. This more than anything else makes these reformers strangers to the individuals of the twentieth century whose concept of morality is relative and eminently flexible. Indeed, the feminist reformers' hope for progress was dependent on an improvement in morality. As feminists they did not think this hope a utopian one which required a change in human nature. Historically, men had forced women to conform to a higher standard of morality than they felt incumbent on themselves. The feminist reformers' purposes would have been served if men regarded the standard of morality they imposed on women as their own as well. Women's greater influence and power was intended to accomplish this.

Herbert Butterfield has called attention to the fact that historians tend to dwell on those personalities and movements that won in the struggles of the past. He insisted that the losers be given their due since the outcome of such conflicts is never preordained. It was during the much maligned Victorian Age that the masculine cause was defined as an obstacle to social progress, and for the first time in history, seriously challenged. The assault on the citadels of the masculine cause was a determined one, and the issue hung in the balance until World War I. One cannot argue that male imperatives have prevailed despite the advances women have won in educational opportunities and legal rights. But the fact that the traitors to masculinity lost does not mean they deserved to lose; another fallacy of those who identify with the victors. In retrospect the male feminists' fears of heightened violence, both domestic and international, have indeed materialized, and mankind would appear to be the poorer for their defeat.

The tradition they hoped to fulfill and which best embodies the moral idealism of the male feminists is humanism, in both its secular and religious manifestations. To rediscover the traitors to masculinity is to refamiliarize oneself with a tradition that stressed cooperation in lieu of competition; refused to measure progress by advances in technology; and emphasized priorities that were social rather than egoistic. Perhaps there is no better time to reclaim a heritage which predicated its humanistic concerns on feminine values than the present, when the moral idealism of these men has been preempted by patriarchal stalwarts of the right whose aim is to curtail the free flow of ideas which nourished feminism, who glorify all the acquisitive instincts, and whose ultimate salvation is in military might.

NOTE

1. Joseph McCabe, *The Religion of Women: An Historical Study* (London: Watts & Co., 1908), p. 51.

"Traitors to the Masculine Cause"

FATHERS OF FEMINISM *1*

As feminists of the twentieth century began to look back at the origins of their movement, they saw it emerging from the writings of Mary Wollstonecraft and Mercy Otis Warren, with the leadership exerted by Elizabeth Cady Stanton, Susan B. Anthony, Millicent Fawcett, and Emmeline Pankhurst. These women are now part of the pantheon of the mothers of feminism, their lives and deeds significant to the women's movement and to all those who identify with feminism. That none of them laid claim in their writings or memoirs to the distinction of giving birth to the women's movement says a great deal about their self-image, their status, and the relationship between men and women in the centuries past. Theirs was a self-image that could not encompass a concept of motherhood other than the biological one, which most of these women had fulfilled. Their economic dependence led to emotional dependence. In male-female relationships, as exemplified in the marriage bond, the male was the natural leader, the female the tireless worker in a cause—the family—that transcended self-interest.

Since women's intellectual deprivation and economic dependence would have made it almost impossible for them to mount the organizational skills to launch a women's movement and to fund it, it is not unreasonable that the historic movement that changed women's lives had no acknowledged mothers, but it did have a proud father in the person of George Jacob Holyoake. Holyoake, closely associated with Robert Owen and the communitarian tradition, claimed parentage in his memoirs, *Sixty Years of an Agitator's Life*, published in 1893, when the struggle for equal rights was well under way and attracting a great deal of public attention. In his memoirs, Holyoake recalled that as late as 1840 there was no sign of a women's movement, even though the systematic exclusion of women from the political process—confirmed in England by the Reform Bill of 1832[1] —and the thoroughgoing exploitation of women in factories by unscrupulous industrialists and in the home by tyrannical husbands were matters of record. In 1840, married women in both England and the United States were not considered legal persons. They could not sue nor be sued; could not sign a contract nor make a will; could not own property in their own right. The woman was obliged to live

Plate 2. Robert Owen by John Cranach, painted in Washington, D.C. in 1845. Credit: Frick Art Reference Library. In collection of the Indiana Historical Society, Indianapolis. Used with permission.

wherever her husband chose. Her wages were not her own; her husband had the right to collect his wife's wages from her employer, and anything she purchased with her earnings belonged to him. In 1840, women could not initiate a divorce. The husband had a legal right to imprison his wife and to chastise her "with a stick no thicker that his thumb." If a woman deserted her husband, anyone who harbored her or assisted her could be sued by him. By deserting him, no matter what the provocation, she forfeited all claim to maintenance or to custody of her children. But if she was the deserted party she had no power to obtain maintenance without proving her need in the courts, and could not recover property that had belonged to her at the time of the marriage. Adultery on the part of the wife enabled the husband to obtain judicial separation and terminated his legal responsibility to maintain her; infidelity on the part of the husband, however, was not considered sufficient justification to enable her to separate from him. To add small indignities to large, a wife could not even bring friends to her home without the husband's permission.

Holyoake marvelled that women who knew of the wrongs being perpetrated against them did not have the esprit de corps to unite against their oppressors as men had in a variety of political movements. "Why have they not formed a society for their own protection?" he asked. There were other suggestions, phrased as rhetorical questions: "If they want political rights why do they not themselves ask for them?" "Where are the women's political unions, self-originated and self-sustained?" The questions evolved into solutions as he recommended that women establish their own journals, staffed by women rather than by men, which was rarely the case in 1840.[2] He further challenged women "to take their affairs into their own hands" ". . . to draw up a list of their legal disabilities and then to take the constitutional means of redress by forming societies and organizing public meetings."[3]

Holyoake is important for the note of urgency he sounded and because he followed through by exerting continuous pressure through his journal, *The Free Press*. But his feminism and his prescription for organizing, propagandizing, and agitating, along with the self-help philosophy behind it, were part of a radical tradition that had its roots in the Enlightenment and in the revolutionary turmoil of the late eighteenth century.

It was the abiding faith of the French philosophes of the Enlightenment that mankind was perfectible. Alone of all the species, mankind could reason, and reason could be fostered through education. The philosophes were firmly on the side of nurture rather than nature. They refused to believe that individuals entered the world with innate mental capacities fixed by nature. Helvetius proclaimed that mind was the creation of education and experience and that despotism dehumanized the human character. He further recognized that despotism was not restricted to the power of kings over their subjects, but extended to the power of men over women in general. He directly challenged the prevailing view that it was the prime function of a woman to affirm a man's superiority through her submissiveness, passivity, and chastity, and he did so in the name of progress:

The domestic subjection of wives to husbands, the education of girls in a specialized morality, the fetters of custom and fashion, the experience of economic dependence, the denial of every noble stimulus to thought and action, these causes were making a sex condemned to an artificial inferiority and induced parasitism. The amiable weaknesses of women fostered characteristics of a class bred in subjection, the trading habits of a profession which had bent all its faculties to the art of pleasing.[4]

To Helvetius, the result of women's upbringing was to place them in the same category as the aristocrats of eighteenth-century France. Like the aristocrats they were mannered, genteel toys, and a hindrance to the changes requisite for the rational utopias that the philosophes projected for the future. Helvetius was convinced that this state of affairs could be changed by the liberating effects of education, and he advocated it for women.

Baron d'Holbach exposed the universality of male dominance and implied that it had unfortunate effects on both males and females. He wrote:

In all the countries of the world the lot of women is to submit to tyranny. The savage makes a slave of his mate and carries his contempt for her to the point of cruelty. For the jealous and voluptuous Asiatic, women are but the sensual instruments of his secret pleasure. Does the European, in spite of the apparent deference he affects towards women really treat them with more respect? While we refuse them sensible education, while we allow them to busy themselves only with playthings and fashions and adornments, while we seek to inspire them only with the taste for frivolous accomplishments, do we not show our real contempt while we mask it with a show of deference and respect?[5]

Holbach was critical of the absurdities of women's education, insisting that it perpetuated their helplessness. It left marriage as the only career open to women and these unions were based not on love but on mercenary considerations. A loveless marriage of convenience was a burden both for the woman and the man. Holbach pointed out that esteem was essential in a good relationship and asked, "But how is one to esteem a mind steeped in trivialities?" To restrain excessive male power Holbach wanted to adopt Plato's idea that women should participate in politics, but lamented that the results of allowing the corrupt women of his time any power would be catastrophic.

The feminist reformers not only criticized the political, social, and economic institutions of divine right monarchy; they also cast a baleful eye on the sexual dissipation endemic among their royal and aristocratic masters. Holbach believed that the result of distorted and unequal marriage relationships was fashionable conjugal infidelity whereby both partners revealed their scorn for one another. Holbach showed an especial concern about the libertinism of aristocratic men who did not restrict their sexual peccadilloes to their own class, and worried about the dangers—for example, venereal disease—to which working-class girls were exposed by their seducers. He injected the theme of moral reform when he suggested that seduction of innocent girls be punished as a crime no less serious than murder.

The reformist impulses of Enlightenment feminists made equal education for males and females a central objective. Their assumptions as well as their ultimate goals were clearly set forth by the Marquis de Condorcet in *Sur L'Instruction Publique* (1792). Condorcet recommended to the French legislature, which had undertaken to reform French society in the wake of the French Revolution, a system of national education that would be the same for both sexes. He avowed that women had the same natural right to knowledge and enlightenment as men, and he believed that women who had an intellectual background could render useful service to society. Moreover, Condorcet was convinced that the preservation of revolutionary ideals made it essential that women be educated. He pointed out that mothers are the first teachers of their children, and that mothers who remained ignorant would be regarded with contempt by their sons; moreover, grown men would not retain their intellectual vigor if they could not share their intellectual life with their wives. Condorcet also revealed certain moral priorities in his contention that coeducation, where males and females learn the same subjects and relate on the basis of common interests, would further morality because males would not see females exclusively as sex objects nor would females see males merely as foils for their wiles. Condorcet enunciated a principle to which all the subsequent male feminists sedulously adhered—that it was dangerous for a society with democratic ideals to allow inequality to survive between men and women in the family context. The last vestiges of divine right kingship could never be extirpated among men who knew that they could reign as absolute monarchs in the home.

The French concern for women's low estate echoed that of the English rationalists in the wake of the Revolution of 1689. Shortly after John Locke proclaimed experience to be crucial in the shaping of character, Daniel Defoe wrote an *Essay on Projects*, which in 1697 became his first published work. Defoe (1659-1731) denounced those who deprive women of a meaningful education and then go on to criticize them for being foolish:

We reproach the sex every day with folly and impertinence; while I am confident had they the advantages of education equal to us they would be guilty of less than ourselves. . . . To those whose genius would lead them to it, I would deny no sort of learning but the chief thing in general is to cultivate the understanding of the sex, that they may be capable of all sorts of conversation; that their parts and judgment being improved, they may be as profitable in their conversation as they are pleasant. [Defoe was convinced] that all the world are mistaken in their practice about women. For I cannot think that God Almighty ever made so delicate, so glorious creatures, and furnished them with such charms, so agreeable and delightful to mankind; with souls capable of the same accomplishments with men; and all to be only stewards of our houses, cooks, and slaves. I would have men take women for companions, and educate them to be fit for it.[6]

Significantly, Defoe subtitled his work *Effectual Ways for Advancing the Interests of the Nation.*

Popular journals of the eighteenth century, which were opinion molders for the rising middle class, took up the theme of improving women's education. In their publication, *The Tattler*, Joseph Addison (1672-1719) and Richard Steele (1672-1729) chided "ladies" for their "frivolities" but also criticized the system that produced women of such little substance. They ascribed the follies of the female sex and the contempt characteristically leveled at women by men to the lack of educational opportunities for women. Some examples of the fare which women of the upper classes could read in Steele's *Ladies Library* (1714): "The fair sex are as capable as men of the liberal sciences"; "The general mistake among us in educating our children is that in our daughters we take care of their persons and neglect their minds." Steele disavowed the notion that the ability to please was the essential ingredient in a happy marriage, and in fact could not comprehend how a marriage could be enduring where one of the parties was a fool. Knowledge and self-awareness, he proclaimed, were necessary preparation for marriage, and "the rule for pleasing long is, to obtain such qualifications as would make them so, were they not women."

That the education of women was purely sexual was the consistent complaint of the feminist reformers; women were taught nothing except how to get husbands. While acknowledging that there were differences between the sexes, the feminist fathers would not exaggerate these differences through the educational process. To the Enlightenment rationalists, the basis of character was wisdom and virtue, and neither of these attributes was determined by gender. Addison concluded, "We ought to consider in this particular not what is the sex, but what is the species to which they belong. Women's amusements seem contrived for them rather as they are women than as they are reasonable creatures, and are more adapted to the sex than the species." In the pages of *The Tattler*, the women's issue took on political overtones as Steele declared that it was impossible for society to be happily constituted while one half of it was kept in a state of ignorance: "The great happiness of mankind depends upon the manner of educating and treating that sex." Addison and Steele also adumbrated the close connection between reason and morality, indicating that "intellectual idleness is the parent of vice."[7]

Jonathan Swift (1667-1745), a biting satirist of eighteenth-century pieties, showed great sympathy for women and joined the chorus that declared that the reason for women's inferior status was their lack of education. In *A Letter to a Young Lady on Her Marriage* (1723), he advised the daughter of a friend to avoid the feminine trap. Her parents, he let her know, failed when they neglected "to cultivate [her] mind; without which it is impossible to acquire or preserve the friendship and esteem of a wise man, who soon grows weary of acting the lover and treating his wife like a mistress, but wants a reasonable companion, and a true friend through every stage of his life." Swift declared that lack of education had earned women contempt from men and insured their virtual segregation in a trivialized world—something he deplored: "It hath sometimes moved me with pity, to see the lady of the house forced to withdraw immediately after dinner, and this in families where there is not much drinking, as if it were an established maxim that women were incapable of all conversation." Swift disavowed theories about male and female roles that supported a double standard of morality: "I am ignorant of any one quality that is amiable in man which is not equally so in women. I do not even except modesty, and gentleness of nature. Nor do I know of one vice or folly which is not equally detestable in both."[8]

The early eighteenth century feminist reformers in England advocated better education for women to promote domestic tranquillity, in the literal sense. Respect for women was a means of upholding family values at a time when the family was becoming the center of emotional and social life. They addressed themselves to a resurgent aristocracy, which had thrown off divine right kingship and no longer had to fawn on absolute monarchs for status and influence, and to the rising middle class, whose economic power was achieved through sober dedication and single-minded purpose, and who had little time for or patience with the frivolous behavior and trivial concerns of their wives. In this context, better education for women was desirable to foster harmony and a sense of common purpose between husbands and wives.

Feminism did not become a political issue until the agitation preceding the American and French revolutions, when middle-class reformers grew increasingly frustrated with their failure to gain political rights. They elaborated theories of inherent natural rights belonging to all human beings, which to the logically inclined had to include women. Feminism ultimately became the touchstone of radical reform when it became clear that the eighteenth-century revolutions had won signal victories for middle-class males, but left working people and all women to bear the inequities that middle-class men had thrown off.

Before Tom Paine wrote *Common Sense* or *The Rights of Man*, he raised the banner of feminism in his vigorous dissent against the disabilities of women. Paine (1737-1809) believed that the extension of political rights for which radicals on both sides of the Atlantic were struggling should include women, and that women should join in demands for equality. In *An Occasional Letter on the Female Sex* (1775), he imagined what a woman might say were she to advocate women's rights. The work was also an implicit wish that she would:

How great your injustice? If we have an equal right with you to virtue, why should we not have an equal right to praise? The public esteem ought to wait upon merit. Our duties are different from yours, but they are not, therefore, less difficult to fulfill, or of less consequence to society....Permit our names to be sometimes pronounced beyond the narrow circle in which we live. Permit friendship, or at least love to inscribe its emblem on the tomb where our ashes repose; and deny us not that public esteem which, after the esteem of one's self, is the sweetest reward of well doing.[9]

An Occasional Letter expressed sympathy for women's degraded status, anger at their physical exploitation by men within marriage and for the vulnerability to economic hardship, social ostracism, and legal harassment of unmarried women.

Paine wrote the *Letter* shortly after the breakup of his own marriage to Elizabeth Ollive. In acquiescing to the separation, Paine refused to take advantage of his right to retain all of his wife's property, including everything she might earn after the separation. He stipulated in the agreement of separation that she should henceforth be treated as a single woman with rights to her property and the fruits of her labor.

When Paine returned to England after making common cause with the American revolutionaries, he became involved with a circle of radical intellectuals that included William Godwin and Mary Wollstonecraft. The circle formed around the publisher Joseph Johnson, who had established his radical credentials when he published Benjamin Franklin's *Collected Essays* while England was at war with her American colonies. Franklin was strongly identified in the minds of the English with American ideals of liberty and equality; that Johnson chose to publish the *Essays* during the Revolution was a clear indication of where his sympathies lay. The entire group of radicals was inspired by the American example, and was convinced that the institutions which perpetuated oppression in England, such as the monarchy, the House of Lords, and the established church, would soon be toppled by revolution.

The members of Johnson's circle constituted a staff of writers on whom he drew to stir up public debate by challenging conservative and orthodox viewpoints. One of his vehicles was *The Analytical Review*, which published articles demanding reform and book reviews of controversial books. Shortly after she met Johnson in 1788, Mary Wollstonecraft became a member of the staff of the *Review*. By 1789 she contributed a large portion of the reviews of dramas and gave consistently good notices to the feminist playwright, Thomas Holcroft. Johnson introduced her to William Godwin and was the mentor who saw her through her personal crises, sheltered her, and, by employing her, enabled her to meet her financial obligations to her family.[10]

It was through the political discussions that Johnson sponsored in his home that women's rights was put on the radicals' agenda along with men's rights. Paine's *Rights of Man* and Wollstonecraft's companion volume, *Vindication of the Rights of Women*, were published within a year of each other by Johnson. Both were intended to counter the conservative doctrines Edmund Burke put forth in his criticism of the goals and tactics of the French Revolution.

William Godwin's *Political Justice* (1792) was also a Johnson publishing venture, and set the issue of women's rights in a larger framework. Godwin (1756-1836) was typical of Enlightenment thinking with his faith in infinite progress through the perfectibility of mankind. He looked forward to a world where religious and political institutions ceased to distort and stunt the human personality—a prerequisite for the reign of peace and justice. Godwin thought of government itself as a prime evil responsible for all the wars and misery that marked the pages of history, and he regarded the family as an extension of government authority, which had to be abolished along with other oppressive institutions. Godwin described marriage as a selfish monopoly of property and as an obstacle to social harmony: "So long as I seek to engross one woman to myself and to prohibit my neighbor from proving his superior desert and reaping the fruits of it, I am guilty of the most odious of all monopolies. Over this imaginary prize men watch with perpetual jealousy.... As long as this state of society continues, philanthropy will be crossed and checked in a thousand ways."[11] Godwin was convinced that dispensing with government and its adjunct, the family, would lead neither to chaos nor to immorality. His faith in reason was so unbounded that he believed the extinction of the family would improve morality, since rational creatures were *ipso facto* moral and would naturally prefer one mate even if not coerced in that direction. Rights for women were essential for Godwin as a means of hastening the arrival of his utopian vision. He favored equal education for males and females and rights of divorce for women. Godwin acted on his convictions against marriage. He and Mary Wollstonecraft formed a free love union, and married only when she became pregnant, because both realized that in a corrupt world their child would suffer because of their principles. Godwin justified his behavior, widely criticized as immoral, writing, "The doctrine of my *Political Justice* is that an attachment in some degree permanent between two persons of opposite sexes is right but that marriage as practiced in European countries is wrong. Nothing but a regard for the individual which I had no right to injure could have induced me to submit to an institution which I wish to be abolished."[12]

The fact that the American Revolution stopped conspicuously short of granting liberty and equality to all was a disappointment to Charles Brockden Brown. For Brown (1771-1810), the first professional man of letters in the United States, the Revolution was decidedly unfinished since the poor, blacks, and women were excluded from the benefits conferred by the Declaration of Independence and the Constitution.

In *Alcuin: A Dialogue* (1798) Brown made it clear that of all these lapses the ill treatment of women was the most egregious. *Alcuin* is a dialogue between Alcuin (historically, a medieval scholar), and an elderly widow, Mrs. Carter, "who is always at home." That phrase in itself speaks volumes about the condition of women in eighteenth-century America. A paragon of domestic virtue, Mrs. Carter is absolutely essential to the well-being of her brother, whom she is looking after. She is a constant and comforting presence, but just as unobtrusive as the furniture in the house over which she presides. When Alcuin, at a loss for conversation, politely asks Mrs. Carter if she is a Federalist, she displays a stereotypical femininity by disclaiming any knowledge of political affairs: "Surely you are in jest. What! Ask a woman—shallow and inexperienced as all women are known to be—especially with regard to these topics—her opinion on any political question! If you inquire the price of this ribbon, or at what shop I purchased that set of china, I may answer you. These things, you know, belong to the women's province."[13]

It turns out that Mrs. Carter has very definite opinions, and she is goaded into expressing them when Alcuin, probably chosen as protagonist to suggest his medieval thinking, justifies separate spheres for men and women. Voicing a view common to masculinists, he insists that women, who have only to perform domestic work and are required "only to be skillful in the superintendence of a tea table, show affability and modesty, promptness to inquire and docility to listen," have an easy time of it compared to men struggling in the workaday world—implying that women have no cause for complaint. Mrs. Carter warms to the argument, pointing out that women's sphere is a narrow one: "They are obliged to wander, at times, in search of variety. Most commonly they digress into scandal; and this has been their eternal reproach."

Alcuin is quick to appreciate the disadvantages under which women labor, but suggests that these are not insuperable. He taunts Mrs. Carter by pointing to individual women such as the bluestockings who have exerted themselves and gained an education, and who have been able to overcome the obstacles to success in the male world.[14] Mrs. Carter is not impressed with the token woman whose upper-class status makes it possible for her to gain public attention. She speaks for all women and argues that the leisure for thinking is not generally available. The women who have babies, nurse the sick, and remain in the house—the great majority of women—are actively discouraged from learning. It is hypocritical, naive, and self-serving for men to suggest otherwise. Moreover, those women who, like the bluestockings, have the means and leisure to gain an education and achieve distinction in the male world have not opened new possibilities to their less fortunate sisters. They are used as proof by both sexes that those women who fail to find the loopholes in the patriarchal structure are deserving of the low esteem in which they are held.

"What think you of female education?" Mrs. Carter asks by way of getting to the heart of the matter. "Mine has been frivolous. I can make a pie, and cut a gown. For this only am I indebted to my teachers." The constant refrain voiced by the feminist philosophers throughout the eighteenth century, that women's education trivializes them and makes them contemptible to men, is now articulated through Mrs. Carter. She maintains that women are the victims of a sexually segregated education which determines their natures with little hope of escape. Such an education serves to foster economic dependence and the physical bondage that comes with marriage. Women and men come to marriage as strangers, each from disparate, self-contained worlds, one taught to be a master, the other a slave. The distinct worlds that men and women inhabit have separate moral standards, expectations, and goals. Communication between them is conducted through artifice and deceit. The habit of dishonesty in their dealings with each other fosters mutual contempt and further widens the yawning gulf between them. Marriage becomes a charade for both men and women, but men are allowed other interests, while women can never escape its demands.

The oppressions of marriage for women are systematically explored in *Alcuin* and elicit some choice invectives from Mrs. Carter; she complains that in marrying, a woman loses all she owns, literally as well as figuratively, giving up her property as well as her name to become a nonperson: "The will of her husband is the criterion of all her duties. In all contests with him, she must hope to prevail by blandishments and tears, not by appeals to justice or addresses to reason. She will be most applauded when she smiles with the most perseverance on her oppressor, and, when, with the undistinguishing attachment of a dog, no caprice or cruelty shall be able to estrange her affection."

Mrs. Carter is an extremely effective advocate of the causes of coeducation and political rights for women. The device of using a woman to make the case for women's rights is revealing of the thinking of the feminist fathers. They tended to group women into a class with common grievances and interests and believed that these could best be expressed by one of their own group.[15] Mrs. Carter is thus put in the precarious position of speaking for all women even though she herself has not suffered all the oppressions referred to. When Alcuin questions the reliability of her across-the-board charges, again trying to divide women, she will not have it, and attests that women are united by a common oppression imposed by men: "I believe the picture to be generally exact.... Man is strongest. This is the reason why, in the earliest stages of society, women are slaves."

Brown indicates that if women are to overcome legal and educational disabilities they must act in concert and, in effect, become political. It develops that Mrs. Carter's earlier disclaimer to any interest in politics is born of despair that even in the New World, widely viewed as called into being to redress the wrongs of the Old, women are given short shrift. When Alcuin repeats his question, "Are you a Federalist?" her answer is no longer framed with feminine coyness. She responds forthrightly and vehemently attacks the new republic, touted as the freest in the world, for totally ignoring the oppression of women. She repeatedly uses animal images as metaphors for women's lot: "Lawmakers thought as little of comprehending us in their code of liberty, as if we were dogs or sheep. That females are exceptions to their general maxims, perhaps never occurred to them. If it did, the idea was quietly discarded, without leaving behind the slightest consciousness of inconsistency or injustice.... This Constitution is unjust and absurd."

Brown was mindful that the poor and the black also did not receive justice in America, but he gave the liberation of women a higher priority than that of the others. He considered women's oppression to be of longer duration than that of any other group, and believed their liberation to be more important to the realization of the American dream. It was a general dictum of the male feminist that women must not only articulate their demands as an aggrieved class, but must also cease to sacrifice themselves on behalf of others. Mrs. Carter voices this belief in self-help and in the doctrine that liberation is meaningful only as the individual struggles for it himself or herself in its pure form: "Let the black, the young, the poor, the strange, support their own claims. I am a woman. As such, I cannot celebrate the equity of that scheme of government which classes me with dogs and swine."

The utopia Brown looked forward to attaining with the help of women was a moral order where absolute equality reigned between males and females. Women would be part of the productive force, all work necessary for the substinence and shelter of the community being apportioned equally among males and females. Sharing, Brown believed, made all work less arduous, and would prevent either sex from envying the lot of other. There would be no arbitrary restrictions with respect to education, conversation, employment, or even dress, which was to be unisex.

Women were to be the moral guarantors of the community. When Alcuin, the deviser of grand blueprints, suggests abolishing marriage in the William Godwin mode, the intimations of promiscuity give Mrs. Carter pause. She herself puts the finishing touches to a scheme that advances reform rather than revolution. Marriage would be retained, but liberalized. Women would be allowed to own property. Fidelity would be required of both sexes, and rights of divorce would be granted to both partners. Women would be able to have private lives even when married. To this end, married couples might even live apart, seeing each other when it was mutually desired. The rejection of Alcuin's drastic solution indicated certain second thoughts raised about revolution because of excesses such as those that occurred during the Reign of Terror in France. That women were conservers of what was useful, reformers rather than revolutionaries, was an integral tenet of post-revolutionary male feminism, and a major reason the feminists wanted to increase the influence of women in society.

The last part of *Alcuin*, in which Brown provides his own version of utopia, was not published until 1815 (five years after his death). It is a scathing indictment of the new American republic, which was a symbol of hope and progress for the oppressed of the Old World. Mrs. Carter's ascription of tyranny to those who limited her to her assigned role, "to listen and obey," and her heartfelt "No, I am no Federalist," hinted at deep divisions in a free society whose institutions were designed by Enlightenment philosophes, and which were intended to produce a new man. For Brown the test of the new man was his willingness to share his freedom with women and other outgroups. Reformed marriage, as Mrs. Carter described it, was a union much like the American ideal, which had not been realized because of class, race, and sex divisions. Mrs. Carter stipulated that marriage should be a union "founded on free and mutual consent. It cannot exist without friendship. It cannot exist without personal fidelity. As soon as it ceases to be spontaneous, it ceases to be just. This is the sum. If I were to talk for months, I could add nothing to the completeness of this definition."[16]

Through Thomas Spence, a working-class radical, English working-class women found a voice. Spence (1750-1814), whose version of the rights of man included economic well-being, proposed nationalization of land in his socialist utopia, which he called Spensonia. In Spensonia, all men and women attained citizenship and full equality on reaching the age of twenty-one, and all men and women were entitled to the fruits of their labor as well as use of the land. Spence was a revolutionary, repeatedly arrested for selling such works as Paine's *Rights of Man*, for leafletting radical handbills and broadsheets, and for allegedly allowing his bookshop to be used as a cell where agitators drilled for a future uprising.

Spence took up the issue of women in a tract entitled *The Rights of Infants; or the Imprescriptable Right of Mothers to such share of the Elements as is sufficient to enable them to suckle and bring up their young* (1797). Spence, like Brown, resorts to the device of dialogue, and has a woman challenging an aristocratic member of the male establishment. She not only articulates women's grievances, but sounds a call to action. Since women have found their husbands "woefully negligent and deficient about their own rights we women mean to take up the business ourselves." In a later pamphlet, Spence turned his spotlight on the plight of abused wives and advocated rights of divorce for working people. He sardonically noted, "This subject is so feelingly understood in this country, that it is supposed the Chains of Hymen would be among the first to be broken . . . in case of a Revolution, and the family business of life turned over to Cupid who though he may be a little whimsical is not so stern a jailor-like Deity."[17]

The device of women arguing for their rights in dramatic confrontations with males is not used by William Thompson, who passionately addressed himself to the issue of women's rights in the most comprehensive terms by making a direct appeal to women to assert their own interests in the name of human dignity and for the benefit of society. Thompson (1775-1833) was an Irish landlord and whimsically referred to himself as "one of the idle classes." Indeed, he was one of the privileged few, a member of the Protestant ascendancy in Catholic Ireland. He might have aspired to political power, an acknowledged right of a member of his economic and social class. Instead he spent his life trying to insure the extinction of his own class. Thompson, a thoroughgoing rationalist, thought it possible to discover a social science by which the social forces operating on mankind would be revealed, and which would be used to eradicate social ills, to the benefit of all. Like the rationalists of the Enlightenment, he believed organized religion to be an obstacle to progress and felt completely confident that reason would triumph over the unproven dogmas of revelation. He travelled widely and made contact with the French St. Simonians, who were severe critics of laissez-faire capitalism. Thompson became convinced that the industrial revolution was working against the interest and well-being of the working classes and for the exclusive benefit of the "idle rich." He vociferously denounced the capitalist system, maintaining that "those who labour are overcome with toil, while the idle classes who live on the products of the labourer are almost equally wretched from lack of occupation."

In 1814, Thompson took over his estate at Glendore and was confronted with the poverty and squalor in which the tenants lived. His fellow landlords generally absented themselves from their estates and had no contact with the abject peasantry. Thompson managed his estate himself, gave leases on generous terms to the tenants, and instituted improved methods of cultivation. Despite his wealth, he was a man of Spartan habits, who for the last seventeen years of his life was a nonsmoker, vegetarian, and teetotaller, declaring that his spare regimen enabled him to read and write better. His faith in human nature was not tinged with sentimentality and did not prevent him from castigating idleness and demanding conscientious work from his tenants, yet he was universally loved by them.

Disconcerted at finding himself one of the exploiters, Thompson determined to use his position to enhance the welfare of the poor. He entered politics in 1818 as a champion of popular education. He advocated a system of free, secular education and believed everyone should and could be trained to appreciate "general literature. . . the poets and prose writers of his native tongue, and dead and foreign writers by means of translation."[18]

Thompson became acquainted with other radicals, among them Robert Owen, and the utilitarians, Jeremy Bentham and James Mill. But he strongly dissented from the accommodation that the utilitarians were making with laissez-faire economics and middle-class capitalism. His critique of capitalism is contained in his magnum opus, *An Inquiry into the Principles of the Distribution of Wealth Most Conducive to Human Happiness, Applied to the Newly Proposed System of Voluntary Equality of Wealth*. Thompson wrote the book to answer three vital questions, which summed up the failures of the capitalist system: How was it that a nation with the resources and the productive capacity of England, where wealth abounded, should have so much poverty in the midst of plenty?; why should it be that the fruits of the labor of the productive classes—the workers—should be systematically denied to them?; why was it that the industrial system which promised to raise the standard of living for everybody enriched a few at the expense of the mass of producers "to make the poverty of the poor more helpless?" Thompson, in effect, anticipated Karl Marx in formulating the labor theory of value; in demanding an end to the exploitation of workers inherent in the ownership of private property; in citing the family as the pillar on which the capitalist system rested; and in indicting competition as inimical to human progress and happiness. Thompson was not, however, a revolutionary, as Marx was. He proposed a plan for the redistribution of income based on production, and ultimately he envisioned a society based on cooperation.

Thompson disputed that the pronouncements of the classical economists, who consigned the working classes to a secondary role in the productive process, were free of value judgements or were in any sense scientific. His own moral judgments were expressed in virtually every sentence he wrote: "Capital was the mere creature of labour and materials, not their creator. . . the dead material is nothing; the active mind and the hand are the sole objects of philosophical and moral regard."[19] Thompson's critique of capitalism embraced its social and political drawbacks as well as the economic ones. Since capitalists exploited labor to amass their wealth, they could only perpetuate their system by naked power and force. Thompson charged that they kept the masses ignorant, and directly or indirectly monopolized the command of the armed forces and all political offices that promised the most power, required the least trouble, and were the most remunerative. They (the capitalists) imposed on the poor the burdens of taxation, the costs of sinecures for the rich, and state administrations from which they alone benefitted and rationalized their injustices in the name of "rights" and "privileges" which were "little more than a tissue of restraints of one class over another." Thompson described capitalism as a system which made selfishness and materialism the only motives in life and the only incentives for work. To this traitor to his class as well as to his sex, a system that fostered competition encompassed a mean set of values. Everyone sought to amass his own individual "pile," inevitably at the expense of others. "Get wealth, if possible, honestly, but at all events, get wealth" became the established maxim of society.

Thompson described the psychological effects of competition as deadening for both exploiter and exploited. For Thompson, there could not be any

tranquillity, no peace of mind so long as rivalry and distrust, the necessary effects of competition universally prevail. . . . Among the fortunate, a universal fever of excitement, not to increase enjoyment but to outrun each other burns through society. . . . Among the poor rankle universal langour, depression, discontent, and unhoping ignorance.[20]

In the writings of William Thompson capitalistic greed and exploitation were seen as manifestations of the masculine cause, which distorted all relationships— those between the sexes no less than those between classes. Marriage under capitalism was simply another expression of the male power drive. Thompson comments:

Seldom can natural feelings display themselves—connections of what are called friendship and love are made with the view of wealth and domination. Envies, jealousies, and hatreds are generated even after such connections are formed, or their formation is prevented by trifling differences of station. . . . The mere animal part of sexual pleasure is bought by the richer of the dominant sex at the lowest price of competition and enjoyed as heartlessly and as selfishly as any other purchased gratification. The weaker, poorer, selling parties, when used, are thrown by and trampled upon, generally to terminate life after a few years of feverish riot.[21]

It was Thompson who incorporated feminism into radical theory and made it the quintessential ingredient of reform, as opposed to revolutionary, socialism. Thompson's feminism was adumbrated in *Inquiry* when he charged that the unpaid labor women perform in their subservient positions in the family is a mainstay of the capitalist system. He saw women's liberation as a necessary precursor to a socialist society. Thompson avowed: "While women continue to be condemned to the seclusion and drudgery of. . .slaves, all their exertions and duties limited to looking after the domestic comforts. . .of their masters and children, they will never rise in the scale of social existence."[22] It was the issue of feminism which brought a final parting between Thompson and the utilitarians. Thompson wrote the *Inquiry* to dissent from what he considered a craven surrender on the part of the Benthamites to capitalism, and he write *Appeal of One Half of the Human Race, Women, Against the Pretensions of the Other Half, Men, to Retain Them in Civil and Domestic Slavery*, because of James Mill's abandonment of the utilitarians' original commitment to equality for women. When James Mill, in an article on government for the 1824 edition of the *Encyclopedia Britannica*, declared it as "pretty clear" that all individuals whose interests were indisputably included in those of other individuals could be denied political representation without inconvenience, he lumped women and children into a class whose interest was "involved in that of their fathers or in that of their husbands." His defection sent shock waves through the community of progressive thinkers, with Mill's mentor, Jeremy Bentham, and his own son, John Stuart Mill, protesting this violation of principle. When the elder Mill remained unmoved and refused to withdraw the article, Thompson wrote his response, denouncing Mill in the most scornful terms and asserting that the emancipation of women was a prerequisite to abolition of private property, the state, and organized religion.

Thompson was particularly incensed that the willingness to consign women to an inferior state—motivated, as he repeatedly stated, by the self-interest of males—was being promoted not by the "vulgar hirelings of everyday bigots of existing institutions" but was "put forward under the shield of philosophy" by the eminently esteemed and respectable utilitarians. He gave Mill credit for espousing the political rights of men but thought it inexplicable that a philosopher who sought the greatest happiness for the highest number of people should "deliberately in the very threshold of his argument, put aside one half of the human race, of all ages and all characters and conditions, as unentitled to consideration." Mill's argument for the rights of men was predicated on his conclusion that, historically, men had abused their power over others. That he was now asking his disciples to believe that men would restrain themselves when given absolute authority over women was to Thompson incredible and hypocritical.

Thompson proceeded to use the deductive logic based on facts and extolled as the only avenue to truth by the utilitarians to demolish Mill's statement that women's interests were included in men's. For one thing, he pointed out, between one-fourth and one-sixth of the population of adult females possessed neither a father nor a husband and therefore had no man in whose interest they could be included. The logical deduction from Mill's argument would be that these women, like men, were entitled to political rights since they were completely vulnerable to the exploitative tendencies that Mill considered to be part of men's nature. Indeed, because women were denied all opportunity to earn an independent living due to the deficiencies of their education and because they were physically weaker than males, one class of females—the unmarried—had an even greater title to representation than males. Yet they were totally ignored by Mill's hasty generalization.

Thompson insisted that in making his argument for "inclusion of interests," Mill was simply reasserting prevailing conventions, which demanded that a woman get married if she wanted to have any security or respectability. With that same passion and indignation that characterized his arguments on behalf of exploited workers in the *Inquiry*, Thompson turned his attention to the oppressed status of married women, whom he referred to as "involuntary breed-

ing machines and household slaves." The marriage contract was a farce to
Thompson:

Each man yokes a woman to his establishment, and calls it a *contract*. Audacious false-
hood! Where are any of the attributes of contracts, of equal and just contracts? A contract
implies the voluntary assent of both the contracting parties. Have women been consulted
as to the terms of this pretended contract all of whose enjoyments are on one side, while
all the pains and privations are on the other—a contract giving all power, arbitrary will
and unbridled enjoyment to the one side; to the other unqualified obedience, and enjoyments meted out or withheld at the caprice of the ruling and enjoying party?[23]

Having proven that the interests of women were not included in those of men,
Thompson insisted that even if inclusion existed it could never justify a denial of
civil and political rights. Women were one-half of the human race, and if political rights were necessary to happiness and self-respect, as the utilitarians maintained, women had as much right to them as men. The happiness of society could
not be attained without making all its members happy, and to use such phrases as
"the public good" in any other sense was a distortion of reality.

Thompson addressed his *Appeal* to both men and women. The men he admonished to relinquish their despotic power over women:

Be consistent! Ye stronger half of the race, be at length rational! Three and four thousand
years have worked threadbare your vile cloak of hypocrisy. Even women, your poor,
weak, contented slaves, at whose impotence, the result of your vile exclusions, you have
been accustomed to laugh, begin to see through it and to shudder at the loathsomeness
beneath. Cast aside the tattered cloak before it leaves you naked and exposed. Clothe
yourselves with new garments of sincerity. Be rational human beings, not mere male
sexual creatures. . . .

For women, Thompson painted a horrific picture of their degradation under
male authority:

Whatever pleasures you enjoy are permitted you for man's sake; nothing is your own;
possession of person and of property are alike withheld from you. Nothing is yours but
secret pangs, the bitter burning years of regret, the stifled sobs of outraged nature, thrown
back upon your own hearts where the vital principle itself stands checked or is agitated by
malignant passions until body and mind become the frequent prey to overwhelming
disease, now finding vent in sudden frenzy, now plunged in pining melancholy, or
bursting the weak tenement of reason, seeking relief in self-destruction. . . thus degraded
to the level of mere automatons, the passive tools of the pleasures and passions of men,
your actions are regulated, like those of slaves, by the arbitrary will of your masters, to
whom, by the necessities of existence uniting yourselves, you are compelled to vow
uninquiring obedience.

In words worthy of a religious divine calling his flock to a new vision, he
wrote:

Women of England, women in whatever country ye breathe—wherever ye breathe degraded—
awaken! Awake to the contemplation of the happiness that awaits you when all your
facilities of mind and body shall be fully cultivated and developed; when every path in
which ye can exercise those improved facilities shall be laid open and rendered delightful
to you, even as to them who now ignorantly enslave and degrade you....O wretched
slaves of such wretched masters! Awake, arise, shake off these fetters.

Thompson, true to the feminist reformers' doctrine of self-help, advised women
that they would have to get involved in political struggle if they were to achieve
liberation, since "freedom is never received as a gift from the masters." He urged
them to fight for educational opportunity, civil rights and political rights with as
much tenacity and single-mindedness as men did when they revolted against their
royal masters and divine right authority. Women would have to reject men's
definition of femininity, a definition men had employed and justified by the label
"natural" to keep women in an inferior position. He admonished, "You must be
respected by them; not merely desired like rare meats to pamper their selfish
appetites. To be respected by them you must be respectable in your own eyes; you
must exert more power, you must be useful!" He suggested that women would
realize the full measure of their talents in the socialist communities he advocated.

While addressing himself to women "in whatever country ye breathe!" Thompson made a more direct plea to Anna Wheeler, his acknowledged collaborator, a
woman he hoped would fill the shoes of Mary Wollstonecraft by articulating the
grievances of her sex and raising women's consciousness with respect to their
lowly estate. Anna Wheeler was Thompson's intellectual comrade-in-arms, the
early nineteenth-century prototype of the emancipated woman the feminist fathers wanted all women to become. Born in 1785, Anna Doyle was the youngest
daughter of Archbishop Doyle, an Irish Anglican clergyman. At the age of
fifteen she married Francis Massy Wheeler, and discovered that such terms as
"slave" and "breeding machine," which the feminist reformers used to describe
married women, were not mere rhetorical devices. Wheeler was a drunkard who
provided his wife with six children in twelve years, but not the means to support
them. Throughout her travail, which involved the progressive degeneration of
her husband and the death of four of her children in infancy, Anna Wheeler
found some comfort through her intellectual curiosity. She educated herself by
sending to London for the works of the current social and political philosophers,
an act of self-assertion for which she was roundly censured by public opinion.
The community commiserated with Francis Wheeler, whose wife didn't share his
interests, even though these were exclusively limited to liquor. Anna Wheeler
nevertheless persevered, and came in contact with the works of Mary Wollstonecraft
and Holbach, from which she undoubtedly derived a feminist perspective. In
1812, she took her two remaining children and fled from her husband, finding
refuge at the home of a relative who, as governor of Guernsey, was well enough
situated to provide for them. Her departure meant that her husband had not the
slightest legal obligation to her. Anna Wheeler was more fortunate than the great

majority of women. Through her connections she was able to reenter respectable society despite what was considered her desertion of her husband, who died in 1820. She was able to travel widely, and in France established connections with the Saint Simonians, socialist radicals, who, like their English counterparts, considered the emancipation of women essential to their utopian visions. She introduced the youthful Charles Fourier to Robert Owen, hoping a meeting of their minds might produce an international movement. In fact she served as a link between the Saint Simonians and the English socialists, translating extracts of the Simonians' writings for them. By the Saint Simonians she was hailed as the Goddess of Reason and "the most gifted woman of the age." Anna Wheeler became a frequent contributor to the English cooperative press. She urged women "not to leave the bitter inheritance of ignorance and slavery" to their daughters. Throughout the social fabric, she protested, were "vice, crime and social anarchy"; happiness was "lost to all because security was unknown to any." She insisted that, were she to die without a sign expressive of her "horror, indignation, and bitter contempt for the masked barbarism of so-called civilized society," her regret at having lived only to serve and suffer in the capacity of "slave and woman" would be complete.[24]

Significantly, Anna Wheeler never appended her own name when she wrote these noble sentiments. Hence Thompson's *Appeal*, in which he wrote: "I am anxious that you should take up the cause of your prostrated sex, and state to the world in writing, in your name, what you have so often and so well stated in conversation and under feigned names in such periodical publications of the day as would tolerate such a theme."

Thompson exhorted Wheeler in the name of that dream of a future of sexual equality and social harmony that they both shared:

You look forward, as do I, to a state of society very different from that which now exists, in which the effort of all is to outwit, supplant and snatch from each other; where interest is systematically opposed to duty, where the so-called system of morals is little more than a mass of hypocrisy preached by knaves but unpracticed by them, to keep their slaves, male as well as female, in blind uninquiring obedience; and where the whole motley fabric is kept together by fear and blood. You look forward to a better state of society, where the principle of benevolence shall supersede that of fear; where restless and anxious individual competition shall give place to mutual cooperation and joint possession; where individuals, in large numbers, male and female, forming voluntary associations shall become a mutual guarantee to each other for the supply of all useful wants, and form an unsalaried insurance company where perfect freedom of opinion and perfect equality will reign, and where the children of all will be equally educated and provided for by the whole.[25]

Anna Wheeler did not heed the call. The only reason expressed for her unwillingness was the statement made to Thompson that she rejected "the boon of equality with such creatures as men now are." Wheeler, in effect, adopted the posture of moral superiority with which the savants of the nineteenth century credited women, and which at the same time made it easy for women to shun public affairs. Anna Wheeler was torn between her feminist sympathies and a desire to maintain some semblance of respectability in the court of public opinion, which judged women who stepped out of their sphere harshly. Wheeler discovered that ostracism by society for her revolutionary ideas might extend to her daughters. Wheeler's daughter, Rosina, married the novelist Edward Bulwer-Lytton over the strong objections of his mother, who found her radicalism repugnant.

That the career of Frances Wright as a feminist, communitarian, and social reformer was launched under the auspices of Robert Owen gave him a unique standing among the feminist fathers. Robert Owen (1771-1858) was a one-man task force, who sought to implement the ideals of the Enlightenment radicals and to illustrate their pragmatic value. His career can be summed up in the labels he acquired during a long and active life: businessman, philanthropist, social reformer, communitarian, labor leader, cooperator. He was above all a socialist visionary, a rationalist who derived his credo—that the aim of society should be to make people happy—from the philosophes of the Enlightenment. This could be accomplished without violent revolution by reshaping social institutions to make them humane and reasonable, and by educating all citizens so that they would willingly cooperate in a society of equals. On the women's question, he was unequivocal, declaring that there was not a social, a property, or a political right which men enjoyed to which women were not "justly and equally entitled."

Owen first attained recognition as a successful businessman who had strong differences with the prevailing laissez-faire philosophy that guided his colleagues in the business world. In a day when the term *laissez-faire* rationalized human greed and equated it with the public good, when there were no legal guidelines with respect to the hours of work and the conditions of labor that industrialists imposed on their workers, and when subsistence wages were the rule in an unpredictable economy, Owen believed that the profits which served as the justification for capitalism would actually improve if industrialists treated their workers decently. To prove his point, Owen bought several textile mills in New Lanark in Scotland, and turned them into an industrial showplace. The visitors from all over the world who came to see this marvel for themselves found workers living in neat houses with cleanup crews maintaining sanitary conditions. Owen provided high quality food in the company store at low prices. In the factory, the working day was eventually reduced to ten and a half hours, considerably less than was standard. Corporal punishment was prohibited and job security was guaranteed except in cases of persistent infraction of the rules. Workers were treated as human beings, not as machines. They had the right to appeal to Owen himself if they were dissatisfied with the performance ratings of their supervisors. Workers had free medical care and facilities for social activities during their leisure time. Most impressive to the visitors was the fact that young children were in schoolrooms and not working in the factories. These schools were the most astonishing feature of New Lanark and attracted wide publicity, no less for the fact that all children—girls and boys—attended from the day they could walk, than for the methods, which stressed spontaneity, and the curriculum, which was devoid of any religious instruction.

Owen hoped that the success of his community and its schools would convince other industrialists to initiate similar reforms from the same paternalistic concerns which motivated him. He was, in effect, seeking a revolution of reason led by the wealthy to forestall the violent one that the masses were sure to precipitate given the conditions under which they lived and worked. However, the industrialists Owen hoped would follow his example, and the political leaders to whom he addressed pleas for legislative reform to curtail the worst abuses of the industrial system, remained unmoved.

Owen became a critic of property relations in the family as well as in industry. Like Godwin, and like Thompson, whose *Inquiry* made a powerful impression on him, Owen believed that the family isolated people, promoted individualism and competition, and was a bastion of inherent inequality, the wife and children becoming the property of the husband, who was given absolute authority in the domain of the home. Owen wrote: "Separate interests and individual family arrangements with private property are essential parts of the existing irrational system. They must be abandoned with the system." And, instead there must be "scientific associations of men, women and children, in their usual proportions, from about four or five hundred to about two thousand, arranged to be as one family."[26]

The cooperative communities that Owen established in the 1820s were to serve as an alternative to the family and the tyranny of property that it symbolized. Owen considered that the United States would provide a more hospitable climate for his communitarian experiments than England, where class privilege was deeply rooted, and in 1824 he established New Harmony in Indiana. According to the plans drawn up by Owen, there would be no private property in New Harmony. Whatever the land and industry produced would be collectively owned and used by all members of the community. The community was to be economically self-sufficient and politically self-governing, and would provide a total environment for maximum social interaction among the inhabitants. To this end he proposed communal kitchens and communal eating places. Women were to be full participants in all the enterprises of New Harmony. Their involvement in communal affairs was made possible because they were unencumbered with the responsibilities that marriage and family life entailed.

A logical extension to Owen's assault on the family was his opposition to Christian marriage. As a secularist, Owen believed that religion and reason could not coexist. In this he was consistent with Enlightenment thinkers, to whom religion was mere superstition and to whom marriage sanctified by religion represented permanent bondage with virtually no escape for a woman except death. In the canon of the male feminist, a marriage entered into without love became synonymous with prostitution and slavery. Owen felt that Christian marriage reenforced the isolation of the family vis-à-vis society, while within the family it emphasized prudery and guilt and prevented a satisfactory sexual relationship between the two partners.

Owen referred to New Harmony as a "moral" community and was categorically opposed to promiscuity. The communities, where men and women were equal shareholders, would provide individuals with a large choice of partners. Owen advocated early marriage without the benefit of clergy ("natural marriage") and, since he regarded the indissolubility of Christian marriage as venal, devised a scrupulously regulated system of divorce for the inhabitants of his communities. Owen's fear that the carefully worked out proportions in his community might be upset by a population explosion brought about his advocacy of birth control, a further boon to women who, under ordinary circumstances, were restricted from any community role, if only because of frequent confinements during their childbearing years.

New Harmony failed. The failure was predictable to William Thompson, a critic of Owen's paternalistic approach, and an avid believer in self-help for all oppressed groups. Thompson did not believe that capitalists could or should be induced to provide the means to establish the cooperative projects he advocated. Owen turned next to cooperation, which, as Thompson defined it, depended on the men and women directly involved to form their own associations within a democratic framework. Owen achieved a mass following when he began to urge workers to take their destiny into their own hands by establishing cooperative networks.

Ironically, the movement launched by this rationalist, who hoped to convince followers through the sheer force of reason and logic, was enormously aided when it was infused with the feminist millennial ideas of James Elishana (Shepherd) Smith. A Presbyterian minister, Smith (1801-1857) was closely associated with the Southcottians, a sect which regarded Joanna Southcott as its prophetess by virtue of the revelations which she made public in some sixty-five books and pamphlets. Smith was convinced that a new dawn would come about through the intervention of a second messiah, a female to complement the first messiah, who was male. Introduced to the radical social ideas of Owen by Anna Wheeler, Smith fit them into his apocalyptic vision, stating that "whenever the fundamental character of Christianity, namely social love and equality, was received as the basis of political government, then it might be positively asserted that Christ was come, and that the Messiah had begun to reign."[27]

In a lecture on the Christian community delivered in 1833, he completely identified Owen's communitarian ideas with his own millennialism, maintaining that the establishment of the Owenite social system would be nothing less than the Christian millennium. He argued that true Christianity had never yet been established in the world, and could exist only in a "system of society where equality of rank and privileges, as well as a community of goods, is acknowledged." The apostles had considered Christianity in terms of a community, and the fact that Jesus had denounced the rich and respectable caused Smith to label the existing Christianity of the well-to-do as Antichrist.

In practice, the millennium envisaged by Smith would be based on Owen's communitarian principles. It would begin in England as "the reign of righteousness" and would convert every nation in the world by its "moral power." The wealth produced in Britain would be sufficient to ensure a good life for all if properly distributed. A liberal education would be available to all men and women, and every form of work would be equally respected. Women would be emancipated from their dependence on men, and the present degrading system of marriage would be replaced by the "marriage of nature."

The feminist views Smith shared with the Owenites were further elaborated in the *Doctrine of the Woman*. In *Doctrine*, Smith expressed his belief that the universe was made up of two principles, the invisible, spiritual world, which was male, and the visible, material world, which was female. His insistence on the equality of men and women was based on his conviction that each was essential to the whole and that the new moral world would be an offspring of both.

In 1844 the Rochdale Equitable Pioneers Society was established in Lancashire, England. It represents the most enduring legacy of Owenism. The Rochdale cooperative established stores, apartment dwellings, factories, and farms owned and operated by the workers, who shared equally in the profits. The rules and business practices of the Rochdale pioneers set the pattern for successful consumer cooperatives throughout the world and kept the radical social and economic doctrines of the Owenites, their feminism included, alive. Owenism became a veritable sect, with branches all over England. Owen's disciples offered lectures and discussions, printed literature about their aims, and sent missionaries all over England to convert those who were alienated from capitalistic-patriarchal society.

Women were encouraged to express themselves and become active in all Owenite activities. The Owenites opened their classes to women and urged them to become lecturers. They admitted women on an equal footing to traditional masculine social rituals such as the ceremonial dinner held in lieu of religious services by the secular Owenites. Frances Wright, an avid pupil of Owenite principles, personified their hopes for liberated womanhood and exemplified their socialist and feminist ideals.

The development of a grassroots radical culture was proof to George Jacob Holyoake, a friend and disciple of Robert Owen, the cooperator, that men and women could raise themselves from oppression to achieve a socialist society based on cooperation. If Holyoake's claim to fatherhood of the feminist movement can be sustained, it is because of the zeal with which he addressed himself to the problems of organizing and of convincing women to assume leadership roles—an area where success had so far eluded the feminist fathers.

Holyoake (1817-1906) shared with Owen the goal of a socialist society brought about by education and rational persuasion rather than through revolutionary violence. This tactic of nonviolence was labelled "moral force." Holyoake was born in Birmingham during the depression following the Napoleonic wars. Grinding hard times rather than ivory tower speculation motivated his radicalism. His mother, who was his own model of an emancipated woman, had a button business employing several hands which she established before her marriage and retained afterwards. He described her as an entirely "self-acting managing mistress," and he started to work at the age of eight, helping her out. His father was a foreman in a foundry, which Holyoake himself entered at the age of nine. Working sixty-three hours a week, he learned to read in Sunday school, but could not write until he reached the age of fifteen. Even so, Holyoake's family situation was better than the average worker's, and he considered his background to be middle-class. In 1832, he began to attend the Mechanics Institute, a workers' school where he was inspired with Owenism, as a number of Owenites taught there. His political consciousness was honed during the 1832 struggle for suffrage reform in which the radicals participated. The Reform Bill of 1832 was very limited in scope, excluding the working classes and excluding women of any class. Although disappointed, Holyoake was impressed with the power of the middle-class political organizations such as the Birmingham Political Union. These organizations exerted considerable pressure on the government in favor of reform. Their tactics could be adopted by other groups, such as the working classes and women, and Holyoake consistently recommended that they should be.

It was under the auspices of the Owenites that Holyoake launched his career as an agitator. The Owenites divided Britain into dioceses much as the church did, and sent missionaries to all their dioceses. They preached secularism, or rational religion, a basic tenet of the cooperative movement. The message which Holyoake, among others, disseminated was that secularism substitutes the piety of usefulness for the usefulness of piety. Holyoake himself had remained a Christian until the age of twenty-four. It was not only the influence of the Owenites, but his perception that the established church opposed every reform for the working classes and consistently counselled passive resignation in the face of economic hardship that made Holyoake an atheist. His refusal to compromise his convictions led to a trial for blasphemy in 1842, and six months' imprisonment after he was found guilty. He was the last man to be tried for atheism in England and to go to prison after being convicted.

The triad of causes for which Holyoake agitated, as a speaker and through a variety of journals he published, was secularism, cooperation, and feminism. In Holyoake's version of the feminine mystique, women were natural cooperators and women's achievement of civil rights would hasten the day when cooperation became the rule by which people conducted their lives. He stated that he was moved to speak on behalf of women's rights,

seeing how much faster political and social amendment would proceed were the quick discernment and decision of women engaged in public affairs. The fine scorn of women to delay in doing what can be done and ought to be done was much wanted in politics, where men who declare an evil to be intolerable will desist from abating it on the appearance of the first fool who tells them the time is not come to act against it.[28]

Holyoake was convinced that the sisterhood of women was necessary to balance the pernicious consequences of the brotherhood of man. He lamented:

We have a race of women but no order of women. . . . The police courts of the metropolis are satiated with complaints of half-murdered women against brutal husbands who escape with comparative immunity. But where are the women out of court to demonstrate? If it is unwomanly to ask for their rights, it will be unwomanly to exercise them when granted— in short, unwomanly to have them. . . . The impunity with which women are despoiled of property, liberty, and even of their children at the caprice of their husbands, as some melancholy instances in our law courts have lately shown, is an imputation more powerful than any conceivable argument upon the womanly spirit of this nation.

Holyoake reiterated Thompson's warning that freedom is never given by the masters. He expressed the view that an enterprising woman of wise will, who would undertake to train her unpracticed sisters in the art of self-emancipation, would be more of a practical benefactor than the authoress of twenty volumes in favour of their rights. Holyoake advised women not to worry about missteps when they begin to conduct their own affairs—

to generate an *esprit de corps* among themselves, to discuss their own questions in public. There will be blunderings committed, weaknesses displayed, exaggerations perpetrated; but let them remember that men blundered and exaggerated times without number before they arrived at their present facility. . . . Were women to attempt to legislate for men, and exclude them from their Parliament while doing it, and suffer no information of the rights or claims of men to come before them save through their wives—what an outcry there would be from men against what they would call one-sided, ignorant, blundering, unjust, insolent, feminine legislation.[29]

Holyoake's herculean exertions bore fruit on both sides of the Atlantic. He was connected with what are considered to be the landmark events of the women's movement both in England and America. In the United States, the women's rights movement was launched under the auspices of Elizabeth Cady Stanton and Lucretia Mott, who acquired their first experiences in public life as abolitionists. It was acknowledged by both Stanton and Mott that they were inspired to call for a feminist convention because of an experience suffered at an antislavery convention they both attended in London in 1840. Not only were they prohibited from addressing the convention because they were women; they were also segregated and forced to sit behind a curtain during the entire proceedings, which featured eloquent speeches demanding the emancipation of slaves. Holyoake was present at this convention, for in his call to action he expressed his bewilderment that the women accepted their humiliation without demur. The Seneca Falls Convention took place in 1848, a year after Holyoake issued his call for a women's movement. That the convention adopted a statement of principles, a program of action, and techniques of agitation similar to those suggested by Holyoake (who corresponded with the American reformers) indicates the equation the feminist fathers made between slavery and the status of married women had no little impact with the American reformers.

In England, Holyoake had contacts with Bessie Rayner Parkes, Barbara Leigh Smith Bodichon, Harriet Martineau, and Harriet Taylor Mill. It was Holyoake who arranged to circulate at his own expense Harriet Taylor Mill's article, "Are Women Fit for Politics? Are Politics Fit for Women?" much to her own dismay. In 1857, Bessie Rayner Parkes and Barbara Leigh Smith launched *The Englishwoman's Journal*—a title suggested by Holyoake when he urged a journal advocating women's rights "edited by women, contributed to by women, and in every sense an exponent of womanly thought." *The Englishwoman's Journal*, however, did not issue any manifestoes or clarion calls for sweeping reforms. The *Journal*'s aim was to set forth the reasons for women's discontent and to suggest remedies. The readers were treated to articles urging wider employment opportunities for women, and to a steady diet of inspirational pieces about women achievers such as Florence Nightingale and Rosa Bonheur.

By the 1850s, women's rights was as significant a tenet of the radical tradition as was the emancipation of slaves, and had the same emotional force. William Thompson had, in fact, referred to married women as "white slaves." The feminist reformers, however, were still in the embarrassing position of having unfurled a banner that attracted few female recruits. The male feminists' dilemmas and frustrations, both personally and politically, are vividly illustrated by John Stuart Mill. Mill (1806-1873) was without doubt the most influential of all the male feminists. His major contribution, *The Subjection of Women*, started with the premise that married women were the last legal slaves. It went on to trace the source of women's inferior status to subtle and pervasive social conditioning; to answer the objections of the critics of women's rights; and to build a case for the rights of women based on humanitarian ideals of simple justice and on empirical grounds that increased happiness would result for both sexes, who together would advance progress.

According to Mill, his partner in this as in other of his works was his wife, Harriet Taylor Mill. *The Subjection of Women* was written in 1861, three years after Harriet Mill's death; it was not published until 1869, over ten years after her death; but Mill attributed the most "striking and profound portions" of the work to conversations with her. His praise of her was effusive. Her mind was "a perfect instrument."[30] According to Mill, her genius was incomparable; her profundity incalculable; her judgments infallible. The casting of Harriet Mill as the fount of all wisdom and himself as something of an amanuensis transcribing her thoughts is difficult to countenance and has made their relationship something of a puzzle to historians, who generally view feminism as informing all of Mill's writings because of Harriet Taylor Mill's determined influence.[31] The question of who inspired whom with feminism can be answered with some accuracy. It sheds light on the importance of feminism within the radical tradition and the strength of the radicals' commitment to women's rights.

John Stuart Mill stated that he did not derive his feminism from Harriet

Taylor. In his *Autobiography* he wrote, "These convictions were among the earliest results of the application of my mind to political subjects, and the strength with which I held them was, I believe more than anything else the originating cause of the interest she [Harriet Taylor] felt in me." Women's rights was a much discussed subject in the radical circles in which Mill was raised and in which he moved his entire life. His father, the utilitarian James Mill, was determined to groom his son for the tasks of philosophy from the moment of his birth. The educational regimen he designed for him was to prove utilitarian principles that a rational being is made, not born, and Mill described his father's influence over him as pervasive. He described his mother, who was, like his wife, named Harriet, as a good woman whose whole life revolved around her family, who drudged tirelessly and worked her fingers to the proverbial bone, and yet inspired neither love nor respect in either her nine children or in her husband, the renowned philosopher. Mill believed that her misfortune was the inevitable result when the two partners in a marriage are unequal in power and totally mismatched with respect to interest and intellect. Mill's writings on marriage are suffused with indignation that women, because of their disadvantaged state, should serve as mere breeders—the vessels for their husband's "animal passions"—and that a boy should imbibe contempt for his mother and think himself superior to her, "owing her perhaps forebearance but no real respect."[32] His strong feelings bespoke his own boyhood. Mill disagreed with his father when the latter, in 1824, sought to abandon the feminism in utilitarian philosophy, and the event marked his intellectual declaration of independence from his father. The fact that he described Harriet Taylor Mill as "equal to his father in the power of influencing by mere force of mind and character over convictions and purposes of others and in the strenuous exertion of the power to promote human progress" is psychologically significant and reveals how difficult it was to break with his father, whom he continued to regard as an apostle of progress.

In all probability, Mill's feminism was confirmed when he suffered a nervous breakdown in 1826. His education had turned him into a veritable thinking machine, and he complained of an inability to feel, which manifested itself in a severe depression. He was on the verge of suicide when he turned to reading fiction and poetry, an activity that was part of the female world of sensibility, and was generally excluded from the male domain of sense. His zest for life returned when he found he was able to weep copiously over the human tragedies that befell the characters in the fiction he read. Weeping was considered a woman's prerogative. The importance of a balance between male and female traits was thus borne in upon him in a very personal way.

By contrast, very little is known about Harriet Mill before she was proclaimed to the world as a philosophical prodigy. She was born Harriet Hardy in 1807, the daughter of a "surgeon and man-midwife." Nothing specific is known about her education. Speculation has it that the Hardy home was not a happy one and after her marriage to John Taylor at the age of nineteen, her contact with her parents was minimal. It was John Taylor, a republican radical who looked after foreign exiles seeking refuge in England, who introduced his wife to a radical group centered around William Johnson Fox, a Unitarian minister with a pronounced bent for feminism. He published a magazine, *The Monthly Repository*, which featured articles advocating women's rights, and encouraged women writers to contribute. Harriet Taylor started writing for *The Monthly Repository* after Fox introduced her to Mill in 1830.

That the relationship between Mill and Harriet Taylor was a master-pupil one is revealed in their earliest correspondence on the subject of marriage, about which Harriet Taylor asked to be enlightened. Mill responded with an impassioned discourse. In one eloquent paragraph this feminist father portrayed the ideal woman and her role:

And the truth is that this question of marriage cannot properly be considered by itself alone. The question is not what marriage ought to be, but a far wider question, what woman ought to be. Settle that first, and the other will settle itself. Determine whether marriage is to be a relation between two equal beings, or between a superior and an inferior, between a protector and a dependent and the other doubts will easily be resolved.... The great occupation of women should be to beautify life; to cultivate for her own sake and that of those who surrounded her all the faculties of mind and soul and body; all her powers of enjoyment and powers of giving enjoyment.... If in addition to this the activity of her nature demands more energetic and definite employment, there is never any lack of it in the world.[33]

To this exposition, Taylor responded with some doubts whether "in the present state of women's mind perfectly ineducated" and raised for dependence, his high hopes could be realized. Taylor's last paragraph suggested that Mill's tutelage could be all important: "It is for *you*—the most worthy of the apostles of all the highest virtues to teach such as might be taught, that the higher the kind of enjoyment the greater the degree. Perhaps there is but one class to whom this can be taught—the poetic nature struggling with superstition; you are fitted to be saviour of such."[34]

There is every reason to suppose the relationship that Taylor and Mill formed was a platonic one.[35] The fathers of feminism were not only rationalists: they were moralists who were convinced that a rational world, devoid of institutions which distorted the human personality, would be a moral world. Sex was more ideology than biology to them, and Mill veered decidedly in the direction of conservatism. Control over "mere animal passions" was a test of whether reason could triumph over instinct, and for a man like Mill, for whom the personal was distinctly the political, sexual discipline was an obligation as well as a commitment. The ire expressed by Holyoake, William Thompson, and Mill because women were raised to be "sensualists and sex objects" suggests that to women they offered the friendly hand of comradeship and the promise of intellectual companionship rather than the passionate embraces of the lover or visions of eternal romance. In his essay on marriage to Harriet Taylor, Mill defined love as intellectual intimacy, and explained that he objected to marriage because it was made "by sensualists, for sensualists, to bind sensualists." Harriet Taylor Mill shared the prevailing nineteenth-century notion that women had no sexual desires per se and engaged in sexual intercourse only because their marital obligations, framed by men, demanded it.

The Mill-Taylor friendship, begun in 1830, did provoke rumors of scandal. The intellectual landscape of the 1830s and '40s was littered with broken friendships between Mill and those who advised him that his constant companion, Harriet Taylor, was causing talk. It is very probable that their friendship had the benign approbation of John Taylor himself. Mill hinted at this in describing Taylor as "a most upright, brave, honorable man but without the intellectual or artistic tastes which would have made him a companion for his wife." That this was the function that Mill filled is the clear implication.

Harriet Taylor became Mill's wife in 1851, two years after the death of her husband. During their twenty-year friendship and their seven-year marriage, Harriet Mill undoubtedly provided Mill with the encouragement and support needed to pursue his intellectual endeavors. It was after her death in 1858 that Mill pronounced their association a partnership of intellectual equals which produced the philosophical works that revised laissez-faire liberalism and gave feminism its moral and intellectual rationale. In making this claim Mill left the world to suppose that the ideal relationship the feminists thought possible when women were emancipated had already existed in his case. He described it in glowing terms in *Subjection*:

What marriage may be in the case of two persons of cultivated faculties, identical in opinion and purposes, between whom there exists that best kind of equality, similarity of powers and capacities with reciprocal superiority in them—so that each can enjoy the luxury of looking up to the other, and can have alternately the pleasure of leading and of being led in the path of development—I will not attempt to describe. To those who can conceive it, there is no need; to those who cannot, it would appear the dream of an enthusiast.[36]

While there can be no doubt Mill felt deep personal anguish over the loss of his wife, his determination to foster the image of an incomparable mind and talent may have been partially motivated by the politics of male feminism. In effect, he provided that model of intellectual accomplishment, an example of emancipated womanhood, that other women could look to as they struggled to end their subjection. Mill refused to let any biography be written about Harriet Mill. His response to a request that he release her papers is instructive. After agreeing that a portrayal of "the formation and growth of a mind like hers would be a valuable benefit to mankind," he demurred: "But such a psychological history is seldom possible, and in her case the materials of it do not exist. All that could be furnished is her birthplace, parentage, and a few dates, and it seems to me that her memory is more honored by the absence of any attempt at a biography than by the presence of a most meagre one."[37] Mill, in his refusal, made certain that the legend he had created could never be challenged by any objective examination of the record.

The Subjection of Women was so persuasively and cogently argued that it became the veritable handbook of the women's movement. It was a more sophisticated analysis of women's inferior status than earlier ones, which lumped all women into a class, in effect making class synonymous with gender. Mill was particularly acute and perceptive about the psychological dilemmas women confronted as an oppressed group which must live with its oppressors—oppressors who subjected them to systematic brain washing to keep them in thrall. He noted:

All causes, social and natural, combine to make it unlikely that women should be collectively rebellious to the power of men. They are so far in a position different from all other subject classes, that their masters require something more from them than actual service. Men do not want the obedience of women, they want their sentiments. All men, except the most brutish, desire to have, in the woman most nearly connected with them, not a forced slave but a willing one, not a slave merely but a favorite. They have therefore put everything in practice to enslave their minds. The masters of all other slaves rely, for maintaining obedience, on fear, either fear of themselves, or religious fears. The masters of women wanted more than simple obedience, and they turned the whole force of education to effect their purpose. All women are brought up from the very earliest years in the belief that their ideal of character is the very opposite to that of men; not self-will, and government by self-control; but submission and yielding to the control of others. All the moralities tell them that it is the duty of women, and all the current sentimentalities that it is their nature to live for others; to make complete abnegation of themselves, and to have no life but in their affections. And by their affections are meant the only ones they are allowed to have—those to the man with whom they are connected, or to the children who constitute an additional and indefeasible tie between them and a man. When we put together three things—first, the natural attraction between opposite sexes; secondly, the wife's entire dependence on the husband, every privilege or pleasure she has being either his gift, or depending entirely on his will; and lastly, that the principal object of human pursuit, consideration, and all objects of social ambition, can in general be sought or obtained by her only through him, it would be a miracle if the object of being attractive to men had not become the polar star of feminine education and formation of character. And, this great means of influence over the minds of women having been acquired, an instinct of selfishness made men avail themselves of it to the utmost as a means of holding women in subjection, by representing to them meekness, submissiveness, and resignation of all individual will into the hands of a man, as an essential part of sexual attractiveness.[38]

Mill thus made clear the special difficulties women faced in rebelling against men. Nevertheless, the premise of the rationalists was that human aspirations could be enhanced, and the social goals of the male feminists—cooperative socialism through peaceful democratic means—required it. Mill exerted himself strenuously to recruit women as the spokespersons and the organizers for the petition drives that were the strategy of the "moral force" radicals. The pressures that male feminists exerted on women and the conflicts they engendered are vividly exposed in correspondence over the course of seven years between John Stuart Mill and Florence Nightingale.

The name Florence Nightingale is synonymous with the profession that she founded. In contemporary terms, it is a sex-stereotyped profession, with nurses often performing the work of doctors without the status or earning potential that doctors have. In the Victorian age, however, nursing was an exciting advance for women who wanted gainful employment, an opportunity for independence, and a meaningful life of service to humanity which might be an acceptable alternative to marriage and motherhood. The theme of wider employment opportunities for women was one consistently sounded by feminists at a time when the fields open to women were very limited. Many women working for meager wages in factories were forced into prostitution to supplement their incomes. To those feminists who considered job opportunities the most important means of raising women's status in society, Florence Nightingale was a heroine and a living legend. Moreover, she was a rebel with whom middle-class women were able to identify in a way they could not with feminist ideologues such as Mary Wollstonecraft and Fanny Wright, who defied middle-class conventions. Indomitably respectable, yet with a character resolute enough to overcome the open hostility of the doctors she worked among during the Crimean War, she was described by Mill as "more universally admired than any other living person." Since the support of the Lady with the Lamp would have given instant credibility to the women's movement he was trying to foster, Mill used all his considerable powers of persuasion to convince her of the importance of political rights as well as equality of opportunity for women.

Their debate on women's rights began in 1860, when Mill asked Nightingale to support a movement enabling women to qualify as doctors on the same basis as men. It was a cardinal tenet of the feminist fathers, and one in which Mill firmly believed, that the capacities of men and women were equal. With the proper education and training, they should be allowed into any field that men entered. In Mill's words, women should "not be excluded by law or usage from the liberty of trying any mode of assertion open to men at their own risk in case of failure." He staunchly disagreed with those who felt that a woman's physique might make it more it more difficult for her to perform certain jobs, especially those which required extraordinary strength. Therefore, he was somewhat nonplussed when Nightingale suggested that women ought not to enter the male professions. Her objections stemmed from her experience as a nurse in the Crimean War. The unsanitary conditions she had to contend with, and the indifference of the doctors to the dismally inadequate medical facilities which were the cause of more deaths among the soldiers than bullets or cannon fire, did not inspire her with respect for the medical profession. She founded nursing schools to provide career opportunities for women who wanted to help the sick, and she believed that from that vantage point they could effectively influence doctors and humanize the medical profession. Nightingale was critical of Elizabeth Blackwell who, in 1849, became the first women to receive an M.D. She said, "While the medical profession is what it is there should be fewer women doctors, for mind you women have made no improvement. They have only tried to be men and they have only succeeded in being third-rate men."[39]

Nightingale's views went to the heart of many women's conflicts. She, like Anna Wheeler, felt that if women were to go into the male world they would "become men," code words for materialism and callousness to feminists of both sexes, who were united in their common opposition to the institutions and values of the man-made world which they inhabited. Feminists were not united, however, on how women's moral values could best be put into effect. Nightingale did not believe that the entrance of women into male professions would bring about any improvement in the masculine character, nor that it would humanize male institutions. Women would simply be co-opted and "masculinized." She hoped that women's unique values could in and of themselves be a constructive force without attaching them to a political cause. In effect, she argued for a separate but equal doctrine with respect to male and female spheres. Mill was relentless in communicating his conviction that there is no such thing as separate but equal. Women could not gain recognition of their values except in the public world; they could not moderate men's excesses without exerting political pressure. Within the domestic sphere, women's moral and humanistic values were conjoined with their inferiority, and could not appreciably influence men.

Male feminists, from Thompson to Holyoake to Mill, maintained that failures and disappointments had to be risked. Ultimately, determination and concerted action would result in reform of the institutions men had developed to perpetuate their own superiority. He wrote Florence Nightingale: "It is too much to expect that they (women doctors) should have made an improvement. But if the medical profession is to be improved it must be reformed from within. There is more chance of that happening when entrance to it is widened."[40]

In 1867, John Stuart Mill, then a member of Parliament, introduced an amendment to a bill enfranchising working-class men, to include women. The amendment failed, but it seemed a propitious moment for women to establish the organizations and support structures which might bring victory in the future. In London, a women's suffrage committee was formed. A number of prominent women, among them Florence Nightingale, were asked by Mill to be sponsors of the organization. Nightingale balked, earning a stern rebuke from Mill. He wrote her:

I know how fully you appreciate a great many of the evil effects produced upon the character of woman-kind operating to the destruction of their own and others' happiness. The new society aimed at the very sort of all the ends you deplore and have passed your life in combatting. As I am convinced that this power [the vote] is by far the greatest that it is possible to wield for human happiness, I can neither approve of women who decline their responsibility of wielding it, nor of men who would prevent them from the right to wield it. Until women do wield it to the best of their ability, little or great, I am convinced that evils of which I know you to be peculiarly aware, can never be dealt with.[41]

Evidently stung, Nightingale quickly responded, citing the reasons for the misgivings she harbored. She was not averse to reform, but the vote was not a priority on her agenda:

It is important for a woman, especially a married woman, to be a person. But it will probably be years before women obtain the suffrage. And in the meantime are there not evils which press more hardly on women than not having a vote? When obtained will women be in a position from those who withhold those rights to retard still further the necessary legislation? [*sic*] Married women must [be] able to possess property. It is possible that the suffrage will delay these rights, since the agitation and confrontation that are necessary to gain them might produce greater hostility to women.[42]

She concluded with a parry typical of women who achieved distinction without a movement behind them, citing her absorption with the administrative duties of the nursing school which had preoccupied her for the last sixteen years. These duties kept her too busy to think about the vote, and she reiterated her preference for staying in the background on this issue.

Mill was familiar with all the arguments Nightingale put forth, for he was thoroughly prepared to answer them point by point. With respect to Nightingale's doubts as to the efficacy of the suffrage in achieving other—perhaps higher—priorities, such as property rights, Mill asserted: "Disabilities can be swept away. The question is, has it ever seemed urgent to sweep away these disabilities until there was a prospect of the ruled getting political power? It is probably a question whether it is in human nature that it ever should seem to be urgent?" Human egotism being what it was, Mill averred, even if unjust property laws were to be abolished today, there would be nothing to prevent new ones from being proposed tomorrow if males retained control of the political process. He assured her that the suffrage reform would be the easiest to accomplish, and that all others "will flow from it."

With respect to an escalation of the war between the sexes if women were to become so bold as to publicly demand their rights, Mill pointed out that conflicts—"political partisanship"—would cease only if women consistently surrendered. He noted, somewhat sarcastically, "No doubt when you have death you have none of the problems of life." He sought to calm Nightingale's fears with his assurance that the prospect of heightened antagonism between men and women was negligible: "I see no danger of party spirit running high between men and women and no possibility of its making things worse than they are if it did." The risk, Mill believed, was worth it for the sake of posterity, to which women owed "the struggle for the advancement of opinion."

Mill assumed that the resistance of women stemmed from the passivity, the habit of obedience—"the servile character"—that social conventions imposed, and that their dependence on men strengthened. He chided Nightingale and at the same time appealed to her pride in the work to which she was dedicated, and in which she had invested all her talents and energies:

I cannot help thinking that the world would be better if every man, woman, and child could appear to the other in an exactly true light; known as the doer of the work that he does and neither to be under or overvalued. It is to be regretted that good women are often fond [of] false appearances asking to hide their good deeds as others hide their bad ones. I know that it is not pleasant to the inactive character fostered by the present influences among the best women, but it is to me a question whether the noble and as I think, heroic enthusiasm of truth and public good ought not in this age to name women.

He asked the skeptical Nightingale to consider the historical example of the early Christian women, who made "so courageous a sacrifice of their most justly cherished delicacy," but in doing so left an example for "the reverent love and admiration of all future time." He pointedly remarked, "I have no doubt that the Roman ladies thought them very indelicate."

Mill, the political economist and moral philosopher—the Saint of Liberalism— again showed himself to be an astute politician in the cause of feminism. He closed his letter to Florence Nightingale on a conciliatory note. More in sorrow than in anger, he wrote: "Therefore, while I have seen with much regret that you join in so few movements for the public good, I have never presumed to think you wrong because I have supposed that your abstinence arose from your devotion to one particular branch of public spirited work."[43]

Appeals to civic virtue, obligations to posterity, and her own self-respect had a powerful impact on Florence Nightingale. She succumbed, as did other doubters to whom Mill personally appealed, and enlisted in the struggle for the suffrage. In doing so she implicitly accepted premises that the feminist reformers had spent years elaborating and refining. These included the notion that the capacities of men and women were equal and that inequalities were the result of laws and social conventions instituted by men. Gaining political rights was the best means of sweeping away disabling laws and conventions, and the result would be a bright future of cooperation, equality, and social justice which would work to the mutual benefit and happiness of both sexes. The radical reformers believed that women were naturally more progressive, more community-oriented, and more pacific than men, and that their influence in society could reap only benefits.

Women who were about to enter the heretofore exclusively male domain of politics were assured that their distaste was a function of their sheltered lives, and that their inexperience would be compensated for by the support given by their male allies who had attained positions of power and influence. In this the women were not disappointed.

NOTES

1. In order to get the Reform Bill of 1832 (enfranchising a number of middle-class men) passed, its advocates agreed that the franchise would never be extended to women. Women subsequently lost municipal voting rights in 1835.

2. In the 1820s factory women in Lowell, Mass., had put out *The Lowell Offering*, but there were no journals in general circulation edited by women that promoted women's causes.

3. George Jacob Holyoake, *Sixty Years of an Agitator's Life* (London: T. Unwin, 1906), p. 222-23.

4. Quoted in H. N. Brailsford, *Shelley, Godwin, and Their Circle* (New York: Henry Holt, 1913), p. 188.

5. Ibid., p. 197.

6. Daniel Defoe, "Essay on Projects," in *The Works of Daniel Defoe*, 3 vols. (London: V. Clement, 1840). See also Katharine Rogers, "The Feminism of Daniel Defoe," in Paul Fritz and Richard Morton, eds., *Women in the Eighteenth Century* (New York: Garland Press, 1980).

7. Richard Steele, *Guardian*, no. 172, n.d.; Richard Steele, *Tattler*, no. 248, n.d.; Henry Addison, *Guardian*, no. 155, n.d.; Richard Steele, *Tattler*, no. 141, n.d.; Richard Steele, *Spectator*, no. 66, n.d.

8. Jonathan Swift, "A Letter to a Young Lady on Her Marriage," in *The Works of Jonathan Swift* (Dublin: George Faulkner, 1742), p. 266.

9. Thomas Paine, "An Occasional Letter on the Female Sex," in Philip Foner, ed., *The Complete Writings of Thomas Paine* (New York: The Citadel Press, 1975).

10. Gerald P. Tyson, *Joseph Johnson, A Liberal Publisher* (Iowa City: University of Iowa, 1979), p. 103-6.

11. William Godwin, *An Enquiry Concerning Political Justice and Its Influence on General Virtue and Happiness*, vol. 2 (New York: A. Knopf, 1927), p. 272.

12. Ibid., Introduction, p. xxxiii.

13. Charles Brockden Brown, *Alcuin: A Dialogue* (New York: T.&J. Swords, 1798).

14. The bluestockings were learned Englishwomen who wrote poetry, novels, and essays. They were examples of women achievers in the eighteenth century.

15. The conviction that women's rights could best be advanced by a female spokesperson suggests that Sophia, a Person of Quality (the anonymous author of a 1739 tract, *Woman, Not Inferior to Man*), was most likely a man.

16. Lee R. Edwards, ed., *Alcuin: A Dialogue by Charles Brockden Brown* (New York: Grossman Publishers, 1971), p. 88.

17. E. P. Thompson, *The Making of the English Working Class* (New York: Vintage Press, 1963), p. 163.

18. R. F. K. Pankhurst, *William Thompson* (London: Watts and Co., 1954), p. 12.

19. Ibid., p. 25.

20. Ibid., p. 119.

21. Ibid., p. 118.

22. William Thompson, *An Inquiry into the Principles of the Distribution of Wealth Most Conducive to Human Happiness Applied to the Newly Proposed System of Voluntary Equality of Wealth* (1824, reprint ed., London: W.S. Orr & Co., 1850), p. 261.

23. All quotes are from William Thompson, *Appeal of One Half of the Human Race, Women, Against the Pretensions of the Other Half, Men, to Retain Them in Civil and Domestic Slavery* (1825; reprint ed., New York: Burt Franklin, 1970), pp. 55, 125, 187.

24. Pankhurst, *William Thompson*, p. 74.

25. Thompson, "Introductory Letter to Mrs. Wheeler," in *Appeal*, p. ix.

26. J.F.C. Harrison, *Quest for the New Moral World: Robert Owen and the Owenites* (New York: Charles Scribner's and Sons, 1969), p. 60.

27. Ibid., p. 117.

28. Holyoake, *Agitator's Life*, p. 223.

29. Ibid., p. 224.

30. John Stuart Mill, *Autobiography* (New York: P. F. Collier and Son, 1909), chap. 6.

31. See Gertrude Himmelfarb, *On Liberty and Liberalism: The Case of John Stuart Mill* (New York: A. Knopf, 1974).

32. John Stuart Mill, *The Subjection of Women* (Philadelphia: J. B. Lippincott & Co., 1869), p. 138.

33. F. A. Hayek, *John Stuart Mill and Harriet Taylor* (London: Routledge Kegan and Paul, 1951), pp. 64-66.

34. Ibid., p. 67.

35. See Alice Rossi, "Sentiment and Intellect, The Story of John Stuart Mill and Harriet Taylor Mill," in Alice Rossi, ed., *John Stuart Mill and Harriet Taylor Mill, Essays on Sex Equality* (Chicago: University of Chicago Press, 1970).

36. Mill, *Subjection of Women*, p. 163.

37. Hayek, *Mill and Taylor*, p. 15.

38. Mill, *Subjection of Women*, p. 28.

39. Florence Nightingale, to J. S. Mill, September 12, 1860. In British Museum, London.

40. Mill to Nightingale, September 23, 1860.

41. Mill to Nightingale, August 9, 1867.

42. Nightingale to Mill, August 11, 1867.

43. Mill to Nightingale, December 31, 1867.

A SINGLE STANDARD OF MORALITY: THE SEX CONSERVATIVES

2

For the traitors to the masculine cause, the slave and the prostitute were metaphors for women's historic condition of oppression. The use of slavery as a code word for the legal subjection of women dominated the early writings of the feminist fathers. "Sexual slaves" was a term denoting married women who had to submit to what feminists considered the lowest degradation possible for a human being—that of being made "the instrument of an animal function contrary to one's inclinations."[1] For these men the word "slavery" summed up that tenet of the masculine cause which equated property and power, and which defined the possession of human property as the acme of power. Their perception that slavery was a masculine invention and an inevitable concomitant of capitalism contributed to their feminism. Since the institution of slavery did not exist in England, references to it as a paradigm for women's condition had little effect in raising the consciousness of English women but the analogy had a powerful impact on women in America where slavery was a legal reality and where feminists such as the Grimké sisters were able to identify with the degradation of their black sisters. It is hardly an accident that the most prominent American feminists of the nineteenth century, Elizabeth Cady Stanton, Lucretia Mott, and the Grimké sisters, gained their apprenticeship in public life through the abolitionist movement, from which they diverged to form a women's movement.

For English women the prostitute, whose number was increasing throughout the nineteenth century, was the more compelling and uniquely feminine symbol of male oppression. The slave was indicative of man's inhumanity to man as well as to woman, while the ubiquitous prostitute brought about a vivid awareness of women's special exploitation by all men, regardless of race, creed, ethnic origin, or social status. The image of the prostitute as a victim of male lusts energized the English women's movement, made it a major force by bringing disparate groups of women together, and gave it that potential for advancing democracy and social justice on which the hopes of the feminist fathers were predicated.

The goal of eradicating prostitution embodied the idealism of the Victorians. Their goals of social harmony and sexual equality required the abolition of the double standard of sexual morality, whereby adultery and promiscuity were considered a male prerogative, but condemned and harshly punished when committed by women. Feminist idealism established as a precondition for continued progress a single standard of morality which would make debauchery as reprehensible in men as it was in women. Thus sexual conservatism was profoundly imbedded in the Victorian conscience, not merely as a result of religious teachings which had traditionally stressed a virtuous life for salvation's sake, but as a means to attain the secular ideals of human progress as well. For the Victorian reformer, whether he was a secular rationalist, a religious sectarian, or a member of the established Anglican Church, the progress of civilization was incompatible with sexual license.

A religious revival movement in the eighteenth century was part of the background for the moralistic impulses that resulted in concerted campaigns against vice. Prostitution came to be regarded as the greatest challenge the crusaders confronted. Methodism, which emerged from the religious awakening of the eighteenth century, had particular impact on the working classes, from whom the Bible-thumping preachers exacted commitments to sobriety and continence at their emotion-charged meetings.[2] But the evangelical fervor of the movement also percolated up and inspired establishment politicians such as William Wilberforce; the visible expression of his rebirth was his arduous campaign to end slavery in the British Empire, and, closer to home, to stamp out pornography. Opposition to obscenity was consistent with the desire on the part of the eighteenth-century reformers to raise women's status from that of sex objects to that of human beings worthy of the same rights and dignities to which men aspired. Obscene literature was not considered fit reading matter, either for males, whom the reformers were trying to imbue with respect for women, or for females, who were being encouraged to become more intellectual and more conversant with the world outside their immediate domestic concerns.

In 1788, members of the Proclamation Society successfully prosecuted the publishers of *Fanny Hill*, and, having tasted success, continued to exert pressure on Parliament to strengthen the obscenity laws and to apply them stringently. Since the image of women was at stake, women were invited to participate in the antivice organizations which were formed to influence manners and morals. In 1802, the formation of the Vice Society, which included as founding members William Wilberforce, Hannah More, and Zachary Macauley, exemplified the common interests that were so significant in making feminism in large part a moral uplift movement.

That religion and science were in total agreement on the necessity for sexual discipline explains the strength of the Victorian sexual code which, seen from the vantage point of the twentieth century, was repressive in the extreme, but which was an inevitable outgrowth of the matrix of fears and hopes generated by the eighteenth-century revolutions. When the French Revolution broke out in 1789, it heralded a new dawn for radicals in England, who hoped it would start a chain reaction that would topple the English monarchy. Tom Paine's works were so outspoken in this respect that they were eventually banned. "Bliss was it in that dawn to be alive," rhapsodized the young William Wordsworth. But some years later, when England was at war with Napoleon, who was widely perceived as having made a mockery of the revolutionary slogans—Liberty, Equality, Fraternity—a chastened Wordsworth was writing in a patriotic vein, buoyed by the fact that England alone was standing up to Napoleon as "the last that dare to struggle with the Foe."[3] Wordsworth was not alone in his odyssey.

The French Revolution generated a major debate in England between radicals who favored revolution and opponents of revolutionary upheavals. When Edmund Burke expressed his misgivings about the benefits of revolution, the radical publisher Joseph Johnson rushed into print with Tom Paine's *Rights of Man* and Mary Wollstonecraft's *Vindication of the Rights of Women* as a counterattack. Burke had voiced skepticism that reason would prevail over human passions once traditional restraints such as religious authority were removed. The excesses of the Reign of Terror appeared to confirm Burke's pessimism about human nature. The violence unleashed when the French monarchy was abolished was indelibly associated in the public mind with sexual license due to reports of atrocities that filtered into England. Incidents of aristocratic ladies being raped by former servants, mutilations of clergymen, and "republican marriages," where men and women suspected of counter-revolutionary activities were tied together naked and then drowned, served to cool revolutionary ardor.

That sexual continence and social order were equated can be seen in the experience of William Godwin. Just after the French Revolution, when confidence in its salubrious effects still prevailed, he experimented with sexual freedom in *Political Justice* by advocating the abolition of marriage. He operated on the assumption that human nature was monogamous, and that reason would triumph over instinct when malevolent institutions were swept away. In the late 1790s, he was severely taken to task by Thomas Malthus, who pointed to the pervasive sexual passions of men as the reason why Godwin's ebullient optimism was unjustified. To reenforce his point that sexual passions were an inexorable force that drove men to act against their reasonable interests, Malthus used mathematical evidence to predict a coming population explosion that would write a calamitous finis to the hopes for progress held by the Enlightenment philosophes. Malthus's warnings about the dire consequences of man's passionate nature reverberated strongly in the radical community, and the population question became a perennial concern of nineteenth-century progressives.

The shift on the part of the English Jacobins from revolution to reform reenforced their feminism, and figures in Charles Brockden Brown's demand for equal rights for women in *Alcuin*. Reformers considered women their natural allies, not only because women's claims for a voice in government had been rejected by the revolutionaries in both France and America, but because women were perceived as sexual conservatives who would thus be guarantors of social stability.

When scientific authorities published conclusions that sex was dangerous to men's health, the trend toward sexual conservatism was precipitously accelerated. Simon André Tissot (1725-1797), a Swiss physician, had as decisive an influence over sexual behavior in the nineteenth century as Freud has had in the twentieth; but Tissot has been as thoroughly purged from the annals of science as those medieval philosophers who declared that the sun revolved around the earth. Tissot's theory of male sexuality was based on the sex drive as a form of energy which had to be conserved for its primary purpose, reproduction. He regarded semen, the visible consequences of the sex act, as a nonrenewable energy resource, the rash expenditure of which brought on a variety of ills, ranging from minor complaints to terminal diseases. Throughout the nineteenth century, "to spend" was the word for orgasm. "Lassitude, feebleness, a weakening of motion, fits, wasting disease, dryness, fevers, aching of the cerebral membranes, obscuring of the senses—above all the eyes—a decay of the spinal chord and other like evils," were all attributed to sexual indulgence.[4]

Any individual who thought to avoid these horrors by self-stimulation was quickly disabused of this notion by Tissot, who declared that *la souillure manuelle* (manual defilement) carried with it even greater dangers than "excès avec les femmes."[5] At the very least, masturbation lowered one's resistance to such killers as smallpox, and was a primary cause of epileptic fits, stones, scrofula, asthma, migraines, and inflammation of the sexual organs. Pleasures enjoyed in solitude were also suspect to the reform-minded philosophes, who wanted to open all human activities to public scrutiny and rational analysis; they were convinced that masturbation was an antisocial activity which would lead to madness. Even involuntary sexual activity such as nocturnal emission did not escape Tissot's condemnation, since that resulted in slow circulation and a pervasive fatigue that prevented sufferers from working more than a few hours a day—a calamity to a Calvinist like Tissot. The one consolation for those afflicted with the latter syndrome was that Tissot offered a viable remedy which consisted of a strict diet.[6]

Tissot's influence was all the greater since he went to great lengths to discredit opponents of his ideas, whom he labelled "quacks, mountebanks, and conjurers." Warning that anarchy in medicine is the most dangerous anarchy, he avowed that the designation "quack" was not applied to as many as deserved it, and asked for severe regulations to prevent charlatans from imposing their nostrums on a gullible public. He was affronted that quacks often effected cures when "trained physicians" could not, and would reserve the most draconian measures for them. He was also incensed that "country people" put their confidence in quacks, and attributed this misplaced loyalty to their lower fees and to an incomprehensible hostility to trained physicians.[7] That the trained physicians spoke with the utmost authority and prescribed harsh treatments (heroic medicine) for ills that they themselves invented, while they were more helpless than the quacks when confronted with the acknowledged diseases that plagued mankind, may have accounted for the popular resistance of which Tissot bitterly complained.

Tissot did much to establish public dependence on the medical profession by driving out the untrained practitioners. Hence the wide acceptance of his views. He was translated into English and his works were published both in England and in the United States. In the United States, Benjamin Rush (1746-1813), the most prominent physician in the early American republic, was a disciple of Tissot and reaffirmed the need for sexual discipline by males. The obverse of this sexual conservatism was feminism, and was expressed by the demand for a single standard of sexual morality.

Rush's theories on male sexuality were part of a comprehensive investigation undertaken to find a common factor that linked all diseases, whether physical or emotional. He further expanded the domain, as well as the authority of the medical profession, when he proposed that the underlying cause of all disease (whether it be yellow fever, which had reached epidemic proportions in Philadelphia; insanity; or social diseases such as crime and drunkenness) was physical, and was subject to treatment by medical authorities. Rush acknowledged the influence of Tissot when he maintained that all outward manifestations of inner disturbance were caused by inordinate excitation of nerves and blood vessels. Insanity, for instance, could be produced by overburdened nerves in the head. It followed that the cure for all diseases was the avoidance and removal of such excitation, the most egregious of which was the sex act. Rush, like Tissot, ascribed a long list of diseases to "excitation of nerves and waste of semen." These included impotence, dyspepsia, blindness, vertigo—and the usually fatal consumption.[8]

Rush firmly believed that an ounce of prevention was worth a pound of cure. He recommended abstinence from all those stimulants which promoted undue excitement. Alcohol, already a target for antivice crusaders, was to be avoided. Sex, the most powerful stimulant of all, could not be dispensed with entirely without making human beings an endangered species, and therefore moderation and temperance were prescribed. In recommending that women's procreative needs set the pace for the male's sexual indulgence, Rush in effect made women the moral guardians of America's uncertain future, and gave feminism scientific backing.

The corollary to the theory of male sexuality as an implacable force which had to be contained for the common welfare was the assumption that female sexuality was negligible. An age which demanded evidence for scientific truths saw no visible manifestation in females of the sexual desire exhibited in males, and thus learned men assumed that women were "passionless" creatures whose sexual drives were tied to their procreative instincts. Those philosophes who believed that reason and morality flourished where passion was absent were implicit feminists. When physicians like Rush urged men to make women their guides with respect to sexual activity, they were acknowledging women's greater virtue and higher morality. Women were designated as tamers of the "beast" in men and given the role of leaders in attaining that moral order where the intellect reigned supreme. With its advocacy of moderation and its emphasis on morality, Rush's sexual conservatism was suited to a people in a new land whose self-proclaimed mission was to lead the way to progress, and whose energies had to be channelled for that purpose.

Rush illustrates the connection between sexual conservatism and feminism in a number of ways. He believed that women, like men, had been endowed with reason and should receive the same education as men. Rush worked for free public education for both women and men. He advocated a liberal arts education for women because he saw them as full partners in the American experiment. They were to be taught mathematics so that they could manage property if their fathers or husbands were otherwise occupied. He believed women should have a knowledge of history and politics so that they could appreciate the nobility of the American mission and the distinction between American ideals and those of their European forebears. His faith that women could master higher education made him active in the foundation of the Young Ladies Academy in Philadelphia. Dismissing the view that a higher education would interfere with women's domestic functions as "prejudice of little minds," he proclaimed that the academy's aim was to "remove the present disparity which subsists between the sexes in the degree of their education and knowledge." Cultivation of reason in women, he believed, could not help but contribute to private and public happiness."[9]

An exalted view of women was given greater credence as the medical establishment dwelt with ever increasing intensity on the debilitating effects of the male sex drive. The cures for this affliction became a growth industry in the early American republic. Dr. Sylvester Graham believed that even sexual thoughts put an undue strain on the body in that they might lead to masturbation. In his *Lecture on Epidemic Diseases Generally and Particularly the Spasmodic Cholera*, which went through ten editions between 1838 and 1848 and was translated into several foreign languages, Graham stressed that an ounce of semen was equivalent to four ounces of blood. A man who sustained repeated losses exposed himself to a growing catalogue of ills, all resulting in premature death. Graham spread the word that morality was the key to health through the health societies which he founded and which spread rapidly through grassroots America. Their guiding philosophy was his dictum, "While we continually violate the psychological laws of our nature our systems will continue to be living volcanoes of bad feelings and bad passions, which however correct our abstract principles of morality may be, will continually break out in immoral actions."[10] Women were actively recruited in the struggle for morality and became the most fervent supporters of Graham's health societies.

John Harvey Kellogg underscored that the nervous shock that accompanied sexual activity was the most traumatic to which the system could be subjected and agreed with Graham that sex, even for reproductive purposes, should be limited to 12 times a year, or once a month. Kellogg stressed that the environment was the most important factor in promoting morality: "The exorbitant demands of the sexual appetite encountered among civilized people are not the result of a normal instinct, but are due to the excitements of an abnormally stimulating diet, the seduction of prurient literature and so called art, and the temptations of impure associations."[11] Both Kellogg and Graham promoted diet as a means of controlling sexual desire, Kellogg affirming that "as a man eateth, so he thinketh." Graham advocated the use of unbolted wheat flour, the chief ingredient of the graham cracker, his contribution to a healthy and morally elevated America. Kellogg, who operated a sanitarium in Battle Creek, Michigan, left an indelible imprint on American eating habits when he introduced to the inmates his special-formula breakfast foods—foods billed as essential to the moral development of the all-American boy. Kellogg's fervent belief in temperance eventually led him to leadership of the Moral Purity Division of the Women's Christian Temperance Union (WCTU). He was offered that post by Emma Willard, leader of the WCTU and a disciple of those medical men who advocated purity and demanded as a prerequisite the standard of morality natural to women.

Science having established the perniciousness and pervasiveness of vice and the importance of moral behavior for physical well-being, church leaders were quick to elaborate on the dangers vice held for the soul. They were outspoken in extolling the superior virtues of women and in urging them to extend their moral standards to men. Clergymen could point out that Christianity had been established on the basis of a universal morality. Their traditional advocacy of a single standard took on added meaning as women became the chief supporters of the churches in the nineteenth century. Figures attest to the fact that churchgoing was principally a feminine pursuit, while masculine activity was associated with secular concerns which promised monetary rewards. Church leaders, acutely aware of the growing disparity in the numbers of men and women parishioners, reacted accordingly by idealizing women's virtues and identifying with their concerns. The Unitarian minister Joseph Buckminster always reminded his largely female congregation how little he could do without them.[12] In a novel called *Zenobia*, written by a minister, William Ware, the Rome of the third century A.D. is viewed as a pre-Christian civilization where there are no defined sex roles. The noblest men and women are fighters, lovers of beauty, and philosophers. A Christian neophyte describes the Christian religion as feminine, "but not weak or effeminate." It is characterized by its "gentleness...the suavity of tone...the humanity of its doctrines...the high rank it assigns to the virtues which are peculiarly those of women."[13]

Church leaders linked women's expanded public role to a better education for women. The rationale was that, as future mothers, women were the prime formative influence on the child. Educated women would thus make better mothers for future generations. The cause of women's education thus became closely associated with the new moral world that was to come. Horace Bushnell made it clear that women were uniquely suited to inculcate moral values, starting with their own children. He established a journal, *Christian Nurture*, to promote women's educational function, pointing out that women could make their most important contributions to society by disseminating their values. Bushnell believed that temperance and social purity could be attained through the teaching of moral values, which was women's acknowledged preserve. He was of the opinion that sexual morality was the key to all morality, and he played a vital role in convincing women that their higher standards were essential to preserving civilization, and could play a vital role in attaining a higher stage of civilization—one that would see the "final triumph of love over lust."[14] The temperance movement, largely led by women, resulted from the partnership the churches had forged with women to promote female culture.

The saving of prostitutes was another challenge to which the social purity movement addressed itself. Early in nineteenth-century America, preachers associated with the Second Great Awakening had called attention to the growth of prostitution in the United States. It was especially prevalent in the poorer sections of urban centers. Overcoming a prevailing belief that ignorance is the best guarantee of innocence, Sunday school societies began to disseminate literature warning of the dangers of prostitution. The recognition that environmental factors such as poverty went hand in hand with vice caused them to wage war on poverty as a prerequisite for eradicating vice.

In the mid-1820s, the American Society for the Prevention of Licentiousness and Vice and Promotion of Morality sponsored direct efforts to eliminate prostitution by preaching the Gospel to "fallen" women. Reverend John McDowall went to the slums of New York City to evangelize prostitutes. He eventually combined his resources with William Goodell, editor of an antislavery paper, and together they published *The Female Advocate*, dedicated to the rescue of prostitutes.

The American Moral Reform Association became the most important of the antivice societies. It was dedicated not only to rescue work, but to resisting as well any attempt to legitimize vice by regulating prostitution. Reglementation, a policy that was adopted by a number of European countries, provided for the regular physical examination of prostitutes to make sure they were not diseased, and in some countries provided for their ghettoization in designated areas where their activities could more easily be policed. The policy of accepting prostitution rather than fighting it violated every precept held dear by the moral reformers, and they spared no effort to prevent its adoption in the New World.

There was a great deal of cross-fertilization between America and England on the social purity issue. England followed a pattern similar to that of the United States, where women's status was upgraded because of their presumptive passionlessness. Evangelical preachers in England, like their counterparts in the United States, equated women's greater piety with their regular church attendance. The clergy harped on the theme that women were made for God's purposes rather than man's, and believed that women had a responsibility to society. The writings of Evangelical reformers claimed that female piety and sincerity would bring "effectual reformation...in every department of society" because "all virtues...are ultimately connected with the manners, principles, and dispositions of women." Thomas Gisborne, a prominent Evangelical, maintained that women had "quicker feelings of native delicacy and a stronger sense of shame" than men.[15]

The brand of feminism that these men fostered is perhaps best exemplified by Charles Kingsley. Kingsley (1819-1875), a churchman, believed it was incumbent upon clergymen to be in the forefront of reforming the conditions of the poor and the destitute, many of whom were prostitutes. He was convinced that the Bible prescribed socialism as the millennium God intended for mankind, and his brand of Christian socialism gave renewed faith in the Christian message to working people. Kingsley believed the involvement of women to be crucial to his cause. From the pulpit and in his novels he urged women to tame the "beast" in men. The hero of *Yeast*, Lancelot Smith, regrets the peccadilloes that had led him not only to offend God but also to disappoint his bride: "The contact of her stainless innocence...made him shrink from her whenever he remembered his own guilty career....She would cast him from her with abhorrence if she really knew...that she would bring to him what he could never, never bring to her."[16]

Kingsley's work among the poor had familiarized him with the problem of prostitution. He urged vocational training for women so that they might find suitable employment and avoid the despair that bred prostitutes. He was instrumental in establishing Queens College for the training of governesses as part of the campaign to promote the welfare of women.

Kingsley urged middle-class women to go among the poor and help reform prostitutes, to rescue their fallen sisters on the assumption that it was a task that women, whom he considered to be more altruistic as well as more virtuous than men, were uniquely qualified for. By the 1850s, prostitution had come to be recognized as the single most obdurate obstacle to that moral order the sexual conservatives thought the crowning jewel in the progress of civilization. Vice societies in England could point to improvements in other areas of concern, such as alcoholism and gambling, and could take satisfaction that sexual purity had become the accepted standard for entrance into polite society. The extent to which middle-class morality had filtered down to the working classes was expressed by Francis Place, a working-class radical, when he stated, "I am certain I risk nothing when I assert that more good has been done to the people in the last thirty years than in the three preceeding centuries; that during this period they have become wiser, better, more frugal, more honest, more respectable than they ever were before."[17]

The Caroline Affair was a lesson for the upper classes intended to teach them that their lax morals were no longer acceptable. In this incident, George IV, who had a reputation as a debaucher and lecher, was rejected by the House of Lords when, upon his accession to the throne in 1820, he asked for a divorce from his long-estranged wife, Caroline. The sight of mobs rallying around the putative Queen Caroline and making her their heroine was instrumental in causing the aristocracy to at least pay lip service to sexual morality. Sexual conservatives found a strong ally when Queen Victoria ascended the throne in 1837. She banned from her court anyone who was in the slightest respect tinged with scandal.

In light of these advances, the growth of the phenomenon of prostitution was a glaring rebuke in the eyes of moral reformers. In 1815, after the celebrations of Britain's victory over Napoleon, a journal noted that "notwithstanding our lofty pretension to the character of a religious and moral people, there is no capital in Europe where prostitution is suffered to display itself in so shameless a manner...."[18] Such observations were regularly repeated. Attempts were made to rally public support for the supression of brothels, but these had only short-lived success. In 1812, the Guardian Society formed a committee to discover the best means of driving prostitutes from the streets and providing homes for those who wanted to reform. In 1813, a group of citizens presented a petition to the lord mayor of London, signed by two thousand householders, demanding a crackdown. And indeed, the lord mayor began busily applying himself to closing down brothels and committing streetwalkers to Bridewell Prison, but no matter how stern the measures, the streets never ceased to be infested with prostitutes.

Government action proving counterproductive, private philanthropic efforts were encouraged. Such attempts went back to 1758, when Magdalen Hospital was established as a home for reformed prostitutes. It was the first of three hundred such homes provided by Evangelical reformers, who emphasized that prostitutes were victims of society's neglect, and that efforts should be directed toward saving them, rather than incarcerating them. This stress on rescue derived from evidence that prostitutes were often forced into the profession as children, victims of the industrial dislocation and of the gruelling poverty that technological progress had done nothing to alleviate. The "fallen" woman, fallen because of her vulnerability to remorseless social conditions, but who might be saved through the dedicated efforts of her more fortunate sisters, became an image charged with both despair and hope, a symbol of the corruption of men and of the redeeming qualities of women.

In 1843, there was a concerted attempted on the part of male reformers to involve more women in rescue work. Female auxiliaries of the antivice societies were formed, albeit with male secretaries. It was hoped that they would initiate a "movement of the women of England," and that hoped-for legislation against prostitution would "only be the commencement of a general improvement in the laws for the benefit of women."[19]

While feminist fathers such as George Holyoake were stymied in their efforts to involve women in political activities, the rescue societies attracted such effective spokeswomen as Josephine Butler, Ellice Hopkins, and Catherine Booth. They were an inspiration not only to other women, but to men, as well, who saw them as proof that women's capacities extended far beyond the domestic sphere. Indeed, rescue work itself comprised a number of activities which required diverse talents. It included approaching prostitutes—in order to get their cooperation, a form of proselytizing. Once a prostitute agreed to "convert," she needed pyschological counselling and constant reenforcement to keep her from slipping back. Rescue workers found employment for reformed prostitutes, provided shelter for unwed mothers, and cared for the sick. They thus combined social work, psychiatry, nursing, and administrative skills. The women practitioners were fueled by missionary zeal and altruistic concerns since the work they did was purely voluntary. Josephine Butler, who exemplified the dedication of these social workers, called prostitutes "martyrs of purity." She worked tirelessly to get contributions to open a small refuge for prostitutes in Liverpool and she herself nursed the ones who were most hopelessly ill.

The involvement of women in rescue efforts as part of their moral obligation to society, and women's achievements as leaders in reform movements to whose greater virtue men deferred, belie the contemporary conception that the moralists of the nineteenth century lived in a dark night of sexual frustration, productive of hysterical symptoms defined as neuroses by the Freudians, who reversed the sexual theories of Tissot. To conform to an image of virtue and "passionlessness" may be considered oppressive in the age of Freud, or at least to those of his disciples who consider sexual expression the *sine qua non* for physical and mental health. But for the Victorians, the image of the passionlessness woman had certain compensations which made its examplars loath to surrender it. To the extent that sexuality is a function of complex psychological factors, it is likely that Victorian women's sexual desires per se were minimal. Before birth control became acceptable, the sex act was associated in women's minds with childbearing and all its attendant dangers and responsibilities. The risks sex entailed for men were theoretical; but women had ample evidence that sexual intercourse, resulting in incessant childbearing, was indeed injurious to *their* health—leading to a variety of physical and emotional ills, and frequently to an early grave. Passionlessness was thus an extremely effective form of birth control, to the extent that men did as they were urged by feminist reformers and allowed their sexual lives to be regulated by women's maternal needs. In addition, the higher morality of women, based on their passionlessness, created solidarity among them, and made the women's movement possible. Relationships between women assumed a higher value than heterosexual relationships, since female friendships were by definition devoid of carnal lusts.[20] It may be surmised that the emotional intimacies women were free to enjoy with other women, the sustained satisfactions of power which women derived from their role as moral leaders, and the respect they gained as activists in rescue work in England and in the abolition of slavery in the United States, were adequate compensation for the ephemeral sexual pleasures which they presumably forsook.

While a common identification with the prostitute as a victim of male lusts was helping to bring women together, their conflicts about the oldest profession were polarizing men, and creating a battleground between the masculinists and the traitors to the masculine cause. The masculinists tended to think that prostitution was a necessity given the nature of men. Doctors, beseiged by worried males suffering from spermatorrhea, or wet dreams, advised their patients that releasing their sex drives by resorting to prostitutes was preferable to masturbation, whose baneful consequences might include insanity. The historian W.E.H. Lecky, in a classic masculinist statement, saw the prostitute as the most effective guardian of the virtues of middle-class women, since, without her, they would be the inevitable objects of the male attentions which they neither sought nor desired. The dour heirs of John Calvin tended to regard prostitutes as perverted creatures with insatiable sexual appetites, exemplars of the doctrine of irremediable sin, who embarked on their notorious profession because it was both profitable and easy. For them the prostitute was not salvageable; she was, however, considered to be necessary to entrap the sinner and provide visible evidence of the wages of sin through the venereal diseases spawned by prostitution.

It was William Acton (1813-1875), a prominent physician, who made a political issue of prostitution and the double standard which supported it. His actions brought to a head the sexual antagonisms which were brewing and caused an explosion which reverberated into the twentieth century. They raised fantasies of a sex war and made the woman's question a central concern for politicians, scientists, and philosophers. Acton was an unlikely catalyst for the melee he precipitated. A liberal with reformist and humanitarian impulses, he came to the issue out of a concern for public health. Statistics revealed that prostitution was not diminishing despite the heroic efforts of rescue workers. It was, in fact, on the increase, and one evidence of this was the rising incidence of venereal disease. Acton's specialty was venereology. He had studied in Paris under the American-born venereologist, Philippe Ricord. Their work made it possible to distinguish syphilis from gonorrhea, and it was Acton who established that there were three stages in the progress of syphilis. The third stage was found to be insidious, and might occur years after the disease was first contracted and the original skin lesions gone. Third-stage syphilis was terminal, and included the symptoms of progressive brain and bone deterioration that eighteenth-century physicans generally ascribed to excessive sexual indulgence.

In 1838, when Ricord published *Traité Pratique des Maladies Veneriennes*, cures for venereal diseases were highly problematical. The treatment for gonorrhea was the injection of silver nitrate into the urethra, while mercury was used for syphilis. But these treatments were ineffective, and the incidence of disease kept rising; in 1865, one-third of the members of the British armed forces were infected. This staggering figure made venereal disease not only the number one health problem in the nation; it made it a concern of the War Office as a national security concern as well.

When Acton was asked to address the National Association for the Promotion of Social Science, a liberal group which advocated wide-ranging reforms, including women's rights, he read a paper entitled *Prostitution Considered in Its Moral, Social, and Sanitary Aspects in London and Other Large Cities, With Proposals for the Mitigation and Prevention of Its Attendant Evils*. The paper was published in 1857, and offered a considered approach to the problem which took into account the latest scientific discoveries and put them in the context of political reform. Acton did not think the problems generated by prostitution could be solved by the free enterprise system of voluntary rescue work. He demanded a commitment on the part of the state to deal with this blight on a systematic basis, using resources that only the state could muster. Acton recommended a three-pronged approach, which embraced recognition of the problem, then amelioration and prevention of disease by government regulation.

In recognizing prostitution, Acton made every attempt to humanize the prostitutes— "these miserable creatures, ill-fed, ill-clothed, uncared for, from whose misery the eye recoils, cowering under dark arches and among bye-lanes."[21] He defined a prostitute, in the sympathetic terms of the social reformer, as "a woman who gives for money that which she ought to give only for love, who ministers to passions and lusts alone. . . . She is a woman with half the woman gone, and that half containing all that elevates her nature, leaving her a mere instrument of impurity." Acton emphasized that prostitutes were often victims of a pernicious social order and of an economic system that frequently forced them, or at the very least predisposed them, to enter their profession. His extensive studies of prostitutes revealed that they were transients who had no inclination to make prostitution their life's work, but who traded their bodies until an opportunity for a respectable situation (which might be either marriage or regular employment) came along. Acton was eloquent about the conditions that produced prostitution, such as the overcrowding of families and the lack of employment opportunities for women. In the best liberal tradition he demanded reform: "It is absolutely impossible to exaggerate the suffering entailed by a life of prostitution. Instead of the scorn so freely lavished on the poor lost daughters of shame and misery, I plead for a little pity—nay for more than pity, I plead for justice."

Acton's solution made clear that he was a convert to the concept of the big government welfare state, which the new breed of liberal thought the only answer to the abuses of laissez-faire individualistic capitalism. His program of state intervention involved the physical examination of prostitutes to determine if they had venereal disease; their confinement in state funded hospitals should they prove to be infected; and a practical program of reeducation that would "bring them into daily contact with healthy thought and virtuous life." Acton held out hope that by such positive steps the moral climate of society would improve "by gradual and almost imperceptible stages."

A man of enormous personal probity, Acton was a sexual conservative who paid homage to all the moral verities by which proper Victorians guided their lives. He frowned on the use of prostitutes for sexual release and insisted that "man's plain duty is to seek in honorable love the gratification of manly desire and to wait for enjoyment till he has earned the right to it." Until such a time, Acton recommended the exertions of "the cricket field, the river, or the racket court."

Acton testified to the enduring influence of Tissot, concurring with him about the dangers of masturbation—"loss of intellectual powers, pallor, emaciation, depression, a taste for solitude." His description of the masturbator—"haggard expression, sunken eye, long cadaverous-looking countenance, and downcast look"—constituted an implicit agreement with Tissot that sex relations were preferable to onanism.

Despite Acton's social concerns and good intentions, feminists found a dis-

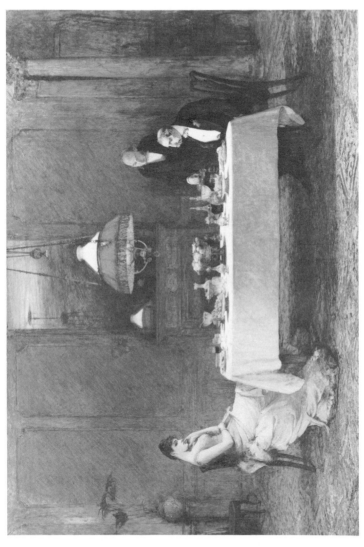

Plate 3. Mariage de Convenance by William Q. Orchardson. This painting and others that follow in this chapter show the hypocrisy of the double standard and the dilemmas of nineteenth-century women. A bored, resentful young woman married to a much older man depicts upper-class marriage as a business arrangement. Used with the permission of the Glasgow Art Gallery and Museum, Kelvingrove, Glasgow.

Plate 4. Past and Present, No. 1 by Augustus Leopold Egg, illustrating middle-class marriage, shows a woman prostrated before her husband. Having committed adultery, her fate is completely in his hands. This first panel from a three-part oil study by the artist, is filled with symbolism. The children have built a house of cards that is collapsing, half of the husband's face is in deep shadow. He has a dark side (angry) and a light side (pained). Used with the permission of the Tate Gallery, Millbank, London.

53

Plate 5. Past and Present, No. 3 by Augustus Leopold Egg, is the third panel in a three-part oil study, showing that the wife's appeal to her husband's better nature has been unsuccessful. Subtitled *No Place to Lay Her Head*, this painting shows the woman with her illegitimate child haunting the docks. Above her is a poster asking help for "Victims." Used with the permission of The Tate Gallery, Millbank, London.

Plate 6. The Poor Teacher by Richard Redgrave depicts one of the few occupations open to women who did not marry. The governess is shown reading a black-bordered letter, isolated and excluded from the family life surrounding her. Used with the permission of the Victoria and Albert Museum, London.

Plate 7. Found by Dante Gabriel Rossetti depicts a rescue. Prostitution was the only recourse for many working-class women. Rescuing prostitutes was a mission for many Victorians and was a means for expressing their distaste for the double standard. The bleating lamb in the net is an allegory for the prostitute. This painting is from the Samuel and Mary R. Bancroft Memorial Collection and is used with the permission of the Delaware Art Museum, Wilmington.

heartening masculine bias both in his philosophy and in his proposals. Acton felt sanguine that prostitution might be diminished, but believed that it would never be abolished because, in the last analysis, the powerful sexual urges to which men are subject made it inevitable. Adverse social conditions might increase the number of prostitutes, but the institution existed because of the nature of the male animal. He noted, "The desire for sexual intercourse is strongly felt by the male on attaining puberty, and continues through his life, an ever present sensible want."

For all the sympathy he displayed for the plight of the prostitute victimized by a callous economic and social system, there were also hints of fear of the temptress who ensnares her male victims: ". . . who are these painted, dressy women flaunting along the streets and boldly accosting passers by?" His belief that male sexual passions can be either encouraged or restrained by women suggested that prostitutes who solicited on the streets were at least as culpable as their clients. Although Acton paid tribute to the virtuous woman (calling her "the sheet anchor of society") and attributed the improved moral climate as "due chiefly to the strength, uniformity, and consistency of her virtues maintained under so many sacrifices and with so much fortitude and heroism,"[22] he evidently did not believe that men were capable of matching women's moral standards. Acton, in effect, accepted the double standard of sexual morality and, because of his prominence in the medical world, left the public to suppose that it had a scientific stamp of approval.

Acton's proposals won the support of a number of political leaders and were embodied in the Contagious Diseases (CD) Acts passed in 1864, 1866, and 1869. The CD Acts, which applied to certain military garrison and seaport towns, gave police officers authority to arrest any woman found within specified areas whom they considered to be a prostitute. The women arrested on suspicion would be brought before a magistrate who, if he agreed with the arresting officer, would order her to register and submit to a medical examination. If found to be suffering from venereal disease, she would be sent to a hospital, where she could be detained for three months or longer at the discretion of the resident physician. If found to be disease-free, she would be released with a certificate of health. If she refused to undergo the mandatory physical examination or to enter a hospital, she was liable to imprisonment with or without hard labor.

The CD Acts addressed themselves specifically to the incidence of venereal disease in the British armed forces which had reached epidemic proportions. This was not only a concern of the public health authorities but of the War Office, which feared for the effectiveness of an army felled by disease. The CD Acts thus had the active support of public health authorities, of the Admirality and the War Office, and of a broad cross section of both the Conservative and Liberal parties. For Conservatives, the CD Acts were entirely consistent with the concept of paternalism to which they subscribed—that the privileged had an obligation to the underprivileged—a philosophy that had already produced landmark legislation restricting the hours of work for women and children. The CD Acts were also expressive of a revised liberal philosophy which foreshadowed the welfare state by designating the government as guardian of the interests of the victims of the industrial process. Liberals had begun to recognize that unfettered capitalism had spawned an underclass whose members could not help themselves, and whose problems could not be alleviated solely by the philanthropic work that many middle-class women had undertaken. In proposing regulation of prostitutes, Acton bore in mind that liberals, with their traditional concern for civil liberties, had to walk a fine line between protecting the community and allowing for a maximum of individual freedom. He maintained that a prostitute had the right to use her body for profit if she chose, but that she did not have the right to transmit diseases endemic to her profession to the rest of the community. Since the CD Acts provided for the rehabilitation of prostitutes, they outwardly conformed to humanitarian principles and could be linked, at least philosophically, to other reform measures calculated to appeal to feminists, including better education for women, improved employment opportunities, and higher wages for working women.

The CD Acts were passed with broad bipartisan support, with little debate and without any fanfare. Well-intentioned though they were, the CD Acts aroused the deepest fears of the feminists and were an affront to their moral convictions. By regulating prostitutes society was, in effect, condoning vice and accepting the double standard as national policy. The men and women who had been inspired by the Evangelical conviction that the fallen could be saved, and who dedicated their concerted energies to that goal, found their work repudiated by the masculinists, who deemed prostitution essential as a safety valve. Feminists were especially outraged at the implied approval of the double standard and at the ascription of the blame for the diseases generated by male lusts to a class of poor women.

In forcing medical examinations on prostitutes, the government was notifying women collectively that they were to be held responsible for the transgressions of men. Indeed, parliamentary supporters of the feminists such as Lord Shaftesbury had tried to insert in the CD Acts provisions for the prostitutes' clients to be arrested and held for medical examinations, and for pimps, procurers, and brothel owners to be prosecuted, but these provisions were resoundingly defeated, reenforcing the feminists' anger. There were ominous signs, perceived by Josephine Butler and James Stansfeld, who eventually joined forces to repeal the CD Acts, that the masculine cause, already associated with economic exploitation and with an array of vices, would evolve into a male tyranny over women through the exclusive control by males of the machinery of the modern state.

Misgivings about male intentions were deepened by the fact that working-class males had attained voting rights in 1867. John Stuart Mill had attempted to add an amendment to the bill that would give the vote to women as well, but had failed. Thus, by 1870, working-class men, many of whom were largely illiterate, had political power, while well-educated middle-class women did not.

The opponents of the CD Acts had support from some liberals who were especially sensitive to violations of civil liberties and who charged that the civil rights of English women were being systematically denied every time a suspected prostitute was arrested for a physical examination. Enforcement of the

CD Acts required that the local magistrates be given freewheeling authority to pick up women who might be prostitutes, causing Sheldon Amos, a lawyer, to complain that "the police may put any women as to whom they have received information on trial as a common prostitute." The police were not given clear guidelines in selecting suspects, and their judgments were often fallible. They tended to single out women of the working classes whose shabby clothes indicated their vulnerability, if not their surrender, to temptation. John Stuart Mill, giving evidence before a royal commission, emphasized that the police had to have considerable discretion if the CD Acts were to be effective, and that excessive zeal could lead to abuse of authority. This might endanger not only the freedoms of the prostitutes, but those of all women.[23] In one case of mistaken identity, a woman arrested and forced to submit to a physical had merely been guilty of walking in a garrison town by herself. The woman was poor but respectable, and she was so humiliated at the indignities to which she was subjected, and so fearful of losing her good name, that she committed suicide.

When it was proposed that the CD Acts be extended to the entire country, the feminists, male and female, decided to wage an all-out campaign for repeal of all the Acts. In addition to clear cut instances of abuse of power, the repealers could point to the dubious success of the CD Acts. In 1870, after six years in force, the supporters of the CD Acts could not point to any precise number of prostitutes who had been rehabilitated, and worse, they could not claim any significant reduction of the incidence of venereal disease. The case for repeal appeared strong, since the CD Acts advocates confounded themselves by their seemingly contradictory goals—on the one hand, reduction of the number of prostitutes through reform efforts; on the other, the retention of prostitution as a safety valve to secure domestic tranquillity, in both the figurative and the literal sense.

The formation of organizations devoted to repealing the CD Acts indicated that sentiment for repeal cut across class, party, and sex lines. The most prominent of these organizations was the National Association for the Repeal of the Contagious Diseases Acts. The Ladies National Association for the Repeal of the Contagious Diseases Acts was formed soon afterward. Josephine Butler, who had been prominent in the rescue of prostitutes, agreed to be its head on the urging of her husband and such antivice leaders as Daniel Cooper, secretary of the Society for the Rescue of Young Women and Children. Cooper avowed, "The ladies of England will save the country from this fearful curse." Petitions against the CD Acts began to appear once repeal associations were formed. They were signed with alacrity by prominent women such as Harriet Martineau, Mary Carpenter, and Florence Nightingale, none of whom had any difficulty identifying repeal as a feminist issue upon which the power and influence that women had acquired hinged.

By common consent and by design, the campaign against the CD Acts was identified as a women's issue. Josephine Butler maintained that central to her decision to assume leadership of the repeal campaign was her meeting with a group of Quaker leaders. "These Quaker gentlemen," she wrote in her autobiography, "put it to me, was I willing to go, because they felt at that period of our crusade, the cause must be presented prominently as a women's cause, and be represented by a woman."[24]

Indeed, women were much in the public eye, demonstrating, making speeches, and canvassing for petitions; but they had extensive behind the scenes support among males, who provided financial backing, gave legal advice, and did recruiting among their political contacts. One of the gray eminences in the campaign was William Shaen (1821-1897). Shaen derived from that liberal feminist tradition which originated in the antislavery and antivice crusade led by William Wilberforce. He worked for higher education for women and was an early supporter of women's suffrage. A lawyer, he was active in rescue work and served as legal adviser to the Rescue Society of London. He was a founder of the Social Purity Association and Moral Reform Union. He launched the Ladies National Association for Repeal and became its honorary president. Shaen had influence among working-class radicals. In the early 1840s, he was a "moral force" Chartist—one of those advocating reform through the political process rather than by means of violence. He later taught in the Working Men's College and was very likely influential in swinging many of the newly-enfranchised working men in favor of repeal. The support of working-class males, who had gained the suffrage in 1867, was considered crucial for both supporters and opponents of the CD Acts.

Repeal quite naturally had the support of church leaders, since it was perceived as a moral issue. At first support came primarily from the nonconformist churches, especially the Quakers, Methodists, and Unitarians. But in 1873, approximately two thousand Anglican clergymen urged Parliament to repeal the CD Acts, and by the late 1870s, Dr. L. B. Pusey, leader of the high Anglican Oxford Movement, had joined the cause as well. For the established Anglican Church, the break with the government over repeal of the CD Acts was significant. The Anglicans' concern about the double standard culminated in the formation of the White Cross Society which helped young men resist the temptations of prostitutes by providing sex education. The White Cross Society agreed that women's moral standards were higher than men's, and in asking members to live up to women's standards, committed themselves to promoting equality of opportunity for women. This ideal was put into practice in the organization itself, where both men and women were encouraged to assume leadership roles.

The brunt of the battle for repeal was necessarily borne by those members of Parliament who had a commitment to women's rights. Noteworthy for their zeal were Jacob Bright and William Fowler, both of whom were in the "aye" column when the roll was called on the first attempt to achieve suffrage for women in 1867. They argued that it was illegal to require women to undergo examinations, Fowler maintaining, "It is unconstitutional for women to be arrested upon mere suspicion. . . . No proof of prostitution is required and no definition of the word, 'prostitute' is given in the Act."[25] Bright also took to the floor, declaring, "A voice is heard from the country—a voice which is growing louder every day— asking for a restoration of those safeguards to personal security which have been handed down to us from generation to generation, and which until now, no government, either Liberal or Tory has ventured to invade."

Those calling for repeal argued that the CD Acts could not be condoned, because they singled out women for punishment. John Stuart Mill maintained that the government had no right to single out one disease and one group of people and force them to undergo treatment. Mill articulated the position that, if any regulation was to be required it should be aimed at the men who spread venereal disease to innocent women and children after having had contact with an infected prostitute. He said, "It seems to me, therefore, if the object is to protect those who are not unchaste, the way to do this is to bring motives to bear on the man and not on the woman who cannot have anything to do directly with the communication of it to persons entirely innocent, whereas the man can and does."[26] This position was entirely consistent with the criteria justifying state intervention that Mill had established in *On Liberty* (1859).

Sir Harcourt Johnstone also argued that one group could not be singled out for special punishment: "I maintain that this house would not pass an Act that would compel a registration of men.... An Act that would arrest men coming out of brothels and require from them a voluntary submission.... You would find it impossible to apply these Acts to both sexes and therefore, I say in common justice that they ought to be repealed."[27] Jacob Bright further pointed out that the CD Acts not only constituted sex discrimination, but were

the most indefensible piece of class legislation of which I have any knowledge. How are these Acts carried out?... Women frightened by the police are induced to sign their names or put their crosses to a paper of the meaning of which they know nothing. Every kind of cajolery and fraud are resorted to to obtain the signature of the ignorant and defenseless women. Then once they have committed themselves, they are subjected to forced examinations every fortnight and have upon them a brand which makes their return to decent life impossible.[28]

In 1871, a royal commission was formed to study the CD Acts and their effects. Charles Dilke pointed out that the commission contained not a single repealer; not a single woman; and not a single member of the nonconformist churches that favored repeal. Not surprisingly, the commission did not produce a report that was acceptable to the repealers. It merely suggested reverting to the 1864 provision of the CD Acts, which applied only to prostitutes suspected of being diseased rather than to all prostitutes. The commission also asked that the age of consent be raised from twelve to fourteen. This attempt at compromise was vitiated by the hard line taken in support of the double standard, which made the commission report anathema to the repealers. The report gave unqualified endorsement to the double standard:

We may at once dispose of this recommendation (that soldiers and sailors should be subject to regular examination) so far as it was founded on the principle of putting both parties to the sin of fornication on the same footing by the obvious but not less conclusive reply that there is no comparison to be made between prostitutes and the men who consort with them. With the one sex the offense is committed as a matter of gain. With the other it is an irregular indulgence of a natural impulse.[29]

It is indicative of the emotion generated by the report that three members of the commission became repealers. They included F. D. Maurice, prominent in female educational reform; Charles Buxton, who promptly resigned as vice-president of the Organization for Extending the Acts; and Holmes Coote, a physician who, subsequent to his change of heart, joined the National Association for Repeal.

In 1872, another attempt at compromise failed. H. A. Bruce, the home secretary, offered a proposal that would have made physical examinations voluntary. It also would have raised the age of consent from twelve to fourteen, and would have provided for the prosecution of brothel owners. Bruce's bill had to be withdrawn for lack of support, since it satisfied neither the supporters nor the opponents of the CD Acts. Supporters felt that medical examinations were crucial to the efficacy of the Acts, and opponents held out for nothing less than repeal on constitutional and moral grounds. There was no room for compromise when, in the words of one parliamentarian, "for the first time in our history, prostitution had become a 'legalized institution'—a woman is made a chattel for the use of men."[30]

The cause of repeal appeared dead after William Gladstone, who was tilting towards the CD opponents, was replaced as prime minister by Benjamin Disraeli, whose Conservative party won a majority in the elections in 1874. Disraeli was an architect of the paternalistic conservatism embodied in the CD Acts, and since the Conservatives did not have the sensitivity to civil rights that the Liberals had, it was unlikely that Disraeli would lend his support to repeal. In addition, a number of repealers were defeated in the elections, including Jacob Bright and William Fowler. The hopes of repealers were thus at their nadir when James Stansfeld, a former supporter of the Acts, decided to risk the odds, and over the next nine years dedicated himself to the goal of repeal with single-minded tenacity until the objective was won.

Stansfeld (1820-1898) is a remarkable example of the talents and the zeal that the male feminists displayed. A profound sense of duty and a lifelong sympathy for the oppressed and disadvantaged, the most salient features in his makeup, were derived from his strong religious convictions as a Unitarian. The Unitarians were one of the nonconformist churches and themselves had historical experience as outsiders with respect to the established Anglican Church. Stansfeld's sympathy for the underdog predisposed him to feminism, and he was confirmed in that cause by an incident described by a number of men and women as crucial to their feminist commitment. This was the antislavery convention held in England in 1840 and attended by, among others, American abolitionists Elizabeth Cady Stanton, Lucretia Mott, William Lloyd Garrison, and Wendell Phillips. When some delegates to the convention expressed disapproval at the presence of women and ordered them to sit behind a curtain, segregated from the males, Garrison and Phillips chose to sit with the women in protest. Stansfeld recorded, "It was that episode, the shame I felt as a man and an Englishman that first turned my thoughts to the position created in England for our mothers, sisters, and wives, that made me resolve that all schemes of education, and of political reform, should include them as equals."[31] Stansfeld married one of the daughters of William Ashurst, a radical lawyer whose working-class sympathies and feminist principles went hand in hand. When asked why he was such a friend of women, Ashurst replied that he had seen a girl tried for murder who had been betrayed by a man, convicted by men, sentenced by a man, and hanged by a man.[32]

Stansfeld made a successful bid for a seat in Parliament as a radical Liberal committed to reform in 1859. He represented the district of Halifax until 1895. He supported women's suffrage when a bill was first proposed in 1867, and in 1869, in company with J. S. Mill, Charles Kingsley, and Henry and Millicent Fawcett, spoke at the first public meeting held in London to demand the franchise for women. Stansfeld was an early supporter of the CD Acts precisely because they were touted as reform measures that would benefit both prostitutes and the larger community. But, in 1869, soundings of opinion among his constituents impressed him with the scope of the opposition. Among the opponents were a large proportion of the working men whose leaders in Parliament and in the trade unions had taken the position that the CD Acts were a form of class legislation with the exploiters, upper-class men, blaming the victims—poor, working-class women—for the evils that their own greed and corruption had brought about. Arguments that prostitution was a necessary safety valve to protect middle-class domesticity only affirmed the image of working-class women as convenient sexual objects for upper- and middle-class men, who were thus able to maintain the purity of their own wives and the sanctity of their property.

Stansfeld was affected not only by the grievances of the working people, but by the outrage of the feminists and by their conviction that theirs was a life-and-death struggle, with the survival of civilization itself at stake. After the Royal Commission Report of 1871 was made public, with its affirmation of the double standard further polarizing opponents and supporters, Stansfeld came out for repeal, stating, "To me, it is impossible to assent to legislation which implies in my mind state recognition and something very nearly approaching state sanction of the vice of prostitution."[33] It was a difficult decision for a radical reformer to make, since opposition or support of the CD Acts was presented by sincere reformers as a choice between the rights of a degraded class and the health and welfare of the community.

In 1874, Stansfeld took command of the small group in Parliament that favored repeal. He became vice-president of the National Association for Repeal and gave up a cabinet seat in the Liberal government, in effect sacrificing a promising career in politics because of his principles. He was roundly criticized by the *Times*, which favored the CD Acts and "regretted to find a statesman of Mr. Stansfeld's eminence identifying himself with the hysterical crusade against the Contagious Disease Acts." Stansfeld fully realized the import of burning his bridges behind him, stating, "I have taken a course lately which very much modifies my political position and probable future. I have cast my lot with those men and women, forever reverenced be their names, who hitherto have had a hope which too long has seemed forlorn, and never will I desist until these degrading laws are blotted out from the Statute Book forever." He whimsically advised Josephine Butler, "I hope to be the best abused man in England in twelve months."

Stansfeld devoted his considerable skills to enlarging the base for repeal among the working-class electorate and the churches; to raising questions about the effectiveness of the CD Acts; and to proposing alternatives. To accomplish the second aim, he turned to the medical profession, which was divided on the issue. In 1875, after an inquiry into the affair of Mrs. Percy, the woman who committed suicide after being arrested on suspicion of soliciting, an influential doctor was encouraged by Stansfeld to form the National Medical Association for Repeal. The Association adopted the premise of the repealers that the CD Acts were more dangerous than the evils they sought to cure, in that these laws created a pariah class of women "set apart for the necessities of men." With increasing vehemence, Stansfeld hammered at the failure of the CD Acts to attain their goals of reducing the incidence of venereal disease and reforming prostitutes. In the debate on the issue in 1876, he unveiled statistics showing that there had been a large increase of the less serious forms of venereal disease in the navy, and no diminution of them in the army.

Eventually, Stansfeld scored heavily by calling on physicians to explain these failures. Two doctors testified that no reduction in the number of diseased persons could be expected under a system which examined only women. One pointed to the difficulty in diagnosing active venereal disease in women. When it became clear that the CD legislation might actually be contributing to disease by making men think they were safe when in fact they were not, and that the forcing of prostitutes to register was creating an underground of resisters, the futility of the legislation was borne in on the majority of the Commons.

To emphasize the moral issue Stansfeld wrote to church leaders, reminding them of the serious implications "of treating prostitution as a recognized social institution and of making state provisions to render it physically as innocuous as possible by the compulsory state medical supervision and inspection of a Pariah class set up for the necessities of men."

Stansfeld was a humanitarian who believed that care of the poor and helpless was indeed a state responsibility. As a radical Liberal he agreed with the principle that government had a role in protecting the health and welfare of those too poor and powerless to protect themselves. He insisted, however, that the sick could be cared for under the amended Poor Law of 1867. Under the provisions of the law dispensaries for the sick (including the infirm and the disabled) were established. They operated for the benefit of the poor, who went there on a voluntary basis, and Stansfeld felt it was unnecessary to have a special system of treatment for sick prostitutes so long as the existing dispensaries were adequately financed and humanely administered. In his determination that repeal should not be simply negative, but should also include positive rescue work, Stansfeld voiced his hope that "wherever there was a Committee for Repeal, there also would be a society seeking to rescue, but desiring also that as much in these as in any other cases of human bodily sickness and suffering, even those not yet dreaming of escape should be charitably ministered to."

In 1880, Stansfeld became a member of a select committee to investigate the effectiveness and the moral consequences of the CD Acts. Amid a welter of conflicting statistics, a majority report was issued that continued to support the CD legislation because of "a diminution in venereal disease." A minority report issued by six members, including Stansfeld, repudiated the statistics, and attacked the report on moral, constitutional, and sanitary grounds. It pointed out that venereal disease had not diminished and that among registered women the incidence of disease had actually increased.

On April 20, 1883, Stansfeld took the floor in the House of Commons to give a long and impassioned recitation of the reasons for his opposition to the CD Acts. He reiterated that, contrary to statements made in the majority report of the select committee, the CD Acts had not accomplished their aim of reducing venereal disease in the army and navy, and he cited figures from medical reports to substantiate his claim. He argued further that the legislation was immoral, and that it was "opposed to the deepest convictions of a large proportion of the most earnest and most active supporters of the present government." In urging an end to the compulsory examinations he charged:

You have built up not merely a wrong system—an immoral system, but an unnatural system against which the appetites and faculties of the bodies of men and women revolt; and the consequence is this—that you have created a Pariah class, the mere instruments of the most brutal, the most disgustingly sensual appetites of men, and they become the media without themselves being infected, of conveying contagion from man to man.

Stansfeld then moved that the House abolish the section of the CD legislation which had aroused the greatest furor—the requirement that all prostitutes in areas subject to the CD Acts undergo periodical medical examinations. When his motion carried by a vote of 182-110, the CD Acts, for all intents and purposes, became a dead letter.

Stansfeld and the army of repealers, vindicated after over ten years of unremitting effort, brought about an emotional polarization over what values the Victorians should pursue—the moral imperatives of the feminists, with their special concern to protect the poor and powerless from exploitation; or the impersonal masculine approach which required, in the interests of efficiency and social order, the legitimization of government intrusion in even the most private concerns, and a vast bureaucracy to accomplish these ends. Stansfeld fully appreciated the dimensions of the struggle and the irony that he, a radical who supported government action on behalf of the defenseless, should lead the fight against laws widely seen as public health measures. In rejecting what he saw as a manifestation of the masculine cause—the CD legislation which condoned exploitation of women—he spoke feelingly:

Sir, I have been obliged to speak largely and mainly of hygiene but I revolt against the task. I have had the weight of this question upon me now for some ten years past. I loathe its details. . . . What I have done I have done for conviction and for duty's sake, and never will I abandon a duty which I have once undertaken to fulfill. . . but no man knows or ever can know what to me has been the suffering, the burden, and the cost.

At least part of the cost to Stansfeld had been his loss of standing in the Liberal party. Stansfeld had held a series of cabinet posts and was president of the Local Government Board when he assumed leadership of the CD Acts opposition. Since Liberal party policy favored the CD Acts, he resigned that post, and put aside his other radical priorities, such as Home Rule for Ireland, to concentrate on repeal. His personal triumph came when, in 1882, he managed to win approval for repeal from the general committee of the National Liberal Federation, a group which was important in setting policy for the Liberal party. Gladstone's assent to repeal followed, and this cleared the way for Stansfeld's return to the cabinet, but in the meantime other Liberal stars, such as Charles Dilke and Joseph Chamberlain, had captured the public's fancy. One consolation for the cost he suffered for adhering to principle may have been a tribute from the *Times*, which had opposed his position. This tribute summed up the esteem in which he was held for taking up the cause of prostitutes—a cause which even the suffragists shunned for fear of a backlash. The *Times* admitted, "It is impossible to approach Mr. Stansfeld without a feeling of respect; his convictions are so heartfelt, his manner so honest, his career so wholly that of a man who has sacrificed everything to what he, in a manner however mistaken, has held to be right."[34]

Another clearcut triumph for feminist moral standards was achieved by William Stead, a crusading newspaperman whose vitriolic campaign against the white slave traffic not only forced total repeal of the CD Acts, but produced comprehensive legislation on behalf of minors who might be induced to become prostitutes.

White slavery was the ultimate outrage that united women into a mighty force with that potential for progressive change to which the feminist fathers had looked forward. Rescue workers such as Josephine Butler had long known that there was a group of prostitutes who were minors and who had been sold into prostitution by their parents or been forced into prostitution because of their helplessness. In trying to impress upon the members of Parliament the inimical effects of the CD Acts, Butler testified on a traffic between England and Belgium of children—some as young as eleven years old—who were being literally kidnapped and forced into prostitution. A select committee of the House of Lords was formed to investigate the charges. After a desultory three-year investigation, the committee duly reported in 1882 that juvenile prostitution was increasing at an alarming rate, citing overcrowding and decreasing parental authority as two of the causes. The report went on to confirm Butler's charges that the girls, many of them under twenty-one, were sent abroad under duress. The girls, according to the report, "were not in the main of good character"—which many took to mean "were in the main of the lower classes"—but the report conceded that "they did not know that they would be practically prisoners."[35] The lords recommended that the age of consent be raised again, this time from thirteen to sixteen, and a bill was introduced to amend the Criminal Law Amendment Acts to reflect the change. It did not pass. In fact, some of the men in Parliament seemed more disposed to lower the age of consent to ten, thus not only conceding that child prostitution was uncontrollable but, in effect, condoning it, much as the CD Acts had winked at adult prostitution.

When Parliament continued to drag its collective feet on raising the age of consent, Butler was induced by Charles Booth, commander-in-chief of the Salvation Army, to present the same findings she had given to Parliament to Stead, who was the newly appointed editor of the mass circulation *Pall Mall Gazette*. Stead was impressed enough to wage a media exposé of the kind which was to become common in the twentieth century, but which was unprecedented when Stead revealed the facts about sexual exploitation of children and hinted that men at the highest levels of government were involved in protecting this racket.

The white slave issue was ready-made for Stead's brand of Christian idealism, with which he infused all the causes into which he threw himself with the utmost fervor. Like so many of the progressives of the Victorian age, his zeal was strongly rooted in the evangelical ideas of the nonconformist churches; these ideas included a belief in the perfectibility of human beings and an abiding faith in the democratic process. Stead (1849-1912) was the son of a Congregationalist minister, and became a writer because of a desire, never fulfilled, to write the history of Puritanism. Politically, his humanitarian instincts and his championship of the underdog made him a Liberal. But like Stansfeld, his capacity for moral outrage often brought him into conflict with the politicians of his own party when he perceived hypocritical or self-serving motives on their part.

Stead believed it was the obligation of a newspaperman not to follow, but to mold, public opinion, and he frequently supported highly unpopular causes. In the late nineteenth century, when Russia was emerging as a dangerous rival to England's Middle Eastern sphere of influence, Stead exhibited sympathy for Russia, even though his patriotism was impugned as a result. He was a self-proclaimed imperialist who believed that it was England's mission to Christianize the world, but somehow always supported the struggling colonial masses in the British Empire when Christian conduct was lacking on the part of their British governors. Consistent with this stand, he became an adamant opponent of the Boer War—which pitted the might of Britain against the resistance of the South African Boers—after the brutality of its prosecution became clear. Stead was succeeded in the newspaper world by a breed of big businessmen—the Northcliffes and the Hearsts—who sensationalized the news and pandered to the lowest prejudices of potential readers to boost circulation and profits. Stead, with his stern moral outlook and unbending standards of Christian conduct, usually pursued his stories at a financial loss, and in the case of the white slavery exposé, at the sacrifice of his personal freedom.

When Josephine Butler approached Stead with the white slavery evidence, he was already her warm admirer and an ardent devotee of the CD repeal cause she espoused. He had become involved with the issue of the CD Acts as editor of the *Northern Echo*, where his last assignment was to write a review of Josephine Butler's book, *The New Abolitionists*. His own strong opposition to the CD Acts was manifested early. In terms that are almost psychological clichés, he traced the source of his antagonism to them and, indeed, of his feminism, to his mother, who was opposed to the CD Acts, and whom he recalled canvassing for signatures on petitions for repeal. Regarding the CD Acts, he admitted:

It was one of the subjects upon which I have always been quite mad. I am ready to allow anybody to discuss anything in any newspaper which I edit; they may deny the existence of God, or of the soul, they may blaspheme the angels and all the saints; they may maintain that I am the latest authentic incarnation of the devil, but one thing I have never allowed them to do was say a word in favor of the CD Acts, or of any extension of the system which makes a woman the chattel and slave of the administration for the purpose of ministering to the passions of men.[36]

Another woman who deeply influenced Stead, and of whom he spoke in worshipful terms, was Catherine Booth, who was described by Stead as the founder of the Salvation Army, although standard sources credit her husband, Charles Booth, with that accomplishment. In his biography of Catherine Booth, he indicated that she had converted him from his Congregationalist faith to the Evangelical credo of the Salvation Army. His ardor for Catherine Booth is a fulsome statement of his own feminism. In the Salvation Army, equality of the sexes was a fact as of 1875, when it was stipulated that women be considered for any position in the Army on an equal basis with men. The prevalence of women in its councils was regarded by Stead as "one of the great secrets of its strengths." He affirmed, "If the Salvationists had rendered no other service to humanity and civilization than that which is involved in revealing to the world the latent capacities and enormous possibilities of usefulness that lie in womankind they would have deserved well of their generation."[37]

Stead formulated a theory that the early relationship between mother and son determined in later life whether the son would be a masculinist with "absurd prepossessions about the natural superiority of man," or a traitor to that cause. Stead insisted that by their adherence to the masculine syndrome of superiority, "many men unwittingly proclaim to the world the misfortune which attended them in their nursery. A man who had a mother as a fool or a fribble [*sic*] or a female whose maternal functions were purely those of the dam and the milch cow naturally grows up a disbeliever in the capacity of women, and therefore is of necessity a sworn advocate of the monopoly of the male." He wryly noted, "Whatever dutiful sons may inscribe on their mothers' tombstones, their only inscription to the maternal memory which is known and read of all men is their sons' comparative estimate of the reasonableness of women's claim to the full rights of a human being." There was never any doubt about Stead's revulsion at "the hateful doctrine which in every age has persistently depressed fifty per cent of its number below the recognized human level."[38]

Stead's sympathy for the downtrodden, and his perception that women—no matter what their differences in social class or ethnic identity—were in that category, made him a consistent champion of damsels in distress. As a newspaperman, his feminism was constantly being tested in the stands he took on the unsavory divorce cases among the upper classes, which were beginning to be publicized after the First Divorce Act of 1857 made divorce easier to obtain. In one such case, a Scottish M.P. named Crawford sued his wife for divorce, naming Sir Charles Dilke, among others, as corespondents. Dilke was a radical Liberal whose inconoclastic approach to politics matched Stead's own. Yet, despite the political bonds between them, Stead could not overcome his antagonism to an alleged philanderer who made sexual objects of women and who was thus associated with a system of male dominance that victimized all women. Stead could not find it in his heart to condemn the adulterous women in such cases, knowing that frequently they had been forced into loveless marriages, which the latter day traitors to masculinity saw as the moral equivalent of prostitution. Stead was all too aware that the husbands who were the accusers were free to indulge with impunity in the crimes for which their wives were crucified. A Charles Dilke, or a Charles Stewart Parnell, who allowed his passion for Kitty O'Shea to undermine his role as leader of the Irish Home Rulers, could expect no sympathy from Stead or any of his fellow feminists, who rejected the masculine cause as it applied to the double standard. Although Stead supported Home Rule for the Irish and recognized Parnell as the most effective spokesman the cause of Home Rule had, he publicly called Parnell a "thorough-paced dissembler," and he used all his media influence to prevent the resumption of Parnell's role as leader of the Irish party in Parliament after the divorce case in which he was named as corespondent was aired.

Stead's moral absolutes did not derive from any disposition to asceticism on his part. He married Emma Wilson in 1873, and they had eight children. He was described as having strong sexual drives that found partial release through verbal ribaldry. Havelock Ellis stated that mastery of his own sexual impulses was a great problem for Stead. Ellis theorized that Stead's zeal for humanitarian causes was a sublimation of his sexual energies, writing, "His repressed sexuality was, I consider, the motive force of many of his activities."[39] It is hard to avoid the conclusion that the moral idealism of the males no less than that of the females, far from limiting their lives, acted as a powerful dynamo to channel their energies into the social welfare work that absorbed their lives. Stead's reform activities encompassed more than feminism. He was a republican who favored abolition of the monarchy and reunion of Britain with the United States. Before World War I, he was an ardent peace advocate. His campaigns for social justice and peace won him international acclaim. He was en route to the United States to fulfill speaking engagements when he went down with the Titanic in 1912.

Upon learning from Booth, Butler, and the other repealers that not even children were safe from the depredations that the male establishment condoned and protected, Stead committed himself with wholehearted abandon to their exposure. His first task was to verify the charges of an illicit traffic in child prostitutes by conducting an investigation, during which he was able to confirm that a young girl, if she was a bona fide virgin, could be purchased for as little as five pounds. Using a reformed prostitute referred to him by the Salvation Army as a contact, he purchased Eliza Armstrong from her own mother. Convinced that he had a case and one of the most significant stories of the century, he made the *Pall Mall Gazette* a powerful weapon in his crusade for decency and justice.

The articles detailing the prevalence of white slavery began appearing in the *Pall Mall Gazette* on July 6, 1885, under the title "The Maiden Tribute of Modern Babylon." Stead made clear his purpose in an editorial accompanying the first installment in which he demanded the immediate suppression of crimes such as the sale and purchase of virgins; the procuration of virgins; the entrapping and ruin of women; the international slave trade in girls; and atrocities, brutalities, and unnatural crimes. The articles were calculated to make further delay on the Criminal Law Amendment Acts, which would raise the age of consent, political suicide. They were serialized over several days, and revealed in sharp detail "How Girls Are Bought and Sold"; "The Confessions of a Brothel Keeper"; and "Why the Cries of Victims Are Not Heard."[40]

Stead jolted Victorians by pulling the veil from a carefully constructed facade of respectability. He could not be ignored, because he satisfied the Victorian penchant for hard facts by providing evidence that there was a wide open market for young virgins—that is, girls usually between the ages of ten and thirteen, and sometimes even younger—who were lured into prostitution by an array of devices: "some are simply snared, trapped, and outraged either when under the influence of drugs, or after a prolonged struggle in a locked room, in which the weaker succumbs to sheer downright force. Others were regularly procured, bought at so much per head in some cases, or enticed under various promises into the fatal chamber." Especially calculated to shock Victorian sensibilities were disclosures that the children were sought by respectable and well-to-do members of society. To emphasize this aspect, Stead used such rhetorical queries as, "Then do you mean to tell me that in very truth actual violation, in the legal sense of the word, is constantly being perpetrated in London, on unwilling virgins, purveyed and procured to rich men at so much a head by keepers of brothels?" Although no names were named, the implication of the existence of a corrupt, venal, and hypocritical power structure was clear, and there were hints that those involved used their political influence to protect their interests.

That the girls were unwilling victims of depraved lust was brought out in lurid detail: "The screams of fear and pain in the seduction chamber avail them nothing since the limit of a scream is but five minutes." Undue resistance would ordinarily call for ropes to restrain the girls, but under certain circumstances screams of pain heightened the experience: "To some men, however, the shriek of torture is the essence of their delight, and they would not silence by a single note the cry of agony over which they gloat."

The existence of prostitution was well known. The Contagious Diseases Acts had revealed its prevalence and had made prostitutes more "visible" than ever before. What was not fully appreciated was how well organized the business was, the nature of the clientele, and how ruthless were the practices of those dealing in human flesh. All the elements of the middle-class laissez-faire business outlook could be detected in this flaunting of masculine power. The girls were referred to as "consignments" or "parcels," and no effort was spared to get the "genuine article," or virgin. Demand was quite high, procurers operated in an expanding market, and the "articles" frequently fetched high prices. An offer of a "situation" or an evening's entertainment was frequently enough to lure an impoverished young country girl to London. The night's lodging she was offered after her putative benefactor saw that she missed her train turned into a permanent prison when all her clothes and belongings were taken from her, making escape impossible. Once a girl lost her virginity—"that which may be lost in an hour could never be recovered"—her prospects were so diminished as to be hopeless. Children below the age of consent were even more defenseless. They were frequently induced to sell themselves into slavery by signing a declaration that put the relationship in the starkest terms, and might read, "I hereby agree to let you have me for a present of four pounds."

In publicizing his findings, Stead challenged some basic Victorian assumptions—that respectability and success went hand in hand with moral rectitude, while a low estate carried with it moral stigma; and that maintaining one's ignorance of reality was somehow protection against it. He charged that sexual crimes were facilitated not only by a conspiracy of silence at the top, but also by a society-wide conspiracy that kept girls—even those of means who had access to an education—ignorant of the facts of life.

Reactions were immediate and served to keep the issue before the public in a highly dramatic way. Some political figures professed to believe that printing the facts was a more serious offense that were the facts themselves. James Stansfeld, however, stated, "I thank God for the disclosures of the last fortnight. They were necessary and therefore they were right." Nor did the revelations of protection surprise Stansfeld, who remarked, "When you have police regulation of sexual vice, it becomes their training, their instinct and their business while they regulate, to protect."[41]

Citing the danger of "polluting" minds and "pandering to the prurient," the masculine establishment sought first to censor, and finally to discredit Stead. W. H. Smith, the wealthy stationer and M.P., refused to allow the offending issues of the *Pall Mall Gazette* to be sold in his stores. The Prince of Wales, the future Edward VII, ended his subscription to the *Gazette*, and several West End clubs banished the newspaper from their premises. The city solicitor began to harass the newsboys who were hawking the *Gazette*, and a defense fund was duly established in case the paper should be sued. Lord Cavendish-Bentinck clamored for the extinction of the *Gazette* and, in a newly acquired concern for the civil rights of the poor, succeeded in having Stead charged and indicted for negotiating the purchase of Eliza Armstrong without the knowledge of her absent father. There were never any charges that Stead had exaggerated or distorted the facts in the interests of sensationalism. Most of what Stead spelled out had already seen the light of day in the Parliamentary Commission Report of 1882. But to protect himself and the paper, Stead asked a commission headed by Cardinal Manning to conduct an independent investigation and to make a public report. Stead very shrewdly used his opponents' spiteful attempts to censor him to gain sympathy and generate further publicity for his exposé.

In exposing white slavery, Stead was able to marshal public opinion on behalf of feminism as never before. The *Pall Mall Gazette* was active in publicizing the numerous demonstrations of support that took place throughout the nation for repeal of the CD Acts, and for passage of the Criminal Law Amendment Acts, which raised the age of consent. As the time for a vote on the Criminal Law Amendment Acts neared, a gigantic rally in Hyde Park in London brought together a coalition of feminists that included socialists, trade union leaders, and suffragists, as well as newly-converted feminists from both major political parties. Its list of sponsors and speakers constituted a Who's Who of radical and reform thought. Included were Millicent Fawcett of the suffragists; Henry Broadhurst, a labor leader and Liberal member of Parliament; Joseph Arch, founder of the National Agricultural Labourers Union; Richard Pankhurst, a socialist reformer and feminist; and John Ruskin, the social critic and essayist.

There was a new consensus that women should be given a role in public life. Many church leaders who had heretofore resisted a role for women in politics were now confirmed suffragists and echoed the suffragists' sentiments that declining morality would be reversed if women had the vote. One minister exclaimed, "By all means, why should not woman enter upon any trade or profession she likes." Shocked by Stead's revelations in the *Pall Mall Gazette*, John Ruskin, not heretofore identified as a feminist, explicitly invited women to participate in public life. "Women are too shut up," he announced. "Outside there is a wilderness of secrets of which you dare not penetrate and sufferings of which you dare not conceive."[42] The practice of child prostitution was indelibly branded in the consciousness of Richard Pankhurst, Frederick Pethick-Lawrence, Keir Hardie, and Philip Snowden, all of whom eventually took up the cause of women's rights.

When the Criminal Law Amendment Acts were passed in 1885, they contained stronger provisions than the ones that had been rejected earlier in the year. The age of consent was raised to sixteen, and the penalties for violations were stringent. The minimum sentence for attempting intercourse with a girl below the age of sixteen was two years; actually having intercourse with a girl below the age of consent might mean penal servitude for life.

The repealers have been faulted for opposing government regulation in the case of the CD Acts and then favoring it when they demanded the age of consent be raised.[43] To regard them as hypocritical or inconsistent in this is to miss the import of their feminism. The opponents of the CD Acts were not laissez-faire individualists opposed to any government intervention to ameliorate the debased conditions of the poor in industrial society. They were radical liberals who supported a government role on behalf of the helpless and disadvantaged. Their dedication to reform was part of a moral commitment as well, born of the Evangelical faith that bettering social conditions for the poor would improve morality—not merely sexual behavior—and reduce crime as well. They did not consider the CD legislation helpful to poor working women, who were driven to prostitution because they had no other opportunities available to them; quite the contrary. They believed the CD Acts oppressed a small group of working women and consigned them to a degraded condition for life—in order to serve the needs of the all-male power establishment. In addition, their concept of civil rights stipulated that the state could not legislate for people whose interests were not directly represented in its councils. Women's—let alone prostitutes'—interests were not represented since they did not have the vote. Thus the repealers were, or became, strong women's suffrage advocates. The Criminal Law Amendment Acts, which raised the age of consent and prosecuted brothel owners suspected of kidnapping girls, were (as the name suggests) not considered social legislation. These laws redefined criminal behavior to protect a class of individuals—children— who could not help themselves, and women, who were outside the political process.

The issue of child prostitution reverberated through England's politics for decades. It was kept alive by the indictment and trial of William Stead for the abduction of Eliza Armstrong, the thirteen-year-old girl he had purchased from her mother to prove the existence of the white slave traffic. Stead's arrest indicated to many to what lengths masculinists would go to protect their privileges over women. Stead was charged on a technicality, because the court knew that the girl was purchased only to gain evidence and that she was not harmed, since she was turned over to the Salvation Army immediately after her purchase. Once the case was made public, Eliza Armstrong's mother had second thoughts about the sale, denied it had ever taken place, and therefore insured Stead's arrest for abduction. He went on trial with Bramwell Booth of the Salvation Army and the reformed prostitute, Rebecca Jarrett, who were both charged as coconspirators. The trial lasted twelve days and the sentences reflected the sentiments of the authorities toward each of the defendants. Bramwell Booth was released, in something of a tribute to the influence the Salvation Army had achieved. William Stead was given three months in prison; Rebecca Jarrett was given six months in prison, under harsher conditions than those endured by Stead. Stead was all the more anguished because he could conceivably have obtained acquittal for both himself and Jarrett had he been prepared to challenge Mrs. Armstrong's marital status on the witness stand. Part of the charges included Stead's neglect in getting the father's permission for the sale. This permission would have been unnecessary if it could have been shown that the Armstrongs were not legally married, which was in fact the case. Characteristically, Stead refused to subject Mrs. Armstrong to this ordeal for, in his own words, "I had frequently protested against the way in which women were insulted in the witness box by a cross-examining counsel."[44]

The capstone of the efforts of the reformers came when the CD Acts, the initial cause of the furor that brought the double standard into politics, were repealed in 1886. For those who had dedicated themselves with single-minded purposefulness to this goal, the victory was sweet, but only a beginning. For the traitors to the masculine cause the deeper issue was women's rights. William Stead articulated the sentiments of the male feminists when he said that women should no longer be "the mere ancillary of man, to be petted or slaved at his will...." She must have an independent voice in the disposal of her life with the right to decide "what best suits her genius, and how best she can develop her faculties."[45]

Victory brought new challenges and opportunities. The cause of feminism had been strengthened by the number of other issues that had become associated with it, and the political potential of women gained credibility. The Marxists were extremely impressed by the gender consciousness women had displayed during the CD and white slavery agitation, and considered the possibility of women becoming a revolutionary force. Marx himself had been extremely skeptical of the Thompson-Owenite ideas of cooperative socialism, with their inherent feminism, and labelled them "utopian" as a means of expressing his disdain. Marx died in England in 1883, unimpressed by the epic struggle where gender appeared to supersede class, but his daughter, Eleanor Marx, and a disciple, Edward Aveling, became intrigued with the possibilities of the women's movement. Richard Pankhurst, an heir of the utopian socialist tradition that believed in democracy as a means of attaining social and economic justice, was more than ever convinced that winning the suffrage for women was the key. Prostitution, which came to be equated with middle-class marriage, was the rallying cry both socialist wings used to impress upon women the need for political action. The tensions generated by the conflicting strategies of the two socialist movements— one revolutionary, the other democratic—insured that the women's question would be a hotly debated item after the stunning victory over the masculine cause achieved by moral reformers.

NOTES

1. John Stuart Mill, *The Subjection of Women* (Philadelphia: J.B. Lippincott Co., 1869), p. 56.

2. Elie Halevy believed that Methodism drained off the revolutionary impulses of the working classes and accounted for the fact that England did not experience a revolution similar to those that occurred in France and America. (*A History of the English People in the Nineteenth Century* (London: Ernest Benn Ltd., 1924).

3. The former verse is from "The Prelude"; the latter from "November, 1806". In *The Complete Poetical Works of William Wordsworth* (Boston: Houghton Mifflin, 1904).

4. Vern Bullough, *Sexual Variance in Society and History* (New York: John Wiley and Sons, 1976), pp. 542-43.

5. S. A. Tissot, *L'Onanisme. Dissertation sur les Maladies Produits par la Masturbation* (Lausanne, n.p., 1758), p. 79.

6. Ibid.

7. S. A. Tissot, *Advice to the People in General with Regard to Their Health* (Philadelphia, n.p., 1771).

8. Bullough, *Sexual Variance*, pp. 542-43.

9. Carl Binger, *Revolutionary Doctor: Benjamin Rush* (New York: Norton, 1966), p. 171.

10. David J. Pivar, *Purity Crusade* (Westport, Conn.: Greenwood Press, 1973), pp. 38-39.

11. Ibid., p. 151.

12. Ann Douglas, *The Feminization of American Culture* (New York: Avon Books, 1977), p. 115.

13. Ibid., p. 138.

14. Pivar, *Purity Crusade*, p. 79.

15. Eric Trudgill, *Madonnas and Magdalens* (New York: Holmes & Meier, 1976), p. 16.

16. Bullough, *Sexual Variance*, p. 539.

17. Trudgill, *Madonnas and Magdalens*, p. 174.

18. Ibid., p. 107.

19. Edward J. Bristow, *Vice and Vigilance: Purity Movements in Britain Since 1700*. (London: Rowman & Littlefield, 1977), p. 62.

20. Nancy Cott, "Passionlessness: An Interpretation of Victorian Sexual Ideology," in Cott and Elizabeth Pleck, *A Heritage of Her Own* (New York: Simon and Schuster, 1971), p. 173.

21. William Acton, *Prostitution* (New York: Praeger, 1957), p. 24.

22. William Acton, *The Circle of Life* (New York: Appleton, 1849), p. 219.

23. Constance Rover, *Love, Morals, and the Feminists* (London: Routledge and Kegan Paul, 1970), p. 79.

24. Josephine Butler, *An Autobiographical Memoir* (Bristol: J. W. Arrowsmith, 1911), p. 275.

25. Margaret Hamilton, "Opposition to the Contagious Diseases Acts," in *Albion*, vol. 10, no. 1 (Spring 1978), p. 17.

26. Ibid.

27. Rover, *Love, Morals and Feminists*, p. 73.

28. Ibid., p. 75.

29. Hamilton, "Contagious Diseases Acts," p. 18.

30. John and Barbara Hammond, *James Stansfeld: A Victorian Champion of Sex Equality, 1820-1898* (London: Longmans, 1932), p. 17.

31. Ibid., p. 183.

32. Judith R. Walkowitz, *Prostitution and Victorian Society: Women, Class, and the State* (New York: Cambridge University Press, 1980), p. 97.

33. Hammond and Hammond, *James Stansfeld*, pp. 189, 191, 209, 270.

34. Ibid., 292.

35. Select Committee of the House of Lords to inquire into the state of the Law relative to the Protection Of Young Girls from Artifices to induce them to lead a Corrupt Life, and into the means of Amending the same, 1882, House of Lords, Parliamentary Papers (188), 1882.

36. J. W. Robertson Scott, *The Life and Death of a Newspaper* (London: Methuen, 1952), p. 96.

37. William Stead, *Life of Mrs. Booth* (London: H. Hovell and Co., 1900), p. 85.

38. Ibid.

39. Frederic Whyte, *The Life of William Stead* (Boston: Houghton Mifflin, 1925), p. 342.

40. William Stead, "The Maiden Tribute of Modern Babylon," in *Pall Mall Gazette*, July 6, 1885.

41. Hammond and Hammond, *James Stansfeld*, p. 275.

42. *Pall Mall Gazette*, August 22, 1885.

43. See Walkowitz, *Prostitution and Victorian Society*.

44. Robertson Scott, *Life and Death of a Newspaper*, p. 129.

45. Whyte, *The Life of William Stead*, p. 321.

A WOMAN'S RIGHT TO CONTROL HER BODY: THE SEX RADICALS

3

It is a contemporary truism that women gained more independence from the pill than from the vote. In an age of individualism, birth control is seen chiefly as enabling women to realize personal freedom and to take advantage of opportunities for self-fulfillment. These results reflected the humanitarian goals of the male feminists. There is little mention today of the political, social and economic necessities which motivated the birth control struggle. The male feminists wanted women to have control over their own bodies, in the firm conviction that reproduction was a political act, and that women would use their power to restrict the number of children they bore, thus preventing the population explosion that threatened to put a precipitous brake on the progress envisioned by feminists.

The fear of overpopulation was one that haunted the thinkers of the nineteenth century. Fear of overpopulation was a major reason for the sex conservatism of middle-class reformers, it having been ineradicably impressed on them that the powerful male sex drive might become the catalyst for disaster. Sexual restraint was a natural reaction for those whose fears of overpopulation conjured up visions of a return to jungle law, with people fighting with each other for living space and for the shrinking resources that growing multitudes would devour. Birth control was the obvious solution for the political economists who pointed to the vast dimensions of the approaching disaster. The debate over who should practice birth control and what methods ought to be used raised conflicts and anxieties that are very revealing about the class tensions pervading the period.

Birth control was initially publicized as a middle-class prescription to alleviate the economic hardships of the working class. Since the working-class males generally resented this imposition upon their sexual rights, it was women who were called upon to be the agents of population control for the working class. The right to control their own bodies was the lure for working-class women to join the women's movement—the introduction for many to equal rights for women. The incentives were extraordinarily appealing. They included longer life, better physical and mental health, enhanced sexual pleasure, and the preclusion of abortion and infanticide.

Plate 8. Alas That It Should Ever Have Been Born by Pierre Vigneron. This shows a woman leaving her baby at a foundling hospital because she lacks the means to support it. This plea for birth control was a frontispiece to Robert Dale Owen's *Moral Physiology* when it was first published in 1830.

Thomas Malthus, who first brought the dangers of overpopulation to public attention, was by no stretch of the imagination a feminist. However, it was his *Essay on the Principle of Population as it Affects the Future Improvement of Society* (1798) that inspired the various organizations styling themselves Malthusian. These groups were devoted to propagating birth control and they did so in a feminist context. Convinced that women had a natural interest in controlling their own fertility, they demanded that women should have the right to control their own bodies.

Malthus, challenging the optimistic view of human nature put forth by William Godwin, insisted that reason was the most fragile of mankind's faculties, and one that exercised little control over passion, by emphasizing one irrefutable fact—"the constant tendency in all animated life to increase beyond the nourishment prepared for it."[1] While the utopians confidently looked forward to a bright future where the benefits of industrialization would eventually be available to all and where technological progress would preclude catastrophes such as famines, wars, and epidemics, Malthus maintained that these phenomena had beneficial side effects by acting as natural checks on population thereby assuring a balance between population and resources. Malthus, a thoroughgoing believer in laissez-faire principles, suggested that the coming population explosion would affect the working classes first, inflicting hardships on them that would surpass the degraded conditions in which they were even then living. In the context of the law of supply and demand, which was as immutable as the law of gravity to classical economists, the working classes were reproducing themselves at a rate which glutted the labor market and thus kept wages low. Malthus believed that if the working classes maintained their prolific habits wages would go below subsistence levels, turning the industrial revolution from a bright promise of progress to a nightmare of unending poverty for working people.

Ever true to laissez-faire orthodoxies, Malthus dismissed demands by radicals that government improve the conditions of factory labor, and well-meaning attempts by charitable organizations to help the poor, because these actions encouraged further breeding and therefore added to the problem instead of solving it. Malthus, a clergyman, left salvation in the hands of the potential victims. It was within the power of workers to prevent the tragedy of mass starvation by the simple expedient of reducing their numbers and having fewer children. However, his middle-class background and his training as a clergyman did not permit Malthus to contemplate any mechanical or artificial measures to prevent conception. He would countenance only late marriage and abstinence within marriage as acceptable birth control measures.

The publication of Malthus's *Essay* set off shock waves in the intellectual community. The work sold well, going through six editions in Malthus's own lifetime. Critics who could not adequately refute his doleful prophesies were reduced to charging that he was a Cassandra who defended smallpox, war, and child murder, and who denounced charity and early marriage. That economics since Malthus has been called the "dismal science" is a measure of the gloom he spread in his wake.

Malthus's assertions were given substance even as he was writing, for the Napoleonic wars had produced economic dislocations. Bad harvests in 1798 sent food prices skyrocketing. Since laissez-faire doctrinaires felt no obligation to raise wages to keep pace with the cost of living, the working classes felt the wage-price squeeze with devastating impact, and their sufferings increased the rumblings of revolt. In this atmosphere of uncertainty, Malthusianism, which became the generic term for population control, was adopted by the radical utilitarian philosophers Jeremy Bentham and James Mill.

Ironically, Malthus's sensational forecasts, put in a religious context of retribution for man's original sin, led to greater awareness by the public of a concern already voiced by the secular rationalists. In 1797, Jeremy Bentham indicated the desirability of birth control for the poor. In *Situation and Relief of the Poor*, he alluded to the use of "sponges" as a contraceptive device to keep down the cost of welfare for the poor.[2] That Bentham should suggest the sponge, a device that women could use, rather than the condom, which was available in England by the 1760s,[3] was indicative of the moral sensibilities of the period, to which radicals no less than conservatives subscribed. The male condom was used to protect against venereal disease, and it maintained this association with immorality and exploitation of women throughout the nineteenth century. Birth control devices for women were sought by male feminists and consistently touted as completely within the scope of the moral outlook of the period. For women to have control over their own fertility fit in with the growing conviction that women were more moral than men and with the perception that women had greater incentives to control reproduction than did men.

The males who advocated artificial birth control were feminists. Their primary treason was to the masculine cause of church authority, which held women strongly in its grip, and which was adamantly opposed to the use of artificial devices to control reproduction. The radical middle-class utilitarians, concerned about class conflict and intent on forestalling revolution, were primarily motivated by their desire to forge an alliance with the working-class men and women against the privileged and corrupt, but still powerful, aristocracy. They recruited working-class spokesmen for their program—which included rights for working-class men and for all women—on the basis of the self-help doctrine they believed to be the key to the liberation of all oppressed groups.

Artificial birth control methods were first publicized by atheistic working-class radicals, members of the utilitarians' network, who were convinced that keeping their own numbers within bounds was a form of self-help that would improve their living standard in the free market in which they operated. Francis Place (1771-1854) experienced at first hand the privations endured by the working classes in a laissez-faire economy, where the worker was considered a commodity subject to the natural law of supply and demand. Trained as a tailor,

Place had just gotten his first job in 1793 when a strike was called which turned into a gruelling yearlong battle for survival. The strike itself lasted six months, during which Place and his wife watched their infant son die of smallpox. The workers eventually had to go back to work on the manufacturers' terms but Place, who had been an activist during the strike, was blacklisted. He survived another eight months of unemployment by subsisting on bread and water. The Places managed to get piecework, which enabled them to get back on their feet, and eventually Place established a tailor shop which afforded the family financial security. His experiences radicalized Place. In 1794, he joined the London Corresponding Society, a political action group which demanded far-reaching reforms. These included universal manhood suffrage, equal representation in Parliament, and payment for members of Parliament. Their goals were greater democracy and an end to the political corruption that enabled the landed aristocrats to purchase seats in the House of Commons, seats they used to expand their wealth and influence. Because England was at war with Napoleonic France, any demands for reform smacked of revolution; the London Corresponding Society was considered a subversive organization and driven underground after its leaders went on trial for sedition. Left on his own, Place began to systematically read contemporary political and philosophical works. He made contact with the Benthamites and became a disciple of their reformist approach to politics.

Having acquired a modicum of economic security, Place began to dabble in politics. His tailor shop doubled as a library and meeting place for fellow radicals who wanted to discuss their common plight. Place's reform, as opposed to revolutionary, outlook was vindicated when, in 1807, Francis Burdett, a radical whom Place had supported, was elected to Parliament. When the workers' right to strike was taken away by legislation passed in 1801, Place was active in the campaign to repeal the Combination Laws, and in 1824 his efforts were crowned with success.

The Diabolical Handbills—information on birth control—which Place anonymously authored in 1823, came to be written through his association with the Benthamites, who used him as a conduit to the working classes. The feminist context in which he presented his message resulted only in part from the feminist principles the utilitarians espoused. Place is typical of many early feminists in that his feminism was deeply rooted in his childhood. He described his mother as "one of the best women that ever existed, clean, neat, kind, cheerful, good-tempered, warm-hearted, and always ready to do services to everybody whom it seemed to be possible for her to serve. She was much respected by all who knew her and greatly beloved by those who knew her best."[4] His recollections of his father were grim. A sometime baker, the father's addiction to gambling resulted in extreme fluctuations in the family fortunes. Place described him as "entirely governed by his passions," frequently absent, indifferent to his children, and abusive to his wife, who confided her unhappiness to young Place. At nineteen Place married a woman of sixteen whom he saw as an incarnation of his mother— mother and future daughter-in-law having established strong bonds with one another. Place credited the women in his life with providing the support and stability he never found in his father, and expressed guilt feelings about irrational outbursts of temper that were typical of his father. He recorded in moving terms his regret at lashing out at his wife under the adverse conditions they both endured:

Instead of doing everything in my power to soothe and comfort and support my wife in her miserable condition, instead of doing her homage for the exemplary manner in which she bore her sufferings, instead of meeting as I ought on all occasions to have done her good temper and affection, I used at times to give way to passion and increase her and my own misery.[5]

Place believed that his early marriage had saved him from a life of debauchery and could hardly be sympathetic to Malthus's prescription of late marriage for the working class, even though he agreed that births among working people should be curbed. Place's wife bore him fifteen children, five of whom died in infancy, and he was not indifferent to the hardships both the births and subsequent deaths caused her. He spoke from experience when he maintained in *The Diabolical Handbills* that large families perpetuated poverty and undermined the health of women. He prescribed as the best method of birth control the one touted by utilitarians, "a piece of sponge, about an inch square, being placed in the vagina previous to coition, and afterwards withdrawn by means of a doubled twisted thread, or bobbin, attached to it." He added a cautionary note that the sponge should be "rather damp, and when convenient, a little warm," and assured his readers that no injurious consequences could in any way result from its use and "neither does it diminish the enjoyment of either party."[6] The latter statement suggests that the working classes did not subscribe to the doctrine of women's asexuality, a fundamental tenet of middle-class morality.

Malthus's *Essay* confirmed the sexual conservatism of some reformers, such as John Stuart Mill, who believed that men's sexual passions constituted the big question mark in their hopes for progress. The refusal to concede that sex was a base animal function and that dire consequences to mental and physical health ensued from its expression, defined sex radicalism during the nineteenth century. One manifestation of sex radicalism was the search for a safe, reliable, and inexpensive means of birth control of which poor women could avail themselves. The sex radicals continued the radical Enlightenment tradition of William Godwin, who was optimistic about human nature and maintained that reason, if systematically cultivated through education, was capable of socializing and moderating the passions. Their special targets were the established church and religion in general because they induced guilt about the expression of normal human instincts, thus distorting them, and spread "fables"—for example, the virgin birth—that flew in the face of reason. A conviction that women, too, were reasonable creatures who could participate in sexual pleasure and control their fertility without becoming promiscuous, coupled with a consistent pattern of atheism, insured that the sex radicals would reap a harvest of troubles.

Richard Carlile (1790-1843) felt the full force of establishment outrage because of his heterodox views, religious, political, and sexual. He spent fully one-third of his life in prison. Born in humble circumstances, he managed to acquire enough schooling, including a smattering of Latin, to aspire to a literary career. He left jobs as a druggist's helper and tinsmith's apprentice, considering them to be degrading; spent several years wandering the English countryside; and launched his career as a writer by sending letters to radical newspapers. These writings were revolutionary in tone, and were thus for the most part rejected. The radicals had nominally sworn off revolutionary goals in order to survive in a class-conscious society whose leaders had been made nervous by the popularity of the French revolutionary slogan of Liberty, Equality, Fraternity. Nevertheless, with the Napoleonic wars having resulted in dislocations and hardship for the working classes, revolutionary plots were discovered, causing the government to suspend the right of habeas corpus in 1817. The suspension left booksellers and publishers extremely vulnerable, for they could be arrested for publishing or selling any work which the government characterized as seditious libel. Among the works so classed were Tom Paine's corpus, including *The Rights of Man* and *The Age of Reason*. Carlile had opened a printer's shop and, although he knew he was risking several years' imprisonment, decided to publish both works. While he was in prison, he evolved from a deist to an atheist. Carlile's wife reopened his printer's shop and operated it with great success until she too was convicted and, together with their baby, joined Carlile in prison. The family circle was completed when Carlile's sister was imprisoned for the same offense. It is a measure of the resentment felt toward the government and a tribute to the intensity with which Carlile communicated his convictions that his shopmen and shopwomen resolutely carried on the fight for freedom of the press and were also imprisoned. There was never any shortage of volunteers to take their places.

Carlile was nothing if not zealous when convinced of the justice of a cause, and it was this quality that caused him to publish *What Is Love?* when Francis Place persuaded him that birth control was necessary to improve the condition of the working classes. Carlile wrote Francis Place from prison in 1822, asking for information about birth control because he was contemplating an article on the subject. He harbored doubts about birth control since he believed it was only the fear of pregnancy that kept girls chaste and married women faithful. When Carlile expressed the more traditional view of women as seething cauldrons of sexuality who, after they pass puberty, "have an almost constant desire for copulation," Place informed him bluntly that promiscuity was inescapable in the lower classes, where children confronted the facts of life from the time of consciousness. Place had himself observed while growing up that because of the early exposure to sex acts and "lewd songs. . . want of chastity in girls is common."[7] Many were seduced into prostitution as early as nine or ten years of age.

Place convinced Carlile that a remedy for overpopulation "would not extinguish vice but would make attainable a larger measure of virtue."

Carlile published *What Is Love?* in 1825. It not only provided birth control information, but put the issue in a completely feminist perspective since he addressed the introductory remarks to women:

What a dreadful thing it is, that health and beauty cannot be encouraged and extended, that love cannot be enjoyed without the danger of conception, when that conception is not desired, when it is a positive danger to self and society. . . . What is to be done to remedy this? There is something to be done; a means has been discovered, a simple means more criminal in the neglect than in the use. . . . Here, as in every other case of disease or other evil, it is better to prevent than to cure, and here prevention is most simply practicable, a means within the reach of all.

In recommending the sponge Carlile tried to anticipate adverse reaction from women by emphasizing the positive benefits:

It shocks the mind of a woman, at first thought, that never dreamt of such a thing, but once practiced, all prejudice flies and gratification must be the consequence. To weak and sickly females, to whom pregnancy and parturition are dangerous. . . the discovery is a real blessing. And it is a real blessing in all other cases, where children are not desired. It will become the very bulwark of love and wisdom, of beauty, health and happiness.[8]

In a section titled *To the Married of Both Sexes of the Working Peoples*, Carlile explained why birth control would improve society. Using Malthusian principles of supply and demand, he pointed out that an oversupply of workers resulted in low pay, with the workers becoming little better than slaves. He continued, "The sickness of yourselves and your children, the privation and pain and premature death of those you love but cannot cherish as you wish, need only be alluded to. You know all these evils too well." He cited higher wages, lower hours, more time for recreation, diminution of vice and debauchery, plus the higher standard of living that all the workers sought, as benefits of birth control. A shrewd psychologist, Carlile appealed to the working-class desire for middle-class status by assuring them of the credentials of the sponsors of the plan—"all elderly men, fathers of families of children grown up to be men and women, and men of first rate moral character and first rate learning, and some of the first politicians and philosophers that ever lived in this or in any other country."

Carlile summed up the utility of the sponge: no married couple need have more children than they wanted and could support; no woman not able to bear children need endanger her life; there need be no illegitimate children; sexual intercourse would be enhanced if the fear of conception were eliminated.

What Is Love? was republished anonymously in 1826 under a new title that made even clearer the audience he was trying to reach. It was called *Every Woman's Book or What Is Love?* When a cookbook also titled *Every Woman's Book* was published at the same time as Carlile's, he heatedly protested that the latter book, pertaining to "culinary matters," "was not every woman's business; but love is in reality the business of every woman."[9] Carlile claimed a sale of ten thousand copies by 1828. That an avid audience existed for birth control information there is ample evidence. But the working-class males Carlile and Place were trying to influence to reduce their numbers tended to oppose Malthusianism for a variety of reasons.

In expressing fears of greater immorality among women, they reflected typical patriarchal attitudes and masculine sentiments. William Cobbett, a Tory turned radical, sounded this note in a diatribe against Place and Carlile in which he called their birth control prescriptions "openly and avowedly teaching young women to be prostitutes before they are married, and in a way so as not to prevent their future marriage."[10] To Cobbett, the exclusive male right to punish wayward girls had to be preserved. It was also suggested that lack of numerous children struck at the manhood of the working-class male. For some workers, completely subservient to exploitative employers, multiple fatherhood was the only proof of manhood they had and enabled them to enjoy a measure of prestige and authority in domestic life that was completely lacking in their working life. In their opposition to birth control, working-class leaders also responded to the fears of their constituents, who saw numerous children as "money in the bank," because they could be sent to work during hard times to make their contribution, small though it might be, to the family income. In old age, children were the only means of support in a laissez-faire society, and production of children had to be maintained because disease and malnutrition, the concomitants of poverty, kept infant mortality high.

That Malthus was a middle-class clergyman whose solution to overpopulation put the entire burden of poverty on its victims, the poor themselves, made him and all those who advocated his prescription appear to be apologists for their class interests and agents of an oppressive state and its ally, the established church. Class appeals against birth control were highly effective and shrewdly adopted by Karl Marx in his efforts to woo the working classes away from his "moral force" middle-class rivals. Carlile and Place—both atheists—were characterized as tools used by the reactionary establishment to promote the ideas of the hated Malthus, who had no sympathy for the plight of the poor and who saw working people as so many pawns on the industrial chessboard.

The editors of *The Black Dwarf*, an influential working-class newspaper in the mining country of northern England, considered birth control an insult to the working classes who were the producers in the country, while the "idle rich" were mere parasites. It recommended that the Malthusians "should dispose of drones who ate without working, rather than check the multiplication of the working bees, in order that more money be left to the drones." Working-class journals insisted that there were adequate supplies of food and that it was a malevolent government that was keeping the poor in a state of virtual starvation. Revolutionaries were opposed to birth control for very pragmatic reasons and saw it as, in effect, cutting their own throats. They did not want to diminish the numbers of the working classes when their chief hope of victory over the upper classes in any revolutionary uprising lay in the advantage of sheer numbers.[11]

Despite the fact that "preventive checks" to population growth received scant support from working-class men, advocates were not deterred. They had become aware that women, who, after all, bore the greater responsibility for children, were sympathetic. Robert Dale Owen and Charles Knowlton, the two men who set out to teach Americans about the benefits of birth control, both indicated that they were responding to poor women's pleas for help.

Robert Dale Owen (1801-1877) was the son of Robert Owen, one of the fathers of feminism. Knowledge of the sponge in England was mistakenly attributed to Owen senior by both Francis Place and Richard Carlile, probably because as an early advocate of "preventive checks," he encouraged Place to disseminate information about the sponge. Owen considered birth control important for the success of the model communities he sought for working people. When New Harmony, the cooperative community he established in Indiana, was in the planning stages, birth control was viewed as essential to keep the resources of the community from becoming strained. Within a few years New Harmony failed, but Robert Dale Owen, who had come to America with his father to help in the communitarian enterprise, continued to preach the gospel of cooperation and feminism, and in 1830 he authored the first tract on birth control to be published in America.

The title (*Moral Physiology: Or a Brief and Plain Treatise on the Population Question*) notwithstanding, America had no overpopulation in the early nineteenth century. Quite the contrary. There was a wilderness to settle and the United States was in the throes of an acute labor shortage, which was eventually remedied only by the large scale migrations from the Old World to the New. Owen's concerns were feminist, secularist, and socialist. He explained that he became America's birth control pioneer after receiving a letter from a young Kentucky wife that showed that the capitalist free enterprise system entailed as much hardship in the New World as in the Old. The woman wrote that she was married to a "mechanic of industrious habits" whose one vice—a tendency to drink—incapacitated him periodically. She had borne three children in less than four years and was in an extreme state of anxiety as to their welfare:

I shudder at the prospect before me. With my excellent constitution and industry, and the labor of my husband, I feel able to bring up three little cherubs in decency, were I to have no more; but when I seriously consider my situation, I can see no other alternative left for me, than to tear myself away from the man who, though addicted to occasional intoxication, would sacrifice his life for my sake. . .or continue to witness his degradation and bring into existence, in all probability, a numerous family of helpless and destitute children, who, on account of poverty, must inevitably be doomed to a life of ignorance, and consequent vice and misery.[12]

Moral Physiology revealed its feminist concerns in the frontispiece, a painting by Vigneron, depicting a mother abandoning her infant at the gate of a foundling home and lamenting, "Alas that it should ever have been born." Owen challenged the ignorance about sexual matters which was considered a proper state especially for middle-class females, many of whom did not find out the facts of life until their wedding night. He urged women to read his book with the reassurance that their chastity would not be compromised. "For myself," he reflected, "I would withhold from no sister, or daughter, or wife of mine, any ascertained fact whatever. It should be to me a duty and a pleasure to communicate to them all I know myself; and I should hold it an insult to their understandings and their hearts to imagine that their virtue would diminish as their knowledge increased."

Owen regarded the use of birth control as a moral necessity for poor people in straitened circumstances, who could be saved from a sordid existence by limiting their progeny; and as a humane solution for the numerous women who suffered premature death due to repeated childbirth:

How often is the health of the mother—giving birth every year, perchance, to an infant—happy, if it be not twins—and compelled to toil on even at those times when nature imperiously calls for some relief from daily drudgery—how often is the mother's comfort, health, nay, her life, thus sacrificed. Some women can never give birth to normal or even living children. Is it desirable—is it *moral* that such women should become pregnant?

Fears of promiscuity did not weigh heavily on Owen. He was a secular rationalist who thought passion could be controlled by reason. He believed that, with the removal of oppressive institutions like the family and the church, people would see their true interests in mutuality and cooperation. The Owenite socialists viewed promiscuity whether male (in the form of the double standard) or female (in the form of prostitution) as functions of private property which would disappear when cooperation became the rule. The sexual double standard was specifically condemned by Owen who regarded it as "unmanly and unchristian" of men to persecute women for behavior they condoned in themselves.

Owen articulated an attitude toward sex that was consistent with the secularist position of the optimistic Godwinites. For them, sex was not an ominous cloud hovering above, an overwhelming biological urge whose expression caused political anarchy, social upheaval, economic deprivation, physical anguish, and mental unbalance. To the sex radicals, it was a social instinct—of small moment in the rational scheme of things. Its indulgence in moderation was, like an after dinner aperitif, soothing to the nerves and conducive to conviviality between the sexes. Owen never doubted that sexual indulgence was something that could be controlled by reason and "chastened by good feeling." He thought it gave to social intercourse much of its charm and zest and considered it the least selfish of all the instincts. Its repression, if not leading to "peevishness, melancholy, incipient diseases, or unnatural practices, at least almost always freezes and stiffens the character by checking the flow of its kindliest emotions, and not infrequently gives to it a solitary, anti-social, selfish, stamp." Sex was thus a form of cooperation which could only further the benign feelings that were essential to the success of a cooperative society. Considered as a social act it was infinitely preferable to the two alternatives that haunted the social reformers of the nineteenth century—masturbation and prostitution. Following the Wollstone-craft-Godwin model, Owen himself lived in a free love union with Frances Wright for several years, partly to politicize the ideas in which both believed.

Most of *Moral Physiology* is an apologia and a philosophical discourse on the necessity for birth control in order to improve the human condition and increase prospects for happiness. For Owen, birth control was the key to human progress due to its salutary and civilizing benefits:

It would reduce crime; it would decrease intemperance and profligacy; it would polish the manners and improve the moral feelings; it would relieve the burden of the poor, and the cares of the rich; it would most essentially benefit the rising generation by enabling parents generally more carefully to educate and more comfortably to provide for their offspring.

In a few pages, Owen considered the pros and cons of all the known methods of birth control. Even though his father was thought to have brought the sponge to England, and even though both Place and Carlile recommended it, Owen did not. He indicated that knowledge of several cases where the sponge had proven ineffective forced him to the conclusion that it was of "doubtful efficacy." The baudruche, or condom, referred to in slang as a French letter, used to prevent venereal disease, was dismissed because the male feminists wanted to maintain a strict line between themselves and the sort of man who used women as sexual objects. Owen wrote, "I do not write to facilitate, but on the contrary to prevent the degrading intercourse of which it is intended to obviate the penalty." Also mitigating against the condom was the prohibitive cost. At one dollar each in the early nineteenth century, the device was too expensive for the poor at whom the birth control advocates aimed their literature.

Owen favored as the most effective birth control method, and one involving no expense at all, withdrawal on the part of the man (coitus interruptus). Answering objections that it required a mental effort and a sacrifice of pleasure, he insisted that it was an effort young men could learn and, once learned, it became habitual "and a matter of course." Owen did not think a minor sacrifice should outweigh "the most important considerations connected with the permanent welfare of those who are nearest and dearest to us."

The only valid objection to coitus interruptus that Owen was willing to consider was that it placed power chiefly in the hands of the man, and not where it ought to be, in those of the woman. To Owen, this meant that "she who is the sufferer, is not secured against the culpable carelessness, or perhaps the deliberate selfishness, of him who goes free and unblamed whatever may happen." He advised women not to have anything to do with any man "void of honor." Owen's admonition was a challenge for women to increase their power as moral guardians of the race, and to become the midwives of future progress through the discriminating choices they made in picking a mate. A man's social reputation

would be placed, as it should be, in the keeping of woman, whose moral tact and nice discrimination in such matters is far superior to ours. How mighty and beneficent the power which such an influence might exert, and how essentially and rapidly it might conduce to the gradual, but thorough extirpation of those selfish vices, legal and illegal, which now disgrace and brutify our species, it is difficult to imagine.

Owen fired another feminist broadside with *Lawyers, Clergy, Physicians, Men and Women* in 1839. Owen charged these all-masculine professions with trading in human misery and having a vested interest in perpetuating vice, crime, and disease since they profited from these phenomena. He accused writers like Washington Irving of having the same self-interest—fame and monetary rewards—in perpetuating an image of women as helpless, dependent creatures who find their only fulfillment in male approval. Asking rhetorically, "May she not be an active being?" he predicted that a time would come when the monopoly of sex will perish along with other unjust monopolies. Owen persuaded the Indiana legislature to pass laws assuring women the right to own and control their separate property during marriage; the right of married women to their earnings; the right of widows to one-third of their husband's property; and the right of women to divorce cruel or habitually drunken husbands. In 1851 he was presented with a silver pitcher inscribed: "Presented to the Honorable Robert Dale Owen by the women of Indiana, and in acknowledgment of his true and noble advocacy of their independent rights to property in the Constitutional Convention of Indiana."

When *Moral Physiology* was published, it was described by ex-President James Madison, a member of the middle class, as "well-written and out of the trodden circle." Such implicit approbation from the power elite did not inspire working-class confidence, and working-class journals were intensely hostile. Owen was called the leader of the "sponge party" in America and "an aristocratical, sophistical, self-contradictory, contemptible Jesuit" despite his palpable atheism.

The English edition of *Moral Physiology* was published by the freethinker James Watson in 1832. English working-class spokesmen, increasingly class conscious, rejected it; and conservative traditionalists lumped socialism, atheism, and birth control into something resembling a pornographic cult that threatened the survival of civilization. When the elder Robert Owen debated the question, "What is Socialism and what would be its practical effects upon society?" his opponent scored his major point by holding up a copy of *Moral Physiology* and describing it as a filthy book "too beastly to be named, that recommended practices of so revolting an order, that I will not even so much as name them." When an indulgent chairman, after glancing at a passage in the book agreed that "for common decency's sake" it could not be read aloud, Owen was completely vanquished.[13]

Moral Physiology became important chiefly for the influence it had on the more enduring work by Charles Knowlton, *The Fruits of Philosophy*. This work brought about Knowlton's imprisonment in 1832 when it was first published in the United States, and forty years later it became the catalyst for the trial of Annie Besant and Charles Bradlaugh in England.

Knowlton was an early traitor to the all-masculine medical establishment, and was penalized not only for the atheism which he flaunted but because his fellow physicians resented his subverting their authority by dispensing cheap medical advice to the poor. Charles Knowlton (1800-1850) was born in Massachusetts, where the Puritan tradition he revolted against had first established roots. He arrived at an early appreciation of the conflict between reason and instinct. Inculcated with the sinful portent of the emission of semen, he was on the verge of despair when he became a victim in adolescence of "gonorrhea dormietum," the arcane designation the medical profession used for the common phenomenon of wet dreams. Consulting ten physicians, he was plied with ten different remedies, including quinine, wine, Spanish fly, iron, balsam, opium, silver nitrate, alum, vegetable astringents, and blisters. Knowlton's problem was resolved when he married the daughter of yet another healer, who prescribed shock treatments as a cure for his malady.

Knowlton's early anxieties and conflicts led him to the study of medicine. He was imprisoned for the first time when, deciding that a doctor should have first-hand knowledge of the human anatomy, he stole a corpse from a local cemetery in order to dissect it. While serving his two-month prison sentence he became an atheist. Knowlton's bout with the law did not prevent him from earning a medical degree in 1824. He opened a practice in Ashfield, Massachusetts, where he scandalized the townspeople by ostentatiously playing his fiddle Sunday mornings while others were going to church.

His medical practice made Knowlton aware that frequent births imposed financial hardships on young couples, and undermined the health of women as well. He realized from his own experience that late marriage, the conservative solution for overpopulation among the poor, was impracticable. In 1831, he decided that a manuscript he had written on contraception, which he was in the habit of lending to those of his patients that needed guidance, deserved a wider audience. Thus was born *The Fruits of Philosophy* (1832). The book was totally ignored by reviewers at the time of publication. It took eleven years for the *Boston Medical Journal* to dismiss the work as promoting "unnatural measures." However, the ever-vigilant antivice crusaders saw to it that Knowlton was prosecuted three times on charges that included giving a "complete recipe of how the trade of strumpet may be carried on without its inconveniences and dangers." A complaint brought by a Cambridge physician offended by Knowlton's challenge to the authority of the medical profession earned him three months hard labor in a house of correction.

In *Fruits of Philosophy*, Knowlton tried to proselytize for the truth, and to teach as well as to give advice on practical methods of birth control. He stated his conviction that everyone has a right to knowledge and that no truth can lead to moral evil. To Knowlton, birth control was an idea whose time had come, one that would lead to happiness and social progress. It was his firm conviction that women were reasonable creatures whose partnership was necessary for progress to take place. He regarded objections that preventive checks would lead to promiscuity and increased prostitution "as an outrageous slander on the fair sex which must be the emanation of a carnal heart which has been peculiarly unfortunate in its acquaintances."[14]

Fruits of Philosophy was principally devoted to an elaborate description of the male and female reproductive organs and their functions. The homespun advice he offered in the remainder of the work was designed to allay fears about sexual matters. Knowlton favored early marriage, thus establishing his credentials as an opponent of Malthus. Late marriage, Knowlton believed, increased vice by forcing young men "to go out in the world and form vicious acquaintances." His sex radicalism is implicit in his view that sex relations had a beneficial effect on both physical and emotional well-being when practiced in moderation. Knowlton assured his presumptive audience of young marrieds that "temperate gratification promotes the secretions, and the appetite for food; calms the restless passion, induces pleasant sleep, awakens social feeling, and adds a zest to life which makes one conscious that life is worth living." Knowlton subscribed to the energy theory of male sex, opposed vice and prostitution, and hoped to improve morality through reason. Both his and Owen's sex radicalism was part of their protest against a patriarchal clergy and a medical establishment that used the fear and guilt they instilled about sex in order to preserve their power and authority.

A desire to promote self-help and self-reliance in women pervaded Knowlton's discussion of birth control methods. The emphasis was on effectiveness as well as on convenience and cost. He rejected the sponge and coitus interruptus on grounds of ineffectiveness. He would not countenance the condom because "it has been used to secure from syphilitic infections," and proposed his own invention, the douche. It consisted "in syringing the vagina immediately after connection, with a solution of sulphate of zinc, of allum, pearl ash, or any salt that acts chemically in the semen, and at the same time produces no unfavorable effect on the female." According to Knowlton, the only drawback to his method was that women would have to leave the bed for a few minutes after intercourse, but he believed the advantages more than compensated for this inconvenience: "In its favor it may be said, it costs nearly nothing; it is sure; it requires no sacrifice of pleasure; it is in the hands of the female; it is to be used after, instead of before, connection . . . and last but not least, it is conducive to cleanliness, and preserves the parts from disease."

The notoriety of his trial helped to publicize Knowlton's work. By 1839, ten thousand Americans had braved censure to buy it. James Watson, the same publisher who brought out Owen's *Moral Physiology*, published *Fruits of Philosophy*. It enjoyed a steady sale of one thousand copies annually until Knowlton's posthumous trial in 1877 catapulted the book into the best-seller category.

While Malthusianism created class conflict because it was viewed as the middle-class solution to working-class problems, William Thompson and John Stuart Mill made it clear that the responsibility for population control cut across class lines. Each asserted that population control was a prerequisite for women's equality as well as for social stability, and that women's equality, in turn, would act as a check on the population because women would be free to engage in pursuits other than motherhood. Thompson spoke for the radical middle class when he insisted that constant childbearing perpetuated women's servitude. In *Appeal*, he pointed out that as long as women were "breeding machines" they could not take their place in the world outside the home.

Mill's Malthusianism was made explicit in *Principles of Political Economy* (1848). He saw the legal equality of women and the expansion of employment opportunities as the surest guarantees of keeping the population down: "Among the probable consequences of the industrial and social independence of women will be a great diminution of the evil of overpopulation." Mill's advocacy of birth control was also influenced by his sympathy for poor women, who not infrequently committed infanticide to get rid of unwanted babies. When Mill was seventeen, he was walking through St. James Park in London when he saw a strangled infant. The sight so moved him that he helped Frances Place distribute *The Diabolical Handbills*. His arrest for the offense did not diminish his support for the right of women to control their bodies. In *Political Economy* he maintained:

It is seldom by the choice of the wife that families are too numerous; on her devolves the whole of the intolerable domestic drudgery resulting from excess. To be relieved of it would be hailed as a blessing by multitudes of women who now never venture to urge such a claim but who would urge it if supported by the moral feelings of the community.[15]

Mill did not discuss methods, but his frequent disparagement of the male sex drive marks him as a pure Malthusian, that is, a believer in abstinence. Mill stated:

It is by devoting one half of the species to that exclusive function (childbirth), by making it fill the entire life of one sex, and interweave itself with almost all the objects of the other, that the animal instinct in question is nursed in the disproportionate preponderance which it has hitherto exercised in human life.... Among the barbarism which laws and morals have not yet ceased to sanction, the most disgusting surely is that any human being should be permitted to consider himself as having a right to the person of another.[16]

George Holyoake serialized *Political Economy* in his journal, *The Reasoner*, so that working people who could not afford the book might benefit from the philosophy.

The feminist case for abstinence—"prudence"—was stated by Austin Holyoake (1826-1874), younger brother of George Holyoake. The brothers took for granted that Mill was assuming the mantle of feminist leadership from the aging Robert Owen and gave him their full support. Austin Holyoake, like his brother, was an atheist, and he wrote the pamphlet *Large or Small Families, on Which Side Lies the Balance of Comfort?*, making clear his secularist convictions, in all probability to dissociate his ideas from those of the divines who proclaimed abstinence to be good for the soul. Holyoake, in an empirical vein, recommended abstinence because it was good for a man's health and his pocketbook, and kept the bloom on his wife's cheeks. With the exercise of prudence, early marriage was possible. Fewer children conserved the charms of women, "which yield so much joy in wedded life"; it assured those offspring one did have a better future; and it enabled one to maintain control over one's own fate and destiny. He admitted that this form of birth control required a "philosophical frame of mind"—something he believed to be within the capacity of every man, for he exhibited little sympathy for those who were unable to discipline their passions. He pointed out that the same passions do not operate on all with the same intensity. Some people desire more sleep than others, some more food and drink. Holyoake complained of the forbearance shown to men who would not master their sexuality: "The sluggard who sleeps half the day and will not work to support his family, he is criticized, but the man who has ten children when he can only afford two, him we pity and subscribe for what is the difference."[17] It is not known when *Large or Small Families* was written, but the fact that it was not published under Holyoake's name till 1892, well after his death, suggests that the radical middle class did not wish to create further rifts with working-class males over the issue of Malthusianism, which generated among them a hostility that their Marxist rivals for working-class allegiance sedulously exploited.

Among the sex conservatives, the practice of abstinence was entirely consistent with the prevailing ideas of the "passionlessness" of women. It is hard to escape the conclusion that Mathusianism was a vital aspect of the feminism of the middle-class disciples of Mill, a means whereby they were making it possible for their wives to engage in public pursuits and to become the intellectual companions and friends that they sought.

It was Mill who provided the motto for the neo-Malthusians, as they styled themselves in the 1850s, with this statement: "Little improvement can be expected in morality until the production of large families is regarded in the same light as drunkenness or any other physical excess."[18] Neo-Malthusianism became uniquely an issue for traitors to masculinity during the halcyon Victorian Golden Age, when all the institutions associated with patriarchy were never more secure. There was a determined militance in the traitors' stance against religion and clerical influence as the tensions between science and religion increased, tensions which culminated in the vituperative debate generated by Darwin's theory of evolution. During the years of prosperity, when it seemed possible that the poor would be absorbed into an expanding economy, the issue of birth control was kept alive by small groups, such as the secular societies, who were devoted to free thought. Atheists who had made complete their break with the masculine cause by rejecting the patriarchal God, whose authority underpinned the complacency of the proper Victorians, adopted the cause of birth control as *prima facie* evidence of their free thinking and as the red flag of their rebellion.

It was a free thinker, Edward Truelove, who agreed to publish George Drysdale's *Physical, Sexual and Natural Religion* in 1855, when no one else was willing to take the risk. Drysdale, like his predecessors, Place and Carlile, published his manuscript anonymously, not wishing to cause pain to his mother because of his challenge to political and religious orthodoxy; but he insisted that he was ready to come out into the open and stand behind it if it was attacked. There was little chance it would not be attacked since Drysdale fulfilled the darkest intimations of the proper Victorians by his iconoclasm on the subjects of sex, marriage, and the family.

George Drysdale (1825-1904) was still a medical student in Edinburgh when he wrote *Physical, Sexual and Natural Religion*. He considered the established church to be responsible for the low esteem in which science and its exponents, among them the members of the medical profession, were held; and he fired as opening salvo this statement: "The noble science of medicine has never yet received due reverence from mankind. This arises chiefly from want of reverence of the human body, the special object of its attention."[19] In trying to shift the focus of attention from the soul to the body, Drysdale articulated a totally mechanistic philosophy of sex as a bodily need no less strong in women than in men. He believed that women were the chief victims of the propaganda the church dispensed about feminine virtue. Chastity, the highest accolade in the eyes of the church, was poor compensation, in his view, for the physical and mental discomfort women had to endure to earn it.

Drysdale considered the church to be responsible for prostitution. Imposing impossible demands on both males and females, it forced men to turn to this class of women, whom Drysdale described as "martyrs" who performed more useful work than many respectable professions. Drysdale, trying to foster the objective view of the scientist, avoided emotionally loaded terms, and he called prostitution "mercenary love." His sympathy for these women was made clear: "That there should be among us a class of unfortunate women who are treated worse than dogs, who are hunted about by the police, despised and abhorred by their own sex, and abused and neglected by men, to whose wants they minister, is a page of human shame too dark for tears."

Drysdale believed the sexual organs to be like any other organs, requiring regular use lest they become atrophied. Total sexual avoidance—a virtue in the eyes of church authorities—was pronounced "unnatural." Drysdale maintained, "It is so unnatural and therefore sinful, that it is totally incompatible with health and happiness, and produces the most widespread and desolating diseases." He insisted that the effects of celibacy on women were ravaging: "Woman's peculiar torments begin at puberty, and from that time on until her marriage, she is constantly prey to anxiety which becomes a pressure for marriage." Drysdale recommended free unions as an alternative to marriage, and as a protest against this pressure.

Drysdale also believed motherhood to be essential to women's well being: "Impregnation and child birth are certainly of the greatest importance to the health and happiness of women and hence every woman should produce her fair share of offspring." His advocacy of sexual freedom for males and females was coupled with a demand that it be exercised responsibly through "preventive intercourse," as he called birth control. Drysdale stated, "The only means by which the virtue and the progress of mankind are rendered possible is preventive sexual intercourse. By this is meant, sexual intercourse where precautions are used to prevent impregnation. In this way, love can be obtained without over-crowding the population."

Drysdale put forth "preventive sexual intercourse" as the panacea that would make possible the liberation of women from their bondage to religious authority, and as a means to safeguard the resources of society. It was the ultimate utilitarian solution for realizing the greatest happiness for the greatest number. In his catalogue of methods, Drysdale made the first mention of the rhythm method, a new importation from the Continent, by which women abstained from sexual intercourse during the part of the month when they were fertile. He looked favorably on this "natural" method, considering that even the limited sexual exercise it made possible would prevent "the evils of sexual morbidity, repressed sexual desires, and unexercised sexual organs, as they are seen in the numberless cases of chlorosis, hysteria, and diseases of menstruation." Since scientific evidence of rhythm's effectiveness was lacking, he indicated his preference for the sponge as the best of all the "unnatural" or mechanical means of preventing conception. Besides passing the test of effectiveness, the sponge did not cause nervous disorders, as withdrawal might, nor did it decrease sexual pleasure or produce impotence (which Drysdale considered a distinct possibility if the condom were used). He followed the sex radicals' tradition in his assurance that all these methods could be used without causing physical or moral evils and that through their use "each woman in our society could have a due share of the pleasures of love and also of the blessings of motherhood."

Drysdale went beyond the economic and social justifications for birth control characteristic of the earlier sex radicals. In describing sex as a biological instinct to which men and women alike must respond as inevitably as they must respond to the impulse to evacuate, he sought to divest it of any moral significance. Drysdale used the rhetoric conventional to the nineteenth century. But in challenging the doctrine of women's asexuality in the name of science, and in seeking to substitute the authority of science for religion, Drysdale has adequate credentials to be considered the forerunner of the sexual revolution that reached fruition in the early twentieth century.

In 1857, three years after the publication of *Physical, Sexual and Natural Religion*, later renamed *Elements of Social Science*, the obscenity laws in England were strengthened. This attempt at censorship made birth control an issue not only for atheists, but for those who believed in the principles of freedom of speech and press as well. A whole cluster of organizations, including the Secular

Society and the Dialectical Society, discussed and promoted Drysdale's book, not necessarily because they agreed with its revolutionary sexual ideas, but because they would not countenance the persecution that Drysdale was subjected to by outraged public opinion.

In 1868, the father of Bertrand Russell, Viscount Amberly, who had been impressed by Drysdale's argument for preventive intercourse, took the chair at a meeting of the London Dialectical Society, where a paper entitled "On the Happiness of the Community as Affected by Large Families" was being given. Among the speakers were Charles Bradlaugh and Charles Drysdale, George Drysdale's brother. Throwing the meeting open to discussion, Amberly suggested that women, if they had any say, would opt for limiting the size of their families, and asked medical men to speak out on the subject of birth control. Amberly's queries were leaked to medical organizations and shortly thereafter the *British Medical Journal* commented: "We believe that our profession will repudiate with indignation and disgust such functions as these gentlemen wish to assign to it."[20] Soon a chorus of medical men joined in deploring the suggestion that they had the function of "teaching females how to indulge their passions and limit their families" or of fostering "dens of obscenity and vice." When in that same year Amberly was designated to run as the Liberal candidate for Parliament for South Devon, the lay media accused him of advocating "unnatural crimes," by which was meant infanticide and abortion. The papers urged the voters of South Devon to do their duty for king, country, and family and defeat his candidacy, because he had insulted the women of England and America and counselled pure wives and mothers to degrade themselves below the "level of beasts." Amberly was dubbed "the vice-count," and, after a heated campaign of innuendo and slander in which the merits of birth control were ignored, Amberly was defeated.

In 1873, John Stuart Mill was posthumously taken to task for his advocacy of birth control. It was not for the Malthusianism of *Political Economy*, where to all intents and purposes he espoused abstinence, but for the youthful indiscretion that occurred when he was seventeen. His arrest for distributing *The Diabolical Handbills* was hushed up at the time because of his father's eminence, but the incident was revealed in an obituary after Mill died. When William Gladstone, the leader of the Liberal party, for which Mill had provided a program and a philosophy, read of the incident, he announced that he was withdrawing his sponsorship of a memorial for Mill. In a twist of logic perhaps typical of an ambitious politician sensitive to the pressures of public opinion, he interpreted his withdrawal as an "act involving no judgment either way on this painful controversy."[21]

The Bradlaugh-Besant trial took place in 1877 in an atmosphere where a married woman who practiced birth control was labelled a prostitute and her husband was considered as no better than a masturbator. Charles Bradlaugh (1833-1891) started his revolt against church authority early in life and continued his challenge to that masculine cause until he was vindicated when Parliament allowed him to take a seat to which he was elected. His education, which included numberless beatings to instill proper respect for authority, ended at eleven. He was clerking for a coal merchant and teaching Sunday school in his spare time when he questioned the pastor about some puzzling discrepancies between the four Gospels and the Thirty-Nine Articles of the Anglican Church. The pastor angrily denounced Bradlaugh as an atheist and suspended him from his Sunday school duties. When the elder Bradlaugh learned of his son's disgrace, he ordered him to appease the pastor, lest he be evicted from his home and fired from his job. Bradlaugh, at fifteen, left, and resumed contact with his mother and sister only after his father's death. He found shelter with the widow of Richard Carlile and made the acquaintance of Robert Owen; through this adopted father he completed the secular radical's rite of passage from Christianity to deism, and finally to atheism. His atheism made it difficult for him to find a job, so Bradlaugh joined the army. Bradlaugh's love of Greek scholarship and his teetotalism at first brought jeers from his fellow soldiers, but his sheer physical bulk and his willingness to use it eventually won the respect of his comrades. While in the army Bradlaugh was stationed in Ireland and acquired a lifelong sensitivity to the plight of the politically oppressed. Always a man to put his principles to the test, Private Bradlaugh led a platoon of soldiers on a mission to tear down a fence put up by a landlord which interfered with a traditional right of way used by the Irish peasants. The fence stayed down, and Bradlaugh was an instant hero to those he had helped.

It was after he bought his discharge from the army with funds donated by an aunt that Bradlaugh began to build a national reputation for iconoclasm. In 1855, he gained notoriety by championing the right of public assembly in Hyde Park. He was the most impressive witness before a royal commission investigating the subject, and his description of police brutality toward peaceful assemblers won the point.

Bradlaugh became a republican after reading the works of Tom Paine, and he aided national liberation movements wherever the goal was the creation of a republic. He supported Garibaldi's struggle for Italian unification; aided Polish nationalism when the Poles revolted against the Russians in 1863; and provided a draft of a proclamation listing the grievances of the Irish toward the British and announcing the establishment of an Irish Republic in 1867. In the early 1870s, after grief over the death of Prince Albert turned Queen Victoria into a recluse, and scandals in the private life of the Prince of Wales rendered the English monarchy vulnerable, Bradlaugh took a leading role in encouraging republicanism in England.

Bradlaugh's feminism was a function of his all embracing belief in human rights—part of the radical tradition. He expressed his feminism by advocating the extension of full civil rights, equal employment opportunities, and the suffrage to women. His categorical support for the latter was expressed in 1862, when some Liberals were arguing that if women received the vote they would be inclined to conservatism and would vote Tory. Bradlaugh wrote in the *National*

Reformer, a newspaper he edited, "Even if it were unfortunately true that every woman would always vote Tory, it would be the duty of radicals to try and obtain the suffrage for them."[22]

In 1859, Bradlaugh was elected president of the London Secular Society and showed his talent for organization by uniting all the local secular societies into the National Secular Society. In his capacity as leader of the NSS, Bradlaugh started a periodical, *The National Reformer*, which provided a forum for attacking social, religious, and sexual prejudices. The paper declared itself to be republican, atheist, and Malthusian, and was therefore required to pay an eight-hundred-pound deposit as a guarantee that the owners could pay damages if charged with blasphemy or seditious libel. Bradlaugh refused to pay and was ordered to stop publishing. He issued a statement that he was going to continue publishing "in defiance of her Majesty's Government." He was twice prosecuted, but the law requiring cheap newspapers to put up such a bond was repealed. He won John Stuart Mill's admiration and support for his "persevering resistance."

Bradlaugh's belief in free thought and freedom of the press were catalysts for a number of political and legal imbroglios; but it was the Malthusian issue that resulted in his and Annie Besant's highly publicized trial, which he himself considered the supreme test of his principles. Bradlaugh was an enthusiastic Malthusian and believed that the use of birth control was the only way the working classes could raise their standard of living. Writing on the subject in *The National Reformer* in 1861, he suggested that Jesus, Shelley, and Malthus had provided separate traditions on how to deal with poverty. Jesus was equated with the religious spirit of submission to poverty, which Bradlaugh repudiated; Shelley represented the spirit of revolutionary socialism which Bradlaugh believed held out empty promises. Bradlaugh rejected socialism in both its revolutionary and evolutionary guises. While he adopted the feminism of his early patron, Robert Owen, he did not subscribe to Owen's socialism. He conceded that Owen's cooperative movement had enormous value, "if only as a protest against that terrible and inhuman competitive struggle, in which the strong were rewarded for their strength."[23] But after the Chartist movement petered out in 1848, Bradlaugh saw little chance for socialism to make any headway in England on a national basis, and put his trust in the power of the democratic franchise and the workers' own efforts to improve their living conditions through birth control. Bradlaugh felt that, even if national income were redistributed more equitably, it would not prevent the population from doubling every twenty-five years and reducing everyone to misery.

For Bradlaugh, Malthusianism thus emerged as the last best hope for the economic advancement of workers, and he hailed it as the modern, scientific way of dealing with the age-old problem of poverty. He said, "No permanent civil and religious liberty, no permanent and enduring freedom for human kind, no permanent and enduring equality among men and women was possible until the subject which Malthus wrote upon is thoroughly examined."[24]

Bradlaugh met Annie Besant in 1874. She shared his views on feminism and birth control, and became a full partner in all his enterprises. He allowed her space in *The National Reformer* to express her views on feminism, and a bond developed between them because of the personal tragedies that both endured through unhappy marriages. Bradlaugh had married Susannah Lamb Hooper in 1855, but the marriage became strained because of her extravagance and her addiction to alcohol. Financially hard-pressed after the medical treatment he had sought for her failed, he sent her and their three children to the home of his father-in-law, with hopes of using this relief from family responsibilities to get back on his feet. While his family was away, Bradlaugh's only son died of scarlet fever. Increasing his pain was the fact that, as a highly controversial figure, he was harshly criticized for what was publicly perceived as desertion of his wife and his family responsibilities. He never defended himself against the charges; but his daughter Hypatia, who wrote a biography of Bradlaugh, insisted that her father's conduct toward her mother was irreproachable under the circumstances, and that the criticisms he encountered were "painful for one who loved her parents equally, and would fain have been equally proud of both."[25]

The Bradlaugh-Besant relationship was a platonic one of shared ideals. To Bradlaugh, Annie Besant was one of those notable and admirable women who were willing to risk condemnation for the causes in which they believed. Thus, she was much like himself, and the sort of woman the male feminists were encouraging to come out into the open. It was in this context that he explained why he allowed Besant to share his ordeal by trial when he was accused, at best, of lack of gallantry and at worst, of hiding behind a woman's skirts. Bradlaugh maintained that he wanted all the world to see a woman with the courage of her convictions, a woman ready to participate in her own liberation and to provide an example to others. He declared, "To me, a woman brave enough to stand by the side of a man in defense of free publication of unpopular doctrines was an incentive to the public to investigate those doctrines and decide for themselves."[26]

Given the violent emotions generated by the birth control issue, a public flogging of proponents was perhaps inevitable. The chain of events that led to the Bradlaugh-Besant trial began in 1876 when a Bristol bookseller named Henry Cook was sentenced to two years' hard labor for publishing an edition of Charles Knowlton's *Fruits of Philosophy*. The book was adorned with "obscene illustrations"; these were most likely diagrams of male and female genital organs, which Knowlton himself had merely described. The book had been published in England without interference for forty-three years by James Watson and Austin Holyoake, both associates of Bradlaugh. After their deaths, Charles Watts, a fellow atheist, bought the plates of *Fruits of Philosophy* from Watson's widow and resumed its publication. The authorities, having successfully prosecuted Cook, decided to go after Watts as well. Watts panicked, and pleaded guilty in return for a suspended sentence. Bradlaugh felt disgusted because the authorities had been given an uncontested victory, and he regarded Watts's surrender as a betrayal of the principles of free speech and press. From his pulpit in *The National Reformer*, Bradlaugh declared that "the struggle for a free press has been one of the trademarks of the Free Thought Party throughout its history, and as long as the Party permit me to hold its flag, I will never voluntarily lower it."[27] Bradlaugh and Annie Besant decided to make a test case. They formed the Freethought Publishing Company, reissued *Fruits of Philosophy* with medical notes by George Drysdale, and informed the authorities of the time and place they intended to sell the book. They were promptly arrested on obscenity charges.

The trial of Annie Besant and Charles Bradlaugh took place in June, 1877, with the two defendants conducting their own defense. They shrewdly aimed their arguments to reinforce the ever growing resentment at the unequal treatment of the rich and poor. They pointed out that wealthy women could get birth control information at any bookstall for two shillings. They insisted that their prosecution was, in effect, the result of their efforts to make the same information available cheaply enough so that poor people could avail themselves of knowledge that they sorely needed to enhance both their lifestyles and lifespans. George Drysdale supported this line of defense by testifying to his knowledge of working women who gave birth twenty or twenty-five times during their fertile years; he called this immoderate breeding "one of the greatest social crimes a man could commit."[28]

Charles Robert Drysdale and his wife, Alice Vickery Drysdale, who were to play an important role in the future of Malthusianism, also testified for the defense. Charles Drysdale further elaborated on the adverse effects of numerous pregnancies both on women and on society. Alice Vickery Drysdale, who was a gynecologist, pointed out that working women desperately wanted some relief from childbearing, but sought it by a method that was harmful. Among working women the assumption was prevalent that so long as they breast-fed their babies they could not conceive. Thus, they often nursed for two years and more, resulting in a condition, described as overlactation, whose effects were detrimental.

In the last analysis, the settled convictions of the solicitor general were in no way altered. He insisted throughout the trial that *Fruits of Philosophy* "was a dirty, filthy book the object of which was to allow persons to have intercourse, and not have that which in the order of Providence is the natural result of sexual intercourse."[29] The jury deliberated for an hour and then agreed on a verdict which could be termed ambiguous at best. They agreed that *Fruits of Philosophy* was injurious to public morals, but absolved the defendants of corrupt motives or of any intent to undermine public morals. Bradlaugh and Besant could have received a suspended sentence had they agreed to cease publication; but they were determined to expose the hypocrisy on which the sentence was based, and announced their intention to continue selling Knowlton's book. At this show of defiance, they were each sentenced to six months' imprisonment and fined two hundred pounds; however, before the sentence could take effect they appealed, and were acquitted on a technicality.

The Besant-Bradlaugh trial was a watershed in the troubled history of birth control. It had served to bring the issue to public attention as never before. After the trial, one hundred twenty-five thousand copies of Knowlton's *Fruits of Philosophy* were sold, more than had been sold in the almost forty-five years since its first publication. The principals went their separate ways, pursuing their own priorities. Bradlaugh, the complete democrat and ardent civil libertarian, took his case to the people, and ran for Parliament on a radical platform that included compulsory free education, separation of church and state, and representation of excluded groups (that is, women) in Parliament. In 1880, he won election but was not allowed to take his seat because of his atheism. Then began a six-year struggle to be seated. The parliamentarians refused to seat him because of his rejection of the required oath of allegiance to the sovereign, which had to be sworn on the Bible. Despite their stand he was repeatedly reelected. Before he was able to take his seat, he was involved in eight legal actions; in the course of one of these he was ejected from Parliament by force and imprisoned for two days.

Annie Besant and the Drysdales devoted themselves to propagandizing in favor of birth control. When the Malthusian League was revived shortly after the Besant-Bradlaugh trial, Besant wrote an updated version of Knowlton's *Fruits of Philosophy*, called *Law of Population*. It was dedicated "to the poor in great cities and agricultural districts, dwellers in stifling court or overcrowded hovel, in the hope that it may point out a path from poverty and make easier the life of British mothers."[30]

The Drysdales turned Malthusianism into a family enterprise, but abandoned George Drysdale's revolutionary sex theories in favor of a conservative approach that implicitly approved of abstinence. They revived the Malthusian League with a two-fold purpose: (1) To militate for abolition of all penalties on the public discussion of the population question; (2) To spread among the people by all practicable means a knowledge of the law of population, of its consequences, and of its bearing upon human conduct and morals. Under the leadership of Charles Robert Drysdale (1829-1907), the organization emphasized the secular, utilitarian, and individualistic philosophy of the Benthamites, which stipulated that the morality of an act should be judged by whether it brings happiness and diminishes evil. The Malthusians dedicated themselves to the proposition that control of fertility would increase private happiness and advance the interests of society.

Drysdale engaged in the struggle for women's rights on a variety of fronts. An expert on venereal diseases, he was involved in rescue work to save prostitutes and was one of the foremost medical opponents of the Contagious Diseases Acts. He believed prostitution would be diminished if women had more fields of employment open to them, but that it could never be controlled by state regulation. He demanded that women be able "to use their industry and talents to the best advantage for themselves." Drysdale encouraged women to go into medicine through his pamphlet, *Medicine: A Profession for Women*, and by teaching medicine to women in the small medical college he opened for women medical students. He was eulogized for the latter action when he died in 1907. It was pointed out that teaching medicine to women during the 1860s and '70s was frowned upon by the medical establishment: "Only the most courageous physicians would take this work in hand. Dr. Drysdale did more than any others for he not only lectured to women students but in the absence of any regular hospital course then open, he allowed his women students to attend on his practice at several hospitals."[31]

The Malthusian League publicized birth control in a number of ways. Its house organ was *The Malthusian*, which educated readers about the effects of overpopulation. For those whom the periodical could not reach, there were missionaries who descended on remote country areas to canvass door-to-door and hand out tracts and leaflets to women. Leaders of the Malthusian League were also available to lecture to any group or organization that asked them to speak.

Doing missionary work for the Malthusians, publishing Malthusian literature, even being associated with the Malthusians entailed risk; and the dissemination of literature advocating women's right to control their bodies continued to be part of the civil libertarian protest against censorship. Since the Malthusians provided no information on actual methods of contraception, it was the civil liberties controversies in which members were embroiled that kept the issue in the public eye and generated interest. Traditionalists considered birth control to be synonymous with public immorality, and the Campbell Law, the same statute that was used to prosecute Bradlaugh and Besant, could still be invoked. Edward Truelove was twice arrested for publishing the enduring *Moral Physiology*. The second time he stood trial he was convicted and sent to prison for four months. Although sixty-seven years old at the time of his imprisonment, he was subjected to harsh prison discipline, which included a skimpy diet for the first three months of his term.

The impact of the Bradlaugh-Besant trial and of the revived Malthusian League was reflected in the demographic records of the 1870s and 1880s. After 1877, the year of the Besant-Bradlaugh trial, the population of England steadily declined. The birth rate in England and Wales fell from 35.5 per thousand of the population in 1871-75 to 14.4 per thousand just before World War I. The decline in population in areas where the Malthusian missionaries were most active clearly indicates that 1877 was a turning point. The causal link between publicity generated by the Besant-Bradlaugh trial and the decline of the birth rate was apparent to contemporary proponents and opponents of birth control. One opponent who feared that Great Britain's imperial role would decline with a decrease in population, and who in retrospect regretted the prosecution of Besant and Bradlaugh, testified in 1898, "We are now becoming quite accustomed to the ever recurring remark in the Registrar General returns: 'This is the lowest birth rate ever recorded.' The serious decline in the birth rate of the United Kingdom can clearly be traced, in the first instance, to the injudicious prosecution of Mr. Bradlaugh and Mrs. Besant."[32]

In 1897, Sidney and Beatrice Webb, founders of the Fabian Society for the peaceful propagation of socialism in Britain, also remarked on the population decline:

There can be no doubt that the practice of deliberately taking steps to limit the size of the family has, during the last twenty years, spread widely among the factory operatives and the skilled artisans of Great Britain. It is interesting to note that the beginning in the fall of the birth rate (1877) coincides closely with the enormous publicity given to the subject by the prosecution of Bradlaugh and Besant in that very year. We attribute this adoption of neo-Malthusian devices to prevent the burden of a large family. . . chiefly to the spread of education among working class women, to their discontent with a life of constant ill-health and domestic worry under narrowing circumstances and to the growth among them of aspirations for a fuller and more independent existence of their own.[33]

In the late nineteenth century, there were a growing number of artificial methods of birth control available. The sponge, first publicized by the sex radicals to give women the power to control their fertility, was refined with the invention of the diaphragm by William Mensinga, a German physician. The diaphragm first received mention in England in Arthur Allbutt's *The Wife's Handbook* (1886). The vulcanization of rubber made the condom cheaper and therefore more practicable for use by the working class.

It is doubtful, however, that artificial methods were in widespread use until birth control became linked with the sexual revolution which separated public and private morality and obscured the importance it had as a political issue for the feminist radicals of the nineteenth century. The proponents of the sexual revolution went far beyond the early sex radicals in emphasizing the personal benefits of sex.

Since the Malthusians only propagated the desirability of birth control among working-class women without endorsing any specific method, and since the female reformers who advocated that a woman should have the right to control her body were sexual conservatives who favored abstinence, it is very likely that abstinence was widely practiced as a contraceptive method, and in large measure the cause of population decline among the middle and working classes.[34] Evidence that middle-class values were filtering down to the working class vindicated, at least for the moment, the political strategy of the feminist radicals, who favored "moral force," and rejected revolution, as a means of meliorating the conditions of the working class.

Demographic studies showed not only a steady decline in population in the late nineteenth century, but a steady increase of females over males as well. A perception that women were destined to play a greater role in society by virtue of superior numbers gave to the woman's question an urgency and immediacy it had previously lacked, and intensified the debate about woman's potential and her role. With a surplus of females over males it was impossible for all women to find husbands to provide for their economic support and enable them to fulfill their traditional domestic role as the fulcrum of the family. Open discussion on women's sexuality and encouragement of its expression by the sex radicals heightened anxieties about promiscuity and free love, and gave the debate about women an acerbic character. Ultimately, it produced two distinct versions of the new woman and her role in society.

NOTES

1. Thomas Malthus, "An Essay on Population As It Affects the Future Improvement of Society," in J. Bonditch and C. Ramsland, eds., *Voices of the Industrial Revolution* (Ann Arbor: University of Michigan Press, Ann Arbor Paperbacks, 1968), p. 51.

2. The introduction of the sponge has been a source of some dispute. Early birth control publicists attributed it to Robert Owen, who was said to have learned of the device while on a trip to France. It is probable that the idea of the sponge was introduced to England by Joseph Townsend, a utilitarian and a friend of Jeremy Bentham who had learned of its use in France and wrote about its possibilities in *A Dissertation on the Poor Laws* (1786; London: Ridgeways, 1817).

3. Angus McLaren, *Birth Control in Nineteenth Century England* (New York: Holmes & Meier, 1978), Chap. 1.

4. Mary Thall, ed., *The Autobiography of Francis Place* (London: Cambridge University Press, 1972), p. 21.

5. Ibid., p. 115.

6. *The Diabolical Handbills* are in the Place Collection, British Museum.

7. Thall, *Francis Place*, p. 57.

8. Richard Carlile, "What Is Love?," *The Republican*, vol. 11, January 7-July 1, 1825, pp. 562-64.

9. Peter Fryer, *The Birth Controllers* (London: Secker & Warburg, 1965), p. 70.

10. Ibid., p. 79.

11. Annie Besant addressed this issue in *The Law of Population* (1877). Reprint in John Saville, ed., *Selections of the Social and Political Pamphlets of Annie Besant* (New York: Augustus Kelley, 1970).

12. All quotes are from Robert Dale Owen, *Moral Physiology, Or a Brief and Plain Treatise on the Population Question* (New York: Medsell, 1835), pp. 2, 30, 21, 36.

13. Fryer, *Birth Controllers*, p. 95.

14. All quotes are from Charles Knowlton, "Fruits of Philosophy," in *Birth Control in America: Two Discussions* (New York: Arno Press, 1972), pp. 16-17, 54, 57.

15. John Stuart Mill, *Principles of Political Economy* (1848; London: Routledge Kegan and Paul, 1965), pp. 765-66.

16. Ibid., p. 372.

17. Austin Holyoake, *Large Or Small Families?* (London: R. Forder, 1892).

18. Mill, *Political Economy*, p. 368.

19. George Drysdale, "The Elements of Social Science; Or Physical, Sexual, and Natural Religion, An Exposition of the True Cause and Only Cure of the Three Primary Social Evils: Poverty, Prostitution, and Celibacy," in E. Royston Pike, ed., *Golden Times: Human Documents of the Industrial Revolution* (New York: Schocken, 1972), pp. 362-67.

20. Fryer, *Birth Controllers*, p. 124.

21. Quoted in Rosanna Ledbetter, *A History of the Malthusian League*, 1877-1927 (Columbus: Ohio State University, 1976), p. 7.

22. Hypatia Bradlaugh, *Charles Bradlaugh* (London: Allen & Unwin, 1908), p. 60.

23. John Saville, ed., *A Selection of the Political Pamphlets of Charles Bradlaugh* (New York: Augustus M. Kelley, 1970).

24. Quoted in Ledbetter, *Malthusian League*, p. 12.

25. Bradlaugh, *Charles Bradlaugh*, p. 58.

26. Ibid., p. 60.

27. Ibid.

28. Fryer, *Birth Controllers*, p. 165.

29. Quoted in Ledbetter, *Malthusian League*, p. 17.

30. Besant, *Law of Population*.

31. Ledbetter, *Malthusian League*, p. 60.

32. Fryer, *The Birth Controllers*, p. 176.

33. Ibid., p. 310.

34. See Linda Gordon, *Women's Bodies, Women's Rights: A Social History of Birth Control in America* (New York: Grossman Publishers, 1976), pp. 95-101.

THE SHAPING OF THE NEW WOMAN: FREE LOVE AND EROTIC RIGHTS

4

The traitors to the masculine cause were convinced that for a woman marriage was the source of all her disabilities and humiliations; for a man it was the most salient affirmation of his power and status. For a woman marriage was a prison to which she was consigned, having committed no discernible crime except that of having been born a woman. For that fault she served a life sentence with no hope of reprieve except the death of her jailer. That she entered her cell voluntarily—often with great anticipation—was due to a lifetime of conditioning that made it appear a gilded cage, and to social and economic pressures that forced her into the realization that her survival and her status depended on her bondage. To John Stuart Mill, her sentence was all the more degrading because the jailer demanded love as well as subservience from his victim, and offered special concessions that the clever, or witty, or beautiful woman might take advantage of, but at the expense of her human dignity, and with the knowledge that she was leaving her less fortunate sisters to a less palatable fate.

According to the analysis of the feminist fathers, marriage was political despotism, economic exploitation, and sexual slavery. Put in these terms, the oppression of women was something with which they themselves could identify. The middle-class male feminists themselves had suffered denial of civil liberties and denial of their rights under a despotic monarchy and its hierarchical established church. For a radical middle-class feminist like William Thompson, who developed the labor theory of value, the fact that married women provided a staggering array of services in return for the minimum of bed and board that the husband legally obligated himself to provide, was unconscionable. The male feminists, equating woman's degraded condition in marriage with their own ignominious state before the American and French revolutions, considered the reform—or, for some, the termination—of this remaining form of bondage a necessary stage in the progress of civilization.

For such feminist radicals as Robert Owen, marriage, which perpetuated church as well as state authority, was the chief obstacle not only to women's rights, but to all social advances. At New Harmony, Owen's experiment in cooperative

Plate 9. John Humphrey Noyes, prophet of free love, about 1851 when the Oneida Community was getting underway.

living, the problem of marriage was not successfully resolved. Owen's criticism of marriage as a source of oppression and as a barrier to harmonious relations between males and females implied advocacy of free love; but Owen prescribed permanent alliances at New Harmony at which lay people, instead of clergymen, officiated. This arrangement was a concession to a moral climate that equated free love with promiscuity and civil strife.

The Owenites regarded the Shakers, the most successful of the communities then under way in the United States, with some degree of envy.[1] The Shakers seemed to presage the coming power of women, since the movement was founded by a woman. The Shakers practiced complete sexual equality, but in a religious context, and without acknowledging the sexuality of either males or females. In the New Jerusalem established by Ann Lee, individuals did not marry, and the Shaker communities were devoid of children. Ann Lee, inspired by a divine revelation after the death of her four children, had become a celibate and had gathered around her a group of disciples consisting of both males and females. They left England for America in 1774 to establish a millennial church. For the thousands she converted, Ann Lee was the female messiah, and her principles were devoutly followed in the Shaker communities that flourished in New York, New England, Kentucky, Ohio, and Indiana.

Ann Lee taught that no one could follow Christ while receiving "the gratification of lust," and demanded celibacy of her followers. Residents of Shaker communities were strictly segregated by sex, the men and women eating separately, working in different areas, and even worshipping separately, but coming together for social intercourse. A characteristic writhing of the body when they danced—an activity they considered to have devotional sanctity—led the Prophets (which was their original name) to be rechristened Shakers. Their ideal was a brother-sister relationship where the individual contributed labor according to ability and where power was vested equally in men and women, who both participated in the running of the communities.

The Shakers established a variety of industries, from distilling herbal medicines, to making tools and furniture, to breeding livestock. Every member of the Shaker communities, including the elders, worked at his or her special craft, and in effect considered work a form of worship, with each worker contributing to the common good. The strength and simplicity of the chairs they made, many of which are part of the valued Americana collections of museums, reflect the values which they espoused and practiced. Since poor workmanship or dishonest dealings were not tolerated, the Shakers found a ready market for their goods, and the communities prospered. The fact that the Shaker communities added population through conversions and thrived despite their extreme sexual conservatism, while the Owenite communities, based on secular values, foundered, focussed attention on the major differences between the two groups. In the Shaker families, strict sexual standards prevailed and the communitarians accepted this discipline, with beneficial results. The Owenites, whose concept of equality included sexual expression, found it difficult to explain away the success of the Shakers. The Shaker communities offered a meaningful life of work and commitment outside of marriage to both males and females. The fact that they failed to provide for the perpetuation of their societal ideal acted as an incentive to Humphrey Noyes.

John Humphrey Noyes studied both the Owenite and Shaker models of community organization and took ideas from each to establish a successful community based on free love. In one of those perversions of the dialectical process, the idea of free love, so crucial to the shaping of one facet of the new woman, was elaborated, practiced, and given substance by a religious zealot. Humphrey Noyes (1811-1886) had his roots in the heady antinomian soil of Puritan New England. He reached young manhood when the United States was in the throes of a religious revival. Its exponents spread the gospel that perfection was attainable in this world, the true believer having it in his power to remake the world in his own idealized image. Noyes combined an eminently rational mind with the religious longings that were part of his milieu. He was originally intent on a career in the law and was already in law school when, at the behest of his mother, he attended a revivalist meeting, certain that he could withstand the blandishments of the preacher. But he emerged convinced that perfection was within his grasp. He abandoned law for a theological seminary, and eventually got his divinity degree from Yale in 1833. Noyes found the hairsplitting arguments at divinity school suffocating, and the dry-as-dust theorizing uninspiring. He was sustained by the certitude of his own perfection and by a faith that he was uniquely qualified to show others the way to remain pure in a world where temptation ensnared and subverted the multitudes. For Noyes, the test of perfection was self-control. He had subjected all his desires, including sex, to intense discipline. Had he belonged to a faith where celibacy was honored, he might have attained sainthood; had he become a Shaker he might have scaled new heights of productivity. But Noyes did not believe that celibacy was part of God's plan for the human race. Through a process of trial and error, Noyes resolved the contradictions inherent in being perfect and living in an imperfect world; of viewing sex as an expression of divine love in a society which sanctioned sex only in the context of marriage and for the procreation of children; of advocating sexual freedom for spiritual enhancement when that would cause women suffering and the unendurable physical consequences of repeated and painful childbirth.

Noyes's way to perfection was embodied in "complex marriage," coupled with "male continence." It was first put to the test in a community he established in Putney, Vermont. At first traditional, monogamous marital relations were maintained and strictly enforced. Noyes's sensitivity to women's oppression in the monogamous setting was heightened after his own wife, Harriet Holton, whom he had married in 1838, experienced a number of excruciating pregnancies. Of the five children she had borne by 1846, four were stillborn. Under such circumstances, where a man inflicted pain on a woman, and where the woman was compelled to endure such pain because the marital state sanctioned it, perfection was possible for neither. Noyes proceeded from a conviction that men and women were equal in God's eyes, both being subject to the same laws and equally capable of attaining the perfect state. A true believer, Noyes examined all the philosophies of his day to find a way of translating sexual equality into communal life. He found much that was congenial in the thinking of the Owenites. He agreed that sex was a social instinct that brought out the unselfish and generous impulses of people, and that it should be engaged in for that reason alone. Marriage, on the other hand, brought out all the selfish impulses of the male, since it gave him absolute authority over the female. Noyes concluded that marriage, which chained a man and a woman together for life, was completely contrary to human nature in that it demanded exclusive love and prevented that sharing which was the essence of an unselfish and loving spirit. Adhering to the notion fostered by modern psychology that the more one loves the more one can love, he stated, "Men and women find universally that their susceptibility to love is not burnt out by one honeymoon."[2]

Noyes accused jealous males of establishing the doctrine that only one woman can be truly loved, and reenforcing it with the romantic ideal that the greater the torment, the more dedicated the love. For Noyes, true love gave peace and rest rather than anguish. He believed that Owen's New Harmony had failed because the Owenites were evasive and hypocritical, rejecting marriage and the nuclear family for valid reasons, but unwilling to carry their beliefs to their logical conclusion by prescribing free love for the communitarians. He felt it was inconsistent to practice economic communism while permitting personal property in the form of wives and children. Noyes was deeply impressed by the strong sense of dedication and commitment to one another that enabled the Shakers to remain a cohesive community, but informed one of the Shaker sisters who explained the system to him that he found their celibacy in total contradiction to God's and nature's laws.[3]

Complex marriage, as Noyes devised it, meant that each was married to all. Noyes elaborated his doctrine of free love as sacrament in the *Berean*, the bible of the communitarians. According to the *Berean*, the purpose of life was to share in the final period of mankind's struggle, the victory and permanent reign of spiritual wisdom and power. To achieve this state, mankind must first strive for perfection, which Noyes defined as uniting the four elements in human nature— the physical, moral, intellectual, and spiritual. Noyes rejected man-made law as being irrelevant to the righteous, who follow God's word through their discipline and spiritual motivation. Man-made law was for the lawless and disobedient. According to Noyes, God commands the righteous to "do as you please for I promise that your pleasure shall be mine. I will write my law upon your hearts." Noyes listed the requirements for regeneration which defined the perfect. They included "a renewed mind—naked and open —which could apprehend divine mysteries"; and a loving heart which had "extinguished all selfishness and with it any need for quarrelling or violence." The perfect had a desire for "unimpeded growth," expressed in Noyes's goal:

"I press toward the mark for the prize of the high calling God in Christ Jesus."[4]

Noyes's feminist concerns went beyond sexual expression. He believed that the act of love must be separated from the act of propagation, and he made the practice of birth control mandatory in the complex marriage system. Noyes's belief that sex was socially and spiritually valuable in and of itself required the practice of contraception, so that women could derive the full benefits of sex without the risks of pregnancy. Noyes was much affected by his wife's acutely painful pregnancies and was sensitive to the fact that women, for whom the consequences of sex meant enfeebling childbirths and possibly untimely death, could not participate in the sex act with the spontaneity that sex as sacrament required. He thus developed a method of birth control—called coitus reservatus—that depended on the discipline and unselfishness of the male for its effectiveness. Its unique feature was that males were required to refrain from ejaculating. The male maintained control "by restricting the action of the organ to avoid the spasmodic crisis."[5] The sex act could thus last as long as the male could maintain his control, virtually insuring orgasm for the woman and, according to Noyes, fully allowing for pleasure and release on the part of the male—a pleasure that was absent with coitus interruptus. In a period that was acutely energy conscious, the conservation of the semen, which was apparently diverted into the urinary tract, also meant that the precious fluid, tantamount to a life force, was not being needlessly expended.

Noyes had mastered the technique he called "male continence" by 1844, and in 1846 introduced complex marriage with male continence to Putney by initiating a select volunteer group. When the Putney townspeople heard of the practice, they reacted by bringing two suits for adultery against Noyes. He fled to New York City in 1847; but during the next year, using eighty of the Putney participants as a nucleus, he reconstituted the community at Oneida, New York, where complex marriage became the basis for community life.

Since sexual equality was a prerequisite for perfection, it was defined and enforced by Noyes. In some respects traditional sex roles were maintained; but in other respects they were interchangeable, and one criterion for perfection was the degree to which traits associated with sex that were considered part of conditioning (such as shyness or submissiveness in females) could be overcome. In the traditional mold, relationships in complex marriage were initiated by men, but not directly. The males made their overtures through a mediator, usually an older woman. There were consultations between the two women, and the object of the man's desire was free to accept or reject his proposal. Any woman or man who wanted to remain celibate could do so; but given Noyes's philosophy about the importance of sex as an element of sharing and the fact that he was considered to be a prophet, the pressure was in the direction of having sexual relationships. Provision was made for inducting males and females into the system of spiritual salvation through sex. Young men were initiated by experienced older women who had passed the menopause, and young women were inducted by older men who had fully mastered the discipline of "continence." The practice was consistent with Noyes's belief that perfection increased with age, and it had the practical effect of ensuring that no one was excluded from any facet of community life because of age or sex.

Striving for sexual equality in all areas was a community imperative. At Oneida, where the population eventually reached 250, all labor was shared. Women were not relegated to the kitchen as a full-time occupation. So that there would be ample time for productive work as well as prayer, only one meal, the morning meal, was prepared. For the other meals, the communitarians helped themselves from a pantry supplied "with a variety of eatables which we invite them to partake of at such times and in such manner as appetite and fancy suggest."

Since Noyes considered women to be, at least temporarily, physically weaker than males, men did domestic chores, such as chopping and carting wood, that required a reasonable amount of strength. Females were encouraged to engage in physical exercise and in all activities considered to be in the male domain in order to bring their physical endurance up to the same level as that of the males. Noyes considered that perfection was a process and that in some areas, such as physical stamina, true equality of the sexes could eventually be realized. The *Oneida Circular* reported: "We have made a beginning in having our girls learn to swim. They have been admitted to a field...which has belonged to men alone, and it appears that they excel in swimming."

In the intellectual arena, women were given full scope. The dictum was: "They shall be admitted to all the sciences, to the whole course of education considered useful to men." It was emphasized that women should develop all their talents to the full and thus they participated in all the labor of the community. Oneida developed a thriving trap industry and later added silk and spoon manufacture. Women, according to their talents, were free to engage in all phases of these industries, up to and including the managerial level. According to statistics released in 1867, of the women who chose non-household work, one out of four was in business; two out of three were artisans or craftworkers; and one in eight was in a professional category.[6]

Sex roles were regularly examined and analyzed at the "mutual criticism" sessions which were held regularly, and in which all members of the community had to participate. Group criticism—a form of encounter therapy— encouraged self-evaluation and the airing of resentments and grievances which might become alienating if permitted to build up. Masculine and feminine traits were frequently the subject of criticism. One man was criticized for having a great deal of what "is usually termed manliness. He has encouraged the stern side of his nature, and discouraged the gentle side. He seems to be ashamed to show the softness and tenderness he feels. He needs to know that these two phases of character are not irreconcilable. They are in fact necessary complements to each other." All the traits that traditional sexual ideology considered natural to females came under sharp attack at Oneida. Women testified that they had overcome bashfulness,

Plate 10. Oneida Community Women at Work. Women at Oneida choose whether to work at domestic tasks like baking (bottom) or in professions (top). From Frank Leslie's illustrated *Newspaper*, April 2, 1870.

melancholia, and hypochondria. One woman revealed, "I have made the most improvement in overcoming effeminacy and false modesty, which was inherent in my nature, and fostered by education. . . . I find myself gaining in courage and true independence of character."[7]

Women played the traditional role of mother for the limited number of babies allowed to be born annually at Oneida only until the children could walk. Socializing the motherhood instinct was a priority for Noyes, and was perhaps the most significant of the innovations relevant to the role of women at Oneida. It demanded of women a sacrifice equal to that made by the male, who surrendered all property to share in community life, and who showed his unselfishness by practicing "continence" during the sex act. Philoprogenitiveness, as the Oneidans called the instinct for motherhood, was a form of special affection which Noyes considered detrimental to a vital pantagamic society. A mother's love that was limited to her biological progeny indicated selfishness and egocentricity and was characteristic of a relatively low level of spiritual development.

Oneidans believed that the maternal instinct could be socialized in small children and, by concentrated effort, in adults as well. As early as 1851, Noyes turned his attention to this goal, which was a major test of whether the community goal of perfection was attainable. An elaborate ceremony was held, during which all dolls were banished from the community. In a kind of rite of exorcism, the expulsion of the dolls was accompanied with a testament:

We think this doll spirit that seduces us from a Community spirit in regard to helping the family and that prevents us from being in earnest to get an education, is the same spirit that seduces women to allow themselves to be so taken up with their children that they have no time to attend to Christ and get an education for heaven.[8]

Children born in the community belonged not to the biological mother but to the community, and they were mothered by all the women in the community, since nurturing was considered instinctual in women—inherent to feminine nature—whether women actually bore children or not.

All aspects of women's issues were considered at Oneida. The fact that women's fashions, which in the nineteenth century included elaborate bustles and tight corsets which made them ornaments and reenforced their helplessness, was turned into a political issue by Amelia Bloomer, who recommended the loose clothing immortalized by the Bloomer girl. At Oneida, the women wore their hair short, and wore virtually the same clothing as the men, clothing designed for comfort and utility. The women's rights movement was discussed at Oneida at the meetings that women held among themselves but was considered irrelevant to their own lives. An issue of the *Oneida Circular* of 1874 stated:

Our readers do not need to be informed that the Community took high ground on the subject of women's rights years and years ago. Curiously enough the movement did not originate with the women nor was it urged forward by Women's Conventions or by the use of the ballot or any of the usual methods of insurrection. Yet, certain it is that some way we have obtained our dearest rights and so have no occasion to get up meetings to talk about them as a separate concern. The spiritual and social questions that agitate women's meetings outside are freely discussed by us, but to confess the honest truth, we find ourselves criticizing ourselves oftener than we do the men.[9]

Oneida endured until 1876, even though the practices of the community constituted a threat to every value middle-class American society held dear, including romantic love, marriage, motherhood, and the proper sphere for women. The community managed to survive in spite of harassment, since their trap shops were a vital element in the area economy. The Oneidans practiced the Yankee ideals of hard work and thrift and were exponents of the Protestant ethic in everything except their unorthodox sexual behavior. Their virtues, plus the fact that they kept to themselves and did not try to proselytize among the townspeople, enabled their neighbors to overlook their eccentricities.

Noyes might have rested on these triumphs, content in the knowledge that he had found the key to cooperative living in a framework of spiritual striving; but this achievement did not suffice for this lifelong rebel. The *Berean* called for constant growth, and having reached his sixties, Noyes decided that success at Oneida must be perpetuated by progeny who would carry Noyes's message to the world at large and thus create a more perfect society. Since its inception in 1848, the community had increased by only two children every year—to two hundred fifty members—thus testifying to the effectiveness of coitus revervatus. Noyes, fascinated by the possibilities of eugenics for improving the species, embarked on a program of controlled propagation through the selection of scientific combinations of males and females. He called his project *stirpiculture*, meaning race culture. As Noyes designed it and carried it out, the program called on men and women at Oneida to volunteer for reproduction. They had to sign a waiver indicating that they were willing guinea pigs in a controlled experiment and that they would not succumb to "envy, childishness, and self-seeking" as a result of it. Fifty-three women and thirty-eight men at Oneida signed the pledge. Actual participants were then selected by a screening process, the standards for selection being good health and physical stamina. Fifty-eight children were eventually produced, with Noyes (who apparently met all the requirements) siring at least nine of them.

The children received the most advanced care the community of surrogate parents could provide. They remained with their natural mothers until they could walk, at which time their care became a responsibility of the community and they were housed in the children's centers provided for them. Excellent health facilities were maintained for their physical well-being, while their emotional health was fostered by the entire community. Records were kept of all the individuals born of this experiment; by 1921, when they were approaching their fifties, there had been only six deaths among the fifty-eight, whereas forty-five would have been the norm. Oneidans who entered the business or professional world when the community ended showed a strong sense of social responsibility through philanthropic endeavors.

The stirpiculture experiment aroused widespread interest in eugenics as a means toward improving both the morality and the physical health of the human species; but at the same time it revived dormant hostility and precipitated a crusade against Oneida by antivice militants. Righteous ministers and zealous prosecutors found a perfect target in Noyes's social and biological engineering schemes, which in their eyes included "degenerate sex practices." Once again Noyes had to flee, this time to a secret hideaway in Canada where he continued to govern the community, albeit in exile. He believed that compromise with convention would enable the community to survive, and recommended that Oneidans abandon complex marriage for the monogamy of which he had been so critical. Celibacy would be an option for those who continued in their opposition to marriage. The proposal was accepted; but once Oneida was divided between the married and the celibate, in effect allowing private property in the form of wives for some, the spirit of cooperation in other areas could not be upheld. This vindicated Noyes's view that the failure of previous communities was due to the maintenance of property in the form of women and children.

The success of the Oneida community, founded on sexual freedom, population control, and selective breeding, had a profound influence on English reformers, especially those seeking a solution to the explosive women's question. The struggle for the repeal of the Contagious Diseases Acts had polarized men and women to such an alarming degree that fears of sex war were regularly voiced in public print and in political speeches. That Humphrey Noyes had offered answers that seemed to satisfy women while maintaining patriarchal authority under his own charismatic leadership was encouraging to those who wanted peace but no surrender of male power.

George Noyes Miller (1845-1904) warned recalcitrant males that their days of power and privilege might be numbered. Women did not have to go to war to topple the old male-dominated order. They could simply go on strike. A nephew of Humphrey Noyes, Miller had been born in the Putney community and received his early education at Oneida. In the preface to *Strike of a Sex* (1891), he articulated the utopian vision of sex and class equality for which the male feminists yearned:

The whole world is plainly in travail to lift the primeval curse of brutalizing labor from man, but the just at least, are beginning to perceive that there is also a principal curse which must be lifted from women [constant childbearing]. When these long borne curses are really lifted from men and women—What then? The Garden of Eden!

In *Strike of a Sex*, Miller's hero arrives at a town in total chaos and disarray. It is a place where slatternly housekeeping is the rule, where the odor of decaying food fills the air, and where there is an "atmosphere of utter joylessness." It is a ghost town inhabited only by men "from which the sweetness and beauty of women and the innocence of children had been banished." Everything is closed except the drugstore from which the men obtained the palliatives to relieve their distress. Upon inquiring where the women are, the traveller is told that they have been on strike for three months to gain their version of Magna Carta. The women are demanding the suffrage, the right to hold public office, equal employment opportunities, the right to property and most important, Zugassent. (This is Miller's term for the male continence practiced at Oneida, which would enable women to control their own bodies.) The women are occupying commodious buildings on the outskirts of town, fully prepared to let the men rot and to let the race die to achieve the free development of their own natures, and "the perfect ownership of their own persons" by determining the number of children they would have. According to a spokesman, the women feel that "the chains which have bound them for unnumbered ages, although artfully garlanded with flowers called by sentimental and endearing names are older and more galling than those of any bondspeople on the globe." The discussion about Zugassent, which the curious hero discovers heads the list of women's demands, is revealing. Miller considers it the prerequisite for that unity and universal love toward which people are striving, the essential that would enable men and women to walk together "hand in hand, ministering to each other from the fountain of eternal affection." He regards Zugassent as a panacea which would eliminate intemperance and prostitution. The restraint and discipline on the part of the man are not only the ultimate proof of love for beleagured women, but are another instance of virtue being its own reward, as the semen which is retained in the body adds enormously to "men's magnetic mental and spiritual force."[10]

The Oneida experiment gave added weight to arguments for birth control and raised the most profound questions about women's sexual nature. George Drysdale, who had scientific credentials and whose opinions could not easily be dismissed, had reopened the question of women's sexuality in *Elements of Social Science*, where he asserted that women had sexual and maternal rights which could be denied only at peril to their health. Drysdale advocated complete freedom of sexual expression for both males and females, but attacked marriage as a major obstacle to the love to which everyone had a right. Drysdale first equated marriage and prostitution, applying that term to the condition of women who traded their bodies for bed and board and enabled their husbands to enjoy total authority over them. Marriage as defined by the church—a permanent bond—was a trap, with male and female drawn to one another in the flush of youthful desire, and chained together for life, often under the most galling circumstances. Under conditions prevailing in the mid-nineteenth century, Drysdale insisted, "it is absolutely impossible to have a free, sincere, and dignified sexual morality in our society as long as marriage continues to be the only honorable provision for the union of the sexes, and as long as the marriage bond is so indissoluble as it is at present."

Since women's sexual nature could not help but have a fundamental effect on society, and since the proportion of women in the population was increasing, making it unlikely that all could get married, the woman's question precipitated a great debate among social reformers. The debate took place within the framework of the two competing socialist movements in England. Members of both the Marxists, who favored revolution, and the Fabians, who favored evolution, as the best means for achieving socialism, saw the woman's question as both a challenge and an opportunity to offer a solution to a problem which had caused stalemate and produced rancor among the traditional parties, who could not even agree on whether women should get the vote or be relieved of their legal disabilities.

When Karl Marx died in 1883, his brand of scientific socialism, which insisted on the inevitability of revolution, had not attracted a wide following in England, even though he wrote his magnum opus, *Capital*, while a resident in England, and used the English industrial system as his model to prophesy the eventual destruction of capitalism. Marx himself believed that the phenomenon of women working outside the home was a vital factor in transforming property relations. In *Capital*, he stated:

However terrible, however repulsive, the breakup of the old family system within the organism of capitalist society may seem, nonetheless, large scale industry, by assigning to women and young persons and children of both sexes, a decisive role in the socially organized process of production, and a role which has to be fulfilled outside the home, is building the new economic foundations for a higher form of the family and of the relations between the sexes.[11]

He was eloquent on the exploitation of women's and children's labor, writing in *Capital* that even after the passage of legislation prohibiting women from doing certain kinds of work and establishing limits on hours for women and children, "women are still occasionally used instead of horses for hauling canal boats, because the labour required to produce horses and machines is an accurately known quantity while that required to maintain the women of the surplus population is below all calculation."[12] Despite the massive documentation of women's exploitation, Marx did not give women's rights any priority. He had no sympathy for the middle-class sponsored women's movement, which he perceived— accurately—as an attempt to meliorate working-class discontent and thereby avoid revolutionary struggle. Equal rights for women were desiderata which would result from the revolution prophesied by Marx.

Marx had a reflexive antipathy to birth control since it was associated with the "bourgeois" Malthusians, and the "naive" Owenites, whose utopian socialism he revised and made "scientific." The Drysdale family had cast the issue of birth control in a light designed to affront all socialists when they insisted that if the poor would use birth control to limit their numbers, "socialism would be unnecessary, and if they refused it would be useless."[13] Commenting on Malthusian proposals, Marx said, "The hatred of the English working class against Malthus . . . is therefore entirely justified. The people were right in sensing instinctively that they were confronted not with a *man of science* but with a *bought advo-*

cate, a pleader on behalf of their enemies, a shameless sycophant of the ruling class."[14]

Marx's attitudes toward marriage and women in general were entirely conventional. He thought submissiveness a desirable trait in women. His wife, Jennie von Westphalen, whom he married in 1843, was a long-suffering woman who bore him seven children, several of them while Marx and his wife were on the run after his exile from Germany. In marked contrast to the Owenites and Millites, who solicited women's ideas and incorporated them into their social philosophy, there is no evidence that the women's point of view was ever sought in Marx's intellectual circle. In his view of marriage as a form of property relations and in his acceptance of the double standard, Marx did not notably differ from the capitalists against whom he relentlessly inveighed.[15]

The English disciples of Marx formed the Social Democratic Federation (SDF) to carry on his ideas. Under the leadership of H. M. Hyndman, they considered the women's movement irremediably bourgeois and demands for women's suffrage a diversion from revolutionary consciousness. They failed to consider even the interests of working women. Instead of insisting on expansion of opportunities for female employment, they demanded the right of women to stay at home and have babies, thus discouraging them from entering the job market and competing with men. Hyndman even viewed prostitution from the viewpoint of the working man rather than the working woman, stating in the SDF organ, *Justice*, that a prostitute's services are bought with the wealth capitalists gain by exploiting her father and brothers.[16]

Publication of Friedrich Engel's *Origin of the Family, Private Property, and the State* in 1884, and August Bebel's *Women and Socialism* in 1885 laid the basis for a feminist perspective in Marxist thought. Engels, drawing on anthropological sources, asserted that married women were the first form of private property, and implied that their potential for class consciousness was enormous on that account. Bebel, too, pointed out that while there were class antagonisms among women, these were mitigated by shared interests. Both insisted, however, that the complete emancipation of women could take place only after a socialist revolution had taken place, and invited women into the movement on that premise.

When women showed solidarity enough to force the repeal of the Contagious Diseases Acts, Edward Aveling began to believe it was possible to recruit women for the Marxist cause. Aveling (1849-1898), had been a vice-president of the National Secular Society before he moved into the Marxist orbit as a result of his acquantance with Eleanor Marx, Karl Marx's youngest daughter. Eleanor Marx and Aveling had criticized the feminist movement for being middle-class, but noted that the one issue which had brought unity to women of all classes was the Contagious Diseases repeal campaign. They believed this display of sisterhood was due to the fact that female sexuality and the male response to it affected all women. Marx and Aveling concluded that socialism must include not only a change in the relationship between labor and capital, but in interpersonal, intimate relationships, that is, marriage, as well. In *The Woman Question* (1886), they launched a concerted attack on the double standard, on marriage as a form of prostitution for women, and on the "bourgeois suppression" of female sexuality. They made women's sexuality a political issue, adopting the view that women had sexual rights; and that marriage was a denial of the free expression of human desire. Weddings, they insisted, were business transactions, and marriages thus arranged "seem to us...worse than prostitution." Chastity was "unhealthy and unholy." *The Woman Question* asked, "How is it that our sisters bear upon their brows this stamp of lost instincts, stifled affections, a nature in part, murdered?" Improvements in relations between men and women would come only when both, "striving after purity, discuss the sexual question in all its bearings, as free human beings, looking frankly into each others' faces." In *The Woman Question* Marx and Aveling predicted that monogamy would gain the day only after a socialist revolution, when "love, respect, intellectual likeness and command of the necessities of life would be assured for a harmonious blending of two human lives."[17]

Until that time when marriage meant dignity for both partners, rather than mastery for the man and slavery for the woman, socialists should protest by loving freely and spontaneously in unions to which they themselves were committed without the sanction of the authorities. Free love, as proposed by Marx and Aveling, was a political statement—an act of defiance against conventional morals, the woman disdaining the exchange of her body for bed and board, and the man rejecting the authority that legal marriage ties gave him. As conceived by Marx and Aveling, free love was a visible manifestation of allegiance to socialist principles and ceased to be an individual expression of rebellion on the Wollstonecraft-Godwin, Robert Dale Owen-Frances Wright model.

Eleanor Marx and Edward Aveling lived their creed in a free union. However, the example they sought to set for their socialist comrades was not an encouraging one. Aveling had character flaws that bordered on the pathological. He appeared to believe that until the revolution changed the exploitative character of societal relationships there was no point in behaving ethically, even though this was the *sine qua non* for a free love union. During their fourteen-year relationship, which started in 1884, he used Eleanor Marx mercilessly, forcing her to pay his debts and to provide for his support while he continued to engage in casual affairs.[18] Marx bore Aveling's transgressions with fortitude; but when he legally married an actress, making a farce of their political ideals and a common mistress out of her, Marx killed herself.

Eleanor Marx's death was a shattering blow to the socialist community. It was a personal tragedy to her friends in the movement, who consistently described her as having all the Christian virtues—love, generosity, compassion—without actually having the faith. Perhaps just as important in the long run were the political ramifications. Through her writings and her actions, Eleanor Marx had dedicated herself to maintaining the legacy of her father. She had sought to incorporate free love, a new relationship between the sexes based on spontaneous feelings rather than property considerations, into the Marxist heritage; but her own experience raised questions as to whether the free love union as long as it was practiced in capitalist society might not make a woman even more vulnerable, and be more demeaning, than middle-class marriage.

Since Aveling was universally regarded as a scoundrel, both branches of socialism sought to dissociate themselves from him. His theoretical contributions on the class solidarity and revolutionary potential of women were regarded as coming from a tainted, self-serving source, and were dismissed by Marxists. When Aveling died a mere four months after Eleanor Marx, not a single one of his former comrades in the socialist movement came to the funeral.

Free love and women's sexual rights were the promises of the postrevolutionary utopia of the Marxists. William Morris established them as the birthright of the new socialist woman. Morris (1834-1896), who hated the aesthetics of capitalism and believed the ugliness of the capitalist landscape symbolized the distorted relationships inherent in the system, was a member of the Social Democratic Federation (SDF) at its inception. In 1884, he left to form the Socialist League because of disagreements with the leadership of the SDF. Morris wrote *News from Nowhere* (1891) to propagate his own socialist ideas for the masses. The book reveals his disagreement with some Marxist orthodoxies, for example the desirability of an industrial society, but demonstrates the powerful influence of Engels, Eleanor Marx, and Aveling on the questions of sex and marriage.

In Morris's blueprint for the future, which brings feminism and socialism together, a revolution in interpersonal relationships has taken place no less dramatic than the one in economic and political relationships, with women gaining complete equality with men. Morris believed that the alienation resulting from machine production outweighed the putative advantages, and he favored the scrapping of all machines and a return to handicraft industry. In Nowhere, females work alongside males at weaving looms as well as in rock quarries to produce the needs of the small communes in which they live. There is no government in Nowhere, the buildings of Parliament having been turned into stables, in which capacity they serve a more useful function. Community affairs are handled democratically, with both males and females participating in the discussions and decision making. The need for a representative government of laws is obviated since there is no crime in Nowhere. Morris saw violent crime as the result of greed and jealousy, the inevitable by-products of the ownership of persons, such as that of a wife by a husband or children by parents. He abhorred the "family tyranny" inherent in capitalist society. In Nowhere, the nuclear family—which placed women exclusively in the home, at the mercy of, first, father and, later, husband— is abolished. Since males and females both engage in production and have economic independence, they form ties based on love and remain with one another only so long as they find their relationship mutually satisfying and fulfilling. Clara, one of the inhabitants of Nowhere, illustrates Morris's idea of the new woman. Clara, after having had two children by Dick, her husband, decides to leave him for another man. Clara does not suffer any stigma because she elects to follow her heart. Nor is Dick regarded as a cuckold with the contempt that designation brings with it. Their children are well cared for by the community since in Nowhere each has a commitment to all. Clara, it turns out, has had her fling, and she and Dick are about to resume married life without the interference of self-serving outside parties. A different morality is possible because there is no greed, envy, or jealousy, such emotions being functions of property. According to the Guide who explains the philosophy of life in Nowhere to the visitor, there is only the "normal unhappiness" that accompanies disappointments in love. It is considered self-centered to dwell on personal unhappiness too long, and foolish to assume "the world must cease" because one man is unhappy. "Youth lasts and there are always fresh opportunities. So we shake off these griefs in a way which perhaps the sentimentalists of other times would think contemptible and unheroic; but which we think necessary and manlike."

Having made clear that sexual freedom exists for women in Nowhere, and that they have opportunities to realize their talents, Morris takes the Marxist anti-Malthusian line that domesticity and motherhood are a woman's ultimate fulfillment. In Nowhere women prepare all the food in public dining halls, do all the housework, and wait on men. "Don't you know," explains the guide, "that it is a great pleasure to a clever woman to manage a house skillfully and to do it so that all the housemates about her look pleased, and are grateful to her?"[19]

Morris considered it a strange, baseless piece of folly that the "superior" women of the nineteenth century wanted to emancipate "the more intelligent part of their sex from the bearing of children." Under the ideal conditions Morris established, maternity is that fulfillment that woman's nature craves. The Guide sums it up: "So that you can see, the ordinarily healthy woman (and almost all our women are both healthy and at least comely), respected as a child bearer and rearer of children, desired as a woman, loved as a companion, unanxious for the future of her children, has far more instinct for maternity than the poor drudges of past days could ever have had."

Despite the multitude of choices theoretically open to women from childhood on, Morris assumed that their natures would sway them in the direction of motherhood. The security which is assured them would cause them to desire more children, and once the mother was secure, free, and happy, the children would be healthier, eugenics inevitably flowing from socialism. Morris's socialist new woman had equal rights and equal employment opportunities but would likely not avail herself of them, seeking instead the traditional female role. The Marxist model of the postrevolutionary woman was hardly as radical as the design that Humphrey Noyes had actually succeeded in realizing at Oneida. At Oneida there was constant striving to change gender traits that Morris accepted as biological. Even the biological maternal instinct was socialized at Oneida. The people of Nowhere are true to Marxist dogmas in disdaining population control even though Morris's version of utopia—an agrarian society with limited resources and no technology—would require that some thought be given to limiting population.

Reformers who wanted socialism without pain in the form of revolutionary upheaval or class struggle came together in 1883 to form the Fellowship of the New Life as an alternative to the Social Democratic Federation. Havelock Ellis was among those who helped organize this group, which demanded that its members should pledge themselves to live according to high ideals of love and brotherhood, and to found whenever possible communities in which such a life could be lived completely. Short of that, they were to put their principles into practice in their day-to-day lives, thus effecting changes in the community through their example. This striving for growth and perfection was very reminiscent of Noyes's ideal and, indeed, Ellis was an admirer of his work.

Within a year, social reformers within the Fellowship concluded that social changes were possible before individuals had attained a perfect character. They were convinced that evolution was tending in the direction of socialism and that this process could be hastened by applying pressure on the government. The offshoot of the Fellowship of the New Life was the Fabian Society, whose goal was the socialization of industry through education, agitation, and organization. Bernard Shaw, who became one of the most effective propagandists for the Fabians, succinctly described the difference between the Fellowship and the Fabians:

Certain members of the Fellowship modestly feeling that the revolution would have to wait an unreasonably long time if postponed until they personally attained perfection wanted the aim to be political and economic action. The Fellowship continued to exist, its members to "sit among the dandelions," the Fabians "to organize the docks."[20]

The Fabians attracted an articulate group of intellectuals which included Bernard Shaw, Annie Besant, and Sidney and Beatrice Webb, who became the leaders of the organization. To the members, ideas were more powerful than weapons, and they brought their unique perspectives as scientists, sociologists, economists, and philosophers to bear on every issue of the day. The issue of feminism divided them deeply. Beatrice Webb was not herself a feminist. Although she eventually supported women's suffrage, as late as 1889 she made her opposition to it manifest when she signed a petition against giving women the right to vote.

Coming from an upper-middle-class family, Beatrice Webb, née Potter, saw women of her class, pampered and catered to, living parasitical lives and being invested by theoreticians with a host of talents and virtues that she did not believe they possessed. Her father encouraged her intellectual bent, and his wealth enabled her to ignore the restrictions that circumscribed most women of the Victorian period. She was never taught to adopt a submissive role and thus was not sympathetic to those of her sisters who were.

Webb's lack of feminist consciousness was a supreme irony, since she was regarded as a model for the new woman by such ardent feminists as Bernard Shaw and Floyd Dell. She was a completely independent and self-sufficient woman. She used her wealth and connections to promote her socialist ideals, and she made the Fabian socialist cause her life's work. Beatrice Potter deliberately rejected Joseph Chamberlain, the man she loved and one who had a promising political future, as a husband, fearing that his awesome masculinity would overwhelm her and that his rigid concepts about women's roles would limit her. She chose instead Sidney Webb, a man she did not love, but with whom she shared common interests and socialist ideals, and whom she could dominate.[21]

The Fabians' leadership, like the Marxists', were not interested in the middle-class women's movement, and were interested in feminism only if it could be put in a socialist context. Karl Pearson's formulations of the women's issue thus appeared promising. Pearson (1857-1936) was a professor of applied mathematics and mechanics at University College, London. During his student days in Germany, he was profoundly influenced by those twin heresies of nineteenth-century thought, Darwinism and Marxism. Pearson spent his intellectual life trying to bring them together, and used feminism as the glue.

Pearson believed the women's emancipation movement to be the most important development of modern times in that it had revolutionary implications which could be harnessed for the benefit of the community. He wanted to subject the entire question of sex differences to scientific inquiry, and proposed a science of sexology for this purpose. The ultimate technocrat, Pearson far outdid Marx in giving socialism a scientific cast. He went to the root of the word and equated *social* with *moral*, and *antisocial* with *immoral*. Socialism in Pearson's lexicon was thus a new morality, denoting "the subjection of all individual action to the welfare of society."[22] A socialist morality was therefore a precondition for a socialist state.

Pearson did not agree with Marx on the necessity for class struggle as a catalyst for revolution. He believed that it was the function of the scientist and of the educated elite in general to bring the classes together rather than to polarize them. A true socialist, in Pearson's eyes, was above class interests and looked to the needs of the entire community. He must educate the governing classes toward a higher social morality and bring about a peaceful revolution by influencing lawmakers in the right direction. Pearson considered it a truism that no great social reconstruction was ever brought about by a revolution, and this theory made his ideas much more palatable to the Fabians than to the Marxists.

Writing during the feminist agitation over the Contagious Diseases Acts, and with an awareness that women outnumbered men, Pearson considered a sex war a greater possibility than a class war despite the depressed economic conditions of the 1880s. Sexology was to determine once and for all whether women were restricted to the domestic sphere for biological reasons or whether their destiny had been determined by long centuries of conditioning. Pearson wanted to know what a woman's physical capacity relative to a man's actually was; what effect reproduction had on her mental and her other physical functions; what effect higher education had on a woman's reproductive functions; whether marriage impeded a woman's intellectual growth; whether a woman's sexual instinct was geared to the maternal instinct; and whether sexual drive could be correlated with intellect—the higher the intellect, the lower the sex drive. Was a new woman— one who could look forward to independence—possible, or were women necessarily subject to men because of the protection they required due to biological inferiority?[23]

The answers to these questions had vital political and economic implications that went to the root of the growing antagonisms between proponents and opponents of the masculine cause. For masculinists, the prospect of women entering the public sphere signalled a crisis in Western civilization. Masculinists were fearful that voting women would cause the decline of the British Empire, and with it the supremacy of the Anglo-Saxon race. They were haunted by the prospect of middle-class women who had acquired an education spurning marriage and motherhood, and leaving the future of the nation in the hands of the least intelligent and poorest individuals.

Pearson was a nationalist as well as a socialist, but he ridiculed attempts to make the suffrage the last stand of beleagured patriarchs. He felt that even if women's mental capacities were inferior to men's, this should not be a bar to their voting, since the vote "was granted to the dullest yokel."[24] The vote and, indeed, politics itself were irrelevant to Pearson's national socialist future, where science would determine the role of woman, a role that would be both in their best interests and in those of the nation.

Pearson reasoned that if women's reproductive function somehow drained them physically and intellectually, then, in effect, women would have to remain second-class citizens despite the claims of justice. Even if they gained equality they would not be able to maintain it and, as far as Pearson was concerned, they would be in the same category as blacks, who, despite their progress from slavery to freedom, were still held to be the moral and intellectual inferiors of whites.[25] Pearson regarded the state as more important than the individual. Since women performed an important function as the bearers of future generations, they would necessarily be well treated and well protected even if they should turn out to be inferior to men. On the other hand, if women were proven to be the physical and mental equals of men, the pool of talents and skills that they represented could be a tremendous boon to society; and those institutions that had held women back and were continuing to stifle them, to wit, marriage and the family, would have to be questioned.

Pearson opened up important questions but was too much of an ideologue to wait for the answers, even assuming that they could ever be attained with scientific accuracy. The next year he emerged with his solutions to the woman's question and made them the keystone of his socialist society. He concluded from his observations of Swabian peasant women who worked long hours in the field that women were indeed the physical equals of men, and reasoned from the existence of talented writers like George Eliot that they were the potential intellectual equals of men. Subscribing to the idea that morality is relative—promiscuity, brother-sister marriages, and slavery all having been considered moral at certain times—he proclaimed that true morality was simply a function of social needs, to be determined by the state. This view permitted him to discard the rigidly circumscribed relations between men and women and to challenge the institution of marriage as well. He called for a totally new relationship between the sexes, where men and women may or may not get married based on their function in society. The new woman, if she was to be man's equal, must be economically independent and therefore must become part of the productive labor force. The economic independence of women, according to Pearson, "will for the first time render it possible for the highest human relationship to become again a matter of pure affection, raised above every suspicion of constraint and every taint of commercialism."

Independent women would form relationships with men based on free love since they would not have to get married to gain subsistence. Pearson called these relationships "sex-partnerships" in lieu of marriage and would encourage the equality they denoted through coeducation, so that boys and girls could become friends, as well as through sex education to teach girls, among other things, that they had a sex instinct. Pearson believed that the abolition of marriage and greater sexual freedom for women was the lasting solution to the gnawing problem of prostitution, so much in the limelight in the 1880s because of the Contagious Disease Acts. He noted, "When marriage is no longer regarded as a profession for women, when men and women can meet on an equal footing," prostitution would cease to exist.[26]

Pearson put the vexing population question in a socialist perspective by combining it with eugenics. The specter of depression that haunted England in the 1870s and '80s brought the fear of overpopulation into focus once again. In that light, Pearson considered woman's childbearing function and her restriction to the domestic sphere to be of dubious value to society. He suggested the possibility of having two classes of women, based on function rather than wealth—childbearing and nonchildbearing women. Sex-partnerships that produced no children could be entered into freely without any interference on the part of the state. But couples that produced children would be subject to state control. Pearson was interested in quality rather than quantity of progeny, believing that the future of the nation required that an improved species be produced, rather than more of the same. Sanctioned births—those which would receive the full support of the government—would make the mother eligible to receive a stipend to insure her independence while performing the functions of motherhood. Unsanctioned births between unsuitable individuals whose progeny were not a eugenic improvement would be punished—presumably by means of a tax.

The new woman who was being shaped in the Fabian mold stood poised on the threshold of drastic changes. She was a sexual being who related to men on the basis of free love because of her independence. Her independence was earned through the productive labor she contributed to the community. If she chose marriage and motherhood, her independence was guaranteed by state endowment so long as she met certain qualifications for motherhood. Her choices, however, were limited by the priorities of the community, since she was first and foremost a member of a community rather than an individual. She was to have no voice in community councils because policies were to be based on scientific data from which there could be no appeal.

Both Pearson and Havelock Ellis showed how the new woman's role could change based on different priorities, new scientific data, or both. As international tensions increased in the late nineteenth century, making war a likelihood, Pearson took a new look at the population question in the light of theories of inferior and superior races, to which he subscribed. He concluded that war was a more efficient way of eliminating inferior stock than the eugenics program, which might take several generations to accomplish its goal. He was strongly in favor of the Boer War, which he justified, saying, "A nation is an organized whole which was kept up to a high pitch of external efficiency by contest, chiefly by way of war with inferior races."[27] Under such circumstances, the state could not afford to allow women to choose whether they wanted to become mothers or not. In the world of the Social Darwinists, where excellence, virtue, and racial superiority were determined on the battlefield and where the needs of power demanded large armies, there might be few choices for women.

A variant of Karl Pearson's national socialism had a very audible echo in the United States. Its American prophet was Edward Bellamy, a Massachusetts-born lawyer turned journalist who became consumed by a desire to find a "method of economic organization by which the republic might guarantee the livelihood and material welfare of its citizens on a basis of equality." Bellamy (1850-1898), loathed the depredations of individualistic capitalism and the chaos and alienation it left in its wake. A self-proclaimed feminist, he touted the importance of feminine culture and its holistic values—cooperation, loyalty, altruism, the capacity for nurture, and respect for human life. His conviction that these values had been etiolated by industrialization made him a champion of women's social, political, and economic rights.

Looking Backward (1888) was the result of Bellamy's search for a harmonious social order and his solution to class conflict and sex antagonisms. In Bellamy's utopia which is situated in Boston in the year 2000, socialism is imposed from above by an elite of middle-class technocrats who preside over a regimented corporate state. In theory, Bellamy considered women to be the only "true socialists" and would integrate them completely into his society. In practice, Bellamy's perception of what women want made his utopia the ultimate consumer society where matter prevailed over mind. Women would be required to perform their domestic functions since Bellamy believed that only married women who were mothers fully represented their sex.[28] Unmarried women could not participate in the councils of the industrial army where military techniques of drill and discipline were used to maintain a grip on the workers. Women had to work in the army but during their leisure time were kept happy by shopping sprees to department stores (an American phenomenon of the 1880s) where they were treated to a veritable cornucopia of goods which they could purchase from conveyer belts and pay for with chits, the reward for their labor. Women in Bellamy's utopia were given the sexual freedom that was mandatory for all future societies since Oneida, but he evidently intended the buying orgies to gratify any erotic cravings they might have.

Bellamy's consumer society exalted the acquisitive instinct of greed to the utmost and depended for its existence on a mindless materialism. He considered memory the enemy of progress and innovation, and therefore, immoral. If he had his way, memory would be extirpated from the human personality. The lobotomized populace would carry "portable memory machines" for remembering those things necessary to carry on their daily routine. Bellamy's virulent anti-intellectualism was the polar opposite of the idealism of the philosophical tradition of male feminism where women's liberation was seen as the culmination of a historical evolutionary process which would also achieve the triumph of reason over instinct.

Havelock Ellis responded to Karl Pearson's call for a science of sexology and considered himself to be the first sexologist. Ellis (1859-1939) was born in the same year that saw the publication of Darwin's *Origin of Species*. His generation was destined to have deep conflicts on where they should place their faith—in the religious traditions of the past represented by their parents, or in the promise that scientific truth held out. Ellis was no exception. He was a child of lower middle-class parents whose father, a merchant sea captain, was absent during much of Ellis's childhood, thus leaving his mother the dominant influence in his life. Ellis's mother was a confirmed Evangelical Christian, but this did not prevent his exposure to such antireligious works as George Drysdale's *Elements of Social Science*. Drysdale, with his advocacy of free love and the necessity for sexual expression, represented the scientific end of the spectrum; but Ellis found that he could not put his faith in the dogmas of science, which reduced life to mechanical laws beyond human control, any more than in those of revealed religion.

Ellis's yearnings reached an acute state when, at the age of sixteen, his father took him on a voyage around the world. Ellis opted to remain in Australia, where he became a teacher in the bush country. Very much isolated, he experienced the first stirrings of his own sexual desire with strong guilt feelings. A reading of James Hinton's *Life of Nature* left him profoundly impressed with its philosophy of life, which was based on a pantheistic belief in nature's oneness with human strivings. Hinton, a physician, combined science with mysticism, and acquired a large and devoted following among women with his conviction—which was similar to that of Humphrey Noyes—that the sexual passions had spiritual significance. Unlike Noyes, he had no deep religious convictions, and propagated his doctrine with such simplistic slogans as "A virtue which harms others is as bad as a vice which harms others," and "Chastity maintained by fear is as unchaste as harlotry."[29]

Hinton remained a lifelong inspiration to Ellis, who returned to England in 1880 to take up the study of medicine, which he saw as a tool which could be used to integrate the human being with his natural environment and to achieve a synthesis between science and religion. On Ellis's return to England, he came in contact with the world of radical politics. He met H. M. Hyndman, leader of the Marxist Social Democratic Federation; Eleanor Marx; and Edward Aveling. In 1883, he helped draw up the constitution of the Fellowship of the New Life (the predecessor of the Fabian Society), which aimed at the subordination of the material to the spiritual, and the cultivation of a perfect character. Through these associations he acquired a belief that human nature was basically good but was corrupted by the greedy, materialistic commercialism of capitalism, and he, as much as any of his radical colleagues, believed that this soul-destroying system would fall. However, he made no political commitment toward that end and was wary of taking any political stand.

Friendships with Olive Schreiner and Edith Lees, whom he married in 1891, nourished Ellis's feminism. He and Edith Lees had wanted to establish a free love union based on the Aveling-Marx model, but Eleanor Marx's unhappy plight convinced them that such an arrangement could not be sustained in the prevailing moral climate. They entered a companionate marriage, which to the liberated intellectuals of the late nineteenth century was the alternative to a free love union. In the case of the Ellises, it entailed separate households, both parties maintaining their own lives and coming together to satisfy mutual needs at agreed upon occasions. Ellis described his marriage to Lees as "a union of affectionate comradeship in which the specific emotions of sex had the smallest part, yet a union, as I was later to learn by experience, able to attain even on that basis a passionate intensity of love."[30]

Ellis is best known as a sexual reformer, a prophet of the modern sexual revolution that liberated men and women, but especially women, from the restraints imposed upon them by Victorian conventions. He defined his mission in his first book, *The New Spirit* (1890), in which he proclaimed a great spiritual awakening which derived from the growth of science, the rise of the women's movement, and the march of democracy. He saw as the great challenge of the day, educating people to realize the enormous potential of these movements.

Ellis started with the premise that since human nature was basically good, impulses and drives which were natural were healthy and therefore could not be judged as evil. In sexual matters, Ellis believed that ancient prejudices and pervasive ignorance were severely distorting and disabling. He was fascinated with the diversity of sexual expression, and his first investigations concerned homosexuality. The sensational trial of Oscar Wilde determined him to enlighten the public on this matter, and the result was *Inversion* (1896), published the year after Wilde's trial.

An amendment attached to the Criminal Law Amendment Acts of 1885—the acts which had raised the age of consent from thirteen to sixteen—had made homosexuality a crime in England. Before Ellis's examination of the subject, there was no neutral term to describe relationships between two members of the same sex. From a religious standpoint such a relationship was discussed in terms of vice and sin; it was considered a disease by physicians. In legal terms it had not been differentiated from masturbation, and was variously called sodomy or buggery. Ellis put the word *homosexual* into the English language. *Inversion* questioned whether any form of sexual behavior should be regarded as criminal. Ellis used historical as well as anthropological evidence to assert that homosexuality was commonly practiced in the past, using ancient Greece as one example. He suggested that morality was not an absolute, but differed according to time and place, and he helped to establish a cultural relativism which undermined Victorian certainties in the most sensitive area of all, that of assumptions on male and female sexuality.

Ellis used the same historical and anthropological method that validated homosexuality to affirm the existence of female sexuality. He asserted that the "myth" denying the sexuality of women was peculiar to the nineteenth century and limited to Great Britain, Germany, and Italy, with previous ages and societies fully acknowledging the sex drive in women. The sexually repressed Victorian woman was a product of a particular time and place, Ellis argued. Ellis advocated erotic rights for women and urged men to recognize them by showing greater sensitivity to women's sexual needs. In *Studies in the Psychology of Sex* (1910), he described sex as "the deepest and most volcanic of human impulses." He elaborately described the physical manifestations of sex, but also rhapsodized on the spiritual significance of the sex act. The message of *Psychology of Sex* was one that he repeated over and over again in the course of his long career—sex was a mysterious gift to mankind which was available to all, regardless of class or sex, and could enhance the lives of everyone. It was the common denominator that united both sexes, and the leveler of all classes.

The Love Rights of Women (also called *Erotic Rights of Women*) is a popular version of ideas contained in *Psychology of Sex* designed for consumption by the masses who might find the sheer length of the latter too formidable. In *Love Rights* Ellis acknowledged that women had never asked for their sexual rights, and indeed that they never would ask for them because of a reserve inherent to their nature. He assured his female readers that they wanted their sexual rights, nevertheless, and that they wanted them more than the political rights and the economic opportunities that they were asking for. He thus effectively denied the feminist fathers' contention that women were rational beings capable of taking control over their bodies. Ellis advised his male readers that women's superficial reserve ("coldness") might best be overcome by a tactical show of force. Declaring that women like to be subdued, he explained: "The ends of courtship may be attained even more successfully by the forceful than the humble male.... In the erotic sphere, a woman asks nothing better of a man than to be lifted above her coldness to the higher plane where there is reciprocal interest and natural joy in the act of love."[31] That women were essentially irrational, and that they received a unique sexual fillip from rape, was communicated to immense audiences through popular journals and magazines whose editors frequently solicited Ellis's views because they took at face value his self assessment as the guru of modern science.

Ellis sought to reassure his middle-class audience that he was no wild-eyed

revolutionary like the youthful George Drysdale who believed that sexual freedom and marriage were mutually exclusive. In Ellis's view, erotic rights for
women could easily be accommodated within marriage. In perceptible stages,
Ellis moved away from the support he had vouchsafed for the women's movement in 1888. He eventually concluded that "women's brains were in their
wombs,"[32] in effect answering in the positive Karl Pearson's question on whether
women's biological functions had any effect on their intellect. Ellis became
convinced that women's unique contribution to society lay in realizing their
biological destiny as mothers. His researches had confirmed that the reproductive
instinct was common to all animals, and he did not believe that females could be
fulfilled except through its expression, although males, whose brains were not
tied to their reproductive functions, presumably could.

Ellis had no more scientific evidence for his declarations about women's
proper role than any of the other social scientists who were dabbling in reform,
and he tended to trim his sails to the prevailing ideological winds. Public opinion, which appeared to turn against the militant suffragettes of the early twentieth
century, reenforced his views about women's role. Persistent evidence that the
majority of women opposed the vote—a poll in 1911 showed that of 18,000
women queried only 5,500 favored the suffrage—was to him confirmation that
women did not want the vote because it was a denial of their femininity. He
concluded that suffrage supporters were subverting their feminine birthright and
imitating men, to the detriment not only of themselves but of society as well. He
proclaimed it to be imperative that each sex should have its unique share in
molding the world of the future, and that women's reproductive functions determined their share. Women could attain power through motherhood by breeding a
superior race of individuals, an exalted role they could never attain as "sexless"
persons in a public world.[33]

Ellis brought together all the features of Humphrey Noyes's Oneida—sexual
expression, birth control, and eugenics—but placed them in a secular framework
where private property was the norm. He was not deterred by the incongruities
inherent in transposing the ideas of a religious prophet, who presided over a
small, cohesive community, to a large society, where all the ingredients that
made the Oneida experiment a success were lacking. Education, he felt, was the
answer. Ellis's study of the past had convinced him that it was the failure of
previous civilizations to properly educate their women that caused their downfall. "We must teach our mistresses," he said, "as we taught our masters"—education
being understood in the Fabian sense of teaching them their duties and responsibilities, as well as their rights.

H. G. Wells, a Fabian socialist, was a dedicated apostle of the new scientific
order that Pearson and Ellis preached. He used his novels to popularize the ideas
of the social scientists and to educate the populace about their values. The new
scientifically designed woman took distinctive shape in his works. *A Modern
Utopia* (1905) gave readers an indication of women's role in the collective state
to which the Fabians looked forward. Wells's utopia is ruled by technocrats, an

elite by virtue of their greater intelligence, whom he calls Samurai. Both males and females are potential Samurai. Procreating in the interests of race improvement is the special responsibility of the Samurai and a female Samurai who does not bear children is liable to expulsion from the order. Evolutionary progress through eugenics would be promoted by preventing weak or unhealthy children from being born. Wells believed that this could be accomplished by assuring the fitness of parents. He maintained:

The state is justified in saying, before you may add children to the community for the community to educate and in part support, you must be above a certain minimum of personal efficiency, and this you must show by holding a position of solvency and independence in the world. You must be above a certain age [21 for women; 27 for men] and a certain minimum of physical development, and free of any transmissible diseases. You must not be criminal unless you have expiated your offense.[34]

Wells would reward women handsomely for their services to society. He believed that a woman who performed her job as mother ably was more vital than any legislator or soldier, and he would provide ample incentives. Every married woman would get a stipend from her husband. She would be given an additional gratuity by the state upon the birth of a child, and would continue to be paid, just as a civil servant might, sums sufficient to keep her child comfortable, but only so long as the child maintained the minimum standards of physical and mental development set by the state. The most competent of the career mothers would get increments if their children's physical and/or mental development were above the average. Wells would forbid women with small children any other employment unless they could get qualified substitutes to care for their offspring, thus completing their restoration to an exclusively domestic role.

Wells's emphasis on the mothering and the nurturing role of women was consistent with a Social Darwinist ideology that stressed sexual specialization and revived hoary shibboleths pertaining to the "weaker sex." Wells believed not only that the sexes have always been specialized accordingly to function, but that evolution was tending toward further specialization. He argued that "the white woman in the materially prosperous nations is more of a sexual specialist than her sisters of the poor and austere peoples; of the prosperous classes more so than the peasant woman." Wells thus equated the fragility and weakness of the Victorian middle-class woman with evolutionary progress, describing the Western woman who had achieved the greatest "sexual specialization as handicapped by her incapacity for great stresses of exertion, her frequent liability to slight illnesses, her weaker initiative, her inferior invention and resourcefulness, her relative incapacity for organization and combination."

The new woman as soldier in the service of the state did not win the converts among Englishwomen that the Edward Bellamy model won in the United States. Havelock Ellis thus made further compromises and blurred the socialist features of the future society. In *The Task of Social Hygiene* (1912), Ellis restored the family to a preeminent place in society, with marriage as a woman's ultimate—and only— goal. Humphrey Noyes's elaborate interconnections between free love, birth control, and voluntary motherhood in a social, propertyless environment were completely robbed of meaning. Karl Pearson and Havelock Ellis after briefy experimenting with women's rights had come full circle in restoring women to their traditional roles. Within the confines of their roles women would enjoy their erotic rights, play their social role of improving the species by having a limited number of children, and devote themselves to rearing their children according to the scientific standards that child experts prescribed.

The new woman, who would have fewer children and thus more time to devote to them, was obviously middle-class. She did not have to engage in productive labor and had no stake in the public interest. Her security, status, and influence rested solely on her family role. In her domestic orientation and her dependence on men for economic support, for sexual rights, for her values, and even for advice on child rearing, she was a far cry from the women who, at the time *Social Hygiene* was published, were fighting in the streets of London for their civil and political rights.

The domestic feminism espoused by Marxists and erstwhile Fabians, with free love and erotic rights as incentives for women to perform their traditional functions, was a caricature of the socialist tradition established by the feminist fathers and of the communitarian principles of Humphrey Noyes. What significantly divided the domestic feminists from the philosophical feminists was their rejection of the democratic faith of their fathers. They assumed that the political process was inefficient, corrupt, and too moribund to deal with the pressing problems of class, sex, and race antagonisms. Edward Bellamy was perhaps the most unabashed in proclaiming that economic equality would "supplant" political equality. But the socialism advanced by the domestic feminists was not based on the cooperation of all groups envisaged by Holyoake, Thompson, and Mill, who distrusted the growing power of the state so long as it was dominated by males; nor on the socioreligious impulses of Noyes; but on an all-powerful, centralized bureaucracy, an elite of technocrats and scientists who would replace the old patriarchal partnership of church and state.

Karl Pearson stated that if women's intellects were connected to their reproductive functions, and if their reproductive functions somehow drained them physically and intellectually, they would have to remain second-class citizens, albeit with a special status, since childbearing was an important service to the state. The domestic feminists made women second-class citizens by downgrading the importance of their political rights relative to their erotic rights, which were more in keeping with feminine capacities as they perceived them. By emphasizing women as sexual creatures and as mothers, and by diminishing the value of their intellectual abilities, the domestic feminists restored women to the traditional function in patriarchal society from which the philosophical feminists were trying to pry them loose so that they could play a social and political role.

Humphrey Noyes made free love the centerpiece of Oneida, but crucial to its success was an overriding religious commitment and the complete absence of private property, whether in the masculine form of marriage, or in the feminine form of motherhood. Noyes, much like the Owenites, thought of sex as a social instinct, the goal of pleasure and well-being requiring cooperation from both partners. For the benefit of the female, who was considered to have a higher sexual threshold than the male, special demonstrations of unselfishness were required on the part of the male. So that the female could gain something comparable to the male experience, sex had to be separated from birth, and both Robert Dale Owen and Humphrey Noyes put the onus for this on the male. Coitus interruptus and coitus reservatus both required feats of self-discipline by the male. In the secular view of Robert Dale Owen, the sacrifice of a degree of pleasure on the part of the male was a valid expression of love. The Oneidan male had the compensatory satisfaction of participating in a religious experience as well.

In the Noyes communitarian concept, even the motherhood instinct was social-ized into an altruistic concern for the entire community. The application of the maternal instinct to society was what the feminist fathers hoped to see when they made motherhood a matter of choice for women. John Stuart Mill stipulated:

Let women who prefer that occupation [motherhood] adopt it; but that there should be no option, no other carrière possible for the great majority of women. . . is a flagrant social injustice. The ideas and institutions by which the accident of sex is made the groundwork of an inequality of rights and forced dissimilarity of social functions must long be recog-nized as the greatest hindrance to moral, social, and even intellectual improvement.[35]

Erotic rights as fostered by Ellis had none of the social and/or religious passions with which the sex act was invested by the earlier breed of sex radical. As Ellis developed the concept of erotic rights, sex was above all an individual experi-ence whose mystic overtones were based on its sheer intensity—an ideal every-one could invest with his or her own expectations. It must be noted that Humphrey Noyes did not think everyone was capable of the transcendent ecstasy of sex as sacrament. It was necessarily limited to the small groups of seekers who put themselves under his charismatic leadership. To all the philosophical feminists, the sex act robbed of its social significance was tantamount to masturbation; or it was no more than the expression of an animal appetite, and one of the primary means by which men exploited women.

Erotic rights was based on the premise that the sexual instinct was equally strong and urgent in males and females. In making this claim, Ellis refuted the opinions of a long list of medical experts, using nothing more definitive than the musings of James Hinton. The sexologists who proposed to answer the questions about women's sexuality claimed the authority of science, but failed to apply the experimental methods by which scientists are expected to validate their claims. Indeed, George Drysdale, Pearson, and Ellis had a political agenda even though they disdained political methods. Scientists seeking recognition and power showed themselves not only prone to expresion of personal bias, but very susceptible to shifts inmasculinist public opinion in their attempt to shape the new woman.

Ellis used various female acquaintances to make the most far-reaching generalizations about all women. That this ultimately served the cause of politics rather than science can be illustrated with the single example of the creation of a lesbian typology. Ellis described his wife, Edith Lees Ellis, as the prototypical lesbian because she maintained deep attachments to other women, rather than investing her entire emotional life in a man.[36] Edith Ellis's involvement with other women was quite conventional by nineteenth-century standards.[37] Raised for the most part in sex-segregated environments, many nineteenth-century women hardly knew a man until they married, and even after marriage their deepest emotional commitments were often reserved for their mothers, sisters, and female friends. Edith Ellis was typical of this pattern. She despised her father, but idolized her mother, who died when she was a small child.[38]

Far from identifying any preexisting species, universally recognizable, Havelock Ellis created a category of inversion and caused enormous anxiety and conflict in women who had heretofore been totally unselfconscious about these feelings and had been living in a milieu in which they were completely acceptable. The pernicious effects of such classifying and labelling, and their potential for social control, were amply demonstrated when all women who bonded together, as in the suffrage struggle, and who found gratification in their common struggle, were suspected of lesbianism, and could thus be dismissed as abnormal.[39] Ironically, it was the capacity of women to form strong networks that had evoked the admiration of the philosophical feminists and caused them to ascribe to them social virtues such as dedication and loyalty—traits which they wanted to see extended to society as a whole.

If women were to be second-class citizens with no political rights, they could take comfort in the fact that they were in the hands of benign authorities, scientific experts who guaranteed progress and happiness in their modern utopias, and who would reward women who performed their designated roles. The scientists who advocated motherhood as women's unique service confidently expected to inherit the societies which the politicians had failed adequately to serve. In lieu of gaining power themselves, they tended to identify with any leader who supported their ideas, and found it difficult to believe that a leadership schooled in the principles they purveyed could be malevolent. When Adolf Hitler passed his eugenics legislation in 1934 to promote the "biological health" of the German people, Havelock Ellis described it as a "carefully framed law," inspired by a reputable work of science, under which people voluntarily apply for sterilization.[40]

The national socialism of Karl Pearson was realized in the National Socialism of Adolf Hitler. The Nazi regime, with its eugenics programs, its racism, and its protection of mothers so long as they fit the approved racial stereotypes, was no doubt a morbid outgrowth of Pearson's thought, but was nevertheless the ultimate fulfillment of domestic feminism. The new woman, who had traded her political rights for her erotic rights and a public role for her biological destiny, could be a sex playmate, a breeder, or a worker, depending on the priorities of the patriarchal authorities into whose hands she had been persuaded to consign herself. A very different vision of the new woman was offered by the philosophical feminists, who continued the traditions of the Enlightenment fathers, and who saw women as primarily reasonable creatures whose unique cultural values comprised an untapped resource which society could ill afford to ignore.

NOTES

1. Robert Dale Owen refers to the Shakers as "ascetics who condoned sex only for the purpose of reproduction" in *Moral Physiology* (New York: Medsell, 1835).

2. Robert A. Parker, *Yankee Saint* (New York: G. P. Putnam & Sons, 1975),p. 102.

3. John Humphrey Noyes, *History of American Socialisms* (Philadelphia: J. B. Lippincott & Co., 1870).

4. Parker, *Yankee Saint*, pp. 109-11.

5. Ibid., p. 180.

6. Louis J. Kern, "Ideology and Reality: Sexuality and Women's Status in the Oneida Community," *Radical History Review*, Spring/Summer 1979, p. 188.

7. Parker, *Yankee Saint*, p. 190.

8. Kern, "Ideology and Reality," pp. 190, 198.

9. *Oneida Circular*, January 1, 1874.

10. All quotes from George N. Miller, *Strike of a Sex and Zugassent's Discovery, Or, After the Sex Struck* (1891; Chicago: Stockholm Publishing Co., 1905), pp. 3, 130.

11. Karl Marx, *Capital* (1867; Chicago: C. H. Kerr and Co. Cooperative, 1908), p. 536.

12. *Women and Communism: Selections from the Writings of Marx, Engels, Lenin, and Stalin* (Westport, Conn.: Greenwood Press, 1950), p. 29.

13. Rosanna Ledbetter, *A History of the Malthusian League, 1877-1927*, (Columbus: Ohio State University, 1976), p. 15.

14. Angus MacLaren, *Birth Control in Nineteenth Century England* (New York: Holmes and Meier, 1978), p. 158.

15. When Helene Demuth, a servant in the Marx household, had a child, the father was reputed to be Karl Marx.

16. McLaren, *Birth Control*, p. 165.

17. Chushichi Tsuzuki, *The Life of Eleanor Marx, 1855-1898: A Socialist Tragedy* (Oxford: Clarendon Press, 1967), p. 125.

18. Ibid., p. 327.

19. All quotes from William Morris, *News from Nowhere* (London: Longmans, Green and Co., 1907), pp. 66, 68.

20. W.H.C. Armytage, *Heavens Below: Utopian Experiments in England* (London: Routledge and Kegan Paul, 1961), p. 331.

21. Norman and Jeanne Mackenzie, *The Fabians* (New York: Simon & Schuster, 1977), p. 135 ff.

22. Karl Pearson, "Socialism and Sex," in *The Ethic of Freethought* (London: Adam & Charles Black, 1901), p. 430.

23. Karl Pearson, "The Woman's Question," in *Ethic of Freethought*, p. 359.

24. Ibid., p. 361.

25. Ibid., p. 363.

26. Ibid., p. 427.

27. Phyllis Grosskurth, *Havelock Ellis* (New York, A. Knopf, 1980), p. 411.

28. Edward Bellamy, *Looking Backward, 2000-1887* (Cambridge: Mass.: Harvard University Press, 1967), p. 266.

29. Edith Ellis, *James Hinton* (London: Stanley Paul & Co., 1918), p. 23.

30. Grosskurth, *Havelock Ellis*, p. 141.

31. Havelock Ellis, *The Love Rights of Women* (New York: The Birth Control Review, 1918), pp. 6, 12.

32 .Grosskurth, *Havelock Ellis*, p. 231.

33. Havelock Ellis, *The Task of Social Hygiene* (Darby, Pa.: Arden Library, 1912) p. 81.

34. H. G. Wells, *A Modern Utopia* (London: Lincoln, 1967), pp. 183-84, 187.

35. John Stuart Mill, *Principles of Political Economy* (London: Routledge and Kegan Paul, 1965), vol. 2, p. 765.

36. Grosskurth, *Havelock Ellis*, p. 127.

37. See Carol Smith-Rosenberg, "The Female World of Love and Ritual," in Esther Katz and Anita Rapone, eds., *Women's Experience in America* (New Brunswick, N.J.: Transaction Books, 1980).

38. Phyllis Grosskurth, *Havelock Ellis*, pp. 136-37.

39. See George Dangerfield, *The Strange Death of Liberal England* (1935; New York: Capricorn, 1961).

40. Grosskurth, *Havelock Ellis*, p. 340.

THE SHAPING OF THE NEW WOMAN: WHAT PRICE FREEDOM?

5

The women's question received a great deal of attention not only from politicians, social reformers, and scientists. It was taken up as well by novelists and dramatists, who were in an excellent position to exert influence on women since women constituted the largest segment of their audience.[1] Thus, these artists freely explored the issues that were of concern to their readership, including education, marriage, work, and eventually, political rights. In the way the writers depicted their characters they presented role models for their readers and different ways of accommodating to changing times. Up until the 1880s, these female role models were well within the conventional norms of the Victorian stereotype. But in that decade, when the women's question reached crisis proportions, male novelists and dramatists began to parade various versions of a new type of woman before the public. They did so as critics of the ideal of true womanhood, and as reformers searching for the conditions which would make for better relationships between the sexes. Some of them used their writing very consciously to teach and exhort.

The female reading public widened precipitously during the nineteenth century, partly as a result of the interest in female education that novelists displayed. It was in the spirit of reform that a number of novelists of the 1840s and 1850s took up the cause of female education. Mrs. Henry Wood, Charlotte Yonge, and Mrs. Henry Gaskell brought the issue to the fore, characteristically through a stock heroine, the governess. One of the few professions open to single women who had to work for a living was that of governess. There was a general consensus that if governesses were better trained for their jobs, they would have a higher status than that of servant, which they were generally considered to be.

Charles Kingsley did much both to promote the education of governesses and to define the parameters within which the woman who had new opportunities opened up to her might move. Kingsley, as a Christian Socialist, believed that God demanded justice for all his children, and in this world rather than in the next. He propagated his views through a variety of roles. Kingsley was a clergyman in the Church of England who became chaplain to Queen Victoria and tutor

Plate 11. George Bernard Shaw. Frontispiece portrait by Frederick H. Evans from *Plays Unpleasant*, 1898.

to the Prince of Wales. He was an amateur scientist who was elected a fellow of the Geological Society; a history professor at Cambridge for nine years; a poet; and a novelist. It was his brand of "muscular Christianity," which insisted on seeing Jesus as a social reformer, that inspired Cardinal Newman to write the *Apologia pro Vita Sua*, a reaffirmation of traditional Christian forms, to silence him. But Kingsley was not to be deterred from his missionary activities. On behalf of higher education for women, Kingsley gave a series of lectures to ladies who were in a position to help their poorer sisters, to advise them of the need for better standards for governesses.

In line with his credo, "Elevate governesses and you elevate society," Kingsley, along with F. D. Maurice, founded Queens College for women in 1848. There was little interest, however, in providing females with the same education as males, and no suggestion at all that equality was desirable in any area. The ideal of womanhood, despite the concession of better education, was distinctly Dickensian; that is to say, women were to be gentle, self-sacrificing, docile creatures whose prime function it was to minister to men. In fact, the better education that was sought for women was intended not only to make them better governesses so long as they had to remain single; since governesses were mother surrogates, improved education was intended to make them better mothers as well. Kingsley himself reminded women that learning was not their true vocation in his novel, *Yeast* (1848). The heroine, Argemone, fancies herself an intellectual with interests that run to Greek drama and chemistry. Kingsley made clear his opinion that a woman simply cannot match a man in brainpower, and that by trying to do so she desexes herself and violates the mind-heart dichotomy so important in establishing sex roles in the Victorian age. Kingsley wrote of Argemone:

Her mind was beside his as the vase of cut flowers by the side of the rugged tree, whose roots are feeding deep into the mother earth. But on all points which touched the heart he looked up to her as infallible and inspired. . . and then half-consciously to himself, he taught her where her true kingdom lay—that the heart and not the brain, enshrines the priceless pearl of womanhood.[2]

Kingsley believed that women's greater sensibilities, their capacity for heartfelt feeling, could work miracles in transforming civilization. In *Alton Locke* (1850), he appealed to middle-class women to come to the aid of the poor and despised prostitutes:

Woman! Woman! Only true missionary of civilization and brotherhood and gentle forgiving charity, it is in thy power and perhaps in thine only, to bind up the broken-hearted, to preach deliverance to the captives. One real lady who should dare to stoop, what might she not do with us—with our sisters?[3]

Kingsley's conviction that women who entered the public sphere would raise moral standards and help to eliminate the manifest injustices to the poor of this world led him to support the suffrage for women after John Stuart Mill made a special plea to him to do so.[4] It was a significant departure from Kingsley's original position, but a logical outgrowth of his conviction that women were morally superior to men.

George Meredith (1828-1909) started his writing career in 1855. He and Kingsley were thus contemporaries, but Meredith's writing signalled an abrupt departure from the depiction of the ideal woman as mindless and all heart. Meredith had developed a strong affinity for the intellectual woman, who tries to shape her world rather than submitting to society's expectations, and who establishes relationships with men on her own terms. Meredith believed in progress through the elimination of legal wrongs and social injustices, and looked to women to perform the "service of helping to civilize the world," much as Kingsley did. But Meredith did not believe that woman could be of service in the form in which she was idealized, as a compliant and self-sacrificing being. So long as women were pitiable victims, they were part of the problem and could not work toward a solution. He stated to his confreres, "Your imagination of the feminine image you have set up to bend your civilized knee to must temper its fastidiousness." Meredith saw women in the same context as oppressed races and nations— as going through a painful process of self-evaluation and change before they could meet the dominant sex/race/nation on equal terms. The foregoing achievement was Meredith's view of progress fulfilled. He asserted that "until men and women learn to be one they are mere morsels for each other to pull on," and their relations would remain in a state of warfare. He did not dismiss the possibility of a revolt of women, and in "Fair Ladies in Revolt" wrote:

> Though few we hold a promise to the race
> That was not at our rising;
> You are free to win brave mates;
> You love but marionettes:
> He who's for us, for him we are.

Far from considering intellectualism in women a drawback, Meredith would foster it, and on an equal basis with men. He favored coeducation for boys and girls as the best means of their learning about one another and overcoming the gulf that existed between them. He would include sex education in the school curriculum, since he believed the lack of it accounted for much marital misery. Meredith always returned to the theme of education when he considered the problem of male-female relationships and the need for women to become social and political beings. He wrote, "I have this feeling for women, because what with nature and the world, they are the most heavily burdened. . . . I can foresee great and blessed changes for the race when they have achieved independence, for they must come of the exercise of their minds."[5]

As things stood, the segregation of males and females reenforced the overweening male ego—the drive for acquisition and dominance—which Meredith held to be responsible for virtually all the conflicts, political, social, and sexual, that existed in the world. The male ego was at fault for the social and economic waste that was laissez-faire capitalism; for the oppression of colored races and nations by imperialists; and for the wars that resulted when male aggrandizement went too far. The ideal of women that Meredith deplored was one that would cater to the male ego. He said:

Men fail to distinguish women as a personal variety, a separate growth. They look upon women in the mass only. They roll her up in her sex and bestow a kick upon the travelling bundle. . . . Men disincline to believe that women grow. Even young women have but a confused idea of the masculine sentiment of complete possession.[6]

The traditional woman catered to the male ego; the emancipated woman challenged it. Marriage was the battleground in which the antagonisms between the sexes were played out, since it was only when a man and woman married that they were finally thrown into proximity with each other. Under such circumstances marriage could be precarious at best. "Modern Love" (1862) depicts a failed marriage with Meredith, as the narrator, attributing its failure to a dearth of intellect and an overabundance of emotion in the woman.

> Their sense is with their senses all
> mixed in.
> Destroyed by subtleties these women
> are!
> More brain, O Lord, more brain![7]

Diana of the Crossways (1885) is perhaps the most comprehensive expression of Meredith's feminism. He based his novel on the career of Caroline Norton, who had singlehandedly brought the plight of unhappily married women to public attention in the 1830s, polarized society by her unorthodox behavior, and created a prototype for the new woman. Caroline Norton was the granddaughter of the playwright Richard Brinsley Sheridan. When her father, Sheridan's son, died, he left the family poor, but highly respected. While his three daughters were accepted in English upper-class society because of their heritage, without suitable dowries, their futures were left up in the air. In 1827, Caroline Sheridan married George Norton, who had no social standing, but who did have money. It was a quid pro quo typical of upper-class marriage alliances, one partner desiring status and the other financial security. Accumulated tension in the Norton household culminated in a sensational public suit brought by George Norton against Lord Melbourne, then prime minister of England, in which he accused the statesman of seducing his wife. The jury rejected the charge, but Norton became abusive and threatening toward his wife, who then left him. Caroline Norton had continued to live with her husband after the trial because, under English law, if she left him she would have no right of support, nor of access to their three children. Once they were separated, Caroline Norton began to support herself by writing novels. She also became a political activist and brought into the open the injustices visited upon women like herself, caught in untenable marriages with no possibility of divorce; no rights to their children if they left their husbands; and no rights even to the earnings gained through their own efforts, let alone a right to support by their estranged husbands. As a result of her outcry, Parliament in 1839 passed the First Custody of Infants Act, which allowed women, under the extreme circumstances exemplified by Norton, custody of their children. Caroline Norton died in 1879, unhonored and unsung. In picking Caroline Norton as his heroine, Meredith expressed his admiration for a woman who not only had the courage to live her own life, but acted as a beacon for other women, some of whom were moved enough by her grievances and identified sufficiently with her situation to form committees to obtain their legal rights.[8]

Diana Merion, the heroine of *Diana of the Crossways*, parallels the career of Caroline Norton very closely. Early in the book, Diana enters a loveless marriage for reasons not clearly stated but which appear to be the need for financial security and protection from the advances of other men. Her husband becomes jealous of an innocent relationship; there is a trial, which Diana wins. Like Caroline Norton, Diana remains married to Augustus Warwick, her husband, but goes out into the world to live an independent existence, earning money by writing novels. A number of men appear in Diana's life to test the extent of her emancipation. Diana marries Redworth, one of her suitors, at the end of the book; this is the only major departure from the actual events in Caroline Norton's life, but a highly significant one in terms of Meredith's view of women's realistic alternatives.

The novel is thus more than a recapitulation of the life of an English public figure and a testimony to her bravery. It is a statement on behalf of feminism and a portrayal of the dilemmas confronting the woman who wants to be independent. While Meredith clearly admires Diana, he depicts her faults as well as her virtues. She does enter a marriage relationship for very questionable reasons, and her extravagant life-style forces her into financial embarrassments that put her at the mercy of the very men from whom she is seeking independence.

Among Diana's virtues are her unconventionality. She goes out alone for early morning strolls, and travels in a third-class railway carriage, to indicate her independence and possibly her identification with those less fortunate than she. Diana's chief virtue is her intellect, which Meredith emphasizes by providing her with succinct aphorisms, on an inordinate variety of topics. These reveal her to be a political liberal like Meredith himself. On the war between the sexes: "Men may have rounded Seraglio Point; they have not yet doubled Cape Turk." On the Irish question: "You have taught them [the Irish] it is English as well as common human nature to feel an interest in the dog that has bitten you." On women: "We live alone and do not much feel it till we are visited." On herself: "I thank God I'm at war with myself."[9]

Brilliance and an independent spirit in a woman were assumed, by masculine standards, to be liabilities when it came to attracting men; but they are a distinct asset for Diana. The only male who fails to appreciate her charms is her husband, who is depicted as totally male ego bound. He sees wives as property and is, according to Meredith, "sour and insupportable. . . who loses all shame in playing the churlish domestic tyrant."[10] Redworth, who becomes her suitor, is constant in his love from the moment he sees Diana, through her ill-fated marriage and her career problems. He is in fact her unknown benefactor in times of financial crisis. Percy Dacier, a politician with a promising future, also finds Diana irresistible until she commits the unforgivable *faux pas* of revealing a state secret he has confided to her. The latter incident replicates one that actually occurred in the life of Caroline Norton. She became involved with a member of the British cabinet and when he told her of the government's decision to repeal the Corn Laws in 1846, she was suspected of leaking the information to the *Times*, causing a great deal of embarrassment to the government. No one will ever know what caused Caroline Norton to betray George Herbert, or even if she actually did. Meredith, in using the incident and making it central to the book, indicates Diana's willingness to deal with men the way they deal with each other in a world that they dominate.

It was the common wisdom that strong-minded women had difficulty in their relations not only with men but with other women, who found their unconventionality a threat to their own respectability and status. Meredith refutes this cliché, depicting a warm friendship between Diana and Lady Dunstane which is just as meaningful and necessary to both as are their relationships with men. Their loyalty to one another is total. Emma Dunstane is always at Diana's side in a crisis, and it is news of Lady Dunstane's illness, and Diana's desire to be with her, that prevents her from consummating her love for Dacier. Meredith suggests that the friendship and support women show each other is essential if they are to effectively challenge the male ego.

Meredith has much to say about his new woman's anguish and the need for those committed to the "process" of liberation to become martyrs. But after much attitudinizing and sermonizing, Diana surrenders her idealistic ambitions through her marriage to Redworth, and the end of the book has her not only securely wed, but suggestively acquiescing to Lady Dunstane's wish to become a godmother. Diana's rationale is that the avenue of marriage and motherhood might lead to a life of service, leaving one to speculate that Meredith may have come to agree that the traditional role of marriage is a form of service for women. Meredith himself had no confidence in his spurious happy ending. He wrote that, having made her take her stand as a martyr, he thought of killing her off, but realized that his largely female audience would find it an unnecessarily harsh fate for Diana: "I could have killed her merrily, with my compliments to the public; and that was my intention but the marrying of her sets traversing feminine labyrinths, and you know that the why of it can never be accounted for."

Meredith's feminist impulses derived from the same radical liberal tradition that inspired John Stuart Mill. The revolutions of 1848, which included demands for liberation from despotic authority as well as justice for the working class, influenced him profoundly. Giuseppe Mazzini, the Italian nationalist who believed that nationhood—the recognition of the unique qualities of a people—would foster equality among races, ethnic groups, and classes, was a hero of his; and Meredith applied Mazzini's philosophy to the sexes as well. He said:

Since I have begun to reflect I have been oppressed by the injustice done to women, the constraint put upon their natural aptitude and their faculties, generally much to the degradation of the human race. I have not studied them more closely than I have men but with more affection and deeper interest in their development being assured that women of independent mind are needed for any sensible degree of progress. They will so educate their daughters that they will not be instructed at the start to think themselves naturally inferior to men, because less muscular, and need not have recourse to particular arts, feline chiefly, to make their way in the world.[11]

He experienced pride in the fact that he had tried in his time "to enlighten them [women] and humanize their males."

Meredith was a strong supporter of the suffrage. He remarked in 1907, "Women who form associations to discuss political matters, whether for one party or the other are taking the right road to the polling booth." So ardent a supporter of the female suffrage as Lawrence Housman paid tribute to Meredith's feminism in *Articles of Faith in the Freedom of Women* (1911). Housman wrote:

Meredith is my leader and I fight under his colours. And those who are working for women's suffrage might well make that phrase their own. . . . Fifty years ago Meredith found in the matrix of English society the germs of a new life and of higher potentialities for the race. He saw clearly at a moment when industrial prosperity had begun to infect the national blood with luxury, pride of wealth, and love of ease that the true 'Wealth of Nations' lay not in commerce but in humanity.[12]

In his feminism, Meredith remained a liberal and a constitutionalist even after the female suffrage advocates had become radicalized. Before he died in 1909, he made it clear that he could not support the militant women who were resorting to violence to win the vote, but continued to support the political efforts of Millicent Fawcett. Meredith counselled patience, maintaining:

I have always stood up for the intellectual capacities of women. I like to see the combative spirit in them. It is as it should be. Certainly they should be given the use of intellectual weapons. But I am not in agreement with anything that is in bad taste and bad strategy. Those rowdy scenes! No, not that. That is not the way. There is a better.[13]

The happy ending no doubt helped make *Diana of the Crossways* an extremely popular book, especially with women. Diana was regarded as a model for the new women, and many of the more advanced tried to pattern themselves after her. But, Diana only partially fulfilled Meredith's hopes for the new woman, which besides "queenly presence, a sense of joyous life, sincerity, fearlessness, and conversational power," included the ideal of social service that transcended marriage and the family. "Above all," he believed, "women should be ready to give, to help, to serve, unstintingly bestowing all that is best in them, bringing forth from their treasure, things new and old."

The fact was that Diana was emancipated without tears. She did not encounter any crisis where there was no deus ex machina to rescue her. She had it all— brilliance, status, the unstinting love of both men and women—while it was becoming clearer that difficult choices lay ahead for the new woman who desired independence. How far could a woman go in maintaining her independence and her integrity under multitudinous pressures from society?

Thomas Hardy (1840-1920) could not be accused of either compromising or obfuscating this issue. Hardy had an abiding interest in the women's question. When Ibsen's *A Doll's House* was produced in England in 1889, taking feminists by storm, Hardy became part of a group, which included Olive Schreiner, Edward Aveling, and George Bernard Shaw, whose purpose it was to keep Ibsen's works in the public eye. Along with George Meredith, he became a founding member of the Independent Theater Association, formed to produce Ibsen's plays. To the English who were involved in this enterprise, Ibsen's work was proof that the multidimensional social problem that comprised the women's question could be treated with artistic integrity.

Jude the Obscure (1895) was considered a veritable manifesto on the controversial marriage question. It is clear that Hardy was extremely pessimistic about the prospects of success for traditional marriage in a rapidly changing society. He sets his two struggling protagonists, Jude Fawley and Sue Bridehead, against a background of change to emphasize their conflicts. Jude is a stonecutter, a craftsman following a traditional trade in an age of machines. He is employed at the beginning of the novel because of ongoing restorations on medieval structures. But he observes that the renovations are done with a precision that the originals decidedly lacked. Hardy explains,

He did not at that time see that other developments were shaping the world around him in which Gothic architecture and its associations had no place. The deadly animosity of contemporary logic and vision towards so much of what he held in reverence was yet to be revealed to him.[14]

Jude's traditional outlook is contrasted with Sue's modern-mindedness. When Jude first meets Sue, she is an ecclesiastical designer, but has absolutely no ties to traditional beliefs as Jude does. She has been taught the evolutionary doctrine that religion and morality need have nothing to do with one another. She reveals herself as a free thinker:

I have no respect for Christminster whatever except in a qualified degree on its intellectual side. My friend I spoke of took that out of me. He was the most irreligious man I ever knew, and the most moral. To be sure, at times one couldn't help having a sneaking liking for the traditions of the old faith, as preserved by a section of the thinkers there in touching and simple sincerity; but when I was in my saddest rightest mind I always felt, O ghastly glories of saints, dead limbs of gibbeted Gods.

The relationship of these two is fated from the start to be a tragic one because of the different emphasis males and females place on love and sex. They meet after Jude is already married to Arabella, a thoroughly feminine woman, whom he marries to satisfy his sexual needs, and who marries him to have a means of support—a conventional marriage in the view of male feminists. Sue, having no sexual interests, sees her relationship with Jude as an intellectual one. When she finds out that he is married and after he reveals more than a platonic interest in her, she marries Phillotsen, a benefactor who has financed her education as a teacher, even though she has displayed no interest in him. When Sue discovers that Jude and Arabella have been divorced, her love for Jude becomes the dominating factor in her life. She pleads with Phillotsen to set her free so that she can follow her destiny. Thus, Jude and Sue come together in a union based on free love and without any legal sanction. Tragedy comes in the person of Jude's son by his marriage to Arabella, whom he and Sue adopt. The boy, depressed by the sinking fortunes of his parents, and feeling himself to be merely a cross they are bearing, kills himself and the two children Sue has borne Jude. This crisis forces Jude and Sue to confront each other and their inner selves, and tests their convictions and values to the utmost. Sue reverts to religion, while Jude loses his faith in all but Sue. He dies after Sue, in a fit of remorse, leaves him to go back and play the dutiful wife to her ex-husband, Phillotsen.

To this highly dramatic plot Hardy appends the underlying issues of the women's question. Sue is Hardy's version of the emancipated woman. She is intellectual, and this is brought out in a number of ways. She is well read and, like all advanced women, has a thorough grounding in the works of John Stuart Mill. Phillotsen confesses that she is more acute than he: "I can't answer her arguments. She has read ten times as much as I. Her intellect sparkles like diamonds while mine smoulders like brown paper." Jude adores her as "a woman poet, a woman seer whose soul shone like a diamond, whom all the wise of the world would have been proud of."

Hardy clearly believes that intellect and sexuality are incompatible, but in men equally with women. Jude has sexual needs, but he is far from being an intellect. He admires learning, although having little capacity for it, and he is attracted to Sue because of her formidable intelligence. Sue is the fulfillment of the philosophical feminists' ideal. She is devoid of sentiment, a rational being who wants men to be soulmates rather than lovers. The belief that males and females have different sexual thresholds is important to Hardy's pessimism about harmony between the sexes. Sue is thoroughly disillusioned to find that Jude does indeed have animal passions, as revealed by his marriage to Arabella. When Sue marries Phillotsen, she makes it clear that sex is distasteful to her by removing herself from their bedroom. She finally becomes involved in a sexual relationship with Jude, but later regrets it and explains it away as womanly weakness and a desire to please her man rather than innate desire. She states:

Your wickedness was only the natural man's desire to possess the woman. Mine, not the reciprocal wish till envy stimulated me to oust Arabella. I had thought I ought in charity to let you approach me, that it was damnably selfish of me to torture you as I did my other friend. But I shouldn't have given way if you hadn't broken me down by making me fear you would go back to her.

To be true to herself, Sue cannot marry. Hardy explans that if she marries she fears it would be breaking faith with Jude to withhold herself "though while uncontracted she feels at liberty to yield as seldom as she chooses."[15] Hardy, in fact, reiterated the view of the sex conservatives that man's sex drive is his undoing, and could be woman's if she succumbs to the male ego and caters to it. When Jude maintains that two people in love could not live forever without expressing it sexually, Sue argues, "Women could: men can't because they won't. An average woman is in this superior to an average man—that she never instigates, only responds. We ought to have lived in mental communion, and no more." Hardy views this situation as an unresolvable conflict between love and passion and it is one which tears both Sue and Jude apart.

Because of her desire to maintain her independence and integrity, Sue cannot come to terms with marriage. Hardy, aware of the debate on the question, stresses that traditional marriage is one of the casualties of the modern world. Mrs. Edlin, an elderly widow and witness to the trials of Jude and Sue, comments on the phenomenon. "Weddings be funerals 'a b'lieve nowadays. Fifty-five years ago, come fall, since my man and I married. Times have changed since then." Hardy accepts the male feminists' analysis of modern marriage— that men marry basically to satisfy their sexual desires, while women have to marry to gain support. Arabella, Jude's wife, is typical in this respect. She advises Sue to marry Jude after she herself has been divorced:

Life with a man is more business-like after it, and money matters work better. And then you see, if you have rows, and he turns you out of doors, you can get the law to protect you which you can't otherwise. . . . And if he bolts away from you, you have the sticks of furniture, and won't be looked upon as a thief.

Jude explains the male point of view:

There seemed to him something wrong in a social ritual that made necessary a cancelling of well-formed schemes involving years of thought and labour, of foregoing a man's one opportunity of showing himself superior to the lower animals, and of contributing his units of work to the general progress of his generation, because of a momentary surprise by a new and transitory instinct which had nothing in it of the nature of vice.

The potential for wrecked lives is self-evident, and Hardy develops it to the utmost.

That Jude's and Sue's relationship is foredoomed is made clear from the beginning. Hardy uses a device familiar in nineteenth-century literature. Jude and Sue are cousins, and a tragic heredity of disease shadows their future. It isn't her genes, however, that make Sue a feminist, but her acute mind and her own insights into the world around her. It is her feminism which makes her shrink from marriage, and Hardy wonders, like many feminists of the period, whether intellectual women like Sue could tolerate the storms and stresses of marriage. He does not think that intellect and sensuality could co-exist in a woman thus always making the physical side of marriage a burden. Neither could an intellectual woman tolerate being a slave—the code word consistently used to state that marriage was essentially a property relationship as it existed in the nineteenth century. Sue cannot reconcile marriage with her identification with feminism and independence. Several times she and Jude decide to get married, but in the end Sue's conviction that the ceremony is a sham prevails. She lives with Jude and bears him children because she loves him freely. The social ritual of marriage would add nothing to their love and would be hypocritical. She maintains, "It is as culpable to bind yourself to love always as to believe a creed always and as silly as to vow always to like a particular food or drink."

In her independence Sue is very much a loner and ahead of her time. Unlike Diana Merion, she has the support of neither women nor men. When tragedy strikes in the form of the deaths of the three children, she is totally devastated, and in her guilt turns to religion. She blames her nonconformity for the tragedy and exclaims, "Perhaps as we couldn't conscientiously marry at first in the old-fashioned way, we ought to have parted. Perhaps the world is not illuminated enough for such experiments as ours. Who were we to think we could act as pioneers?" She begs Phillotsen to take her back despite the fact that he has granted her a divorce. In her regression to the view that marriage is a permanent commitment, she no longer recognizes the divorce as valid. Despite her dislike of sex she grits her teeth, determined to participate even in this aspect of marriage, a surrender considered by feminists to be synonymous with prostitution. This surrender is the ultimate negation of her identity as a free and dignified being.

For all her ambivalence, Sue emerges as a stronger person than Jude. Jude is unable to deal with his losses or to put them in any perspective. Still loving Sue, he remarries Arabella, who has become a comforting and familiar presence. Coming to hate himself for his sexual weaknesses and Arabella, too, because women like her cater to them, he prefers death. Jude's death from overexposure is an interesting reversal of the norms of Victorian fiction, which stipulate that any woman who sins must pay the ultimate penalty in the end. To be sure, Sue loses her children, and by remarrying Phillotsen it is clear that she has chosen a living death; but that she survives at all is Hardy's tribute to the strength of character, self-discipline, and awesome willpower of the segment of womankind Sue Bridehead represents. That Sue has to make self-destructive compromises indicates that Hardy, like Meredith, is pessimistic about the prospects for the new woman's independence under the conditions then existing. In the last analysis, since men's and women's motives are seen to be fundamentally different, equality might be an impossible dream, desirable though it may be.

In *Jude the Obscure*, Hardy reveals that he is in favor of divorce reform so that the step young people often take so lightheartedly need not become an irrevocable one. Indeed, progress had been made since the unfortunate Caroline Norton was compelled to air her marital problems in order to dispel any illusion that marriage was an ideal state. The First Custody of Infants Act of 1839 had been a direct result of her pleas, and further reforms followed, if slowly. In 1857, the First Divorce Act made it possible to obtain legal separation or divorce through the law courts. Injured wives could get maintenance and custody of children. In 1878, a passage of the Matrimonial Causes Act meant that a wife could get a separation order and maintenance and custody of children if the husband was convicted of assaulting her. The Guardianship of Infants Act of 1886 stipulated that a deserted wife could sue her husband for maintenance. In 1891, the courts decided that a husband had no right to forcibly detain his wife in order to obtain restitution of conjugal rights. Perhaps it was this decision that inspired Phillotsen's reasonable behavior when Sue absented herself from their bedroom. Phillotsen is an unusual husband in granting Sue her request for a divorce so that she can follow Jude, since it makes him look ridiculous in the eyes of the community. It would appear that by the 1890s divorce was easier to come by among the middle and lower-middle classes than in the upper classes, where large property settlements might be involved and political alliances at stake. Arabella obtains a divorce from Jude without any difficulty, and Jude wryly comments: "There is this advantage in being poor obscure people like us. That these things are done for us in a rough and ready fashion." Referring to the fact that Arabella remarried before she got the divorce and could have been held liable for bigamy, Jude observed, "I was afraid her criminal second marriage would have been discovered and she punished; but nobody took any interest in her—nobody inquired; nobody suspected it."

Hardy's despair over the state of male-female relationships made him a supporter of the vote for women. He wrote Millicent Fawcett:

I have for a long time been in favor of women's suffrage. . . . I am in favor of it because I think the tendency of the woman's vote will be to break up the pernicious conventions in respect of women, customs, religion, illegitimacy, the stereotyped household (that it must be the unit of society), the father of a woman's child (that it is anybody's business but the woman's own). . . slaughter houses (that they should be dark dens of cruelty), and other matters which I got into hot water for touching on many years ago.[16]

Wherever *Jude the Obscure* was viewed as extolling the emancipation of women, it was reviled upon its appearance in 1895. The *Pall Mall Gazette*, a Liberal journal, headed its review *Jude the Obscene* and called it "dirt, drivel, and damnation." Hardy was designated a member of The Anti-Marriage League, which according to Mrs. Oliphant, who selected the membership, consisted of those novelists who displayed a "disposition to place what is called the sex question above all others as the theme of fiction."[17] In that guise Hardy was pelted with such epithets as "loathsome" and "disgusting." The *Guardian* claimed that the whole novel "affects one like a shameful nightmare." Professing to see a conspiracy against marriage, one critic attacked the new woman as "a victim of the universal passion for learning and culture...full of ologies and isms, with sex problems and heredity, and other gleanings from the surgery and the lecture room." Clearly, in treating women's rights, the literary feminists had hit on a theme that was not only highly saleable, but was capable of swaying their large audiences. The masculinists perceived the threat and reacted accordingly.

In 1895, the same year that *Jude the Obscure* saw the light of day, Grant Allen published a novel called *The Woman Who Did*. Allen (1848-1899) was, in a varied career, a teacher, a writer of travel books, and a popularizer of scientific ideas, such as those of Charles Darwin, which he simplified for a mass audience. *The Woman Who Did* can, indeed, be described as a popularization of the case for free love as well as a comprehensive summing up of the male feminist argument against marriage. That Allen considered the book both a personal and political statement is expressed in the frontispiece, which reads, "Written at Perugia, 1893, for the first time in my life wholly and solely to satisfy my own taste and my own conscience." The preface is equally pointed. It consists of a short, intriguing exchange: " 'But surely no woman would ever do so,' said my friend." " 'I know a woman who did' said I,'and this is her story.' "[18]

The woman who did is Herminia Barton, and what she did was similar to what Sue Bridehead did but without the foreboding and the guilt and with an awareness of its political significance. She refused on principle to marry despite the pleading of the man she loved, and insisted on living with him and bearing their child in a free union. In a total role reversal, perhaps indicative of the unconscious desires of the male feminists, who wanted women to be more like men so that men could be more like women, Herminia carries Allen's political message throughout the book, while Alan Merrick, her lover, is the instrument who tests her resolution and who is easily disposed of midway through the book, after he impregnates Herminia.

In the course of the novel, Grant Allen has much to say about the condition of women in England through the experiences and the voice of Herminia Barton, who expatiates on a variety of subjects. Allen evidently harbored doubts that the much touted advances in female education were a harbinger of emancipation.[19] Herminia, who is described as having the face of a free woman, went to Girton College, but left because she felt too constrained. She complains, "The whole object of the training was to see just how far you could manage to push a women's education without the faintest danger of emancipation." Liberated women learned their credo from John Stuart Mill. So it was with Sue Bridehead, and Herminia Barton is another faithful disciple. She has totally absorbed her hero's philosophy, and becomes expansive about it: "If you begin by educating women you must end by emancipating them," she maintains. She makes clear that she is completely at one with Mill in his goal that men and women should develop equally every fiber of their being and their natures. As a devotee of Mill, Herminia is, needless to say, in favor of women's suffrage, and an active member of the Women's Franchise League.

Allen was a Darwinist in the conflict between religion and reason that Darwin provoked, and it is significant that Herminia rebels against the traditional woman's role despite the fact that she is the daughter of a Church of England clergyman. Having been thoroughly exposed to religious indoctrination, she has rejected it, but has made a religion of her treason much as the feminist fathers whose ideals she fulfilled. Allen believed that faith in religion and a rational belief in ethical conduct derived from the same impulses. Thus, according to the heroine, "The same curiosity that brings one person to faith, brings another to reason." Herminia's intoxication with reason is the basis for her optimism about a future where people who come to think rationally may act rationally as well.

Herminia captivates Alan Merrick, a young lawyer who is described as having liberal views on the women's question. While his fervor for Herminia is unbounded, the author raises reader's doubts about the heroic capacities of Merrick who, as a male, is born to command, and therefore no matter how tolerant he professes to be, harbors the rigid and egoistic traits that support an iniquitous social, political, and economic structure. As far as Grant Allen was concerned, spontaneity was the key to character, and men lacked it. His assessment of his hero: "At 30, he lacked spontaneity which is the essence of love." In Allen's world it is spontaneity which is the antidote to the egoism that George Meredith dwelled on. Allen believed that only a woman could provide it, and if a man has not by the age of 30 responded to a woman, his harsher egotistical traits begin to calcify, an irreversible process which accelerates with age and makes any possibility of change unlikely. Herminia, with her artlesssness, her candor, her openness, is thus on a higher plane of development than Merrick, and he needs her to waken in him the best of which he is capable.

The test of Herminia's commitment comes in a verbal duel between herself and Merrick. Having declared their love for each other, Merrick does what according to all the conventions is the honorable thing, and asks Herminia to marry him. She recoils in horror, just as a respectable Victorian woman might react upon being propositioned, and launches into a discourse on her philosophy of marriage. "Would you have me like the blind girls who go running to the altar as sheep go to the slaughter?...I know what marriage is—from what vile slavery it has sprung; on what unseen horror for my sister women it is buttressed." Herminia vows to become a martyr, if need be, on behalf of her oppressed sisters: "It would be treason to my sex to marry....If I were to turn traitor to my sex for the sake of the man I loved as so many women have before me I should hate and despise myself." Mary Wollstonecraft eventually married William Godwin. Mary Godwin eventually married Shelley; George Eliot married Lewes, her lover; but Herminia vows never to compromise her principles. She would never bind herself for longer than Merrick's love lasted "or if I discover some other more fit to be loved by me."

Meanwhile, Merrick speaks in the name of honor and respectability, a respectability usually mouthed by women, but which the author considers to be really in the male interest, in that once a woman is married her husband controls her; as her husband, he need no longer concern himself with treating her as an individual and can turn his full attention to the economic activities by which the world takes the measure of his worth.

Merrick, a lawyer, makes the brief for marriage. He touches on every point where Herminia, as a woman, might be vulnerable. Why should she, he asks her, sacrifice herself even in a good cause? She answers:

I feel I must face it. Unless one woman begins there will be no beginning. Think how easy it would be for me...to do as other women do...to accept the honorable marriage you offer me, as other women would call it, to be false to my sex, a traitor to my convictions, to sell my kind for a mess of potage, a name and a home, or even for thirty pieces of silver to be some rich man's wife as other women have sold it.

Merrick asks her to be practical, to be a little more moderate in her own self-interest—"to prevent the world from saying the cruel things they are sure to say, and to consider marriage an act of justice to herself and her children." Merrick concludes his argument, "What more could it mean nowadays than that we two agree to live together on the ordinary terms of civilized society?" Herminia sweeps it all away in the accents of the true believer: "The English virtue of moderation," she insists, "has made England the shabbiest, saddest, worst organized of nations."

Once Merrick accepts Herminia's terms, she also insists that they live apart, seeing one another only on mutually agreed upon occasions, and maintaining their separate lives. She considers the relationship a fulfillment of human desires, the desire to love and be loved, but rejects the family ties that "encumber love" and where the women and children are "chattels of the lord and master." In line with her emancipated credo, she stipulates that any children that result from their union will be shared by them equally. Herminia is determined to continue to work at her part time job as a teacher, as well as at the "hack" writing she describes herself as doing. Her work is exactly the same as that of her creator, Grant Allen, and another indication of his identification with her.

Merrick and Herminia embark on their relationship, with few adverse consequences until Herminia becomes pregnant. At this point she permits her lover to convince her to go to Italy until after her confinement in order to avoid the inevitable ostracism. They leave England with the dire warnings of Merrick's father ringing in their ears. The elder Merrick is the voice of the relentless masculine world which punishes unorthodox behavior. To the elder Merrick, Herminia is not a free woman going where love takes her, but a concubine, a mistress, deserving the contempt of society. As a typical masculinist, he would have been proud of his son if he had gone to prostitutes to fulfill his sexual needs, and married a rich heiress whom he did not love to advance his career.

Once pregnant, Mary Wollstonecraft, Herminia's model, married William Godwin; but this is another instance where Herminia will not compromise her principles even under the most extreme circumstances. Alan Merrick contracts a virulent strain of typhoid fever in the dusty hills of Perugia, known so well to the author. As he is dying, his father pleads with him to marry Herminia in order to give their child a name and some status in society. Herminia indignantly refuses and will not even take the money that Merrick senior offers in order to cushion the economic blow of Merrick's death.

Herminia and her daughter, Dolores, return to London, where her experiences further echo those of the author. She decided to write a novel about her life. Grant Allen maintained that women write better novels than men because they have natural intuition, keener interest in social life, and deeper insights than men. Herminia's novel is called *A Woman's World*. However, it is ignored by the reviewers save one, who hails it as a work of genius. Once again the fact that Herminia is a woman is her chief liability in gaining the rewards men consider their due. The reader is left to suppose if she had used a man's name, as did George Eliot and George Sand, her future might have been different.

For Herminia, the road to martyrdom is foreordained, yet it is filled with opportunities to retrace her steps. She resists them all. She joins the Fabians, among whom she meets another man who offers her marriage. Herminia is approaching middle age, when the desire for a more settled life is strong. But she remains consistent. How would she have been able to explain this action to her daughter, to, in effect, say to her, "I wouldn't marry your father in my youth . . . but have consented in middle life to sell my sisters' cause for a man I love and for the consideration of society to rehabilitate myself too late with a world I despise by becoming one man's slave."

Herminia has learned to put her feminism in a socialist context; she recapitulates all the elements of the patriarchal power the traitors to masculinity had long struggled against. There is patriotism—"My country right or wrong—pride of race and lust of conquest; my power to oppress all weaker nationalities; all inferior races; to annex unoccupied territory." Patriotism, Herminia muses, is little more than "collective selfishness." Often it is not even collective, but "my business interests against the business interests of other people and let the taxes of my fellow citizens pay to support them."

Among the defined attributes of masculinity is the monopolist's instinct for property. Herminia thinks of it as: "Me against my fellow citizens. It is the last word of the intercivic war in its most hideous avatar. Look how it scars the fair face of our common country with its anti-social billboards. 'Trespassers will be prosecuted!' It says in effect, 'this is my land, as I believe, God made it, but I have acquired it and tabooed it for myself, for my own enjoyment. The grass on the wold grows green but only for me.' "

To Grant Allen, the monopolist's ethos was worse than the patriot's; the monopolist's ethos was no longer "us against the world," but "me against my fellow citizens." Allen makes a distinction between the monopolist, who controls resources, and the capitalist, who controls the means of production, and who is the next to be assailed in his list of masculine prototypes. The capitalist says:

I will add field to field. I will join railway to railway. I will joggle into my hands all the instruments for the production of wealth that my cunning can lay hold of and I will use them for my own purposes against producer and consumer alike with impartial egoism. The poor shall lack that I may roll down fair streets in needless luxury. Let them starve and feed me.

The monopolists and capitalists also lust after human property. Slavery is abolished, but Herminia reasserts that marriage is its equivalent: "Based upon the primitive habit of felling the woman with a blow. . .and dragging her off by the hair of her head. . .this ugly and barbaric form of serfdom has come in our own time by some strange caprice to be regarded as of positively divine origin." Having felled her, the monopolist treats his wife as he would any other property:

If she ventures to have a heart or will of her own, woe betide her. Let any other man touch her; let her so much as cast eyes on any other man to admire or desire him—and knife, dagger, or law court, they shall both of them answer for it. The Turk drowns the rebellious woman. The Christian Englishman with more lingering torture sets spies on her, drags what he thinks her shame before a prying court and divorces her with contumely. Humanity must transcend these atavisms [Herminia vows] and those who are incapable of giving up their despotic authority would be taught the same lesson the French autocrats learned during the Revolution.

The emancipation of women is held to be a necessary step in that humanization process. Herminia concludes her soliloquy, "Women shall henceforth be the equals of men, not by levelling down, but by levelling up; not by fettering the man but by elevating, emancipating, and unshackling the woman."

Herminia's rejection of the Fabian, Harvey Kinaston, is suggestive of Grant Allen's own rejection of official socialist doctrines in favor of a philosophy he called individualism. The conventional meaning of individualism was associated with laissez-faire capitalism, but to Allen, individualism was a philosophy whereby all people would be able to realize their unique talents and faculties through an equitable environment where they all had free and equal access to the common gifts and energies of nature. He admitted sharing with the socialists a strong sense of injustice over the evils of monopolistic capitalism, and, like them, aimed at a more equitable distribution of goods based on the labor theory of value. But Allen thought this could be accomplished by simply sweeping away the "artificial" monopolies, the state church, the hereditary inequalities, the land-grabbing and coal-taxing, ground rents and tithes, and by establishing in their place a platform from which everyone started equally. He evidently feared the wide-ranging state powers that both Fabian and Marxist socialists envisioned as inherent in a socialist society, seeing them as an expression of masculinity that he opposed, with the centers of power simply being located in different hands. It is indicative of Allen's thinking that he portrays his Fabian protagonist, Harvey Kinaston, as completely orthodox and middle-class on the subject of love and marriage. Kinaston rejects Herminia's standing offer of a free love union, choos-

ing instead middle-class respectability through a conventional marriage to another woman.

His message conveyed in the most clear-cut terms, Grant Allen proceeds to
supply the melodrama mandatory to make a popular novel. Herminia's martyrdom is achieved through her daughter's betrayal and rejection of her mother's
ideals. Grant unaccountably reverses himself on the inevitability of greater rationality through favorable nurturing. Dolores, Herminia's daughter, is completely
immune to her mother's influence. In fact, she is a cultural throwback to an
earlier type of woman, who worshipped success and respectability and who
considered her wildest dreams fulfilled by marrying a handsome, wealthy man.
Dolores actively dislikes and resents her mother for making her life difficult
through her cumbersome principles. Dolores makes her own position crystal
clear when she has an opportunity to marry a rich man who can give her all the
things her mother's ideals have denied her. She confronts her mother about her
origins, finds out that her father's family is well-positioned, and seeks out her
grandfather to ask his protection, disavowing her mother and everything she
stands for. Dolores is not without pride. She will not marry her fiancé so long as
her mother is alive to remind her of the disgrace that society has visited upon
them, an intention she duly communicates to that desolate woman. Herminia
thus achieves the martyrdom she has sought for so long by taking her own life to
insure her daughter's happiness.

Allen was sure his views were so advanced, that no publisher would risk
censure by airing them, and that his message would never reach the world. He
thus made arrangements to bequeath the manuscript of *The Woman Who Did* to
the Bodleian Library, with instructions to the custodians to decide when to
release it. His fears, at least about publication, were groundless. The novel was a
best-seller and went through nineteen editions in one year, leaving Allen well off
until his death. Allen came in for the abuse he expected. That he espoused
Darwinian as well as socialist and feminist ideas made him a tempting target, and
he was castigated for supporting a doctrine of womanhood "more revolting than
the Mohammedans.' " The citizens of his erstwhile place of residence, Hartford,
Connecticut, saw fit to ban the book from their library.[20]

In *The Woman Who Did*, free love as a means for a woman to maintain her
integrity and independence received its most elaborate idealization. Critics who
lambasted the novel as subversive and immoral might have pondered that in the
final analysis, Allen, the romantic novelist, had subverted the message of Allen,
the socialist educator. The fate of Herminia Barton, who staunchly resisted the
pressure of society only to succumb to a mother's sentimental and irrational love
for an ingrate daughter, was hardly one that would instill confidence in women
struggling to achieve new dimensions in their lives. The suicide of Eleanor Marx
a few years after the publication of *The Woman Who Did* vividly exemplified
that the woman who sacrificed practicality for her ideals in a world that was
preeminently materialistic was isolating herself and incurring martyrdom rather
than gaining meaningful independence.

George Bernard Shaw (1856-1950) saw the self-sacrifice and martyrdom that free love entailed as another expression of the traditional feminine role, and advised women to dispense with their chains. Next to John Stuart Mill the most consistent, thoroughgoing, and unflappable of the male feminists, Shaw so integrated his feminism with his socialism, and his politics with his art, that they were inseparable. Shaw used his artistic talent to instruct and believed his tremendous success was proof enough that the aesthete's goal of art for art's sake was a blind alley. He noted in the preface to *Pygmalion*:

I wish to boast that Pygmalion has been an extremely successful play all over Europe and North America as well as at home. It is so intensely and deliberately didactic, and its subject is esteemed so dry, that I delight in throwing it at the heads of the wiseacres who repeat the parrot cry that art should never be didactic. It goes to prove my contention that art should never be anything else.[21]

Shaw was a Fabian Socialist who saw his plays as critical analyses of the institutions of capitalism and as a means of pointing out the injustices, the irrationalities, and the hypocritical moral values that support capitalism. His purpose was to indoctrinate his audiences with the fundamental Fabian dogma of the inevitability of socialism. While other Fabians, including their leaders, Sidney and Beatrice Webb, were dubious about feminism, if not actually hostile to the emancipation of women, Shaw, much like the feminist fathers, viewed feminism as the soil from which socialism would flower. His views were an amalgam of those of Mill, Ibsen, and August Bebel, all of whom he encountered when he immersed himself in the intellectual crosscurrents of London after his arrival there from his native Ireland in 1876. As a member of the Zetetical Society, whose main purpose was to read the works of the "radical Mill," Shaw adopted Mill's premise that woman's nature is a product of conditioning, an artificial construction which, in Shaw's own eyes, served capitalism well, and on which capitalist society based its prevailing morality. Submissive, dutiful, sentimental, irrational—these became the characteristics of the "womanly" woman in Shaw's plays. Self-reliant, courageous, disciplined, intellectual—these were the characteristics of the "unwomanly," or new woman, that Shaw paraded before his audiences for their enlightenment and edification.

It was Ibsen who provided Shaw's new woman with her philosophy of life. Shaw saw Ibsen's works, especially those on women, marriage, and the family, as a revolt against the idealism that Victorians indulged in about love and romance and about the economic institutions of the period. Since they demanded women as human sacrifices, Shaw disavowed these ideals in toto, as did his "unwomanly" women. The concepts of duty and self-sacrifice were favorite Shavian targets. According to Shaw, "The sum of the matter is that unless woman repudiates her womanliness, her duty to her husband, to her children, to society, to the law, and to everyone but herself, she cannot emancipate herself." He elaborated:

The pioneer must repudiate duty; trample on ideals; profane what was sacred; sanctify what was infamous, always driving her plough through gardens of pretty weeds, in spite of the laws made against trespassers for the protection of the worms which feed on the roots, always letting in light and air to hasten the putrefaction of decaying matter.[22]

Shaw saw woman's emancipation from her male-ordained shackles as the first step in the destruction of capitalism, and thus his feminism was integral to his socialism.

August Bebel provided fresh reinforcement that women, once made aware of their condition, would be natural socialists. In *Women and Socialism* (1885), Bebel stressed that marriage was an extension of property relations within the capitalist system. He pointed to the similarity of the position of women and that of the proletariat, and maintained that marriage was the direct result of the bourgeois organization of labor and property. Bebel used the position of women as a litmus test whereby one could gauge whether the ideals of justice espoused by a society matched the reality.[23]

Shaw created a number of vivid women who struggle to find themselves in a male-dominated world that, according to Shaw, does not regard women as ends in themselves, "but solely as a means of ministering to [men's] appetites." Through their struggle the women carry the burden of Shaw's message. *Mrs. Warren's Profession* (1894) presented an experimental version of the new woman. Because of its incisive social criticism, it had the distinction of being banned by the English censors, a ban which was not lifted till 1924. The play was an epilogue to the excitement generated in the 1880s over the struggle to repeal the Contagious Diseases Acts and the labor troubles resulting from depressed economic conditions. The matchgirls strike, organized by Annie Besant in 1888, was as wrenching an exposé of the exploitation of female factory workers as the Stead revelations about white slavery. The strike, coming as it did shortly after the Contagious Disease Acts controversy, revealed the extent of prostitution, explained why so many working girls chose prostitution in preference to, or as a supplement to, their work in factories. The matchgirls were paid wages below the subsistence level, and their work with sulphur involved hazards to their skin and lungs that resulted in permanent damage to their health after only a few years of work. Prostitution might be quite economically rewarding and decidedly less hazardous to a woman's health.

Mrs. Warren's profession is prostitution. Kitty Warren is, in fact, a highly successful madam, who presides over a chain of houses of ill repute with the deftness of the born businesswoman. She has turned the private enterprise system in which, according to socialist critiques, prostitution is inevitable, to her own uses. To Shaw, she is neither a heroine nor a villainess. She is a survivor, who has rejected the role of victim and who has come to terms with capitalist morality, where, if one is not to be a victim, one must be an exploiter. Shaw describes Kitty Warren as "rather spoilt and domineering, and decidedly vulgar," but he also emphasizes her vitality, thrift, energy, and initiative. He admires her because she has found the one male vulnerability that a woman can exploit—his lust—and she does so ruthlessly. She has gained wealth and respectability for herself and opportunity for her daughter, Vivie, who provides the conflict in the drama when she learns where the money for her Cambridge University education has come from. There is a confrontation through which Vivie learns the facts of capitalist life from her mother—that it is a deadening and degrading life for working women, so much so that many choose the alternative of prostitution because it affords greater dignity and, certainly, a longer life.

Vivie Warren, intellectual, unemotional, and calculating, has all the earmarks of the new emancipated woman. She implicitly raises the question of what role the emancipated woman would play in society. Vivie has contempt for her mother's values and way of life. Yet she is no more a "womanly woman," cut out to be submissive and self-sacrificing, than is her mother. All the male feminists agreed that the new emancipated women should look beyond herself and play a role in society. The domestic feminists believed that marriage and motherhood, women's traditional domestic function, could in themselves be a form of service, one women were uniquely fitted for. Shaw, who did not think a domestic career any more natural for a woman than a military career for a man, strongly disagreed.

If Shaw was somewhat uncertain about where emancipation might lead in *Mrs. Warren's Profession*, he was no longer in doubt when he wrote *Major Barbara* (1905). Barbara Undershaft, the Major of the title, has been born to privilege and wealth as an heiress to a munitions fortune; but she rejects the feminine role for which she has been earmarked, and through a process of intense self-examination, under the pressure of outside forces which shatter all her illusions and romantic ideals, struggles through to selfhood.

Barbara, disdainful of her father's profiteering, joins the Salvation Army in a well-meaning effort to ease the rampant poverty she sees around her. Shaw considered religion another trap for women, by means of which their self-sacrificing proclivities are taken advantage of, and through which they perpetuate their own victimization by identifying with the poor wretches they think they are helping. Shaw's quarrel with the Salvation Army arose from his conviction that religion was part of the problem and could not be a solution to social and economic ills. Christianity extolled poverty as a virtue; Shaw thought it was a sin. A morality that forgives the sinner only begets more sinners, Shaw concluded. He acknowledged that he loathed the propagandists of the cross

as he loathed all gibbets.... Forgiveness, absolution, atonement, are figments; punishment is only a pretense of cancelling one crime with another; and you can no more have forgiveness without vindictiveness than you can have a cure without a disease.... You will never get a high morality from people who conceive that their misdeeds are revocable and pardonable or in a society where absolution and expiation are officially provided for us all.[24]

Barbara learns from her own father, an enlightened capitalist in the mold of Robert Owen, that the Salvation Army supports the state and the entire apparatus of capitalism that produced the victims she is trying to reform. Barbara seeks to counter her doctrine of God and salvation to her father's ethic of work and money. She is devastated when the Army accepts a five-thousand pound donation from her father, and when she learns that they have also accepted handsome bequests from the very distillers whose products have ruined the outcasts who come to the Salvation Army for help. In a state of suicidal despair, Barbara opens herself to the visions of Undershaft, the Shavian moralist. Undershaft contends that when society offered him a choice between "poverty or a lucrative trade in death and destruction," it offered him, not a choice "between opulent villainy and humble virtue, but between energetic enterprise and cowardly infamy." Undershaft is using his ill-gotten gains to subvert the system by building cooperative, self-governing villages for his workers. Barbara realizes that it is the people in her father's villages, rather than the pitiful remnant the Salvation Army ministers to, who are the hope of a better future, and accepts his offer to work with them. She finds that they are "not weak souls in starving bodies, sobbing with gratitude for a scrap of bread and treacle, but fulfilled, quarrelsome, snobbish, uppish creatures, all standing on their little rights and dignities, and thinking that my father ought to be greatly obliged to them for making so much money for him. . . and so he ought." In rejecting the religious props that serve as a basis for conventional morality, Barbara becomes a person and acquires some of the godliness that is inherent in emancipation. She announces, "My father shall never throw it in my teeth again that my converts were bribed with bread. I have got rid of the bribe of heaven. Let God's work be done for its own sake; the work he had to create us to do because it cannot be done except by living men and women."

Shaw often used people he knew as prototypes for his characters. Barbara Undershaft is modeled on Beatrice Webb, who after a great deal of soul-searching, dedicated her life to social service, putting domesticity very much in the background.[25] Barbara Undershaft, like Beatrice Webb, does marry, but on her own terms; she requires that her fiancé, Adolphus Cusins, give up his career as a Greek scholar and accept a position in her father's firm as supervisor of the villages. When Cusins asks Barbara what would have happened if he had rejected her father's offer of a job in favor of the esoteric pursuits for which he had been trained, she responds, "I should have given you up and married the man who accepted it."

Whether a woman's emancipation could be sustained within marriage was a question that Shaw explored in a number of plays. A guarded answer might be yes, but only if she shed her illusions about love and romance, and made economic and psychological factors the basis for her decision. Shaw permitted himself elaborate comment on the theme in *Pygmalion*. The heroine, Eliza Doolittle, captivated audiences all over the world. *Pygmalion* became one of Shaw's most popular plays, and after his death was turned into a musical, *My Fair Lady*. On one level, it contains the familiar rags to riches theme. Eliza is picked out of the London slums by phoneticist Henry Higgins, who teaches her to speak proper English, dresses her in fashionable clothes, and enables her to enter middle-class society, illustrating Shaw's point that class differences are the result of unequal educational opportunities and can be easily erased. Higgins emancipates Eliza by freeing her from the poverty to which she has been foreordained by her cockney speech, and enables her to choose her future life. Romantic ideals dictate that she devote herself to the care and feeding of Henry Higgins, who, like his Greek prototype, naturally wants to control the creature he has made. That Eliza, having tasted freedom, should, in gratitude to her mentor, spend the rest of her life fetching Henry Higgins's slippers, was suggested in all productions of the play and movie, over Shaw's strenuous objections.

In a lengthy epilogue to *Pygmalion*, Shaw argued that Eliza's marriage to Higgins went against all feminist principles. Eliza has become Higgins's equal, but a marriage between equals is impossible in a context where the man is given all the power. Eliza could never stand to be badgered and browbeaten by the likes of Higgins without giving as good as she got. She might well marry for pragmatic reasons, to maintain her hard-won middle-class status. Without any background except the speech training that Higgins has given her, supporting herself might mean reverting to working as a flower girl once more. It thus made sense that Eliza should marry the sentimental and weak Freddy Einsforth-Hill, a man who idolizes her, and whom she can easily dominate. Shaw accepted the inequalities of marriage in a capitalist society, but would give women a chance to be in the saddle. He saw marriage as a relationship where one party—the stronger—must be dominant. As a feminist, he did not think it necessarily had to be, or should be, the man, but rather that party who was more realistic and less blinded by the myths that sustained capitalism.

A classic confrontation between the traditional "womanly" woman and the new "unwomanly" woman takes place in *The Philanderer* (1893). It pits Julia Craven, the "womanly" woman who sees marriage as her career, against Grace Trenfield, the independent woman who will not compromise her honesty for the dubious rewards of marriage. At issue is Leonard Charteris, the philanderer, who preys on women like Julia Craven, taking advantage of the spurious love they offer in order to ensnare him but contemptuously discards them once the conquest is made. The womanly woman is herself culpable because she plays the game and encourages the man's advances, deluding herself that she is acting out of love, when all she really wants is a husband who will give her status and support in exchange for unlimited access to her body. Charteris, who represents Shaw himself, expresses his thoughts about Julia's kind:

Then whose fault is it that half the women I speak to fall in love with me? Not mine; I hate it; it bores me to distraction. At first it flattered me. . . . but I soon had enough of it; at no time have I taken the initiative and persecuted women with my advances as women have persecuted me.[26]

Grace confronts Julia in an appropriate place, the Ibsen Club, to which they both belong, but from which Julia is expelled for violating all of Ibsen's criteria for new womanhood. Grace says to Julia:

You calculated to an inch how far you could go. When he is present to stand between us and play out the scene with you, I count for nothing. When we are alone, you fall back on your natural way of getting anything you want; crying for it like a baby until it is given to you. . . . How I hate to be a woman when I see, by you, what wretched, childish creatures we are. . . . I understand now why Charteris has no respect for women.

Charteris rejects Julia, who, none the worse for her experience, marries the obtuse Dr. Paramore. Grace Trenfield triumphs because Charteris, tired of the women he has known all his life, falls in love with her. Grace loves him, but has learned that, in capitalist society, for a woman to fall in love is the moral equivalent of surrender and to give up all hope of being her own person. "I will never marry a man I love too much," she says. "It would give him a terrible advantage over me; I should be utterly in his power."

For Shaw, art followed life and life followed art. Her refusal to entertain sentiment as a proper basis for marriage was instrumental in Beatrice Potter's decision to marry Sidney Webb. In 1892, Shaw himself married Charlotte Payne Townsend more in friendship than in love. The Shaws and the Webbs were successful examples of the partnership or companionate marriage—in which sex was subordinated to social concerns. Many emancipated women saw it as an alternative to a free love union. Both Beatrice Webb and Shaw remained devoted to their respective spouses until their deaths.

Shaw believed it was never too late for the womanly woman to change her ways; but since females were conditioned to their role early in life, it was obviously best to intervene in their education as early as possible. In 1878, shortly after his introduction to feminism via J. S. Mill, Shaw wrote *Dear Dorothea, A Practical System of Moral Education for Females*, which was intended for a five-year old girl. The twenty-one-year-old Shaw, who had recently burned his bridges behind him when he left Dublin, was in a way searching for a new self and making clear the commitments he would spend a lifetime fulfilling by writing to the imaginary girl and attempting to influence her behavior. His evolving socialist outlook was imposed on Dorothea: "You will often feel tempted to take things that you want very badly from people who are weaker than you. But you must not do so, because there are others who are stronger than you, and if everyone were to seize what he desired by force, you would be very miserable."[27] He suggested that emancipation is a process of growth: "You would be an uncleanly, ignorant and unlovable child if you were contented. Therefore be glad that you are discontented and try to remain so." His view that emancipation should foster a responsibility for social justice is likewise adumbrated in his advice to Dorothea: "When a strong person oppresses a weak one, it is said to be tyranny. As long as you live resist tyranny; and never be guilty of it yourself. Never hurt those weaker than yourself and try to prevent others from doing it." He reminded her that the scullery maid was "every bit as good as she was unless you can surpass her by learning more, or by being kinder and controlling your temper better." In the end, Shaw promised to keep addressing Dorothea as she grew older to provide her with further guidelines for unwomanly behavior, and he was as good as his word.

Shaw was very much an activist on behalf of feminism. His commitment was particularly intense during the suffragette campaign waged under the auspices of the Pankhursts. In an interview with a suffragette, Maud Churton Braby, in 1906, Shaw made clear that his concept of equality was indivisible. Confronted with the masculinist charge that women don't fight and that therefore they should not vote, Shaw pointed out that he did not fight and that Parliament was full of civilians who did not fight, many of whom begrudged money for fighting as much as Queen Elizabeth I did. He closed the matter of fighting by pointing out that women could not be sent into battle since they were needed to replenish the species after a war.

Shaw was not fazed by the prospect of women, once they gained their political rights, becoming rulers. He looked forward to that hopefully. Asked whether women should sit in Parliament, he laughed:

Good heavens! What do you want the vote for? Not to give more votes for men, I hope. The suffrage is useless except as a means of getting women into Parliament. That is the whole point of the reform. . . . The only decent government is government by a body of men and women. But if only one sex must govern, then I say, let it be women—put the men out! . . . Women at once discern evils and omissions which men never think of, especially in matters of public health, sanitation, and the like.

Shaw counselled women to use violence in pursuit of their legitimate goals several years before it was even contemplated by militants, noting that governments rarely act until an aggrieved group has succeeded "in making everyone miserable."[28]

In 1907, Shaw gave a speech entitled "Why All Women Are Peculiarly Fitted to Be Good Voters." He made the point that women's immense talents were wasted on the agitation they were forced to mount to obtain the suffrage:

By giving them the franchise England will set free an immense and beneficial flood of political and social energy which is now being taken up by this question. Women's help is absolutely essential to solving the problems that beset humanity. . . . Sweep that one difficulty away. Give women, particularly able women, something else to do than going about on platforms clamoring for this right, which should never have been withheld or denied them, and then you will get a united force of both sexes tackling these social problems, without the solution of which we shall be plunged in the ruin that has overtaken other civilizations in history which have towered in the past. You want the help of women in that.[29]

In "The Root of the White Slave Traffic," Shaw elaborated on the theme he had tackled in *Mrs. Warren's Profession*. Shaw reiterated his view that prostitution is integral to the capitalist system and its profit-making ethos. Under capitalism, hundreds of thousands of women and girls got wages insufficient to support them, and were treated with less respect then any prostitute. Prostitution was supported by the establishment—by industrialists who sweated women mercilessly, by landlords, even by ecclesiastical overseers who rented to brothel keepers. Shaw considered the ordinary law-abiding citizen far from guiltless in remaining silent when women were told to "make up their wages somehow," knowing that the only place they could do so was in the streets. They must have known that "the wages of prostitution were stitched into [their] buttonholes and into [their] blouses, pasted into [their] matchboxes and [their] boxes of pins."[30]

Shaw responded to the charges of various prominent masculinists. When Sir Almroth Wright, a well-known physician, attacked the suffragettes in the *Times* and put forth a thesis, increasingly taken up by scientists, that women's minds as well as their bodies were so different from men's as to make them unfit to make political decisions. Shaw wrote "Sir Almroth Wright's Case Against Woman Suffrage." He charged that Wright was, in effect, "calling every woman a fool," with no shred of scientific evidence for the assertion, and maintained that, in insulting women, Wright was also insulting Shaw, who considered himself totally equal to women.[31]

That many women were prominent among the proponents of the masculine cause was a source of frustration and embarrassment to the feminists. The female feminists found it difficult to confront the opponents of their own sex, since such conflicts played into the hands of masculinists, who pointed triumphantly to division in the ranks of women to make the point that the feminists were renegades and outcasts. Shaw had no such inhibitions. For Shaw, that women like Mrs. Humphrey Ward, who had achieved public acclaim as a novelist, could parrot the masculine line that women were incapable of thinking and should devote themselves to what nature had intended them for—a domestic career— had the makings of high comedy. He wrote *Press Cuttings: A Topical Sketch Compiled from the Editorial Correspondence Columns of the Daily Papers* in 1909, but the action takes place three years in the future, in 1912. *Press Cuttings* is one of Shaw's conversion comedies, where the male authorities are brought to see the justice of the suffragettes' cause when female opponents of suffrage overplay their hand, and expose the real motives for their opposition to acquiring political rights. The typical antifeminist woman is exemplied in the character of Lady Cynthia, who hides her ruthlessness with a veneer of romantic sentimentalism. Lady Cynthia is used to ruling by manipulating men, and stands to lose her power by permitting a democratic free-for-all. She says:

I am one of those women who are accustomed to rule the world through men. When a woman is on the throne the country is ruled by men; when a man is on the throne the country is ruled by women, and therefore well. The suffragists would degrade women from being rulers to being voters, mere politicians, the drudges of the caucus and the polling booth.[32]

The prime minister and his chief of staff are convinced, after listening to her, that democracy may after all be the best way of preventing the Lady Cynthias from manipulating their way into power—a power that entails no responsibility.

Harley Granville Barker (1877-1946), a disciple of Shaw's, made the woman's question and the tensions it was generating in the early twentieth century the central theme of his play *The Madras House* (1909), which is in its own way a social history of the time. The Madras House is a ladies' garment establishment where the fashionable clothes worn by upper-class English ladies are made. In the Madras House, lower-class female labor is exploited in a variety of ways to satisfy the self-indulgent instincts of the leisured class. Among those working in the Madras House is the proud spinster coming to terms with the realities of demography, who says, "I look upon spinsterhood as an honorable estate, as my Bible teaches me to. . .some women marry happily and well. . .and some can't marry at all. These facts have to be faced I take it."[33] One of the women is pregnant with an illegitimate child. She is defiant about her transgression, but her fate hangs on how her employers handle the matter.

The women working in the Madras House are set off against the six daughters of Mr. Huxtable, one of the partners in the firm. Mr. Huxtable's six daughters are all unmarried and living the trivial lives that feminists scorned. They are unmarried because there are no suitable men of their station, or above, available. They have talents—one is artistic, another has administrative abilities—which might be put to good use; but work for ladies of their class is unthinkable, and so they live lives of quiet desperation, albeit in a sumptuous setting.

Granville Barker points out that the Huxtable daughters are as much victims of capitalist profiteering as the workers who sew their clothes and the models who try them on for the buyers. The buyers see none of these women as human beings, but solely as economic units. In one scene the models are paraded in front of the buyers, who are totally absorbed in their merchandising zeal, and as unaware of the models as though they were clothes hangers. One buyer exults:

But it is the middle class woman of England that is waiting for me. The woman who still sits at the parlour window of her provincial villa pensively gazing through the laurel bushes. . . . She must have her chance to dazzle and conquer that is every woman's birthright be she a Duchess of Mayfair or a doctor's wife in the suburbs of Leicester. And remember, Gentlemen, the middle class women of England. . .think of them in bulk. . .they form one of the greatest money-spending machines the world has ever seen.

It is clear that the women's bodies are interchangeable. The models have creations draped over their bodies that they will never actually wear. But the wealthy wearers are as much manikins as the models.

Among the males, there is one diehard masculinist, whose views are set off against those of Philip Huxtable, the feminist manager of the Madras House. Constantine, Huxtable's brother-in-law, is the masculinist ideologue who states his case without any of the hypocrisy affected by some English democrats. Constantine has adopted the Moslem faith and has abandoned England for the Middle East, where there is no woman's question because men dominate by fiat, and there is no pretence of democracy. In Constantine's view, women have their use, that is, breeding, and the world is best served by keeping them strictly to it. He has left England because it is "a country where women are let loose with money to spend and time to waste, and are encouraged to flaunt their charms on the very streets." In the masculinist view Constantine articulates, "women haven't morals or intellect in our sense of the word. It's degrading to compete with them." Constantine's contempt for women does not have to be tempered by the capitalist's need to cater to them as consumers. It is Constantine, the outsider, who makes the devastating critique of the Madras House as a "harem of industry." He uses the models as a case in point:

You coin your profits out of them by putting them on exhibition for 10 hours a day . . . their good looks, their good manners, their womanhood. . . . And when you've worn them out you turn them out . . . forget their very names . . . wouldn't know their faces if you saw them selling matches at your door. For such treatment of potential motherhood, my prophet condemns to Hell.

Philip Huxtable, like Granville Barker himself, is looking forward to a new world of free womanhood but, aware of the vested interests in favor of the status quo, recognizes the difficulties. Ironically, among the chief obstacles are middle-class women like his own wife, Jessica. Born to be pampered, and gaining a renewed sense of her femininity from casual flirtations with other men, she acknowledges, "I've been taught to be charming and to like dainty clothes. It won't be easy for us." Philip Huxtable suggests that they might start with their own daughter, by teaching her about the real world "even if it means not adding her to that aristocracy of good feeling and good taste." He pleads directly to the women who have held back:

There's a price to be paid for free womanhood . . . and how many of you ladies are willing to pay it? Come out and be common women among us common men. If we can't live the bad as well as the beautiful. . . . If we won't share it all out now . . . free air and art and dirt and sin then we good and clean people are costing the world too much.

Philip Huxtable is the consummate male feminist, circa 1909. He looks forward to a better world and believes that equality of the sexes will hasten progress. He invites Jessica into the world of new womanhood by offering her an honest relationship: "I treat you as a man would treat another man."

That friendship and intellectual companionship are the keys to better relationships between the sexes is the message of the philosophical feminists; intellectual interests are a more enduring basis for love than is sex, whose transient pleasures are found wanting when weighed against the sustained flights of which the intellect is capable. The philosophical feminists were united in their belief that there is no equality possible on the basis of sexual rights, because males and females have different perspectives on sex. The woman who consents to being a sexual object is not a new woman at all, but the same traditional woman who has been confined to her domestic role from time immemorial. Men do not take women who are merely sexual objects seriously, and it is doubtful whether they even love them; all the feminist fathers had argued that such creatures, who "cater to men's lusts," and who fail to cultivate their minds, are objects of little more than contempt. Such women are dismissed as soon as their sexual charms fade, as, with age, they inevitably must.

The new woman—à la Meredith, Hardy, Allen, and Shaw—looks beyond the personal to the political. She is educated; she may marry or not; but if she does marry, it is not for the purpose of settling into middle-class domesticity, raising a family, and considering her social functions fulfilled. She is asked to sacrifice her middle-class security, which is maintained at the expense of her poorer, struggling sisters, and to direct her maternal instincts as much to them as to her own biological progeny. She marries—if she chooses that role—a partner, a companion, who shares a commitment to a common cause that transcends the family unit. She is urged to go into the world and challenge the egoistic and materialistic values of men. To do this, her first priority must be to gain a voice in the political institutions that men dominate, in the form of the suffrage.

NOTES

1. Novel writing was an acceptable avocation for genteel women in the early nineteenth century. Critics pointed out that they wrote from the woman's point of view and designated their works for female readership.

2. Quoted from *Yeast* in Patricia Thomson, *The Victorian Heroine: A Changing Ideal, 1837-1873* (Westport, Conn.: Greenwood Press, 1978), p. 60.

3. Ibid., p. 130.

4. Michael St. John Packe, *The Life of John Stuart Mill* (New York: Capricorn Books, 1970), p. 493.

5. Gail Cunningham, *The New Woman and the Victorian Novel* (London: Macmillan, 1978), p. 121.

6. Lloyd Fernando, *"New Women" in the Late Victorian Novel* (College Park: Pennsylvania State University Press, 1977), pp. 74-78.

7. Meredith wrote the poem after he learned of the death of his estranged wife, Mary Ellen Nicholls, in 1861. She had run off with another man.

8. Barbara Leigh Smith Bodichon formed a committee for the legal rights of women partly as a result of Caroline Norton's experience.

9. Phyllis Bartlett, *George Meredith*. Published for the British Council and the National Book League by Longmans, Green & Co., 1963, p. 34.

10. All quotes from George Meredith, *Diana of the Crossways* (New York: W. W. Norton & Co., 1973).

11. Alice Woods, *George Meredith: A Champion of Women and of Progressive Education* (Oxford: Basil-Blackwell, 1937), p. 79.

12. Cunningham, *New Woman and the Victorian Novel*, p. 119.

13. Ibid., p. 129.

14. All quotations from Thomas Hardy, *Jude the Obscure* (London: J. R. Osgood, McIlvaine, and Macbeth-Raeburn, 1896).

15. Fernando, *"New Women" in the Late Victorian Novel*, p. 143.

16. Cunningham, *New Woman and the Victorian Novel*, p. 115.

17. Ibid., p. 45.

18. All quotes from Grant Allen, *The Woman Who Did* (Boston: Little, Brown, 1926).

19. Girton College, Cambridge was founded in 1873. The Girton Girl became synonymous with the new woman in the public mind.

20. Introduction to 1926 edition of *The Woman Who Did*.

21. George Bernard Shaw, *Pygmalion*, in *The Collected Plays of George Bernard Shaw with Prefaces* (New York: Dodd, Mead, 1975), p. 194.

22. George Bernard Shaw, *The Quintessence of Ibsenism* (London: Constable and Co.), p. 41.

23. Norbert Greiner, "Mill, Marx, and Bebel: Early Influences on Shaw's Characterizations of Women," in Rodelle Weintraub, ed., *Fabian Feminist: Bernard Shaw and Women* (College Park: Pennsylvania State University Press, 1977).

24. All quotes from George Bernard Shaw, "Major Barbara," in *The Collected Plays with Prefaces* (New York: Dodd, Mead, 1975).

25. Norman and Jeanne MacKenzie, *The Fabians.* (New York: Simon and Schuster, 1977), p. 309.

26. All quotes from George Bernard Shaw, in "The Philanderer," *The Collected Plays with Prefaces* (New York: Dodd, Mead, 1975).

27. Bernard Shaw, *"My Dear Dorothea: A Practical System of Moral Education for Females* (New York: The Vanguard Press, 1956).

28. Maud Churton Braby, "G.B.S. and A Suffragist," in Weintraub, *Fabian Feminist.*

29. Bernard Shaw, "Why All Women Are Peculiarly Fitted to Be Good Voters," in Weintraub, *Fabian Feminist.*

30. Bernard Shaw, "The Root of the White Slave Traffic," in Weintraub, *Fabian Feminist.*

31. Bernard Shaw, "Sir Almroth Wright's Case Against Woman Suffrage," in Weintraub, *Fabian Feminist.*

32. Bernard Shaw, *Press Cuttings: A Topical Sketch Compiled from the Editorial and Correspondence Columns of the Daily Papers* (London: Constable and Co., 1911), p. 31.

33. All quotes from Harley Granville Barker, *The Madras House* (Boston: Little, Brown, 1920).

"VOTES FOR WOMEN!"
THE MALE SUFFRAGISTS

6

The democratic franchise was central to sexual equality in the thinking of such early feminists as William Thompson, George Holyoake, Robert Owen, and John Stuart Mill. The greater influence of women in society and government was not only required to fulfill the ideals of justice enunciated in the American Declaration of Independence and the French Declaration of the Rights of Man; it was necessary to remedy the egregious elements of the masculine cause against which they revolted. These included authoritarianism, capitalist profiteering, and imperialist domination. To the radicals of the nineteenth century, the expansion of democracy was also a vindication of the historical process, which had been moving from barbarism to civilization in identifiable stages. They saw the enfranchisement of women as the culmination of the process. Without it, no society could call itself civilized, and progress was impossible.

The feminist fathers were rationalists. They held the firm conviction that the franchise could be extended through the political process by educating their leaders and by applying those pressures, including organizing and petitioning, that were permissible under the British Constitution and which were held to be inherent rights in the United States Constitution. Indeed, using these tactics, a number of reforms were achieved. But women's political rights not only did not advance in Great Britain during the first half of the nineteenth century; they actually retrogressed due to Whig and Tory party politics. The Tory party, at the beginning of the nineteenth century, was adamantly opposed to any electoral reform, whether for females or males. Through a system of "rotten boroughs," made possible by electoral laws that had not changed since the reign of Charles II, they securely controlled the government, kept their party in power, and protected their interests.

Within the Whig party there was strong sentiment for opening the franchise to the economically powerful middle-class merchants and industrialists, who were growing restive in a system where British wealth and power depended on their business ventures, but where they were unrepresented in the councils of government. The Whig attitude toward female political rights was expressed by Charles

Plate 12. John Stuart Mill, at the time of his parliamentary election campaign, 1865.

James Fox. Explaining why the franchise for women could never be entertained even though there were many women with greater intelligence and ability than "the uninformed individuals of the lowest class of men," he stated, "And yet why has it never been imagined that the right of election should be extended to women? Why, but because of the law of nations, and perhaps also by the law of nature, that sex is dependent on ours. . . . It has never been in the contemplation of the most absurd theorists to extend the elective franchise to the other sex."[1]

When the dust had settled after passage of the 1832 Reform Bill, the rotten boroughs were, for the most part, abolished; Britain was redistricted so the new population centers—cities such as Birmingham and Manchester—were represented in Parliament; and property qualifications were revised so that upper-middle-class males gained the right to vote. During the acrimonious debates in the House of Commons, "Orator" Hunt, an advocate of universal suffrage, presented to Parliament a petition of one Mary Smith which asked that the vote be granted to unmarried, qualified women. The masculinists of both parties in Parliament responded by substituting for the word "person," which was originally in the bill, the word "male," thus for the first time making sex a criterion for political rights, and effectively removing women from any consideration for participation in government.[2]

It was a result of the tendency to further segregate the sexes into separate spheres—exemplified by the exclusion of women from the voting process and the refusal to allow female speakers at the International Slavery Convention in 1840—that George Holyoake advised women to organize to prevent these calculated insults and to advance their own cause.

Holyoake and the Owenites infiltrated the working-class Chartist Movement in the 1830s, and gave the members, who were also disenfranchised, the same advice they later gave women. They countered the revolutionary sentiments of the Chartists with their own insistence on "moral force" that is, petitioning and organizing, as a means to achieve political rights. The Owenites wanted, in effect, to infuse Chartism with feminism, and to make universal manhood suffrage, which would include voting rights for women, one of their demands. That there was some sentiment for women's suffrage among the Chartists is revealed by R. J. Richardson's *Rights of Women*, written in 1840 while he was in prison. Richardson demanded voting rights for woman, first, because she has a natural right; second, because she has a civil right; third, because she has a political right; fourth, because to vote is a duty imperative upon her; fifth, because it is derogatory to the divine will to neglect so imperative a duty. Richardson went on to elaborate on all these points. Regarding women's civil and political rights, he maintained that is was absurd that in a nation where a woman could be the supreme executive as queen, she should not be admitted to any other executive office. According to ancient constitutional principles, women could hold such posts, and had done so. Richardson was particularly eloquent when he stressed that women not only had ancient prescriptive rights, which had been denied them by arbitrary fiat in 1832, but that they had earned their political rights through their contributions "directly and indirectly to the wealth and resources of the nation by their skill and labour." He described how women were employed in all trades, from agriculture to mining, and how their political impotence guaranteed their systematic economic exploitation.

Richardson was perhaps the first to exhort women to think of political participation not only as a right, but as a duty, to society and to humanity. In doing so he expressed a viewpoint characteristic of the male feminist, that women would be a moderating and humanizing influence in political life:

I think, nay I believe that God ordained women to temper man. I believe for this reason that she ought to partake of his council, public and private, that she ought to share in the making of laws for the good of the Commonwealth in the same manner as she would join with her husband in the council of the household. It is a duty she owes to herself, to her husband, to her children, to posterity, and to her common country.... When we consider that it is to woman we owe our existence, that we receive from her our earliest thought and the bias of our mind—that we are indebted to her for all that makes life a blessing, would it not be unwise, ungrateful, and inhuman to deny them every advantage they can possess in society. It would be equally wrong for women to neglect the making of good laws for the guidance of those she brings into the world.[3]

Richardson's viewpoint was not typical. Although the original Charter of 1837 contained the demand for universal manhood suffrage this demand was later dropped, and only manhood suffrage was included in the six-point program.

Radicals considered the Whig party, traditionally committed to civil liberties and religious freedom, the most promising vehicle for the advancement of political rights for outgroups, which included women. In the early nineteenth century, Henry Brougham was the white hope of the radicals. Brougham (1778-1868), first elected to Parliament in 1812, established contacts with the utilitarians, James Mill and Jeremy Bentham, with Robert Owen and Francis Place; and with the leading radical parliamentarian, Francis Burdett. He had visited New Lanark, Owen's model workers' village, and had been greatly impressed, particularly by its educational achievements.[4] Brougham's willingness to run on a radical program in 1815—a program which included nonintervention in foreign affairs, prison reform, education of the lower orders, the abolition of slavery, and freedom of the press—lent credence to their hopes. But Brougham lost his enthusiasm for radical reform when working-class revolts in 1819 convinced him he was playing into the hands of revolutionaries. Because he believed that its passage would broaden the base of the Whig party, he was a strong supporter of the Reform Bill of 1832. Brougham thought that the clause permanently eliminating women from any consideration for the franchise was regrettable at the very least, and at worst exceeded the authority of the British Constitution. In 1850, in what later became known in suffrage circles as Brougham's Act, he introduced legislation which stated that all acts "importing the masculine gender shall be deemed and taken to include females, unless the contrary be expressly provided." Brougham's Act was to become an important weapon for the women's suffrage supporters.

An immediate result in 1851 was the formation of the Sheffield Female Suffrage Society which, through a sympathetic M.P., presented a petition to the House of Lords asking for the suffrage.

Brougham's more durable interest in education included the education of women. Certain that the extension of educational opportunities to those who were excluded from them or could not afford them would have beneficial social consequences, he supported government funding for the education of the poor. He was instrumental in the founding of both London University (in 1825) and the Mechanics Institute for the education of artisans. The Society for Useful Knowledge and the Library of Useful Knowledge, which he founded, were intended to dispense practical information to the working classes. He became the first president of the National Association for the Promotion of Social Science in 1857. The Association was founded on the premise that political education, through the discussion of important social issues, was as important as practical knowledge. A woman was appointed assistant secretary, and from the outset women were encouraged to come to the meetings and to make substantial contributions. The women's papers were at first read by male colleagues but support for their efforts brought confidence, and in due time they read their own. At meetings of the NAPSS, a number of middle-class women debated feminism as one of the leading issues of the day, got their basic training in public speaking, and went on to bring the woman's question into public consciousness. Barbara Leigh Smith Bodichon, Frances Cobb, and Mary Carpenter all became feminist activists as a result of their political education in the NAPSS.

The most formidable of the Liberal feminists was John Stuart Mill, who exerted his considerable influence on radical colleagues to join the Liberal party in order wrest it away from the laissez faire capitalists and Whig landlords who predominated in its councils.[5] He used the *Westminster Review*, founded in the spirit of radicalism by Jeremy Bentham, to challenge laissez faire doctrines and to substitute for them his own radical ideals, which included feminism. In the course of his writings, *Principles of Political Economy* (1848) and *On Liberty* (1859), he sought to steer the Liberal party away from the selfish individualism that laissez faire capitalism denoted, to a philosophy that put individualism in a social context and attempted to balance individual rights against community responsibilities. Mill saw the need for state interference to prevent laissez faire abuses; but state regulation that might curtail individual liberties could only be condoned if all people, including women, participated in the decision making processes of the state.

In 1865, Mill was asked to stand for Parliament as the Liberal candidate for Westminster. He agreed to run if his platform, which included women's suffrage, was accepted. When it was, he was delighted that because of his candidacy

what are thought the most out-of-the-way of all my opinions, . . . are discussed and canvassed from one end of the country to the other, and some of them (especially women's voting) are obtaining many unexpected adhesions. I reckon this a good stroke of practicality, whether I am elected for Parliament or not.[6]

After his election, he was determined to make women's suffrage his major priority.

The fever for further electoral reform was high in 1865, with the Liberal party committed to extending the franchise to the working classes, but only to the males. There was jockeying between the Conservatives, under the leadership of Benjamin Disraeli, and the Liberals, commanded by Lord John Russell, over who would introduce the legislation, since both party leaders wanted the windfall of working-class voters that would presumably result for the party that achieved the reform. Mill's tactic was to propose an amendment demanding suffrage for women to any electoral reform bill that was proposed. He needed to show that women supported the legislation giving them voting rights, and he and his supporters set in motion the organizational activities and the petitioning central to their strategy for putting pressure on the government.

In January, 1867, a meeting was called in Manchester, a radical center, to plan the formation of a women's suffrage society. Among those who attended were Richard Pankhurst and Jacob Bright, M.P. for Manchester, both strong champions of women's rights, who provided consistent support for the cause in the campaigns that lay ahead—Bright from his position in Parliament, and Pankhurst as a speaker, writer, and lawyer. The meeting resulted in the formation of the Manchester Women's Suffrage Committee, and with the election of Lydia Becker as leader.

By May 20, 1867, when Mill rose to propose his amendment, he could also brandish a petition asking for the suffrage signed by fifteen hundred women, including such luminaries as Barbara Bodichon, Octavia Hill, and Dr. Elizabeth Garrett. Their demands were hardly radical, and they did not ask that all adult women be enfranchised. The petition merely asked voting rights for women who owned property, and, if passed, would have enfranchised approximately three hundred thousand widows and single women who were self-supporting. Mill considered this a first step; but in his speech he demanded the suffrage for women as a class in the name of justice, humanity, progress, and practical politics:

I rise, Sir, to propose an extension of the suffrage which can excite no party or class feeling in the house—which can give no umbrage to the keenest assertor of the claims either of property or of numbers, an extension which has not the faintest tendency to disturb what we have heard so much about lately, the balance of political power, which cannot afflict the most timid alarmist by any revolutionary terrors, or offend the most jealous democrat as an infringement of popular rights, or a privilege granted to one class of society at the expense of another.

Justice demands that we should not capriciously and without cause give these rights to one, and withhold them from another. . . . Can it be pretended that women who manage a property or conduct a business, who pay rates and taxes, often a large amount, and often from their own earnings are not capable of a function of which every male householder is capable. . . . exclusion is repugnant to the particular principles of the British Constitution. It violates the oldest of our constitutional axioms that taxation and representation should be co-extensive.

Much of Mill's speech was devoted to a point by point answer to the masculinists, who brought up a number of reasons why women should not be granted the vote. To the argument that men and women move in separate spheres which cannot and should not be bridged, he responded: "The idea of a peremptory and absolute line of separation between men's province of thought and women's belongs to a bygone state of society. A silent domestic revolution has been taking place where men and women are for the first time in history really companions." Mill raised the idealized relationship he had with Harriet Taylor Mill to a general condition when he said:

The wife is the man's chief associate; his most confidential friend, and often his most trusted counsellor.... Men do not wish for their nearest companions, one whose thoughts are alien from those which occupy his own mind, one who can give neither help nor comfort, nor support to his noblest feelings and purpose.... Sir, the time has come if women are not raised to the level of men, men will be pulled to theirs. When men and women are really companions, if women are frivolous, men will be frivolous; if women care only for personal interests and trifling amusements, men, in general will care for little else. The two sexes must now rise or sink together.

To the argument that the majority of women do not want the suffrage:

If this be so it only proves that nearly all women are still under this deadening influence [their age-old conditioning], that the opiate still benumbs their mind and conscience. How do we know how many more thousands there are who have not asked for what they do not hope to get, either for fear of being ill thought of by men or by other women?... At all events, those who do not care for the suffrage will not use it.

To the argument that women already exercise an abundance of power indirectly through men:

Rich people have a great deal of indirect influence. Is that a reason for denying them the suffrage? Sir, it is true that women have already great power.... Her power is like the backstairs influence of a favorite. She works on him through his strongest feelings without any responsibility. Sir, I demand that all who exercise power should have the burden laid upon them of knowing something about the things they have power over.... I want to make that power a responsible power.

To the argument that women are protected by their husbands and do not in any way suffer:

Sir, this is exactly what has been said of all other unrepresented classes—the operatives for instance, are they not all virtually represented through their employers?... I should like to see a return laid before the House of the number of women who are annually beaten to death, kicked to death, or trodden to death by their male protectors.... Are single females as well represented? Where are the training schools for governesses? What has become of the endowments which the bounty of our forefathers established for the instruction not of boys alone, but of boys and girls indiscriminately?...Hardly any decent occupation save one is open to them. They are either governesses or nothing....As soon as ever women become capable of successfully competing with men in any career, if it be lucrative and honorable, it is closed to them. A short time ago women could be associates of the Royal Academy, but they were so distinguishing themselves, that this privilege has been taken away from them.

I have given these few instances to prove that women are not the petted favorites of society which some people seem to imagine; that they have not in abundance that superficiality of influence, which is ascribed to them, and are not sufficiently represented by the representation of those who have never cared to do in their behalf so obvious an act of justice.

I move, Sir, that the word "man" be omitted and the word "person" inserted in its place.[7]

When the tally was completed, it showed that 73 M.P.s had voted for Mill's motion and 194 had voted against it. Once the woman's suffrage amendment was defeated, the 1867 Reform Bill, enfranchising about one million urban working-class males, duly passed. Mill was not discouraged by the defeat. That one-third of the Commons voted for his amendment was to him evidence that the time was ripe for a concerted effort. To that end, he completely immersed himself in recruiting and in expanding the women's suffrage societies. A month after the 1867 debate he wrote:

It is truly astonishing how the right opinion is spreading both among women and men since the debate. We are now forming a society in London for the Representation of Women, and hope to get others formed in Edinburgh and Dublin and elsewhere (there is already a most efficient one in Manchester, which obtained the majority of the 13,500 signatures to this year's petition). The proposed Society will probably be composed of an Executive Committee of ladies, a General Committee of both sexes subscribing one guinea a year, which will be the ultimate governing body, and ordinary members who will only subscribe a small sum per annum, will receive the reports and circulars but have no part in the management.[8]

Mill designated the women for the executive committee, and included his step-daughter, Helen Taylor, and himself on the general committee.

Within a month he had recruited thirty M.P.s into the suffrage organization. He scored a coup by gaining the adherence of the popular Charles Kingsley to the suffrage cause. The result was a very favorable review of Mill's *Subjection of Women* by Kingsley for *McMillan's Magazine*. In the review, Kingsley complained that the suffrage was being granted to every "illiterate, drunk, wife-beater, and ruffian," while it was denied to the "most virtuous, the most pious, the most learned, the most benevolent women."[9]

Mill aimed his propaganda shafts across the Atlantic to the United States as well. To the editor of the *Anti-Slavery Standard* he wrote, "The disabilities of women are now the only remaining national violation of the principles of your immortal Declaration of Independence."[10] Mill was, in effect, commenting upon the failure to give American women the vote after the Civil War, when freed male blacks received the suffrage by constitutional amendment.

The women's suffrage movement in the United States had in many ways paralleled that in England. American abolitionists Elizabeth Cady Stanton, Lucretia Mott, and William Lloyd Garrison were all in attendance at the 1840 antislavery convention in London, where their feminism was aroused by the refusal to seat women with the men. Garrison, in protest, sat with the women behind a curtain. All three sponsored the Seneca Falls Convention in 1848, which revised the Declaration of Independence to read "All men and women are created equal," and put forth an agenda for women's legal and political rights. Among those attending the convention was Frederick Douglass, a former slave who had become editor of *The North Star*, an antislavery newspaper. He proudly declared himself to be "a woman's rights man" because of women's opposition to slavery. For Douglass (1817-1895), women's support of abolitionism was evidence of that moral sensibility which the male feminists saw as a civilizing force. Douglass wrote in his autobiography:

When the true history of the antislavery cause shall be written, women will occupy a large space in its pages, for the cause of the slave has been preeminently women's cause. . . . Observing woman's agency, devotion and efficiency in pleading the cause of the slave, gratitude for this high service early moved me to give favorable attention to the subject of what is called "woman's rights" and caused me to be denominated a woman's rights man. I am glad to say I have never been ashamed to be thus designated.[11]

At the Seneca Falls Convention, Douglass angrily noted that even to speak on the subject of women's rights was to invite contempt and ridicule, and that a discussion of the rights of animals would be regarded with more complacency by the so-called "wise" and "good" of the land than a discussion of the rights of women. He spoke eloquently in stating the case on principle: "We hold woman to be justly entitled to all we claim for man. We go farther, and express our conviction that all political rights which it is expedient for man to exercise, it is equally so for women."[12]

Abolitionists such as William Lloyd Garrison and Wendell Phillips welcomed women to their ranks and considered that the moral stance women had taken on the issue of slavery in and of itself qualified them for citizenship. The sponsors of the First Women's Rights Convention, in 1850, included Wendell Phillips, William H. Channing, Bronson Alcott, William Lloyd Garrison, and Gerrit Smith. Speeches by Phillips, Theodore Parker, and Thomas Wentworth Higginson were standard fare at women's rights conventions for years.

Higginson (1823-1911) was America's feminist philosopher in the John Stuart Mill mold. Higginson was a descendant of the first minister of the Massachusetts Bay Colony. After getting his training at Harvard University he became a Unitarian minister, but his radicalism cost him his pulpit. Higginson was not only a feminist; his antipathy to slavery was so strong that he favored dissolution of the

Union to cut adrift the half that was slave. Higginson applauded John Brown's raid at Harper's Ferry, Virginia, to free the slaves; during the Civil War he served as a colonel, and commanded the first black regiment ever formed in the United States.

Higginson's abolitionism and his feminism derived from the same impulses, and he became active on women's behalf soon after the Seneca Falls Convention. In *Woman and Her Wishes* (1851), he questioned the education for domesticity that middle-class females generally received: "Nothing can hide from me that an immortal soul needs for its sustenance more than gardening, visiting, the crochet needle, and the occasional manufacture of a sponge cake. Yet what else constitutes the recognized material for the life of most well-educated young ladies?"[13]

In the same work, Higginson declared that women in the United States "were more rigidly excluded from their political rights than the women of any other Christian nation." He arrived at this conclusion after observing that in Europe distinctions were based on "station" (class) rather than sex. Thus a woman could become queen even though women were nominally excluded from participating in politics. Since the United States had no such loopholes in their discriminatory policies, it was all the more important for women to gain their voting rights.

Higginson was in regular attendance at the women's rights conventions that resulted from the Seneca Falls Convention. At the Women's Rights Convention in 1856, there was a debate as to whether women should support the fledgling Republican party which carried the banner of radicalism in mid-nineteenth-century America. The Republicans had been very willing to exploit the feminists' moral stand on slavery, but refused to bind themselves to support of women's rights in their party platform. Higginson was incensed at this duplicity. He thundered: "The Republican Party, if it had any manliness was pledged to support women to whom it had applied to support its cause every day...and if there was such a thing in the land as a Democratic Party, that Party was the Party of women also."[14]

After his service in the Civil War, Higginson turned to journalism as a full-time occupation, and made feminism his cause. He made clear that women's subjection was not natural, since its degree varied according to time and place. He extolled women's talents and identified their virtues. In *Women and Men* (1888) the male ego was a prime target, Higginson declaring, "No matter what a woman does, the stupidest man has always discernment enough to think of something she has not done."[15]

In order to implement his beliefs, Higginson had run for Congress as a Free Soiler, but he was not elected. American feminists did not have anyone in the Congress to carry forward their cause as Mill and his followers did in Parliament. After the Civil War, the Republicans, who had received women's strong support during the conflict, moved to enfranchise the newly freed blacks, but only the males. When pressed by the feminists to include women's suffrage in the franchise reform, the Republicans took the politically expedient position that trying to tack women's suffrage onto the Fourteenth Amendment might bring about the Amendment's defeat, and they proclaimed that "this was the Negroes' hour." Women would have to wait. Since the Democratic party had no interest in women's suffrage, there was no place for the feminists to go. After its abandonment by its erstwhile Republican allies, the American women's movement fell into disarray, and became fractious as the feminists debated tactics and priorities.

In the late nineteenth century, American feminists found a champion in Edward Bellamy who made a major impact with his utopia, *Looking Backward*, in which women were to have equality with men. The book was a resounding success because Bellamy reaffirmed middle-class power over the teeming immigrant masses who were populating the urban centers of the nation. The immigrants were transmitters of the radical philosophies they had imbibed in the Old World. The result was bitter labor strife which raised fears among the middle class that the Atlantic Ocean might not be sufficient quarantine from the European virus of social revolution.

American feminists who had watched in consternation as illiterate black males got the vote after the Civil War, and who saw immigrant males, equally unlettered, gaining political power, were attracted to Bellamy's nationalist philosophy and his reform program in which their talents would be recognized. In retrospect, Bellamy's utopia had ominous overtones. With Boston society restored to its pristine Yankee state; with workers herded into an industrial army in which they had no voice, and where discipline was strictly enforced; with control over workers assured through the elimination of historical memory and critical intelligence; and with the dismantling of political parties and the judicial machinery which guaranteed civil rights, it had all the earmarks of an indigenous American fascism.

Feminists flocked to join the Nationalist Clubs which proliferated from coast to coast shortly after the publication of *Looking Backward* in 1888. They became leaders of the Clubs, and women frequently outnumbered men in the membership. The women invested Bellamy's sterile nationalism, and his authoritarian socialism with their own humanistic concerns. They supported compulsory education and vocational schools, debated the merits of schools for defective children, and backed the development of cooperative industries. American feminists thus deserve a large measure of credit for helping to channel an incipient totalitarianism into what emerged as the modern liberal welfare state with its philosophy that state power and resources should be used on behalf of the poor and disadvantaged. However the feminists' active involvement in the Nationalist Clubs caused rifts. Older feminists such as Elizabeth Cady Stanton, who had achieved a profound radical consciousness because of the influence of the Owenite democratic socialists, pointedly refused to join any of the Clubs. The feminists' identification with social discrimination and with racism, which were inherent in Bellamy's ideas, estranged them from working women and black women and made sisterhood highly problematic in the United States.

The failure of women's suffrage in the United States was especially disappointing since the English radicals' appreciation of the salubrious effects of democracy had derived from their perceptions of the American experience. The ups and downs of democracy in the American republic were carefully charted in the Old World—with approval by radicals and misgivings by conservatives. When Alexis de Tocqueville pronounced a much publicized benediction upon the democratic process as he observed it in America, stressing that democratization was an ineluctable historical force, he encouraged liberals and conservatives alike with his conclusion that, while there were inevitable abuses and dangers in democracy, the cure for these symptoms was more democracy. The English reformers were prepared to take him at his word. In order to keep the issue of women's suffrage in the public eye, they determined to form organizations and to keep the fires of controversy stoked.

The problems and pitfalls of organizing the women's suffrage societies can be illustrated by what happened in Bristol, England. Because of a dearth of women who were willing to risk their reputations by engaging in political activity, the preliminaries for forming a society were undertaken by Matthew Davenport Hill, a radical lawyer who encouraged his daughters, Florence and Rosamund, to become feminists. In order not to shock or inflame public opinion, the invitation sent by Hill's daughters had to be worded with extreme delicacy. Their statement of intent was headed "provisional Suffrage Societies—Bristol Committee." The rest of the message to potential converts to women's rights in Bristol ran: "With a view to forming such a Society, if possible, Mr. Commissioner Hill, who is now at 3 Mall, Clifton, permits his daughter to invite so many as his drawing-room will hold, to meet there on 24th January 1868 at 3 P.M. for a friendly consultation on this public question, although from the narrowness of space the meeting cannot be public."[16] Convinced that the feminists were on the verge of victory, Hill advised those who attended the meeting that the cause of women's suffrage "unlike that of all other great causes will require your support for a very short time." The secretary chosen for the Bristol committee was F. W. Newman, brother of Cardinal John Henry Newman. Francis Newman was fundamentally different from the cardinal in that he belonged to no church and was an inveterate supporter of the unconventional and unorthodox. Francis Newman affirmed that English law toward women was "more unjust than that of the great historically despotic nations and even harsher than that of Turkey with its seraglios."[17]

All the local societies thus formed were merged into a National Society for Women's Suffrage, presided over by Lydia Becker, secretary of the original organization formed in Manchester. The first public meeting in support of female suffrage was held April 14, 1868, in Manchester. It was chaired by the mayor of Salford, Davis Pochin. The first resolution was the model for all subsequent ones in the nineteenth century, and stated that the exclusion of women from voting was "unjust in principle and inexpedient in practice" and that the vote should be granted to women on the same terms "as it is or may be granted to men." Speakers at the meeting were all male with the single exception of Lydia Becker, who shocked public sensibilities by moving the resolution.

The first public meeting in London was held a year later, on July 17, 1869. Among the speakers were Thomas Hare, the father of proportional representation; Boyd Kinnear, a Scottish M.P.; J. S. Mill; Charles Kingsley; Henry Fawcett, M.P. for Brighton; John Morley; and Charles Dilke. In this male galaxy, one female, Millicent Fawcett, who was urged to take a public role by her husband, Henry Fawcett, made a short speech.

Legal efforts were also made to challenge the new voting law, which palpably discriminated against women. The Brougham Act was seized upon to suggest that women who qualified on the same basis as men could in fact vote. Richard Pankhurst asked women so qualified to register for the 1868 elections, and five thousand did so. When they were challenged, Pankhurst prepared the legal brief that was argued in court in the case of *Chorlton* v. *Lings*. Not surprisingly, the feminists lost, with the presiding judge delivering an *obiter dictum* that he hoped the matter had been laid to rest for good.

In order to generate discussion about women's suffrage and hasten its victory, Mill, in 1869, published *The Subjection of Women*, a work written in 1861, which he deemed the fruit of his intellectual partnership with his late wife, Harriet Mill. It was the most compelling and powerful plea on behalf of women's rights since the publication of William Thompson's *Appeal of One-Half of the Human Race on Behalf of the Other*, in 1825. *Subjection* was all the more passionately argued since, in the four decades that had elapsed since Thompson wrote his work, most men had forged ahead to become full citizens, while little had changed for women. In referring to married women as the last legal slaves, Mill was mindful that the suffrage legislation he himself had proposed would have excluded married women, and in dwelling on their plight he emphasized that justice for women had a claim on man's conscience that was equal to the abolitionist cause that had brought about civil war in the United States.

For the sex conservatives, the fact that a woman was never in any position to effectively deny the sexual demands of a husband meant that systematic humiliation and submission to the will of another was her lot. Crucial to their case that married women were sexual slaves was Mill's assertion that "though she may know that he hates her, though it may be his daily pleasure to torture her, and though she may feel it impossible not to loathe him, he can claim from her and enforce the lowest degradation of a human being, that of being made the instrument of an animal function contrary to her inclinations."[18]

In *Subjection*, Mill had much to say about the psychology of women. He charged that what passed for women's nature merely reflected male needs.

Neither does it avail anything to say that the nature of the two sexes adapts them to their present functions and position, and renders these appropriate to them. Standing on the ground of common sense and the constitution of the human mind, I deny that any one knows, or can know, the nature of the two sexes as long as they have only been seen in their present relation to one another. What is now called the nature of women is an eminently artificial thing—the result of forced repression in some directions, unnatural stimulation in others. It may be asserted without scruple, that no other class of dependents have had their character so entirely distorted from its natural proportions by their relations with their masters.

To justify entirely separate spheres for males and females, masculinists argued that history was on their side. Women had always been considered and treated as the subordinate sex and, moreover, they had accepted that position. Mill maintained that the past subjection of women rested on theory only. It had no utilitarian justification:

The adoption of this system of inequity was not the result of forethought or any notion whatever of what conduced to the benefit of humanity or the good order of society. . . . Theorists of black slavery and absolute monarchy have all argued from their origins in nature as an excuse for perpetuating it and have been confounded when these institutions were overthrown.

He pointed to the irony that civilization had advanced beyond the point where might makes right except in the area of women's rights. As for women's passivity being proven by their resignation to their own inferior status, Mill pointed out that some women had over the years registered their dissent from a system that demanded their subservience to male authority. He insisted that countless more would demand their rights "had they not been assiduously taught to repress their desires as contrary to the proprieties of their sex."

Mill was reared in the utilitarian school, and he argued the social benefits of women's rights on empirical grounds as trenchantly as he made his points challenging his opponents on principle. He stated with the deepest conviction that mankind would be better off if women were free. If women were allowed the free use of their faculties, if they were allowed equal opportunity in employment and in education, it would lead to a doubling of the mass of mental faculties "available for the higher service of humanity." Mill thought that humanity could ill afford to lose the talent of one-half of the human race. He considered the influence of women to be "on the whole encouraging to the softer virtues, discouraging to the sterner," and he noted that their "aversion to war and addiction to philanthropy" had had positive effects in his own time. These benefits would be emphasized if women's sentiments were informed by knowledge of public issues. He predicted that, once admitted to public service, their moderating tendencies would be felt in all areas of policy and would diminish the "indulgence of selfish passion."

To Mill, there was no mystery about why males assume their own superiority: "The fact that every boy grows up thinking without any justification that he is superior to any woman including some whose real superiority to him he has daily or hourly the occasion to feel resulted in the cultivation of all the selfish instincts, the self-worship, the unjust self-preference" which marred the relations between men and women. Once he grows up and gets married, the self-fulfilling prophecy of women's inferiority is detrimental to the male as well as to the female. He marries someone who will confirm his superiority and all "that self doubt and questioning which is necessary for growth will vanish." *Subjection* was also a mordant critique of the family. Mill took note of the increasing privatization of family life and the growing tendency to find happiness and security within its confines. He saw this phenomenon as a mixed blessing as long as the family was women's exclusive domain. Mill was in agreement with Robert Owen that family life narrowed one's vision and encouraged selfish interests. If women were not aware of larger issues and did not stimulate their families to take an interest in the larger society—if they continued to regard the family as their personal fief, instead of as a political unit—all would have their horizons bound by "common vanities and common pecuniary objects."

Mill closed by warning his fellow males that, if they persisted in keeping women in a pit, they would inevitably be drawn in with them:

A man married to a woman his intellectual inferior could not advance far in society as he would find her a perpetual dead weight, or, worse than a dead weight, a drag. . . . If the wife does not push her husband forward, she always holds him back. He ceases to care for what she does not care for; he no longer desires, and ends by disliking and shunning, society congenial to his former aspirations . . . his higher faculties both of mind and heart cease to be called into activity.

Mill was defeated in a reelection bid in 1868, but before he left Parliament he spoke on behalf of a bill to permit married women control of their property. Once again he deplored the distorted relations between males and females, and insisted that "it is by remedying the injustice that married women now suffer that real harmony is to be introduced into the married state." Mill lived to see the Married Women's Property Bill he had supported in his last year in Parliament become law in 1870. In the previous year, a modest advance was made in the area of women's suffrage. Unmarried women taxpayers won the right to vote in municipal elections. This was considered an important breakthrough resulting from the dedicated efforts of the Millites, and one that they hoped would be shortly followed by further advances.

Mill's death in 1873 stopped the forward momentum of women's suffrage, permitted the opposition to regroup, and constituted a major blow to the women's suffrage forces. After Mill's death, Jacob Bright, the radical Liberal M.P. from Manchester, took charge of the suffrage struggle. It was Bright who in 1868 introduced a bill to restore the municipal franchise to women taxpayers; to his own surprise, the bill passed. It was also Bright who moved the bill drafted by Richard Pankhurst in 1870 which established the model for future bills relating to the extension of the suffrage. It stated:

That in all acts relating to the qualifications and registration of voters of persons entitled or claiming to be registered and to vote in the election of Members of Parliament, wherever words occur which import the masculine gender, the same shall be held to include females for all purposes connected with and having reference to the right to be registered as voters, and to vote in such elections, any law or usage to the contrary notwithstanding.

Jacob Bright (1821-1899) was the younger brother of John Bright, a Liberal party stalwart who organized and helped finance the campaign to repeal the Corn Laws, making England a free trade country. Both Brights were committed to manhood suffrage, but John Bright voted for women's suffrage with some misgivings in 1867. After he attained a cabinet position in Gladstone's government, he backed off, noting, "I voted with John Stuart Mill three or four years ago but am never free from doubt as to whether my vote was a wise one."[19] Jacob Bright was never beset by the slightest reservations about the justice of women's rights. That the brothers eventually went their separate ways on the issue illustrates the tensions that it provoked within the radical tradition.

Both brothers derived their convictions from their Quaker heritage, which their mother made vivid through her own example. Their nonconformist background inclined both John and Jacob Bright to republicanism and to favor the disestablishment of church and state. Eventually John Bright became convinced that female suffrage might prove detrimental to his pet reforms, fearing that women voters would not support them, and he adjusted his views accordingly. Jacob Bright, on the other hand, was among those whose commitment to feminism was based on a priori principle which stipulated that women must have the vote as a matter of justice despite their political allegiance.

Not only was Jacob Bright instrumental in organizing the women's suffrage society in Manchester, but in 1870, when the issue of votes for women ignited ridicule and was the butt of masculine humor, he stumped for female suffrage at all-male political rallies. When Bright spoke on behalf of his women's suffrage bill in Edinburgh, he rallied his supporters and made the bill a subject of serious debate. He stated in that speech:

I know of no reason for the electoral disabilities of women. I know some reasons, which if there are to be electoral disabilities, would lead me to begin elsewhere than with women. Women are less criminal than men; they are more temperate than men—the distinction is not small, it is broad and conspicuous; women are less vicious in their habits than men; they are more thrifty, more provident; they give more to the family, and take less to themselves.[20]

Bright's efforts resulted in a majority of thirty-three in favor of his bill, the only majority it was ever to receive in Parliament in that decade. It was later killed in committee through the influence of William Gladstone, who was the heaviest of the numerous crosses that the feminists had to bear in the nineteenth century.

Jacob Bright's defeat in 1874 was part of a Conservative tide that brought Benjamin Disraeli to power as prime minister, and brought dissension within the ranks of the suffragists. Lydia Becker, leader of the National Society for Women's Suffrage, believed that the suffrage bill would have a greater likelihood of passage if, rather than being tied to Liberal fortunes, it was a bipartisan effort. The middle-class women suffragists who would benefit from suffrage reform had been encouraged by favorable signals from Disraeli which suggested that he would support a limited suffrage bill. In April, 1866, when electoral reform was being discussed, Disraeli said:

I say that in a country governed by a woman—where you allow women to form part of the other estate of the realm—peeresses in their own right for example—where you allow a woman not only to hold land, but to be a lady of the manor and hold legal courts—where a woman by law may be a church warden and overseer of the poor—I do not see when she has so much to do with the State and Church, on what reasons, if you come to right, she has not a right to vote.[21]

Once Disraeli was in power, Becker, seeking a new sponsor for the women suffrage bill, accepted a Conservative, William Forsyth, who amended the Pankhurst-Bright version by adding a clause "that nothing in this Act shall make women under couverture [married women] eligible to register and vote." The amendment excluding married women from any consideration to the right to vote raised a sensitive political issue. Many Liberals suspected that the comparatively few women property owners who would gain the franchise from the limited bill proposed—elderly widows and unmarried women—would vote Conservative and help to offset the working-class migration to the Liberal party which had resulted from the Reform Bill of 1867. The Forsyth amendment reenforced the idea that the Conservatives expected to reap the rewards of the suffrage bill they supported. This was an important factor in causing original Liberal supporters such as John Bright and Henry Labouchere to switch to the opposition. That the potential women voters were disconcertingly conservative and that most were members of the Anglican Church troubled Bright. When he cast his vote against women's suffrage in 1876, he did so convinced that "women's votes would work to the power of priestcraft in every part of the kingdom." Neither Bright nor Labouchere wanted to see the Conservatives benefit from his exertions on behalf of women. Bright eventually rationalized that suffrage for women would be of no advantage to them, "and I fear at present, and perhaps always, it will tend to strengthen the Party which hitherto has opposed every good measure passed during the thirty years in which I have taken part in public affairs."[22] Henry Labouchere was even more explicit. Informed that a suffrage bill was to have the support of Conservative Lord Salisbury, he quipped, "I thought that a Liberal should pause before going into such bad company."[23]

The flirtation with the Conservatives created a split within the Liberal party between the Millites, who saw feminism as the test of their radical commitment and who considered votes for women a moral imperative no matter how women might vote, and the realpolitik Liberals, who believed that their party purposes transcended any single issue and that considerations of power required rewarding their friends and, at the very least, neutralizing their enemies. The women's gesture to the Conservatives did not produce any positive results. Disraeli did not succeed in convincing his party, dominated by hardline masculinist ideologues, that women's suffrage was either practicable or desirable; and when Jacob Bright returned to Parliament in 1876, he succeeded in having the couverture clause removed, causing the Conservative party to lose interest in women's suffrage.

A confrontation between the Liberal factions—one devoted to the ethical humanism and social radicalism with which Mill tried to infuse Liberalism, the other concerned with consolidating political power—occurred in 1884, when a new electoral reform bill was proposed by the Liberals, who had returned to power in 1880, again with Gladstone as prime minister. The Liberal leadership had committed itself to extending the suffrage to a segment of males heretofore excluded, itinerant agricultural workers.

In 1884, the supporters of female suffrage in Parliament had a variety of new weapons in their arsenal with which they believed they might persuade their former opponents to include women in the electoral reform bill. They could point out that propertied women were, in fact, voting in municipal elections without any of the catastrophes masculinists had predicted would ensue. Women on the Isle of Man, off the coast of England, had gained the suffrage in 1881. The Corrupt Practices Act of 1883, because of its ban on paid election canvassers, had led both parties—the Conservatives and Liberals—to consider the use of women's auxiliary organizations to do the canvassing necessary for an election campaign.[24] Women, as never before, were involved in political issues and were entering the public sphere via their concern over the Contagious Diseases Acts.

In this atmosphere of concerted interest in the woman's question and increasing activism by women in politics, Henry Fawcett, Charles Dilke, and Leonard Courtney, all members of the Liberal government, risked their careers by refusing to put the principle of party loyalty above the greater principle of women's suffrage. Their defiance of Gladstone's leadership presaged the Liberal party split that occurred over the Irish question two years later. Gladstone postponed the inevitable when, in the interest of maintaining nominal party unity for the foreign and domestic storms that lay ahead, he refused to demand the resignations of the three disaffected members of his government.

The crisis which might be described as a struggle for the soul of the Liberal party was precipitated when William Woodall, a Liberal M.P. connected with the Manchester Suffrage Society, emulated the Mill tactic of 1867 by moving an amendment to the new reform bill that would include women in all references to the masculine gender. In his speech, Woodall pointed out that women pay taxes and that 30 percent of them have to work for a living. "If women perform all these functions," he pleaded, "why debar them from dropping a paper in the ballot box once in three or four years along with the labourer who, in many thousands of instances is dependent upon them for subsistence?"[25] Gladstone, who vehemently opposed the amendment on the ground that it would play into the hands of the Conservatives, who would use it to destroy the entire reform bill, threatened to forestall such a contingency by disclaiming the entire reform bill if the women's suffrage amendment passed. With Gladstone adamant, the amendment was defeated 271 to 135, with 104 of the Liberals previously pledged to support women's suffrage voting against it. Fawcett, who was postmaster general, Courtney, who was secretary of the Treasury, and Dilke, who was president of the Local Government Board, were bound by party loyalty to support Gladstone, but agreed they could not acquiesce in this betrayal of their Liberal commitments, and simply walked out of the parliamentary proceedings.

All three defectors had close ties to John Stuart Mill and, although they disagreed on other issues, were firmly wedded to the feminist radical tradition Mill wanted to imbed in the Liberal party.

Henry Fawcett (1833-1884) was elected to Parliament the same year as Mill, and spoke on behalf of women's suffrage in 1867 immediately after Mill had concluded his argument. Both of Fawcett's parents were reformers who thoroughly imbued him with the ideals of the early nineteenth-century utilitarians. His own confidence in Mill was so complete that, as professor of political economy at Cambridge, he would answer virtually every question on economics with the retort, "Read Mill." He acknowledged without any hesitation that Mill's philosophical radicalism had been "the chief education of my mind."[26]

At the age of twenty-five, Fawcett was blinded in a hunting accident; but this did not prevent him from pursuing his economic studies at Cambridge nor from aspiring to political office. In 1867, after he had achieved success in his teaching career and had been elected to Parliament, Fawcett married Millicent Garrett, sister of Dr. Elizabeth Garrett, the first woman to be admitted to the British medical register. Millicent Fawcett described her own feminist inclinations, nurtured by her husband, as being quickened during the memorable evenings the Fawcetts spent at the Mill home. She particularly recalled a conversation between Mill and Herbert Spencer, who opposed women's suffrage on the ground that nature had imposed too heavy a burden on women. Mill's reply, which impressed her, was, "You look upon nature as something we should do well to follow. I look upon nature as a horrible old harridan."[27]

Henry Fawcett was, like Mill, convinced that the franchise would be the most effective way of ending women's economic, social, and educational disabilities, and thus improving society. He believed that so long as they had no influence in Parliament, women's interests would always be neglected, and that the cycle of brutal exploitation for poor women, and enforced idleness and social rounds for wealthier women, would be endless. After Mill's defeat for reelection, Fawcett was constantly on the floor of Parliament answering the objections of those opposed to women's suffrage, countering prejudice with reason. To questions on whether women were intellectually fit for the franchise, Fawcett responded that no intellectual requirement was attached to men's voting rights. To the assertion that men were already protecting women's interests, Fawcett suggested that women might have a different conception of their interests from that held by men, and should, in a civilized society, be given every chance to express it. The fear was frequently expressed that enfranchised women would lose their femininity and the delicacy that accounted for their charms. The male feminists regarded charm as an artifice of the privileged and femininity as a status symbol of the leisured class, having no relevance to the lives of hundreds of thousands of women who toiled in factories for subsistence wages. Their aim was to make clear that women were not creatures apart, but part of humankind, and to challenge men to apply to themselves the criteria they used to express their prejudices. But the attempts to penetrate the opaque and insulated minds of opponents, smug in their masculine superiority, were futile. Only once did Fawcett lose his temper. Confronted for the umpteenth time with the argument that women who had the vote would spend all their time in political activity, to the serious detriment of their domestic duties, Fawcett shouted, "In the name of common sense, does he wish us to believe that every man who has a vote is drawn away from the pursuits of his life...that an artisan working in a mill, a barrister practicing in court, a doctor attending his patients cannot properly study public questions without neglecting his ordinary employment?"[28]

Henry Fawcett was quick to appreciate the need for practical applications of the philosophy of women's rights. When J. S. Mill revised the laissez-faire ideals of his father, James Mill, he made it clear that government had a positive role to play in people's lives by removing the disabilities that hampered individuals from fulfilling their potential. Government, according to Mill, must act as an impartial arbiter between different interest groups, with the aim of protecting the weak from the strong. The latter concept was taken by the feminists as a metaphor for government protection of women from men. Thus, the male feminists who were guided by this philosophy became involved in a variety of feminist concerns, such as education and employment opportunities. Fawcett's earliest feminist involvement was in the area of women's education. Women's inability to get a higher education was regarded as a clear disability which prevented them from attaining their own intellectual level. Fawcett wholeheartedly endorsed Emily Davies in her plan to found a woman's college, and was gratified that Girton College emerged in 1873.

As an M.P., Fawcett was sympathetic not only to women's political wrongs, but to the economic hardships poor women endured. He was certain, given the opportunity, that women could compete effectively with men in any area. Thus, when union leaders pressed for legislation to "protect" working women by excluding them from certain jobs and curtailing their hours, Fawcett perceived their action as a device to protect themselves from competition from women and a means of keeping women out of the job market. Fawcett's concept of individualism supported the protection of children from long hours of work, but not the "protection" of adult women, who needed work to support themselves and who might be effectively forced out of the job market, only to swell the growing numbers of paupers and prostitutes.

Leonard Courtney (1832-1918) was elected to Parliament as a Liberal in 1877. His studies at Cambridge led to an abiding interest in economic problems, and he met Mill after corresponding with him about the question of an income tax They disagreed on that particular issue when they first met in 1861, but found themselves in fundamental agreement on other issues, including women's rights, and Courtney gravitated into the Mill orbit. On his election to Parliament, he gave notice that he was making the woman's question his particular concern; when he got up to speak on the issue, he faced a chorus of ridicule for a half hour. In 1878, he personally introduced that year's women's suffrage legislation. Countering arguments that women were never intended for such things as voting by pointing out that the "considerations now employed against the vote were formerly urged against her education," he managed to get 140 votes in favor of his bill, one of the better showings on women's suffrage.

Because of Courtney's expertise in financial questions, his star rose quickly in the Liberal party, and in 1882 he was appointed secretary of the Treasury in Gladstone's government. In 1883 he married Kate Potter, a sister of Beatrice Webb, thus acquiring important connections for his political career. Any hope that he might achieve a leadership position in the Liberal party was dashed over the women's suffrage stand he took in 1884. He was among those who brought a women's suffrage bill to the floor, despite Gladstone's opposition, and fought hard for its adoption, although without Gladstone's support the chances for its success were virtually nil. In his speeches Courtney affirmed the pragmatic belief of the male feminists that women's suffrage was a vital element in representative government since it would create greater interest in public affairs and strengthen the sense of citizenship and solidarity. But he also firmly held the principle that, whatever the consequences, the risk had to be taken: "Even if her emancipation were accompanied by risk of degradation which had been anticipated, I would face it in consideration of the advantages to be gained." He affirmed Mill's proposition that in "advancing women you will advance men with her," and the result would be "a freer, fuller, nobler woman."[29]

Charles Dilke (1843-1911) was considered a likely successor to William Gladstone as leader of the Liberal party by radicals who had grown restive under Gladstone's heavy-handed methods and moral hypocrisy—so clearly illustrated, to many in his party, by his attitude to women's rights. Dilke and Henry Fawcett became acquainted when Fawcett was a professor of economics and Dilke, a student, at Cambridge. A trip around the world resulted in a book called *Greater Britain*, which elicited expressions of interest in Dilke from Mill, who disagreed with some of the book's basic premises. Mill undertook Dilke's education in radicalism when Dilke entered Parliament in 1868. Dilke became a member of the Radical Club, of which Mill was the soul and center, in 1869, a convinced proponent of women's suffrage. In that same year he joined Jacob Bright in the successful gambit which gained the municipal franchise for women; and in 1870, he managed to get a second reading of the Bright suffrage bill.

When Dilke was appointed head of the Local Government Board he advanced women's opportunities in his own department by appointing women as Poor Law inspectors, bringing them into the civil service for the first time since James Stansfeld appointed women in 1872. In view of Dilke's potential in the Liberal party, his decision to violate party allegiance was a difficult one; but he walked out of Parliament along with Henry Fawcett and Leonard Courtney, refusing to vote against the Woodall amendment. He made his position clear on the issue: "On the merits of women's franchise, I had and have strong opinion. I always thought the refusal of it contrary to the public interest. The refusal of the franchise also affects the whole position of women most unfavorably."[30]

After the debacle on women's suffrage in 1884, Dilke sought an alliance with

Joseph Chamberlain to make the Liberal party more radical than the redoubtable Gladstone would suffer it to be; but this effort foundered because they could come to no agreement on the women's suffrage question. Chamberlain was an adamant foe of women's suffrage, and Dilke noted, "I had a curious talk about women's suffrage with Chamberlain today as that is the only question of importance on which we differ and the only question which seems likely ever to divide us."[31]

Despite their herculean exertions, the results of the feminists' efforts to include women's suffrage in the Reform Bill of 1884 were predictable. The bill, as passed, extended to the county voter the franchise that the Reform Bill of 1867 had given to the urban voter, and increased the total electorate from 3,150,000 to 5,700,000. With the passage of this electoral reform bill all adult males, except for a handful who were still barred because of technical requirements, had the vote. No woman could vote in national elections.

In the last analysis, the opposition of Gladstone had proved decisive, and the Mill tradition was confounded. Particularly galling to the Millites was the decisiveness of the argument that government rested on force and that red-blooded men would never tolerate being outvoted by a minority of men added to a majority of women. The ominous suggestion that in a civilized society the right of the stronger must of necessity prevail was the very antithesis of the democratic idealism of Mill and his followers.

The defeat of 1884 left the suffragists leaderless and disorganized. Henry Fawcett died of pneumonia shortly after the 1884 vote was taken. The December 1, 1884, issue of *The Women's Suffrage Journal*, which was published by the National Society for Women's Suffrage, provided a fitting eulogy:

A great calamity has befallen the friends of women's suffrage in the sudden and premature death of the late Postmaster-General, the Right Honorable Henry Fawcett. No public man has ever endeared himself more closely and universally amongst all classes of his countrymen of all shades of opinion, and it may be said of him what perhaps could not be said of any other politician in any degree of prominence that no one had an unkind word or an unsympathetic thought for him.[32]

Charles Dilke's potential for leadership was disastrously compromised because of his involvement in a highly publicized sex scandal in 1886. He was named corespondent in a divorce suit. Although the judge in the case found no evidence "worthy of the name" against him, Dilke's clean bill of health contrasted oddly with the obloquy heaped on the woman who made the charges against him and was suggestive of the double standard that was at the time a matter of vituperative debate. He lost his seat in Parliament and wandered in the political wilderness for six years. On his return to Parliament in 1892, he devoted himself to labor questions, another facet of his radicalism. He was especially interested in improving the conditions of women in the sweated trades, such as those of the matchgirls, whose strike in 1888 had brought their plight to public attention. His solution was a minimum wage, one which the Liberal radicals adopted when the Liberals were swept to power in the election of 1905. In the early twentieth century, when the women's suffrage struggle reached a crescendo, Dilke expressed the viewpoint of the Peoples' Federation, which demanded the franchise for all adult men and women. He warned that a limited franchise,

if it is ever carried, will be carried as a Conservative measure intended to aid conservative opinion and to root the franchise upon an unassailable limited base, and it will be carried in that case against the counter proposal of the suffrage of all grown men and women made by those representing the advanced thought of the country.[33]

His position, in favor of complete democracy, thus remained consistent with the Mill tradition.

Leonard Courtney resigned his post at the Treasury in 1884. His resignation came not over women's suffrage, but over another issue on which he differed with Gladstone, proportional representation, which he saw as the solution to the Irish question. He finalized his break with Gladstone on the Irish question. When Gladstone chose to stake Liberal party fortunes and its commitment to principle on this issue, Courtney joined the Liberal Unionists. Ironically, he justified his opposition to Irish Home Rule with the same argument many Liberals had used to rationalize their opposition to women's suffrage—that there was no popular majority in favor of it.[34] With the women's suffrage issue dead so long as Gladstone determined Liberal party policy, Courtney devoted himself to other concerns. During the 1880s and '90s, women's suffrage was regularly brought up in private members' bills, that is, bills that had no government support. Even though these bills stood no chance of passage, Courtney always put in a dutiful appearance to speak on their behalf. During the 1897 debate, Kate Courtney warned Millicent Fawcett—while both women were watching from the gallery—that under present circumstances, "it is not likely to go much further." Courtney's radicalism was vindicated when he was recommended for a peerage in 1906, after the Liberal sweep of 1905. His last political prediction, in 1917, was that the next election, to be held in 1918, would surely revolve around proportional representation and women's suffrage, the two issues that had absorbed his political life.

Gladstone left the Liberal party a legacy of opposition to women's suffrage which lasted into the twentieth century, impairing the party's credibility and weakening its hold among its radical constituency, which went into the Labour party; opposition to women's suffrage may be accounted one of the factors that led to the strange death of the Liberal party after World War I.[35] Gladstone cast his vote against women's suffrage when Mill first brought the issue up in 1867, and he never relented. His motives were a mixture of the personal and the political.[36] His stated reasons were a pastiche of all the suffrage opponents' arguments, the most telling being that women's suffrage did not have widespread support. There is little doubt that the Millites were vulnerable because they could not adequately refute the charge that there was no popular mandate for women's suffrage, even among women. Indeed, the female opposition to women's suffrage was vocal and organized, and included Queen Victoria in its ranks. Female suffrage became a favorite target of media celebrities such as Lynn Linton and Mrs. Humphrey Ward. Ensconced in her privileged sanctuary as a staff writer for the virulently antifeminist *Saturday Review*, Lynn Linton spouted the masculinist line with unstinting fervor. She set the pace with an anonymous article called *The Girl of the Period*, which she wrote in 1868. She found the fame and fortune as an antifeminist that had eluded her as the rebel she originally was, and kept up the pressure until her death in 1898. She dubbed the suffragists "the shrieking sisterhood," "the epicene sex," and "the Wild Women." In her articles, the educated and intellectual Girton Girl came to symbolize all the social ills that afflicted England. Mrs. Humphrey Ward was one of the most prominent signers of a petition against the further extension of women's suffrage, addressed to *The Nineteenth Century*, which stated in part that "the political ignorance of women is irreparable and is imposed by nature."[37] The traitors to masculinity were not moved by these evidences of dissension among women on the issue of voting rights. They considered women's opposition a symptom of the conditioning of untold generations the result of which was that they must echo their masters' wishes. It could not be gainsaid that some women had achieved indirect power analogous to that wielded by a court favorite through what the male feminists referred to as "frowning and fawning,"[38] and had vested interests to protect. The male feminists were encouraged by the number of women who joined the suffragist ranks despite the pressures of masculinist opinion, and believed that their courage and forthrightness would set the example for others. They rested their case for female suffrage on humanitarian grounds and constitutional principles rather than on public opinion polls.

With the women's suffrage issue effectively stalled, and the Liberal party preoccupied with the Irish question, the feminists took stock. Richard Pankhurst's disenchantment with the vacillating leadership of Lydia Becker, who persisted in courting the Conservatives through her willingness to support a couverture clause, caused a split in the National Society for Women's Suffrage. Dissidents, who included Richard and Emmeline Pankhurst, Josephine Butler, and Jacob Bright, formed the Women's Franchise League in 1889. Two pioneer feminists from the United States, William Lloyd Garrison and Elizabeth Cady Stanton, gave the new organization an Anglo-American cast. The Women's Franchise League adopted as its suffrage bill the Pankhurst draft that Jacob Bright had introduced in 1870, which ignored couverture for qualified women. To their proposed bill was added a clause declaring that no person should be disqualified for election or appointment to any office on grounds of sex or marital status. Meetings of the league always ended with a resolution that "this meeting resolves itself into a lobbying committee," after the passage of which the more zealous members would repair to Parliament to pressure the M.P.s. Under the guidance of Richard Pankhurst, the league explored the feasibility of aligning itself with the incipient Labour party as a means of putting more intense pressure on the Liberals. This maneuver was to bring the women's suffrage issue surging back to life in the early twentieth century.

In 1897, the remnants of the 1889 split in the National Society for Women's Suffrage reconstituted themselves into the National Union of Women's Suffrage Societies. They demanded the suffrage "as it is, and may be given to men" and were determined that no government, regardless of party, should take up questions relating to the franchise without removing the electoral disabilities of women. Millicent Fawcett, who had described her political education as beginning at the time of her marriage to Henry Fawcett, who had joined the first suffrage society in London, and who articulated the demand for the enfranchisement of women with skill and effectiveness, appeared to be the natural choice for leader of the NUWSS. In her insistence on reasonable discourse as well as on the constitutional process in achieving the goal of women's suffrage, she became the guardian of the Mill tradition.

In a unique tribute, George Holyoake, one of the feminist fathers who survived into the twentieth century, summed up the meaning of Mill's politics of civility in an age increasingly disposed to political extremism. In *John Stuart Mill, Teacher of the People*, he expressed his intention of dwelling on those personal qualities which had won for Mill "the regard and honor of the insurgent industrial classes—insurgent not in the sense of physical rebellion against authority but of intellectual rebellion against social inferiority and insufficiency of means." Holyoake revealed that it was Mill's stern uprightness that cost him his seat in Parliament in 1868. Mill took the position that no candidate for public office—the holding of which he considered a public service, and for which, in his day, one received no salary—should contribute to his own campaign expenses. At the same time, Mill felt it was proper to contribute to the campaigns of those whom he supported, and made a contribution to the campaign of Charles Bradlaugh. Since Bradlaugh was a self-proclaimed atheist, the contribution was used against Mill by his Tory opponent with telling effect.

Holyoake made clear Mill's conviction that the pursuit of truth could only bring advantage. Mill's instruction to all people was "never to take authority for truth but truth for authority." His only rancorous feelings were reserved for those who hinted at untoward conduct in his relationship with Harriet Taylor, and "he never communicated again with any who injected dishonorable motives into the relationship."

Holyoake was eloquent about what the world had lost with the death of Mill:

What would you not give to hear Mill's calm voice again? What would you not give to see him apply the plummet of justice and reason to the crooked iniquities of the front benches? For even the most foolish understood more or less dimly that they were listening to something exalted, spoken from another sphere than that of the professional politician. [Holyoake concluded,] By his protest against the subjection of women he brought half the human race into the province of politics and progress. They have not all appeared there as yet but they are on the way.[39]

NOTES

1. *Speeches of the Right Honorable Charles James Fox in the House of Commons* (London: Longmans, 1815).

2. Some property-owning women had been exercising voting privileges and holding public office before the Reform Bill of 1832 excluded them.

3. Dorothy Thompson, *The Early Chartists* (Columbia: University of South Carolina Press, 1971), pp. 116-25.

4. See Arthur Aspinall, *Lord Brougham and The Whig Party* (Manchester: University of Manchester Press, 1927). See also *The Life and Times of Henry Lord Brougham Written by Himself* (Edinburgh: William Blackwood & Sons, 1861).

5. Michael St. John Packe, *The Life of John Stuart Mill*, (New York: Capricorn, 1970), p. 214.

6. Ibid., p. 448.

7. All quotes from John Stuart Mill, *Suffrage for Women*. Reprint of the speech Mill made in Parliament, May 20, 1867. (London: National Society for Women's Suffrage, 1869).

8. St. John Packe, *Mill*, p. 493.

9. Charles Kingsley, *Women and Politics*. Reprint of review of "Subjection of Women" in *McMillan's Magazine* (London National Suffrage Society, 1869). In Museum of London.

10. St. John Packe, *Mill*, p. 493.

11. Frederick Douglass, *Life and Times of Frederick Douglass* (New York: Pathway Press, 1941), p. 521-23.

12. Elizabeth Cady Stanton, Susan B. Anthony, and Matilda Joslyn Cage, eds. *History of Woman Suffrage*, 6 vols. (Rochester: Fowler & Wells, 1881),vol. 1.

13. Thomas Wentworth Higginson, *Woman and Her Wishes*. Women's Rights Tracts, no. 4. (Rochester: Steam Press of Curtis Butt & Co., 1851). pp. 6–11.

14. *Proceedings of the Sixth National Women's Rights Convention*. Held in New York City, 1856.

15. Thomas Wentworth Higginson, *Women and Men* (New York: Harper & Bros., 1888), ch. 51.

16. Roger Fulford, *Votes for Women: The Story of A Struggle* (London: Faber and Faber, 1947), p. 61.

17. Ibid., p. 63.

18. All quotes from John Stuart Mill, *The Subjection of Women* (Philadelphia: J. B. Lippincott, 1869), pp. 56, 38, 36, 138, 163.

19. George Trevelyan, *The Life of John Bright* (New York: Houghton Mifflin, 1914), p. 380. See also Herman Ausubel, *John Bright: Victorian Reformer* (New York: John Wiley & Sons, 1966).

20. Fulford, *Votes for Women*, p. 83.

21. Ibid., p. 48.

22. Ibid., p. 88.

23. Constance Rover, *Women's Suffrage and Party Politics in Britain, 1866-1915* (London: Routledge and Kegan Paul, 1967), p. 105.

24. The Primrose League (1885) was the women's adjunct to the Conservative party; the Women's Liberal Federation and Women's Liberal Unionist Association (1886) canvassed for the Liberal party.

25. Charles Dilke, *Woman's Suffrage Speeches* (London: Swann, Sonnensbein & Co., 1885), p. 14.

26. Leslie Stephen, *Life of Henry Fawcett* (London: Smith, Elder & Co., 1888), p. 102.

27. Millicent Fawcett, *What I Remember* (New York: G. P. Putnam's Sons, 1925), p. 61.

28. Henry Fawcett, *Speeches* (London: Macmillan & Co., 1873), p. 160.

29. G. P. Gooch, *Life of Lord Courtney* (London: Macmillan and Co., 1920), p. 138.

30. Roy Jenkins, *Victorian Scandal* (New York: Chilmark Press, 1965), p. 176.

31. Stephen Gwynn, *The Life of the Rt. Honorable Sir Charles Dilke* (New York: The Macmillan Co., 1917), p. 8.

32. *Women's Suffrage Journal*, December, 1884.

33. Charles Dilke, *Women's Suffrage and Electoral Reform* (People's Suffrage Federation League, 1910).

34. Gooch, *Life of Courtney*, p. 240.

35. See George Dangerfield, *The Strange Death of Liberal England* (1935; reprinted ed., New York: Capricorn, 1961).

36. Rover, *Party Politics*, pp. 118-20.

37. Duncan Crow, *The Victorian Woman* (London: George Allen & Unwin Ltd., 1971), pp. 190-98.

38. Charles Anthony, Jr., *Social and Political Dependence of Women* (New York: Longmans, Green, & Co., 1880).

39. George Jacob Holyoake, *Bygones Worth Remembering* (London: T. Fisher Unwin, 1906), pp. 273-74.

"VOTES FOR WOMEN *NOW!*": THE MALE SUFFRAGETTES 7

The Women's Social and Political Union (WSPU) was founded on October 10, 1903, its chief demand being "Votes for Women Now!" with an emphasis on the *now*. It was an explicit challenge to the NUWSS constitutionalists who, it was felt, had had their chance to apply the methods of rational persuasion and education, and muffed it. Emmeline Parnhurst, the leader of the WSPU, expressed the distinction between her organization and the National Union of Women's Suffrage Societies (led by Millicent Fawcett), saying, "We shall work not by means of any outworn missionary methods but by political action."[1] One might add that the differences between Millicent Fawcett and Emmeline Pankhurst exemplified the differences between Henry Fawcett, an orthodox nineteenth-century liberal with a strong belief in individualism and a distrust of intrusive government, and Richard Pankhurst, a committed socialist and one of the founders of the Labour party, who believed that a democratically elected government would eradicate the injustices endemic to the capitalist system.

Emmeline Pankhurst derived both her socialism, which was short-lived, and her feminism, which became the driving passion of her life, from her husband, Richard Pankhurst. Emmeline Pankhurst was born Emmeline Goulden in Manchester. She was one of ten children in an upper-middle-class family, where Robert Goulden, the father, was a fervent Liberal. The current events of the 1860s, such as the American Civil War, the national liberation revolts in Italy, and the Irish Fenian uprising of 1867, gave Goulden the opportunity to inculcate his children with his own strong antislavery sentiments and his sympathy for national liberation movements. Manchester was a major center of liberal and radical causes, one of which was feminism. It was there that the coordinated drive for suffrage undertaken by J. S. Mill in 1867 was launched. One of the founders of the committee, which eventually became a national suffrage society, was Richard Marsden Pankhurst. By the time Emmeline Goulden attended her first meeting of the suffrage organization at the age of fourteen, Richard Pankhurst had a long career of service on behalf of unpopular causes—feminism among them—behind him. Pankhurst (1838-1898) derived from a

Plate 13. Richard Marsden Pankhurst, architect of militant feminism. Used with the permission of the International Instituut voor Sociale Geschiedenis, Amsterdam.

Plate 14. Keir Hardie, first leader of the Labour party, from a campaign poster, 1895.

Plate 15. Frederick Pethick-Lawrence, at the time of his trial, 1912. Photograph from Pethick Lawrence: A Portrait by Vera Brittain, Allen & Unwin, 1963. Used with the permission of the publisher.

middle-class, nonconformist family and had already received his law degree from the University of London in 1858, the year Emmeline Goulden was born. His first interest was in better educational opportunities for working people. He initiated evening classes for the poor at Owens College, and donated his services as an instructor at the college. He was an original member of the National Association for the Promotion of Social Science which had elected Lord Brougham as its president, and which was the breeding ground for various reform movements, including that for female emancipation.

When Pankhurst was called to the bar in 1867, he immediately began using his legal skills on behalf of women's voting rights. Feminists believed that there was a loophole in the Reform Bill of 1867 which might enable women to vote even though the Mill amendment had not passed. Women had been excluded from the franchise in 1832; but in 1850 the Brougham Act made it clear that the word *man* is a generic term, such as *mankind*, which also includes women, and that future legislation which specified males and excluded women must use the term *male person*. Since that term was not used in the Reform Bill of 1867, Pankhurst seized on this slim reed, writing an article for *The Fortnightly* suggesting that women, indeed, had the right to vote, and urging female householders who would have been enfranchised had the Mill Woman Suffrage Amendment passed to register and vote. During the general election of 1868, over 5,000 women in Manchester did so. When women were challenged, it was Pankhurst who argued the case known as *Chorlton* v. *Lings* before the court of common pleas. The judge who decided that women did not have the right to vote unless it was expressly granted to them by Parliament at least cleared the air and let the suffragists know the formidable nature of the task that lay ahead.

In 1870, Richard Pankhurst drafted the bill for the enfranchisement of women which was introduced by Jacob Bright. It stipulated that gender be eliminated as a criterion for the granting of voting rights. Pankhurst was instrumental in drafting both the Married Women's Property Act of 1870, which was watered down, and the stronger act of 1882, which passed, allowing married women to retain their personal earnings. When married women won the right to vote in municipal elections in 1888, again it was Richard Pankhurst who supplied the legal know-how by helping to frame the law.

Though he had vowed to remain a bachelor because of his commitment to reform, Pankhurst refused Emmeline Goulden's offer of a free love union and married her in 1879. Robert Goulden was an admirer of Pankhurst, who was known in Manchester as "the Doctor," and introductions were made after the Goulden family heard Pankhurst address a large audience, criticizing Disraeli's jingoism and demanding that the Russo-Turkish crisis of 1878 be resolved peacefully. Pankhurst and Emmeline Goulden fell in love at first sight and married despite her father's objections. While he respected Pankhurst for using large portions of his barrister's fees to finance his reform activities, Robert Goulden did not fancy this sort of altruism in a son-in-law. The gap in their ages insured that Emmeline Pankhurst would regard her husband as teacher as well as husband, and she quickly entered his radical world. Upon their marriage, she was immediately drafted for the Married Women's Property Act committee. Pankhurst also mapped out a reading program for her.

In the 1870s and '80s Pankhurst's radicalism comprised an amalgam of causes that put him on the extreme left of the political spectrum. His avid republicanism and his admitted atheism put him at odds with the Liberal establishment and resulted in his being defeated all three times he ran for Parliament. His first attempt was made in 1883, on a platform of new "liberal" principles which he himself formulated, and which were latter day applications of Owenite socialist and Chartist ideas. These included abolition of the monarchy and the House of Lords; adult suffrage for both sexes; payment of a salary to members of Parliament and other public officials; disestablishment of the Anglican Church and removal of all religious restrictions; free compulsory secular education; nationalization of privately owned land; transfer to Parliament of the power to make peace and war; a proviso for an international tribunal which was to lead a united nations commonwealth; drastic cuts in military and naval armaments; and Home Rule for Ireland.

Pankhurst's candidacy aroused a great deal of excitement; it was hampered not only by the opposition of the Liberal party newspapers, but also by his own integrity, which prevented him from spending more on the campaign than the new Corrupt Practices Act allowed, even though the act was not yet in force. His opponent did not harbor such a nice sense of propriety. He had plenty of money to distribute handbills calling Pankhurst an "atheistic corrupter of morals." When Pankhurst brought suit against the man, the judge in effect asked the jury to find for the defendant, and against Pankhurst.

His second attempt in 1885 was impugned because he allegedly boasted about his atheism, but, more significantly, the Irish party did not support him even though he was the first candidate to come out for Home Rule in Ireland. The Irish, under their parliamentary leader, Charles Stewart Parnell, had devised a tactic for bringing the issue of Home Rule to the attention of the public by opposing all the candidates of the "ins," whatever their particular position on the Irish question, as a means of showing their muscle and winning support from the "outs." Within Parliament, their tactic was to support no legislation, no matter how commendable, without first making a deal with the sponsoring party for support of Irish Home Rule. Pankhurst lost the election; but he assured his wife, when she inveighed against the duplicity of the Irish, that their policy was politically sound. It constituted the new politics of disruption, which Emmeline Pankhurst herself was to adopt when she became a militant on the women's suffrage issue.

By the time Pankhurst made his third try for Parliament in 1895, he had abandoned his Liberal party ties altogether and stood as a candidate for the fledgling Labour party, which he had helped to found. He lost when the Liberal party candidate from the district refused to stand aside. The Labour party could not match the campaign funds available to the Liberal candidate.

The list of organizations Pankhurst helped start or with which he was associated reveals him to have been a restless soul constantly seeking new avenues to express his radical idealism. He was a member of the National Association for the Promotion of Social Sciences; the Royal Statistical Society; the Society for the Reform of Codification of the Law; the Manchester Chamber of Commerce; and the Committee of the Union of Lancashire and Cheshire Mechanics' Institutes. He was elected a governor of Owen's College, later Manchester University.

With regard to women's rights, he stood for adult suffrage, no more and no less. He was appalled by the timidity of the suffragists who, under Lydia Becker, were willing to compromise to the point of adopting Conservative demands that married women should be completely excluded from the suffrage. This concession gave new legitimacy to the concept of couverture just when Pankhurst was winning victories for the rights of married women to control their own property and to gain custody of their children in case of divorce. Pioneers of women's suffrage such as Jacob Bright and Pankhurst insisted that the clause discriminating against married women be eliminated and, when overruled by the executive committee of the National Suffrage Society, formed their alternative organization, the Women's Franchise League, in 1889. The Franchise League wanted an end to sex discrimination in all areas, and they were willing to use the direct method of public demonstrations to secure publicity and exert pressure. After one meeting of the Franchise League which took place in the Pankhurst home in 1890, Pankhurst, who had forcefully reiterated the standard women's suffrage pitch about the stupidity and cruelty of denying women their political rights and thus stultifying half the population, was exasperated enough to exclaim to his wife, "Why don't you force us to give you the vote? Why don't you scratch our eyes out?" It was a *cri de coeur* that later found an echo in Emmeline Pankhurst's own consciousness.

It was Richard Pankhurst who made women's rights an integral part of the Labour party platform. Pankhurst's Manchester origins, together with his given names, Richard Marsden—those of a revolutionary Chartist—almost predestined him for socialism. His early struggles for education for the working classes were followed by support of trade unions and their right to strike. The Pankhursts were early members of the Fabian Society, and they would have joined the Marxist Social Democratic Federation as well were not H. M. Hyndman's dogmatic antifeminism unacceptable to them. It would be safe to say that Richard Pankhurst was also put off by the authoritarian tendencies evinced by the Marxists. He believed firmly in democracy as the essential prerequisite for socialism. Even the Fabians, under their pivotal figures, Sidney and Beatrice Webb, exhibited a middle-class elitism that, coupled with their antifeminism, drove Pankhurst to make common cause with the radical union leaders who wanted to form a new party to represent labor's interests in Parliament. A close and fruitful relationship with Keir Hardie, first leader of the Labour party, was the result. The Pankhursts met Hardie while attending the International Socialist Conference in 1888. An immediate bond developed between Pankhurst, who was looking for new radical paths to break, and Hardie, who had succeeded in organizing the Scottish miners and who was intensely disappointed with the alliance older union leaders of the skilled trades had made with the Liberal party. From the Lib-Lab alliance, the unskilled workers of the "new unionism" which Hardie represented, and which included many women, reaped no benefits at all. Hardie's determination to bring the new unions' influence to bear in Parliament was reenforced with his own election as a Labour candidate in 1892. He formed the Labour Representation Committee, forerunner of the Independent Labour party, of which Richard Pankhurst was a member. Pankhurst agreed to run as a Labour candidate in 1895; his established reputation as "the Doctor" and his middle-class background gave the party a credibility it did not have with its union base of unskilled workers. When Pankhurst died suddenly in 1898, an effusive outpouring of working-class people turned his funeral into a demonstration of support for his socialist and feminist ideals. He was eulogized as "one of the most beautiful figures of our time who would fill one of the rarest pages of history."[2]

After the death of Richard Pankhurst, the issue of women's rights was as much a test of the principles of the Labour party and of the integrity of its leaders as it was of the dedication of Emmeline Pankhurst. The labor unions which were the underpinning of the Labour party had taken a positive position on women's suffrage in 1884; but Keir Hardie had no illusions about the depth of the workers' commitment to women's rights. The struggle of working women for recognition in unions in many respects paralleled the struggle of middle-class women to gain their rights in Parliament. Women were organizing their own unions because the ones that admitted both men and women had no disposition to fight for equal wages for both sexes, and used the fact that women paid lower dues because of lower earnings as an excuse to keep them out of the leadership positions. Women union organizers like Emma Patterson, secretary of the Women's Trade Union League, often regarded their male colleagues in the unions and the male workers themselves as more implacable opponents than their employers. Fearing competition from women, male union members wanted to keep women off the labor market, even though statistics showed that there were more women than men so that not all women could get married, even if they so desired. The attitude of the male workers and their leaders was succinctly expressed by Henry Broadhurst, a trade unionist elected to Parliament during the period when the Liberals formed the so-called Lib-Lab alliance for the advancement of their mutual interests. Broadhurst maintained, "They [the men] had the future of their country and children to consider, and it was their duty as men and husbands to use their utmost efforts to bring about a condition of things, where their wives would be in their proper sphere at home, instead of being dragged into competition for livelihood against the great and strong men of the world."[3] Such attitudes, supported by the Marxists,[4] filtered down to the unskilled "new unionists" as well. Leaders of the new unionism, such as Keir Hardie and Philip Snowden, did not defend such attitudes but recognized their existence. It was a measure of Snowden's own commitment to feminism that he could admit that men on the whole were hostile to women's rights "from selfish dislike of sharing with women the privileges they had won for themselves. Even working men in arms against their own oppressors liked to feel there was something a little lower than themselves."[5]

Feminist Labour party leaders thus confronted at least the same odds as the Liberal male feminists who had struggled during the nineteenth century for a broader interpretation of woman's sphere. What made Keir Hardie, Philip Snowden, and George Lansbury such convinced and wholehearted advocates of the cause of women's rights was, first of all, the practical consideration that a growing proportion of their constituency were, in fact, women—those who were sweated the most and paid the least in the "dark, satanic mills" in which they worked. Female labor was powerfully concentrated in the textile mills of the Northwest of England and its growing numbers could be denied no longer. The new generation of traitors had also absorbed the earlier Owenite tradition that stressed the importance of the feminization of culture, which would lead to a greater sense of community and to less masculine aggressiveness and individualism, all trends which conformed to their idea of progress. Hardie expressed this vision when he wrote in 1907, "We witness on every hand unchallenged male dominance, arrogant armaments, harsh and unfeeling administration of the law. . . . with the incoming of the mother element into politics this would be gradually changed."[6]

Philip Snowden made the point about future progress, stating, "I support the enfranchisement of women because I believe the active partnership of men and women will raise politics to a higher, holier, and purer atmosphere."[7] Fanning the idealism of these new men was a Christian sense of mission. The chief difference between the twentieth century Labourite feminists and their nineteenth-century Owenite forebears was that the Labourites were not freethinkers. Nor were they optimistic rationalists convinced of the evolutionary inevitability of their goals. Their roots went back to the radical Protestant tradition of the sixteenth century, which saw a future utopia in both social and religious terms. Snowden was a Methodist who thought of socialism as a practical application of the New Testament. Lansbury and Hardie were evangelical Christian Socialists who believed that the socialist millenium might require its share of martyrs.

It was Keir Hardie who assumed the burden of the women's suffrage cause when Richard Pankhurst died. James Keir Hardie (1856-1915), born in Lancashire, was the illegitimate son of Mary Keir. When she married David Hardie, a ship's carpenter, he gave the boy his name. Hardie went to work at seven, and became a miner at the age of ten. He went to night school and learned to read at the age of fifteen. Hardie came from an atheistic background, but was converted to Evangelical Christianity by a Christian Socialist minister who taught the New Testament from a humanistic point of view and emphasized the compassion for the poor explicit in the Sermon on the Mount. His stepfather's alcoholism led to an interest in the temperance movement, where he gained his first experience in public speaking, but his energies were soon diverted into union organizing.

Hardie grew increasingly frustrated with the Lib-Lab alliance as he watched Liberals sworn to support radical principles being co-opted by the Establishment the moment they were elected to Parliament. To assure his radical union constituency that this would not happen to him, he shocked the members of Parliament by wearing his miner's outfit on his first day in that body after his election in 1892. Hardie's knowledge of socialist theory was prodigious because of an early affiliation with Hyndman's Social Democratic Federation. He frequently referred to Engels's theory that women were the first form of private property in the marriage bond, and he averred that capitalism had much to answer for in its exploitation of women. Socialism meant to him that the sexes should meet on terms of freedom and equality: "It is only by recognizing the perfect right of every human being to equal treatment because they are human beings that we can hope for better days for the race."[8]

Hardie encouraged Emmeline Pankhurst to continue her husband's work with the Labour party. The Women's Social and Political Union was originally called the Women's Labour Representation Committee. It was intended as a support group for the Labour party much as the Women's Liberal Federation was an adjunct of the Liberal party, and the Primrose League was one of the Conservative party. Christabel Pankhurst, the eldest Pankhurst daughter, renamed it out of a desire to give the organization a more independent cast in order to attract a broader following. Despite these early intimations that the female Pankhursts' ties to labor were tenuous, Hardie raised three hundred pounds to give the organization its start, and encouraged female union members to give it its full support. Annie Kenney, the most durable of the working-class suffragettes, whose loyalty remained unshakable even when the WSPU sustained various splits and schisms, was thus recruited.[9]

Hardie's intention of putting a woman's suffrage plank in the Labour party platform was all the more complicated because the Labourites who did favor women's suffrage favored adult suffrage, that is, the enfranchisement of all adult males and females. Hardie thought this a noble goal—and the ultimate one—but, ever the realist, thought it absolutely impossible to achieve in 1903, especially with a Conservative government in power.[10] He was convinced that "Votes for Women Now!" was possible only if the Labourites supported the enfranchisement of women on the same basis as that of men, and this still included a property requirement. He argued that all reform, including that of male suffrage, had come slowly, since it had to contend with the "conservative, plodding, timid mind of the average man."[11] Hardie's advocacy of essentially the same bill for which the Liberals had futilely struggled in the nineteenth century made him appear suspiciously bourgeois even to the women in the Labour party, who considered the limited version a "ladies bill" which would give voting rights to middle-class property-owning and conservatively inclined women. Hardie denied that it was a "ladies bill" and noted that the support for voting rights for four categories of women—female lodgers, property owners, householders, and those in service—would add one million working women to the voters' rolls. A powerful speaker, Hardie won endorsement for his women's franchise bill at the Labour party's annual conference in Cardiff in 1904.

During the election campaign in 1905, the WSPU first got the publicity it sought on behalf of women's suffrage. Hardie believed that heckling political candidates and demonstrations in front of Parliament were the kind of direct activism that had been missing from the genteel petitioning of the nineteenth-century suffagists. When Christabel Pankhurst and Annie Kenney questioned Sir Edward Grey at a public meeting about his intentions on women's suffrage, they were arrested for causing a disturbance. Thus the WSPU achieved the limelight and their aggressive tactics earned them the nickname suffragettes to distinguish them from their more decorous sisters in the NUWSS.

The Liberals swept to power in 1905, with Henry Campbell-Bannerman as prime minister. They were committed to wide-ranging reforms which included old age insurance, a minimum wage, health insurance—a veritable war on poverty as David Lloyd George, the president of the Board of Trade in the new cabinet, referred to their program. Labourites were feeling triumphant with good cause, for it was their concerted pressure and their remarkable showing in the election that had forced the Liberal party to the left.[12] Hardie determined to challenge the Liberals to make good on their oft-repeated lip service to the cause of women's suffrage by bringing in a women's suffrage bill. Pointing out that the new Parliament was overwhelmingly on record in favor of the limited suffrage bill, he invoked the spirit of John Stuart Mill in asking Liberals to support it, and noted that the bill he had introduced merely "removes from women the category of idiots, lunatics, and paupers, and recognizes that woman though she be, she is a human being who may be a citizen."[13]

Hardie's parliamentary maneuver to get women enfranchised on the basis of a limited bill met the same fate as all the previous ones which Liberal parliamentarians had introduced in the nineteenth century. It was killed. The pressure on the Liberal government was therefore stepped up to include direct encounters between delegations of women and parliamentary leaders. Thus, in 1906 Hardie led a delegation which included Emmeline Pankhurst, Annie Kenney and Emmeline Pethick-Lawrence to see Campbell-Bannerman in order to demand his support. The prime minister was mildly encouraging and told the women "to keep on pestering,"[14] but he made no commitments; after the disappointing meeting the delegation addressed a crowd of seven thousand people to inform them of their failure and of their determination to fight harder.

Hardie believed that heckling and confrontation would prove effective; but the Pankhursts decided that the stalemate called for the use of the Irish tactic of asking the electorate to vote against all the "ins," no matter what their stand on the relevant issue, as a means of punishing them. When the suffragettes used this tactic in the by-elections of 1907, the Conservatives made gains. Even though they were the beneficiaries, the Conservatives were not moved to any exertions on behalf of women's suffrage; and the Labourites were furious with Emmeline Pankhurst, who was still a member of the Labour party's executive committee, for causing losses in their parliamentary delegation. At the party conference in Belfast in 1907, Hardie found that his close association with the Pankhursts was not considered a point in his favor, and his leadership of the party came under serious challenge. Hardie's dilemma was acute. He was aware that the Pankhursts were turning to the right in their desire for middle- and upper-class support in the form of membership and contributions. Yet the zeal and determination with which they pursued their aims, even though their demonstrations in front of Parliament resulted in the jailing of WSPU members, moved him, and he was mindful that even as the conference was taking place twenty suffragettes were languishing in prison. He asked the conference to support the women's enfranchisement bill, but was overwhelmingly rejected as the Labourites affirmed their support of adult suffrage instead. Their vote had the practical effect of killing any chance for "Votes for Women Now" or in the immediate future, as adult suffrage was considered outrageously radical. Hardie threatened to resign from the party if the resolution was made binding as a matter of party loyalty on Labour M.P.s. Almost overcome with emotion, he told the assembled delegates, "The Party is largely my own child; I cannot part with it lightly or without pain.... if it is necessary for me to separate myself from my life's work, I do so in order to remove the stigma resting upon our wives, mothers, and sisters of being accounted unfit for citizenship."[15] Hardie's stand helped to delineate the left and right wings of the party. Those later identified with the right wing of the Labour party, such as Ramsay MacDonald, refused to entertain any idea of a reversal; but Hardie did succeed in getting approval to allow Labour M.P.s to vote their conscience on the suffrage issue. He also succeeded in squashing a motion to censure Labour party members of the WSPU for dissociating themselves from Labour candidates and, over the opposition of MacDonald, succeeded in getting a resolution congratulating the suffragette prisoners, thus maintaining official Labour party support for the feminist cause.

When Herbert Asquith succeeded Campbell-Bannerman as prime minister in 1908, the suffragettes met as intransigent a foe of women's suffrage as the previous generation had had in William Gladstone. Lacking even nominal support from the Liberal party leadership, the women's suffrage bill was once again reduced to the status of a private member's bill which had even less chance of passage than in the nineteenth century because of tighter party organization. The suffragettes in the WSPU decided to escalate their war with the government by storming Parliament. Individuals would enter and chain themselves to the grill railing of the ladies' gallery in the House of Commons. Calls went out for volunteers to go to prison, as that was the fate of the demonstrators who participated in the "Women's Parliaments." Once in prison, the suffragettes went on hunger strikes as another form of protest. The government, loath to release the starving prisoners, started a policy of forcibly feeding the women. The process entailed holding the prisoners down, forcing their mouths open, inserting a tube into their throats, and pouring some nourishment into the tube.

The tactic of direct confrontation with government power left the male suffragettes in a dilemma. They were opposed to any activity that could lead to violence but felt that, as men, they were in no position to tell the women to desist in a cause which concerned them exclusively and about which they felt so strongly. The tradition of feminism to which they adhered encouraged women to play leadership roles, make their own decisions, and take the risk of making mistakes. For some, the dilemma was deepened since women's militancy subverted their belief that "moral force" would have a special validity for women, who were held to be more pacific than men.

The male suffragettes came to grips with the issue of militance in various ways. For Keir Hardie, who was opposed to the demonstrations, the focus of his support for women's rights shifted to questioning government leaders on why women were being singled out for special abuse for making legitimate demands. He rose in Parliament to protest the extraordinarily long prison sentences they were being given and to demand that they be treated as political prisoners instead of as common criminals. Forcible feeding was considered a species of torture designed especially to humiliate the helpless women. It was indicative of the vast and growing gulf between the outlook of the male feminists and that of the masculine establishment that when Hardie took the floor of Parliament to protest forcible feeding as a "horrible, beastly outrage," M.P.s in the government backbenches roared with laughter. Hardie wrote, "Had I not heard it I could not have believed that a body of gentlemen would have found reason for mirth and applause."[16]

A truce in militancy was called in 1910 when the Liberal government promised to support a conciliation bill as an attempt to accommodate Conservative objections to a Liberal-Labour suffrage bill. A conciliation committee was formed, of which Philip Snowden became the secretary. Snowden (1864-1937) was the son of a Lancashire weaver whose radical inclinations made politics of consuming interest in the family. Philip Snowden's father was one of those enfranchised by the Reform Bill of 1884. Snowden had a moderately good education which was helped along by a small library that his father, who had intellectual interests, kept in the house. He opted for a career in the civil service and, after passing the examinations, worked in the excise department of the Board of Inland Revenue until paralysis from what was probably spinal tuberculosis caused him to be discharged with a small pension. Snowden remained handicapped for the rest of his life but recovered sufficiently to enter local union politics. He had read socialist theorists during his convalescence, and switched from Liberal to Labour after being asked to give a speech on socialism before a local group of Liberals.

Snowden wrote an eloquent letter which was published in the London *Times* about the plight of the weavers in his home district of Cowling. It was an indictment of Imperial Britain, whose rule in the 1890s extended over one-quarter of the earth—due as much to the industriousness of the weavers of Cowling as to the might of the armed services—but where the standard of living was rapidly declining. He noted in his letter that 70 percent of the weavers' wives had to work in factories, and that 90 percent of children over the age of eleven were factory operatives. He cited a report which showed that the 30 percent of wives who were not working would gladly do so, but that many were elderly and had been driven out by younger hands.[17] As a result of Snowden's effort, he was urged to enter national politics as a Labour candidate for Blackburn in 1900. He lost the election, but took over the pamphleteering activities for the Labour party, and ran in subsequent elections until he became one of the twenty-nine-man delegation that the Labour party sent to Parliament in 1906.

Snowden had given little thought to the suffrage question until he met and married Ethel Annikin. She was a schoolteacher, as dedicated a socialist as he was, and a strong women's suffrage supporter. His own commitment was made manifest when he became Keir Hardie's staunch ally in insisting that women's rights be incorporated into the Labour party platform. Snowden believed that feminine influence in politics would in itself be a social reform, and that socialism without women's votes would be unworthy of the name. Both he and Ethel Snowden considered that women spent too much time on "recipes and babies," to the neglect of their social concerns—an attitude which made Snowden the polar opposite of the masculinists, who could not entertain the thought of women in any way neglecting their domestic duties. He proclaimed that he was not appalled by the prospect of the country being led by a woman.[18]

Snowden was opposed to the escalating militancy of the suffragettes, although he maintained that his criticism was always muted when he saw "their tattered faces."[19] He undertook his duties as chairman of the conciliation committee aware that, with the feelings of the suffragettes running so high, the conciliation bill might be a last opportunity to avert violence. What emerged from the conciliation committee was a bill which would have given the national franchise to women who already had the municipal franchise—about one in every thirteen women. Snowden and Hardie were all too aware that it was a compromise of a compromise; but in a House growing increasingly polarized, and with women's suffrage opponents given to dogmatic posturing, it was the best they could get. When Snowden rose to present the bill he said, "I speak from conviction of the truth and justice of the cause which I support. Women have no one in this House of Commons of their own sex to speak on their behalf. I esteem it to be one of the greatest privileges of my life to speak for them here."[20] He freely predicted that if the conciliation bill failed to pass, militancy would increase, and implied that the Commons would have only themselves to blame.

Much to the dismay of the feminists in Parliament, Snowden's prophecy was realized when the bill fell victim to Conservative-Liberal antagonisms. David Lloyd George and Winston Churchill, both members of Asquith's Cabinet, wanted to dissociate their party from a bill which had Conservative support, as long as the Conservatives were gutting their social reform legislation. They discovered that the bill was "undemocratic" in that only female property holders would benefit. Asquith heaped insult upon injury when he refused to consider a revised bill, and shortly thereafter announced a new electoral reform bill in which women would not be included. Hatred for Asquith's betrayal burned brightly among the suffragettes, and militancy resumed with greater intensity.

"Black Friday," on November 18, 1910, saw a massive demonstration in which 120 women were arrested. The temper of the opposition may be gauged from newspaper reports of the incident. *The Daily Sketch* headlined "Suffragists Storm Westminster Again." A subheading read, "Over a Hundred Women Arrested After Deplorable Scuffling Outside the Houses of Parliament." The lead column reporting the event noted, "It was an unending picture of shameful recklessness. Never before have otherwise sensible women gone so far in forgetting their womanhood."[21]

Because of what he considered extraordinary provocation, George Lansbury fully supported the militants' tactics, and he went to extraordinary lengths to demonstrate his support. Lansbury (1859-1940) was the son of a railway time-keeper whose work for the railroads kept the family constantly on the move. Lansbury initially derived his radicalism from his grandmother, a Methodist and a strict Sabbatarian, whose one indulgence on the Lord's day was to buy a political newspaper. Eventually the Lansbury family settled in London's East End, whose denizens, which included a rich variety of anarchists, nihilists, and social revolutionaries, fed his radicalism. Lansbury vividly recalled the election of 1868, which he was taken to see. The candidate his father supported was a Jew, David Salomans. It was the fourth election since a Jew was enabled to sit in Parliament. In the days before the secret ballot, elections were raucous affairs where all the voters had to publicly declare their candidate. His father's support of Salomans was an occasion for anti-Semitic reactions, and Lansbury commented, "How we came back alive, I cannot tell."

At his father's death in 1880, Lansbury and his brother took over the family business, carting coal for a railway company; but times were difficult, and Lansbury decided to take his wife and growing family to Australia to seek better opportunities. When he got to Australia he found that, contrary to the claims of local agents, there were no jobs awaiting them, and he took his family back to England, determined to try to end this kind of fraud. This first effort in public life resulted in the secretary for the colonies providing an emigrant information department. The Marxist H. M. Hyndman completed Lansbury's education in class consciousness. Hyndman, a member of the upper classes, was given to distributing his Marxist leaflets in Hyde Park wearing striped pants, a frock coat, and a top hat. When asked by local working people why he sported such finery on his working-class missions he would deliberately respond, "Because your class are idiots enough to enable people like me to do so."[22] His candor and directness appealed to Lansbury. Hyndman advised Lansbury to enter Liberal party politics and get a thorough training in government because competent people would be needed after the anticipated revolution. Lansbury ran as a Liberal for the Board of Local Guardians, and won; but he left the Liberal party in 1892 to work as a full-time propagandist for the Social Democratic Federation. Lansbury was uncomfortable with the authoritarianism of the Marxists, and began to feel that workers under state socialism would become the slaves of the state as soon as they ceased to be the slaves of capitalist employers. His political odyssey came to an end when he joined the Labour Representation Committee in 1903 after he had become a pacifist and could no longer countenance the violence implicit in Marxism. Lansbury became a Labour M.P. in 1910, dedicated to the principle of independence and dignity for every working man and woman. He entered Parliament at the height of the furor over the conciliation bill. The government's use of violence to deal with the protesting women so enraged Lansbury that it eclipsed his pacifism and his socialism and filled his whole horizon. He justified his support of the militants by saying, "When you are tricked and deceived, when Parliament betrays its sacred trust, you have a right to rebel. Let all of us stand shoulder to shoulder with the militant women."[23]

For Lansbury, the die was cast when he rose in Parliament in 1912 to demand release of the suffragette prisoners. In their frustration at the failure of the third conciliation bill, the suffragettes had gone on a window-smashing spree. Emmeline Pankhurst was sent to prison and, along with other suffragettes, was subjected to forcible feedings when she went on a hunger strike. When Lansbury was told by an impassive Asquith that the prisoners were free to leave the moment they agreed to abandon their militancy, a distraught Lansbury left his seat to confront Asquith directly and, waving his fist in his face, shouted, "You know they cannot. You know it is dishonorable to ask them. You disgrace yourself. You are beneath contempt. You drive women mad and ask them to walk out. You will go down in history as the man who tortured innocent women." Then addressing the amused Conservative backbenchers as he left, he sputtered, "You ought to be driven out of public life. These women are showing you what principle is. You should honor them instead of laughing at them."[24]

In his autobiography, Lansbury noted laconically, "I left the House of Commons in October, 1912 because of disagreement on the subject of the franchise."[25] Lansbury had wanted to go along with Emmeline Pankhurst's demand that the supporters of women's rights in Parliament vote against every government measure—even much needed reforms that they were sworn to support, such as Irish Home Rule and a national health insurance plan—until a women's suffrage bill was passed. This went considerably beyond the policy favored by Keir Hardie and Philip Snowden, of opposing only new electoral reforms that did not include women. Lansbury was rebuked by members of his own party for his support of the militants' position and he resigned his seat. The Labour party's union constituency did not appreciate Lansbury's putting feminism before socialism at a time of economic crisis, when his presence in Parliament was sorely needed. Because wages were not keeping up with rising prices, the workers, too, were becoming militant. In 1910, a strike of Lancashire cotton workers idled 120,000. It was followed by a sympathy walkout of 30,000 miners. A seaman's strike in Liverpool in 1911 led to rioting with two men being killed. Nevertheless, Lansbury made women's suffrage his first priority.

After his resignation from Parliament, Lansbury ran as a women's suffrage candidate in order to test voter attitudes on the issue. Without any party funds, with only the suffragettes canvassing for him in the working class East End of London where he ran, Lansbury lost the election by seven hundred votes.

During his campaign, Lansbury told the voters:

I want especially that you should join me in a supreme effort to raise the question of womanhood to the highest position. The women of our country live hard, laborious lives. I have grown to understand what poverty and destitution mean to women. We men have wanted to use votes to improve our social condition. I want our wives, sisters, and mothers to join us in that fight. The women's struggle is part of the struggle for the emancipation of humanity all over the world.

Referring to his resignation from Parliament to campaign for women's rights, he said:

Some will tell you that I have acted stupidly. I ask you to believe that I am activated by one purpose only, and that is that if I am your representative, I want to faithfully represent your views and that I believe the policy which I urge you to follow is the only policy in these days worth fighting for. Many men will come to you and talk of party and principle but believe me we have been caucus ridden and party ridden for too long. The House of Commons is dragooned and controlled by a small handful of men. To vote according to one's conscience is to be untrue to party. I want you to send me to the Commons to vote for those principles which you have supported, irrespective of government and party. [He exhorted the electorate,] Come on and help me in what will be one of the historic fights of our time and that will give us the satisfaction of knowing that we have done our part toward raising and ennobling womanhood and motherhood in our land.[26]

His loss was considered a major defeat for the feminists, who had thrown their all into his campaign, but Lansbury put it in a different perspective:

To talk about one election being lost [he said,] and to talk about one man's defeat at the polls being a defeat for the suffrage movement is to talk arrant nonsense. This movement is bigger and more important than all the parties in the country. The East End working people now know what is at stake—that votes for women and the poverty question are one.[27]

Lansbury was proud that his campaign was one in which working men and women had participated and gained the political experience necessary for future battles. Nor was Lansbury's support of the women ever constrained by considerations of personal safety. At one point he devised a ruse that enabled Sylvia Pankhurst to speak at an East End suffragette meeting. Destined for arrest as soon as she left her quarters for the meeting, Lansbury's daughter, Rose, pretended to be Sylvia Pankhurst; she was arrested, enabling the real Sylvia to speak as scheduled at the meeting.[28]

Lansbury's support of the suffragettes' militancy eventually led to his own arrest. While Emmeline Pankhurst was in prison in April, 1913, he, in effect, incited to riot. In his autobiography, he confessed:

I appealed to the women to close up the ranks and for every one in prison another should take her place; that if they burned and destroyed they were only doing what others had done before; no life had yet been taken—on behalf of the suffragettes no life would be taken; but human life and human happiness were much more valuable than all the property in the world.[29]

Lansbury was served with a summons, went to Pentonville Prison, and went on a hunger strike for four days before being released under the Cat and Mouse Act. Lansbury believed that, through his actions, he was following the traditions of England's Protestant martyrs. This is revealed by his response to a prison chaplain who remonstrated with him for hunger striking, thus "defiling the temple of the body." Lansbury told him, "You are able to come here and insult me because two men named Latimer and Ridley allowed the temple of the Holy Christ to be destroyed by fire because they would not submit to the laws of the land just as I will not submit to the laws of the land as to what I shall say in regard to political agitation."

Lansbury's stand on the basis of conscience kept the women's suffrage issue in the forefront of Labour politics. His extreme position made the Hardie-Snowden plan—that of putting Labour on record as being opposed to any electoral reform which did not include women—seem moderate in comparison. At the Labour party executive committee meeting in 1913, Philip Snowden passionately argued for this proposal. When the miners protested, he turned on them and accused them of being willing "to steal more votes for men at the expense of women."[30] The result was the passage of a joint Hardie-Snowden resolution instructing Labour members of Parliament to vote against any electoral reform legislation that did not include voting rights for women.

In truth, treason to the masculine cause was a growing phenomenon in the years before World War I. It was linked not only with democratic socialism, but with pacifism and the New Humanism, a movement on the part of intellectuals to revitalize a society they thought decadent. In the tension-ridden years of the early twentieth century, socialism, pacifism, and feminism were part of the same equation for a growing number of idealists. Perhaps the prototype of this genre was Frederick Pethick-Lawrence. Pethick-Lawrence (1871-1961), born Frederick William Lawrence, was a privileged scion of a Liberal nonconformist (Unitarian) family. At Cambridge, he showed aptitude in a variety of fields and found it difficult to choose between a career as a mathematics professor, one as an economist, and one in government service. In his economics studies his mentor was Alfred Marshall, who influenced him deeply. As Pethick-Lawrence later put it, "He really cared passionately that a knowledge of economics should be applied to bettering the lot of humanity and, in particular, the underdog."[31] Lawrence studied law as the surest path to a career in public service, and joined the Labour party (breaking with his family's Liberal tradition), seeing it as the more effective vehicle for the attainment of social reform. He served an apprenticeship in social service by working as treasurer in a settlement house in Camden. There he became familiar with the problems of the poor and came into contact with such stalwarts of the socialist movement as Beatrice Webb, Keir Hardie, and Ben Tillett. The Boer War, which broke out in 1899, made Lawrence a pacifist. The issues raised by the war caused divisions in all the political parties in England. Lawrence's conversion was similar to that of many pacifists, who initially supported the war with South Africa in the interest of progress which was commonly considered to be synonomous with the extension of British power. Olive Schreiner, a native South African, convinced Lawrence that the Boer War was a brutal undertaking by British imperialists, resulting in untold anguish for a helpless population which wanted only to maintain its independence, even if that independence was unprogressive by British standards. A personal trip to South Africa confirmed Schreiner's reports for Lawrence; he became an advocate of peace. In order to further the cause of pacifism and socialism, he bought a defunct newspaper, *The Echo*, and turned it into an organ for the advancement of his socialism and his pacifism.

While working at Mansfield Settlement House, Frederick Lawrence met Emmeline Pethick, and they became lifelong partners in their commitment to each other and to the social causes in which they believed. Emmeline Pethick was a "new woman" whose financial independence allowed her to consider a career in social service as an alternative to the traditional one of wife and mother. Lawrence had to use all his considerable powers of persuasion to convince her to marry him. His determination that the marriage should be in all respects a partnership of two equals led him to ask his family for permission to add her name to his. Thus Frederick William Lawrence became Frederick Pethick-Lawrence. Pethick-Lawrence did not think that marriage should inhibit his wife's career. He provided her with her own apartment so that she could continue to pursue her interests, free of the domestic inbroglios that marriage, at least for women, involved.

Keir Hardie introduced the Pethick-Lawrences to Emmeline Pankhurst shortly after the formation of the WSPU. The organization showed promise of revitalizing the issue of women's suffrage in a socialist context. But the Pankhursts had no money, since Emmeline and Christabel's insistence on independence from the Labour party precluded the use of party funds. Emmeline Pankhurst also had no experience at organizing. At the time the Pethick-Lawrences were encouraged to aid the Pankhursts, the WSPU lacked even a headquarters and such rudimentary essentials as letter paper and paper clips. Emmeline Pethick-Lawrence became the treasurer of the WSPU, and Pethick-Lawrence provided a headquarters in the building where he and his wife shared an apartment. He also financed the organization's operation through his personal fortune. Pethick-Lawrence remained on the periphery of the WSPU until the suffragettes began to go to prison as a result of their militancy. He had watched the suffragist movement in the nineteenth century sputter and die because of female indifference.[32] But the suffragettes' willingness to make extreme sacrifices for their cause aroused his admiration and, as a consequence, his full-time commitment.

It was the Pethick-Lawrence family fortune which provided the bail money for the release of the suffragettes. Pethick-Lawrence also instructed volunteers on how to defend the women prisoners, and was affectionately dubbed "The Godfather." Pethick-Lawrence's strategy was to keep the suffragettes highly visible through intensive leafletting, public meetings, and large parades, rather than through demonstrations, which led to arrests. He staged these parades like a master showman, providing the full complement of banners, floats, and armbands, as well as marchers.

Pethick-Lawrence committed himself more profoundly at a time when other supporters of the suffragettes were becoming deeply disillusioned with the Pankhursts. In 1907, Emmeline Pankhurst ended democratic participation in the WSPU, giving members the choice of either submitting to her personal authority or leaving. This stand brought about an exodus of women, led by Charlotte Despard, who formed their own organization, the Women's Freedom League, along democratic lines.[33] The defectors could not countenance the paradoxical situation whereby Pankhurst was demanding democratic rights for women from the government while curtailing them in the WSPU.

Pethick-Lawrence provided the WSPU with an extremely potent propaganda device by financing a weekly newspaper called *Votes for Women*. *Votes for Women* was founded in October, 1907, and was dedicated "to the brave women who today are fighting for freedom: to the noble women who all down the ages kept the flag flying and looked forward to this day without seeing it; to all women all over the world, of whatever race or creed or calling whether they be with us or against us in this fight."[34] The paper's original purpose was to supply information on the activities of the WSPU and to act, in essence, as its house organ. It had a characteristic format which was maintained until the publication of the last issue in February, 1918. The cover carried a cartoon, usually one exposing the hypocrisy of Liberal leaders' attitudes to women's suffrage. There was a rundown on "The Outlook," sometimes gloomy, sometimes optimistic, depending on the latest dispatches from Parliament; bulletins on meetings or demonstrations that were scheduled; and reports on meetings that had already taken place. Most of the paper was given over to background articles, written either by one of the Pankhursts or by Emmeline Pethick-Lawrence, who, with her husband, appeared on the masthead as coeditor. By 1909, *Votes for Women* had a circulation of fifty thousand and was making profits from advertising revenues.[35]

In 1910, Pethick-Lawrence published several works of his own to help turn the tide in favor of the conciliation bill. He turned his background in law and economics to educational purposes and revealed a flair for making suffrage meaningful and dynamic to every level of society. In *Women's Votes and Wages*, he explained how getting the vote would affect working women's wages in the most direct way. Noting that women earn only a fraction of the wages men earn, while being expected to perform domestic functions for nothing, he insisted that women's votes could affect both the demand for, and the supply of, their labor, which according to classical economists was the reason for their low wages. Demand for women's labor would be dramatically increased if a law were passed requiring children to stay in school even one extra year, till the age of fifteen, keeping them off the labor market for that extra year. A law forcing a husband to support his wife and prohibiting a "bad husband" from spending the whole of his wages on himself, as he then had a right to do, would, in effect, remunerate women for their domestic services, and keep at least some married women out of the work force. According to the prevailing economic wisdom, when the supply of labor went down, wages should rise, thus benefitting the single women who had to work to subsist. Pethick-Lawrence noted that the government was a major employer in an increasingly bureaucratic state. Women were getting neither those jobs controlled directly by the government—such as jobs for factory inspectors— nor those in government-controlled industries, because they did not have the vote and could be safely ignored. The vote, he insisted, could remedy this situation, and might eventually lead to the establishment of new hiring policies for the private sector as well.[36]

Pethick-Lawrence perceived that in the bureaucratic state, which was totally impersonal, the ability to influence legislation was all-important if any semblance of balance was to be maintained between competing interest groups. In *Is English Law Unjust to Women?*, he painted a grisly picture of women's status under the law to emphasize the need for change, which could only come with the vote. Pethick-Lawrence showed how a woman was exploited by the law at every stage of life, starting in girlhood when she could easily be victimized by white slavers. As an unmarried woman, she was barred from well-paid professions and was paid less than men in the jobs that were open to her. As a married woman, her relationship with her husband could not be one of equality because the laws favored his interests. As a mother she had no rights over her own children; and as a widow she might find herself destitute because the law did not stipulate that a husband had to leave any of his property to his wife.[37]

At the height of the struggle for the conciliation bill in 1910, Pethick-Lawrence wrote *Women's Fight for the Vote*, in which he cogently and incisively summed up the arguments for the enfranchisement of women to yet another generation. He noted that voting was a symbolic act of citizenship. Women desired the vote "firstly in order that they may play their part in the life of the nation and introduce their point of view and their unique capacities which excel in the care of all living things," into the government of the country; and secondly, in order that the interests of women might be safeguarded.

In the tradition of the defense of others, Pethick-Lawrence pointed to the patent injustices and to the double standard built into the law whereby the single woman is treated differently from the single man, and whereby she is hampered at every turn when she tries to maintain her independence. Thus, her only alternative is to get married where her status is still one of total subservience to her husband, "bad man" though he might be.

In view of the fact that an antisuffragist society had been founded in 1909 which boasted a petition signed by 250,000 individuals, Pethick-Lawrence felt compelled to answer their arguments. Most of the antis' arguments were not new. They continued to insist that the majority of women did not want the vote. Pethick-Lawrence questioned their premise, pointing out that by 1910 more women had signed petitions for the suffrage than for any other cause in history; but he also insisted that, if the cause were just, the opinion of the majority had no bearing whatsoever on the issue. The "separate spheres" argument was still very potent, but losing its sting. When the masculinists claimed that politics is a male world and that women could enter it only at risk to the adequate performance of their duties as wives and mothers, feminists could now point out that in the various areas where women already had the vote—for instance, in Australia, New Zealand, the Isle of Man, and several of the United States—civilization had survived and women were able to perform their civic responsibilities without precipitating domestic havoc.

The foregoing arguments, and the argument that females who expressed political concerns did so at the risk of losing their femininity, were by 1910 repeated almost by rote. Several generations of activist women, as Pethick-Lawrence could attest, had not diminished their attractions by their commitment to social concerns. Indeed, for philogynists and traitors to masculinity such as Pethick-Lawrence himself, their activism had heightened their allure. One argument resurfaced to confirm the male feminists in their longstanding belief that masculinity condoned and entailed naked aggression and exploitation as means of perpetuating itself. In the early twentieth century, the most potent masculinist argument was made by those who identified themselves with imperialism and England's global dominance. With growing competition from Germany and Russia, the imperialists increasingly advocated the use of physical force to protect England's interests, whether in Ireland or India, and they applied this logic to opposing women's rights as well. Stated with classic simplicity by A. V. Dicey, and supported with fervor by Lords Curzon and Cromer, the argument against women's rights rested on the need to preserve the physical force by which males had always maintained their dominance over the weak. It can be accounted another sign of the times that Dicey argued not only that government rested on physical force, but that the integrity of the British Empire—then being threatened by nationalist movements in Ireland, India, and elsewhere—must also be maintained by physical force. Masculinists could now regard their retreat from democracy as their patriotic duty, since Dicey insisted that preservation of national greatness frequently involved denying human rights. It must be admitted that he had the Irish, who were clamoring for Home Rule, foremost in mind, but the argument was equally viable against women. The unfavorable character traits which those who opposed Irish independence found in the Irish, and which they used to justify their stand against Home Rule for Ireland, were also discovered in women, "who lacked active courage; firmness of judgement; self-control; steadiness of conduct; a certain sense of justice that was maintained even in the heat of party conflict by an Englishman even of ordinary type."[38] Thus, the most learned woman could not measure up even to an illiterate man since she could not fight for her country; and male chauvinism attained a new respectability, presented in the guise of concern for national security. In asserting on behalf of women's rights that government rested on intelligence rather than force, feminists like Pethick-Lawrence were also establishing their credentials as peace advocates in the tumultuous atmosphere of the years preceding World War I.

Despite misgivings born of his pacifism, Pethick-Lawrence supported the suffragettes' militancy. He took the stand characteristic of the feminist pacifists: that resigning oneself to the brutality of the all-masculine government was too high a price to pay for peace, since it meant forfeiting one's dignity and self-respect. He maintained that before the advent of the WSPU, suffrage had been a dead issue, and he stated, "The fact was that the day for peaceful agitation was past; politicians had turned a deaf ear to the claims of justice; they had to be forced to listen by very different means." He went even further when he avowed that "submission was not inherently beautiful—it was generally cowardly and morally wrong" and women particularly had been for too long led astray by this doctrine. Militancy was a way for women to become aware of stern realities, and it put the women's movement in the mainstream of an honorable revolutionary tradition which gained for Englishmen such basic rights as those included in Magna Carta and the Bill of Rights.[39] The perception that women's historical submissiveness had merely incurred martyrdom therefore defined the limits of pre-World War I pacifism.

In 1912, the Pethick-Lawrences and Emmeline Pankhurst were put on trial for going beyond militancy, to violence. Emmeline Pankhurst, in the face of ever greater hostility on the part of the Liberal government, began to think in terms of sedition—destruction of property—to achieve the goal of women's suffrage, since demonstrations had failed. As the third conciliation bill came to the floor of Parliament and was defeated, the suffragettes included smashing of windows in their tactics. Both Pethick-Lawrences and Emmeline Pankhurst were arrested, subjected to forcible feeding, and brought to trial. Pethick-Lawrence conducted his own defense and used the trial as a means of conveying to the public the intensity of the suffragettes' commitment. Before the trial began, Pethick-Lawrence wrote to his wife, "We are to stand where the great and noble have stood before us all down the ages. We are to be linked with those who have won the everlasting homage of the whole human race. If next week you and I were to be crowned King and Queen in the presence of an adulating people, how paltry would be the honor in comparison."[40]

During the trial, Pethick-Lawrence summed up what he considered to be man's burden in the women's struggle, which included, an empathetic understanding of women's feelings and their historical validity. In making common cause with the women, an unrepentant Pethick-Lawrence addressed the court:

I am a man, and I cannot take part in this women's agitation myself, because I am a man; but I intend...to stand by the women who are fighting in this agitation. Knowing what methods have succeeded in history, I am not going to say that these methods have been a mistake. I say that because I think in the first place it is not merely a woman's battle, it is not merely a battle for women—I think it is a battle for the good of the people of this country, a battle waged by one half of the community whose deeds are valuable to the other part of the country. And when I see other men standing out against this agitation, then I am more determined to stand in with it; and I feel this further, that but for some of those men who have stood in with this agitation there might be a danger of this agitation becoming a sex war. I think a battle of women against men is an ugly thing—a thing to be deplored, and I say it is because of the men who have shared in the battle that a sex war has been prevented.

[He continued,] I say that children are dying because women's points of view are not understood, and I say: "How long are women to have no say in the government of the country?" I say: "How much longer is it to go on?" You cannot say to the women: "You are not to go out to throw stones. You should have gone out and had your bodies broken, your persons assaulted, had yourselves arrested for doing nothing at all." I say to you that you and I as men who have not got to face these things have not a right to say that to women.

Pethick-Lawrence concluded by quoting William Gladstone on the uses of violence. Since Gladstone was an opponent of women's rights, this served to highlight the double standard that the antis were employing with respect to violence. Pethick-Lawrence quoting Gladstone:

But while I eschew violence, I cannot, I will not adopt that effeminate method of speech which is to hide from the people of this country the cheering fact that they may derive some encouragement from the recollection of former struggles, the recollection of the great qualities of their forefathers, and from the consciousness that they possess that still. Sir, I am sorry to say that if no consideration had ever been addressed in political crises to the people in this country except to remember to hate violence and love order and exercise patience, the liberties of this country would never have been obtained.[41]

Pethick-Lawrence was found guilty. Moreover, he was ordered to pay all the court costs, and when the damages to the shopkeepers whose windows were broken were assessed, Pethick-Lawrence was ordered to pay these as well. His financial underwriting of the suffragettes bankrupted him, and, as a further sign that the masculinists would not tolerate traitors to their cause, he was expelled from the Reform Club, which ostensibly adhered to enlightened Liberal principles.

Perhaps the unkindest cut of all was Emmeline Pankhurst's sudden break with the Pethick-Lawrences and the socialism that gave birth to the WSPU. Christabel Pankhurst had concluded that it was Conservatives who would eventually give women the vote. She saw a reprise of the 1867 triumph, when Disraeli had proposed a more comprehensive measure for working-class suffrage than Gladstone in order to "dish the Whigs." The departure of the Pethick-Lawrences precipitated shock waves throughout the WSPU, causing one wag to project a conversation between two feminists, one asking the other, "Are you a Peth or a Pank?" The humourous comment did reflect the dilemmas the suffragettes confronted. It was not the first time the members of the WSPU had had to choose between the Pankhursts and their view of the vote as an end in itself, and the humanistic tradition in which feminism had its roots, that saw the acquisition of voting rights as part of a wider struggle for social justice. Emmeline Pankhurst retained her socialist ideals as long as her husband was alive. Left to her own devices or, as has been suggested, under the influence of her determined eldest child, Christabel, she reverted to her upper-middle-class values and associations, and cut herself off from the dynamism of the working-class movement.[42] Increasingly, the WSPU revolved around the Pankhurst personality cult. The disdain Emmeline Pankhurst had shown for democracy and her purge of the socialists brought about a rift between Emmeline Pankhurst and her younger daughter, Sylvia, who decamped to take up residence in London's East End so that she could combine the socialist and feminist concerns that had made her father a hero to the Labour party he helped found.

The Pethick-Lawrences took their leave of the organization to which they had devoted their fortunes, in every sense of the word, with forbearance and good grace. In his autobiography Pethick-Lawrence, commenting on the incident, noted, "It was of course open to us to drag the issue into public controversy. But that could serve no useful purpose, while it would give the enemies of the movement occasion to blaspheme and we refused to pull down stone by stone, the edifice which we had with such care and at such cost assisted to build up." He respected the women who had chosen to be led by women exclusively, without any "masculine opinion," and thought that this could be a significant step in the development of their unique capacities.[43] About the Pankhursts, he stated that there were some men and women who were destiny's children. "They seem to be used by destiny for some purpose, whether of beneficent constructive reform or of blind destructive retribution, they cannot be judged by ordinary standards of conduct, and those who run up against them must not complain of the treatment they receive."[44]

The men who made women's suffrage an overriding cause and who tirelessly donated their time to making speeches and writing articles came from a variety of backgrounds and interests. Israel Zangwill (1864-1926) was a novelist, poet, dramatist, and essayist whose works illumined his late Victorian world. It was his own Jewish world that he painted with loving strokes as, above all, Zangwill was a committed Jew. He was the son of an East European immigrant. His father was part of a wave which came to England toward the latter part of the nineteenth century to settle in London's East End, where Zangwill was born and lived his entire life. Zangwill's father was a traditional Jew. His mother was a fiercely independent woman whose indomitable strength summed up womanliness for Zangwill. His admiration for Ibsen's works reenforced his concept of the new woman as determined, courageous, and self-contained.

Zangwill's services to the Jews went beyond such works as *Children of the Ghetto* and *King of the Schnorrers*, which made vivid the Jewish experience and validated it for the faithful who chose to resist the assimilationist pressures imposed by devotees of modernity. Zionism had its effective beginnings when Theodore Herzl visited the highly acclaimed Anglo-Jewish writer and, after introducing himself, made a direct plea: "Help me to build the Jewish state."[45] Zangwill was a passionate admirer of "the noblest soul in Judah," as he called Herzl, and he readily lent himself to the Zionist dream. Zangwill's anguish about the immediacy of the plight of "suffering Jewry," combined with his English loyalties, complicated his Jewish nationalism. Since at that time the dream of a Jewish homeland appeared to be a long-range vision, he believed that the urgent needs of the Jewish people might be better served in the short run if they obtained some territory in what was to him the Promised Land—the British Empire. His conflict of loyalties gave a special imperative to his feminism.

Zangwill stopped writing in 1904 in order to concentrate all his energies on the various causes to which he was devoted. All his activities were in some sense a service to Judaism, and his support of women's suffrage was no exception. For Jews, the extension of the democratic franchise to males exclusively had not fulfilled the optimistic expectations of liberals. Nor had it been accompanied by progress. The late-nineteenth-century rise in racism and anti-Semitism held premonitions of disaster for Zangwill. The characteristic Victorian optimist believed that man was destined to move upward, leaving the ape and tiger in him behind. Zangwill, like his fellow male feminists, knew the ape and tiger were very much alive in men. All over Europe demagogues were attaining power by tapping and exploiting the latent anti-Semitic prejudices of the male electors. The anti-Semitic fever had been comparatively mild in England. But to Zangwill, the suffragettes—struggling for their rights; wanting to break free of their assigned domestic domain (the ghetto) but labelled inferior; ridiculed and refused acceptance on an equal basis; and humiliated by forcible feeding—were participating in the Jewish experience. He was convinced that women's involvement in politics would act as a corrective to the "male beast" that was asserting itself through jingoism, racism, and anti-Semitism.

Because of his intense admiration for the women working "with unfaltering spirit and energy to break down one of the last barriers that shut them out from opportunities and responsibilities," Zangwill was a frequent speaker at suffragette meetings. In a speech given in 1907, he showed as little patience with female antisuffragists as he did with Jewish anti-Semites: "Some ladies do not want the vote. Poor things. There are ladies in China who are content to have their toes crippled. But why keep back the ones who want natural feet?" Were the female antisuffragists womanly? To Zangwill they were masculine—"their action redolent of all that sneaking mutual hatred of women by women which was unhappily engendered by woman's old over-dependence upon men." Zangwill gave his support to militant methods on the ground that, in asking for the vote, which represented human dignity, the suffragettes had made an unanswerable argument. In 1912, while the second conciliation bill was being debated, Zangwill insisted that the only mistake the women had made was in not turning to militancy earlier. He labelled the opposition to the suffrage as the "Hithertos," people "who are effectively dead but who don't know it and have not yet departed. We," he proclaimed, "are the Henceforwards. We have done with their man ridden world."[46]

Laurence Housman (1865-1959) was a prolific dramatist and an exponent of the New Humanism, a cultural movement which attempted to reassert the primacy of the intellect over the irrational forces that seemed to be engulfing the world. The movement stressed the importance of art as an outlet for the irrational, which was viewed as a function of increasing technology. New Humanists were impressed with the efflorescence of artistic and intellectual endeavor among women as a result of the new woman phenomenon. They believed that a change in the relations between males and females was essential so that the potential exhibited by women could be fulfilled. Housman thought that male domination had been a social and political disaster and that the women's movement was a necessary stage in the achievement of the New Humanism. He envisioned an androgynous world where the best men "have the woman in them without being womanized and the choicest women are those who yield not a feather of their womanliness" for some amount of man, namely determination. He denied that the suffragettes were instigating sex war by their militant methods. He considered the sexual games men and woman play—such as the use of seductive allure by women to incite the sexual beast in man—as the chief symptom of sex war. Rape, prostitution, and the double standard were further evidence of sex war. According to Housman, sex peace would come when men who used sex as a weapon and voiced degrading sentiments about women were no longer considered representative of their sex.

Housman was a pacifist who was alarmed by the exaltation of brute force as a sign of virility, and tied this directly to the fact that the male sex drive was being encouraged by sexual rights advocates. He identified "libidinous men" as imperialists reaping wealth and power at the expense of colonials. He hoped that greater political involvement by women would see the sex instinct channelled into constructive work rather than being indulged in for its own sake, and the motherhood instinct socialized to encompass the larger community. To answer the question, "What is womanly?" he counterposed the questions "What is manly?" Manliness was defined as the ability to possess oneself, and to develop one's faculties, which called for discipline as well as freedom. Womanliness was defined in exactly the same way.[47]

One of Housman's contributions to the suffragettes was a one-act play, *Alice in Ganderland*. It is peopled with Alice-in-Wonderland characters and has a suffragette Alice demanding the right to vote. The Mad Hatter and the Dormouse represent the two major parties in England who, when confronted with their old war cry, "Taxation without representation is tyranny," have conveniently revised it so that, for women, "taxation is representation." Throughout the exchanges, which reveal political duplicity and hypocrisy, the dormouse interjects, "Three cheers for the British constitution."[48]

Henry Noel Brailsford (1873-1958) left the halls of academe—he was professor of logic at the University of Glasgow—to influence a wider world with his socialist ideals. He became a journalist and freedom fighter. Brailsford fought as a volunteer for the Greeks in a war against Turkey, and then stayed to offer his services to help solve the refugee problem that followed in the wake of war. Brailsford joined the Labour party in 1907 and made his commitment to women's suffrage clear two years later, when the Liberal government began forcibly feeding the suffragette prisoners who were hunger striking. The suffrage supporters in Parliament demanded that the brutality be stopped and that Herbert Gladstone be removed as home secretary. Brailsford and Henry Nevinson were both on the staff of *The Daily News*, a Liberal newspaper. Both resigned their positions as a protest against the editorial policy of the paper, which supported the government. In a joint statement they maintained, "We cannot denounce torture in Russia and support it in Britain, nor can we advocate democratic principles in the name of a Party which confines them to a single sex."[49]

Subsequently Brailsford wrote an article for the *Newcastle Daily Chronicle*, expressing his views in greater detail. It was called "Militant Suffragists in Newcastle," and described a demonstration that took place there in October, 1909. He saw the demonstration as a drastic step taken by high-minded women fully aware of the consequences to follow. He noted,

For a week or more before they had counted the cost—the weakness and misery of hunger, and then the forcing of a steel instrument between their teeth, the insertion of a gag, and outrage of the stomach-pump. Even to men it is . . . loathsome . . . to a woman it is a violation. . . . The thing was done at Birmingham, and there the worst sufferer was a working woman. . . . Mr. [Herbert] Gladstone presumably supposed that by torturing six women at Birmingham he would deter their comrades. The only result has been that with a superb chivalry twelve women have come forward to face the worst at Newcastle.

Brailsford suggested two ways out of the dilemma.

Let it be frankly recognized that these women, despite the fact that they have committed a sort of symbolical violence, and injured Liberal or Government property, are political offenders, entitled to the honours of war, and there will be no hunger strike. The strike is not against imprisonment. It is against the degradation of ordinary criminal treatment. . . . Or when they have starved for three, four, five, or six days, as their predecessors did, let them be released.

Newcastle, which welcomed Garibaldi should not forget the honor due to political prisoners who face outrage and possible death in a just cause. Is the political offender entitled to less honour because she happens to be a woman not an Italian soldier or a Russian conspirator, but an English woman? . . . Years ago the country was ripe for the reasonable and moderate measure of enfranchisement which these women demand. Nothing stands in the way save false pride of one or two Ministers who are trading on the popularity of their colleagues. The Government cannot make up its mind either to give or refuse the vote to women. It is firm and unanimous only in its resolve to violate the bodies of its political opponents.[50]

Besides their feminism, the common denominator that united Zangwill, Housman, and Brailsford was their pacifism. That they did not consider support of the women militants to be inconsistent with their pacifism reveals that in no sense did they believe pacifism to require turning the other cheek. The pre-World War I pacifists believed in self-defense, and gave their support to those who chose to struggle for human rights, whether they were women or ethnic minorities. These men were opposed to wars of "steel and gold," in Brailsford's phrase—wars of aggression which they associated with capitalism and imperialism. Such wars were part of the masculine mystique to which they were traitors. That they considered aggression to be a manifestation of the male sex imperative made them sex conservatives, like so many of the male feminists before them.

Criticism of the policy of forcible feeding led government leaders to change their tactics, but no concessions were made on the suffrage issue. In April, 1912, Parliament passed an act enabling the government to temporarily free starving women prisoners so that they could return home and regain their strength. Once their health was restored they were subject to rearrest to serve the remainder of their sentences. The legislation was promptly dubbed the Cat and Mouse Act by Robert Cecil, a supporter of women's suffrage, and inspired a highly evocative cartoon of a large, complacent government cat lying in wait to pounce on a hapless and thoroughly terrorized suffragette mouse.

With the formation of the antisuffrage societies, led by such die-hard antis as Lord Cromer, the male supporters of the suffragettes began to form their own organizations to demonstrate in a public and palpable way their solidarity with the women. The Men's League for Women's Suffrage; the Men's Political Union for Women's Suffrage; the Men's Federation for Women's Suffrage; the Men's Society for Women's Rights; the Male Electors for Women's Suffrage—these were the organizations men formed to generate support for women's suffrage and to put their sentiments on record. The most active of these groups were the Men's League for Women's Suffrage and the Men's Political Union for Women's Suffrage. These two organizations embrace the wide spectrum of ideas covered by the male feminists.

The Men's Political Union for Women's Suffrage (MPU)—founded in 1909—was the male counterpart of the WSPU, and thus supported the Pankhursts in all their policies, including attacks on property. The MPU was formed by Victor Duval, who described himself as an active member of the Liberal party until 1906, when he resigned because of the leadership's failure to support women's suffrage. The objective of the organization was "to secure for women the Parliamentary Vote on the same terms as it is or may be granted to men." The methods it endorsed were: (1) action entirely independent of all political parties; (2) opposition to whichever party was in power till women's suffrage was granted; (3) participation in parliamentary elections in opposition to the government candidate, and independently of all other candidates; and (4) vigorous agitation and the education of public opinion by all the usual methods, such as public meetings, demon-

strations, debates, distribution of literature, newspaper correspondence, and deputations to public representatives. Toward these goals Duval welcomed "men of
all shades of political opinion, to show the Government that they are in deadly
earnest and are prepared to make sacrifices in order that justice should be done to
the women of the country."

The MPU exactly paralleled the goals and methods of the WSPU, and their
closeness is further evidenced by the fact that the weekly report of the MPU was
published in the suffragette newspaper, *Votes for Women*. MPU support was
important because, as males, they could do more than simply cheer the women
on with such slogans as, "Stand fast and let your tyrants see that fortitude is
victory." Since MPU members could actually exercise the suffrage, they could
punish recalcitrant politicians at the polls. MPU members took over the heckling
of government spokesmen at political meetings, causing a great deal more embarrassment to the politicians than did the women, who were summarily ejected
from such meetings and often imprisoned for causing a disruption. Several
members of the MPU also were imprisoned, Victor Duval among them. Duval
thought it important that men show their support by joining women in prison. He
proudly recorded the events of his week-long stay in Pentonville Prison in 1910.
He described how he was arrested while trying to question Lloyd George about
the government's intention on the conciliation bill. When Lloyd George tried to
escape, Duval grabbed him by his coattails to force an answer out of him and,
when his captive resisted, called him a "traitor and a hypocrite." Duval was
given a choice of paying a fine or receiving a seven-day sentence; he chose
prison because he would not, on principle, pay a fine for any work he did for
women's suffrage. Once in prison, he regarded himself as a political prisoner and
refused to wear prison clothing or eat prison food. Unwittingly, Duval drama-
tized Pethick-Lawrence's assertions that women were mistreated precisely because they had no recourse at election time. Duval, who was a voter, was granted
every request he made. He was allowed to wear his own clothes, buy his food
and have it brought to him, and even to exercise when he demanded it.[51]

The second annual report of the MPU in 1911 recorded the deeds by which the
men showed their support. They opposed those candidates at by-elections who
refused to vote for the conciliation bill; held meetings on forcible feeding; spoke
out at political meetings, asking candidates to take a stand; took action against a
constable "who appeared to be abusing a woman"; and smashed two windows of
the Home Office, which incurred a fine of "a few pounds." The report noted that
in two years eight members had gone to prison.[52]

Henry Nevinson (1856-1941), chairman of the Men's Political Union, wrote
numerous articles justifying the policy of militancy on which the suffragettes had
embarked. Nevinson proclaimed his belief in freedom as the noblest goal of
mankind, and the ultimate destiny of civilization. Giving women their freedom
would accelerate the benefits of freedom for all and would more quickly bring
about a reduction of armaments, the extension of rights to other oppressed
groups, including the Irish and the Indians, and the curtailment of vices such as

alcoholism and infidelity. He looked for an improvement in the species as women became more independent and more discriminating in their choice of mates. Nevinson noted that the most cherished liberties were never won without a struggle. Magna Carta, parliamentary government, the Reform Bills of 1832 and 1867—all these victories taught Nevinson that "it is only by defiance that our liberties have been won." Nevinson was convinced that democracy had the sweep of history behind it and that women's votes was the predestined culmination of the process.[53]

The Men's League for Women's Suffrage (MLWS), founded in 1907, was more attuned to the educational methods of the suffragists than the militant stances of the suffragettes. Its membership included every shade of political opinion from the socialism of Philip Snowden to the liberalism of C. V. Drysdale, to the conservatism of the Earl of Lytton, president of the organization. The league had branches throughout England and published a monthly newspaper to keep the membership up to date on the suffrage situation and the activities of the members. The issue of November, 1910, was published to apprise members of the progress of the conciliation bill and to remind them of the urgent need for their support. It denounced David Lloyd George for his statement that he could not approve the bill but would always vote for one which would enfranchise the women who were suffering most. The article pointedly asked how he defined women who are suffering and added, "What we do know is that the Conciliation Bill bestows the franchise on just the women who have most practical need of it—the householders, the working women who have no one but themselves to depend on." Questions were provided for MLWS members to ask members of Parliament: "Will the member do his utmost to obtain further facilities for the Conciliation Bill, even though the proposal is opposed by the Government?" There was notice of a demonstration that the MLWS was holding in Trafalgar Square. Men were advised "How You Can Help Distribute Handbills," "Exhibit posters at [your] homes," and "Assist in chalking pavements."[54]

The MLWS solicited endorsements for women's suffrage from the literary, artistic, military, scientific, educational, legal, and religious establishments of the population to show how large a cross section of the population favored the vote for women. The list published in 1909 showed eighty-three present and past officeholders in England in the Liberal and Conservative parties who favored votes for women; twenty-four high ranking army and navy officers; forty-nine church leaders of both the established and nonconformist churches; eighty-six educators, among whom were Bernard Bosanquet, J. B. Bury, and Gilbert Murray; and seventy-three scientists. The literature and drama contingent included J. M. Barrie, E. M. Forster, John Galsworthy, Thomas Hardy, John Masefield, Arthur Pinero, George Bernard Shaw, H. G. Wells, and Israel Zangwill among the fifty-four listed. Thirteen actors, including Granville Barker, Dion Boucicault and Edmund Gwenn, signed their names, as well as thirty-three musicians and artists.[55]

In the *Men's League Handbook on Women's Suffrage*, supporters were given the opportunity to make their case. Sir John Cockburn introduced the first women's suffrage bill in Australia and wrote *The Colonial Experience*. Australian women were given the vote in 1902, while in New Zealand women received the vote in 1893. Cockburn was able to assure the English that none of the calamities the masculinists had warned of had come to pass. To wit: Chivalry had not declined; domestic quarrels had not increased; and homes had not been neglected. Cockburn, in fact, confirmed the predictions of supporters who believed that the moral climate of society would improve and that public health would benefit from women's votes. That infant mortality had shown a steady decline in Australia, and was the lowest in the world in New Zealand, was attributed by Cockburn to women's having a voice in framing social legislation.

The lord bishop of Lincoln gave no succor to those antis who insisted that the confinement of women to the domestic sphere was ordained by God. In making his points he gave a liberal rather than literal interpretation of the Bible where it pertained to women. The lord bishop made clear in "The Moral and Religious Aspect" that nothing can be inferred from the silence of scripture on women's rights, noting "that our Lord and his Apostles accepted the social life of his time as it stood is clear from the New Testament. Against wealth, indeed, Christ made a vehement stand, and Himself lived a life of mendicancy by way of protest. But we find nothing said against slavery, against despotic government, against war, and other existing institutions." Neither was the status of women disturbed by the Christian fathers; according to the lord bishop, it would it appear that "St. Paul was anxious only that the women of the Christian Church should demean themselves with all (and more than all) the modesty, the gentleness, the reserve, which were expected of good women in society." The bishop argued that any attempt to revolutionize ancient social life would have made the spread of the Gospel impossible. The New Testament, he warned, should not be treated as a final codex of laws and regulations. That is what has enabled Christianity to progress "while other religions such as Islam and Brahminism have been left behind in the march of progress."

C. V. Drysdale ("*The Economic Aspect*") demanded equal pay for equal work for women, not only as a measure of justice for women, but as "imperatively necessary in the interests of men." He pointed out that there were 1,300,000 more women than men in the United Kingdom. Most of these women were compelled to enter the labor market to earn a living. Men, he noted, had been quick to recognize the danger of nonunion labor in terms of other men, but had been content to let women become "coolie labor"—5.5 million women wage earners were earning an average weekly wage of seven shillings, while the average male earned thirty shillings. He asserted:

The lower remuneration of women for equal work has inevitably led to the selection of women in place of men in every case where the two compete on equal terms, and there are only two possible ways of checking this displacement. Either female labour must be entirely prohibited or placed under rigid restriction, which is most impracticable; or, on the other hand, the principle of combination must be extended to women, so that they shall not accept lower remuneration for given services than men do.

Drysdale concluded the Liberal argument in favor of the competitive system as the guarantor of progress for both men and women by asking for women's suffrage.

Suffrage supporters from the scientific community were frequently called upon to answer charges of the opposition that women's brains were smaller than men's and that they were therefore unable to deal with weighty political matters. Sir Victor Horsely, a prominent physiologist, declared that the human brain grows were it has a chance to develop. In asserting that women do see things differently from men, he took the male feminists' stand that this was beneficial for society. Horsely noted that the British Medical Association had expressed its confidence in women's mental ability by admitting them to membership in 1892 .[56]

A barrister, J. Arthur Price, refuted the historical argument for keeping women in an inferior position in "The Argument From History." He made it clear "that to exclude women from suffrage in a modern state is to place her in a worse position than that in which she stood in the Middle Ages." Price showed that the great obstacle to women's enfranchisement throughout the ages has been Roman law, which insisted that a woman was incompetent to act on her own behalf and that she could not perform public functions. As proof that while Roman law was influential in England, it had not been incorporated in English law, Price cited examples of medieval English women exerting authority. Women inherited the office of sheriff; some were elected to the office of churchwarden. Price showed that much of the work being done in the modern state by Parliament was previously done by religious and craft guilds in which women had had adequate representation. To deny women participation in the form of the vote in a modern state, a vast impersonal bureaucratic machine "restrained only by the voting power of those possessed of the suffrage, a Press-directed public opinion, regulating life and industry, and seeking to effect great schemes of social reconstitution," was to leave them even more vulnerable than at any time in the past. He charged that widows and children, protected by the Church and by guilds in the past, received absolutely no protection in the modern state:

Anti-suffragists do not protect them, they exploit them. . . . The truth is that the opponents of Women's Suffrage are the enemies (perhaps unconscious) of the Christian civilization in the West. They stand for the strong against the weak, and they are forced to fight their battle by weapons of brutality. Their triumph can only be . . . the victory of a theory of human life which even the Middle Ages rejected with horror, the theory that would see in women "an animal not of a very high order."[57]

Price's arguments had especial impact on Conservatives, who valued tradition and feared the materialism of their times, and who looked with a jaundiced eye at the "progress" that the proponents of the modern bureaucratic state claimed to

have inaugurated. Two members of the Conservative party who regularly spoke
on behalf of women's suffrage and who strongly supported the conciliation bill
were Robert Cecil and Robert Lytton. Cecil (1864-1958) admired the women
achievers of the past and regretted women's exclusion from public life. He
reminded his audiences that England had produced Boadicea, who instigated a
revolt against the Romans, and Queen Elizabeth I, whose reign rendered devoid
of any substance all arguments that women could not discharge public functions.
Cecil characterized the opposition to women's suffrage as mandarin, reactionary, and un-English. It suggested to him an Oriental view of woman which
stipulated that she should be "shut up lest she lead men into evil and women into
error."[58]

In the case of both Cecil and Lytton, support of women's rights was a family
tradition as well as a political principle. Cecil boasted that his father had voted
with the "radical Mill" for women's rights and that he was not ashamed to vote
with the "radical Hardie." Lytton (1876-1947) was the great-grandson of the
same Anna Wheeler to whom William Thompson directed his *Appeal*. His sister,
Lady Constance Lytton, was a member of the WSPU and enlisted a number of
her personal contacts among Liberals and Conservatives in the suffragettes'
cause. She was arrested for participating in a demonstration in 1910, and was
given special treatment in prison partly because of her rank and partly because
she suffered from a heart condition. Anxious to show that women were united
and could not be divided along class lines, she wore working-class clothes in
subsequent demonstrations. When she was arrested again the next year, she gave
her name as Jane Wharton. This time, like her sisters of less imposing status, she
was forcibly fed after going on a hunger strike, until her identity was discovered
by embarrassed leaders of the government. Her experiences contributed to a
precipitous decline in her health and undoubtedly were responsible for Lytton's
compassion for the militant suffragettes. He told opponents of the suffrage:

You see in it only the folly and the wickedness; but I also see in it the pity and the
tragedy.... I have seen the exhibition of human qualities which I consider to be as rare
and as precious as anything which a nation can possess. I have seen these qualities given
to a cause which is in itself as great and as noble a cause as you could well find, but given
in such a way as to defeat the very objects that they sought to obtain . . . and that to my
mind is a tragedy.[59]

Lytton made his most powerful plea for women's suffrage in the House of
Lords in 1914, just before the outbreak of World War I. In the classic conservative tradition of Edmund Burke, he argued that the struggle for women's suffrage
was a great principle and a test of whether sex alone should permanently and
under all conditions debar any woman in the country from voting at parliamentary elections. He assured fellow conservatives that giving a vote to the woman
"who is alone; single-handed; unmarried and working for a living was a pace of
change that was moderate, deliberate," and therefore true to conservative pre-

cepts. He warned of the danger that exists for any party identified with "anti-democratic tendencies" and he concluded that to deny women the vote after they had demonstrated their demand for it and shown by participation in local elections that they were adequate to perform their civic responsibilities, would be to confirm that their disability was a legal rather than a natural one and would be denying them elementary justice.[60]

The Men's League for Women's Suffrage had an overseas branch in the United States, with Max Eastman as its guiding light. Eastman's philosophy was expressed in a pamphlet, *Is Woman Suffrage Important?* He explained that there was no militance in the United States because there was nothing to militate against: "What we have to overcome is a polite but perfectly useless acquiescence." Eastman's quarrel was with America's leisured, moneyed class, which maintained the image of women as ignorant, silly, and helpless: "If you add to these ethics. . . a tendency to erect her enforced feebleness into a holy thing, and add a sentimental subservience of the man to this enslaved queen in matters of no moment, you have the attitude of the leisure class of our day." Eastman had the faith of the liberal optimist that the modern state was destined to progress if led by the social-minded rather than by the moneyed interests. That progress would be achieved if male and female were brought to cooperate in the venture as "the sexes are more idealistic together than in what they do apart."[61]

The international ramifications of women's suffrage were brought out when the Men's League for Women's Suffrage and its overseas affiliates evolved into the Men's International Alliance for Women's Suffrage, which held its first congress in London in 1912. Among the English delegates were C. V. Drysdale, Victor Duval, Laurence Housman, George Trevelyan, and Sir John Cockburn.

The constitution of the Men's International Alliance stated that the establishment of women's suffrage was the sole object of its existence, and unanimous resolutions were passed demanding the enfranchisement of women "in the interests of justice and good legislation." Other resolutions pertained to the international problems that women's suffrage might relieve. The white slave traffic, an issue that had repercussions around the world as a result of William Stead's exposure in 1885, was a major concern. Regarding this problem, the resolution stated, "This Congress calls attention to the serious evils to the race consequent upon the White Slave Traffic and the social subordination of women, and considers that the enfranchisement of women is imperatively demanded in order to obtain rational and just legislation concerning these matters." It pointed out that in every country where women's suffrage was passed the age of consent had been raised and the white slave traffic reduced. A final resolution affirmed the belief of the members "that the influence of women in politics will be in the direction of assisting the peaceful settlement of international disputes."[62]

When World War I began, all reform was postponed pending an Allied victory. The British government asked all subjects to do their duty to insure a successful outcome. The suffragettes, who had been in a state of war with the government, were, in effect, asked to forget their antagonisms and to make, in the name of democracy, sacrifices for a leadership which had consistently denied them their democratic rights. Not all complied. Emmeline and Christabel Pankhurst, after years of militant action and calls for sedition, did a complete about-face. They became superpatriots, dropped their demand for the vote, and turned their zeal to recruiting men for battle and women for war work.

The Pethick-Lawrences continued to publish *Votes For Women* and continued to demand the suffrage. In July, 1914, *Votes For Women* stated that the question of war and peace is preeminently one on which women should be consulted, since the men who fight in wars are fashioned by women "at the cost of anguish, blood, and life, itself." It called for the immediate enfranchisement of soldiers' wives. In 1915, *Votes* took up the equal pay for equal work issue, demanding that women in war work be paid what the men were getting. The last issue, in February, 1918, carried a clarion call for men and women to work together to rebuild humanity.[63] The Pethick-Lawrences were joined by other suffragettes, both male and female, in their activities on behalf of peace. Frederick Pethick-Lawrence worked for the Union of Democratic Control, which favored peace by negotiation, and eventually became a conscientious objector.

The fact that women's suffrage was granted in June, 1918, has often been seen as a reward for the suffragettes' wartime activities.[64] There is no evidence to support this interpretation, any more than there is reason to suppose that their prewar hostilities prevented suffrage from passing earlier.[65] The suffragettes' arch-foe, Herbert Asquith, had always maintained that his position against suffrage was based on "public expediency."[66] Translated into power exigencies, women could always be sacrificed to other priorities precisely because they did not have the suffrage. The decision to deny women the vote was unilateral in the case of William Gladstone as well as Asquith and shows the growing power of the party leaders in the Commons and in the executive.[67] The male suffragettes had consistently pointed out that the enlarged authority of the party leaders, responsible only to males, meant that they would continue to sacrifice the interests of women in order to maintain their constituencies.

The suffrage was granted to women after Asquith was replaced by David Lloyd George as prime minister. With Asquith's war policies called into question, his other policies were also discredited, and Lloyd George was able to make a fresh start. Because of the war, other parties were brought into a coalition government. The Labour member, Arthur Henderson, was a women's suffrage supporter, and brought to bear the stand Labour had taken on this issue at the 1913 executive committee meeting. The Conservative member of the coalition, Robert Cecil, was also a women's suffrage supporter. Both made it clear as early as 1915, when they entered the cabinet, that they would support no electoral reform that did not include women's suffrage.[68] There was still ample opposition to women's suffrage in 1917, the antisuffrage societies being very much alive; but once the decision was made in the cabinet, with a coalition of women's suffrage supporters forcing the issue, the outcome was foreordained. The speaker of the House of Commons, who had made arbitrary rulings against the suffrage supporters, made rulings—just as arbitrary—in their favor. The bill that gave women the vote passed without any fanfare, with 385 in favor and 55 against, and almost as an anticlimax.

NOTES

1. Roger Fulford, *Votes for Women* (London: Faber and Faber, Ltd., 1947), p. 119.

2. All information about Richard Pankhurst was taken from: E. Sylvia Pankhurst, *The Life of Emmeline Pankhurst* (London: T. Werner Laurie, 1969). See also Emmeline Pankhurst, *My Own Story* (London: Eveleigh Nash, 1914), David Mitchell, *The Fighting Pankhursts* (New York: The Macmillan Co., 1967); Fulford, *Votes for Women*.

3. Sheila Rowbotham, *Hidden From History* (New York: Random House, 1974), pp. 60-61.

4. Angus McLaren, *Birth Control in Nineteenth Century England* (New York: Holmes and Meier, 1978), p. 163 ff.

5. Philip Snowden, *An Autobiography* (London: Ivor Nicholson & Watson, 1934), p. 273.

6. Fulford, *Votes for Women*, p. 171.

7. Colin Cross, *Philip Snowden* (London: Barrie & Rockliff, 1966), p. 114.

8. Keir Hardie, "Socialism and The Women's Question," in *From Serfdom to Socialism* (London: George Allen, 1907).

9. Anne Kenney, *Memoirs of a Militant* (London: Arnold & Co., 1924).

10. The Conservatives were in power from 1895 to 1906, with Lord Salisbury as P.M. until 1902. From 1902 to 1906 Balfour was P.M.

11. Keir Hardie, "Citizenship of Women," in *Review of Reviews*, 1905. (Reprinted by ILP, 1906.)

12. The Labour party won twenty-nine seats in the election of 1905.

13. Hardie, "Citizenship of Women."

14. Fulford, *Votes for Women*.

15. William Stewart, *Keir Hardie* (London: National Labour Press, 1921), p. 237.

16. E. Sylvia Pankhurst, *The Life of Emmeline Pankhurst* (London: T. Werner Laurie, 1969), p. 92.

17. Cross, *Philip Snowden*, p. 288.

18. Ibid., p. 114.

19. Snowden, *Autobiography*, p. 288.

20. Cross, *Philip Snowden*, p. 109.

21. *The Daily Sketch*, November 19, 1910.

22. Raymond Postgate, *George Lansbury* (New York: Longmans, Green, and Co., 1953), p. 32.

23. Ibid., p. 130.

24. Ibid., p. 142.

25. George Lansbury, *My Life* (London: Constable, 1928), p. 120.

26. Speech reported in *Votes for Women*, November 15, 1912.

27. *Votes for Women*, December 6, 1912.

28. Lansbury, *My Life*, p. 120.

29. Ibid, p. 123.

30. Snowden, *Autobiography*, p. 295.

31. Vera Brittain, *Pethick-Lawrence: A Portrait* (London: George Allen & Unwin, 1963), p. 21.

32. Ibid., p. 32.

33. Charlotte Despard, *Women in the New Era* (London: The Suffrage Shop, 1910). Emmeline Pethick-Lawrence, *My Part in a Changing World* (London: V. Gollanez, 1938).

34. Votes for Women, October, 1907.

35. Brittain, *Pethick-Lawrence*, p. 53.

36. Frederick Pethick-Lawrence, "Women's Votes and Wages," *Votes for Women*, October 21, 1910.

37. Frederick Pethick-Lawrence, *Is English Law Unjust to Women?* (London: Womens Press, 1910).

38. A. V. Dicey, *Letters to a Friend on Votes for Women* (London, 1909). In Museum of London.

39. Frederick Pethick-Lawrence, *Women's Fight for the Vote* (Women's Press, 1910). Ch. 8.

40. Fulford, *Votes for Women*, p. 251.

41. Frederick Pethick-Lawrence, "The Man's Share," in Museum of London.

42. See David Mitchell, *The Fighting Pankhursts* and *Women on the Warpath*.

43. Frederick Pethick-Lawrence, *Fate Has Been Kind* (London: Hutchinson and Co., 1942), p. 100.

44. Brittain, *Pethick-Lawrence*, p. 69.

45. Joseph Leftwich, *Israel Zangwill* (London: James Clarke, Ltd., 1956), p. 181. Also Maurice Wohlgelernter, *Israel Zangwill: A Study* (New York: Columbia University Press, 1964).

46. Israel Zangwill, "One and One Are Two," 1907; "Talked Out," 1907; "Old Fogeys and Old Cogeys," 1909; "The Sword and the Spirit," 1910; "The Lords and the Ladies," 1909. "The Immoral Effect of Ignorance in Sex Relations," 1911. "The Hithertos," 1912; "The Militant Women," 1913. All the above were originally speeches and printed in *Votes For Women*.

47. Laurence Housman, "The New Humanism," 1913; "Articles of Faith in the Freedom of Women," 1910; "What is Womanly?" 1914; "Sex War and Woman's Suffrage," 1912. Men's League for Women's Suffrage; "The Physical Force Fallacy," 1908, all in Museum of London.

48. Laurence Housman, *Alice in Ganderland* (London: Women's Press, 1911).

49. Fulford, *Votes for Women*.

50. H. N. Brailsford, on "The Militant Suffragists in Newcastle," October 11, 1909. Reprint in Museum of London. See also *Women and the Reform Bill* , in Museum of London.

51. Victor Duval, "My Week in Prison," in *Votes for Women*, November 4, 1910. *An Appeal to Men*, 1915. In Museum of London.

52. Men's Political Union for Women's Enfranchisement. Second Annual Report, 1911. In Museum of London.

53. Henry Nevinson, "Women's Votes and Men," in *The Growth of Freedom*. In the Museum of London.

54. Men's League for Women's Suffrage Monthly Paper, No. 14, November 1910. In Museum of London.

55. Men's League Handbook on Women's Suffrage. Published by same. 1913. In Museum of London.

56. Men's League for Women's Suffrage Speeches. Demonstration at Queen's Hall, January 26, 1909. In Museum of London.

57. Selections by J. Cockburn; Bishop of Lincoln; C. V. Drysdale; J. A. Price. All from Men's League Handbook on Women's Suffrage.

58. Address of Robert Cecil to Conservative-Unionist Women's Franchise Association, December, 1908. In Museum of London.

59. Fulford, *Votes for Women*, p. 302.

60. Lord Lytton, *The House of Lords and Women's Suffrage*. Reprinted by National Union of Women's Suffrage Societies, 1914.

61. Max Eastman, "Is Women Suffrage Important?" Reprinted by Men's League for Women's Suffrage.

62. First International Congress Men's League for Women's Suffrage. *More Light on the Women's Question*. 1912. In Museum of London.

63. *Votes for Women*, July 31, 1914; December 31, 1915; February, 1918.

64. See Christabel Pankhurst, *The Story of How We Won the Vote* (London: Hutchinson & Co., 1959); Millicent Fawcett, *The Women's Victory and After* (London: Sidgwick and Jackson, 1920); Ray Strachey, *"The Cause" ; A Short History of the Women's Movement in Great Britain* (London: G. Bell and Sons, 1928).

65. Constance Rover, *Women Suffrage and Party Politics in Britain 1866-1914* (London: Routledge, 1967).

66. Brian Harrison, *Separate Spheres* (New York: Holmes & Meier, 1978), p. 204.

67. David Morgan, *Suffragists and Liberals* (Oxford: Basil Blackwell, 1975), p. 156.

68. Harrison, *Separate Spheres*, p. 208.

THE PAST, PRESENT, AND FUTURE OF WOMEN

8

In the nineteenth century, and up until the suffrage was won, it was the unwavering assumption of the traitors to the masculine cause that for women the present was insufferable, involving as it did indignities men themselves had endured as part of a less civilized past and oppressions men had precipitated revolutions to eliminate. They believed the future progress of mankind depended on changes in the depressed status of women, and the realization of political equality. John Stuart Mill made clear that it was not only a matter of justice for which he made a *prima facie* case, but for the pragmatic reason that society would benefit if all available talents were used without regard to sex.

To emphasize the inevitability of their goals in what they saw as the march of progress, the male feminists made a concerted appeal to the past. The uses of history were manifold for feminists. Firstly, the evolutionists, who held a linear theory of history which presupposed that mankind had been steadily progressing upward, could show that women's equality was predestined by tracing the struggle backward in time. Analogies to the struggles males had won through both evolution and revolution engendered certainty that the achievement of women's equality was only a matter of time and simply another step—to some the final step—in that long upward climb from barbarism. In addition, past instances of women's rebellion lent credibility and gravity to the ongoing struggle, gave it historical dimensions, and made it more than a temporary wave of hysteria that, according to the masculinists, had seized a small minority of women. Exhuming examples of women who had served in capacities other than the domestic gave the lie to the masculine mindset that women were inferior and belonged exclusively in their traditional domestic role. Evidence that, despite the obstacles, women had made significant contributions to society, fueled demands that they receive the just rewards of recognition and power commensurate with their contributions. For the moralists of the nineteenth century, history was an important teaching tool. It provided models of heroic individuals for present genera-

Plate 16. Floyd Dell, the Intellectual Vagabond. Photograph courtesy of
Christopher Dell.

tions to follow and told of great deeds that have pushed civilization inexorably forward. Inspiring men—and now women—to emulate the deeds of the great was part of the task of the reformer. Thus, the first women's histories were written as part of the male feminists' educational efforts and political activism.

For the socialists, women's prehistoric past was an ideal state of peace and sexual harmony which needed to be reestablished. This was one of the justifications offered for a revolution against capitalist economic, political, and social values. Basing his theories on the anthropological evidence of Lewis Morgan, Friederich Engels (1820-1895) wrote *The Origin of the Family, Private Property, and the State* (1884). It was a work that had a decisive influence on feminists. Engels challenged the assumption that women had always been in a state of subservience and therefore cut the ground out from under those who insisted that, since it had always been so, it must remain so. J. S. Mill could only take issue with conservatives by using empirical logic and historical analogies, and by making appeals to justice. After Engels, feminists could use anthropological evidence to support their claims.

Engels used Morgan's three-fold classification of the stages of history—savagery, marked by gathering and hunting; barbarism, marked by animal breeding and agriculture; and civilization, marked by art and industry—to show that women's position had progressively deteriorated from the earliest stage, which was both matriarchal and communistic. In the earliest savage societies, group marriage or unrestricted sexual freedom prevailed. Paternity was unimportant, and only the female line, or Mother Right, prevailed. In this communist structure, women were part of the work force, and hence were highly esteemed apart from their childbearing and rearing function.

In the next stage of barbarism the pairing family emerged, and with it private property. To insure the paternal line women were held to strict fidelity. Labor was segregated according to sex, since men, no longer needing to hunt, gravitated to agriculture, which was discovered by women and which was the focus of their productive work. Private property and patriarchy brought about the overthrow of Mother Right, and women were rendered economically dependent. With the advent of civilization monogamy was established, and the male solidified his authority over the female by legal enslavement in the marriage bond. Thus emerged the first class struggle, that between the sexes, since in the family the male is bourgeois, the female, proletarian.

According to Engels, the overthrow of Mother Right was the "world historic defeat of the female sex" and made her subsequent oppression inevitable. Monogamy, according to Engels, was never the desire of the female, and in the savage or matriarchal state where females had a voice, it did not exist. It was brought about by the male, exclusively for the perpetuation of private property. "In order to make certain of the wife's fidelity and therefore of the paternity of the children, she is delivered over unconditionally into the power of the husband; if he kills her he is only exercising his right."[1]

When the man took command in the home, the woman was degraded and reduced to servitude, becoming "the slave of his lust and a mere instrument for the production of children." In marriage as it evolved in patriarchal society, the woman's helplessness was further exacerbated by the fact that only the man could dissolve a marriage. Deriving as it did from male aggrandizement, marriage could not in any way be the culmination of a love relationship; rather, it was based solely on convenience. "It was the first form of the family to be based not on natural, but on economic conditions—on the victory of private property over primitive, natural, communal property."

Associated with marriage and private property were the critical social and economic issues that concerned the feminist reformers. Monogamy, through which women became the first private property, brought in its wake adultery, prostitution, and slavery. Since marriages were made to secure property, both men and women sought love outside of marriage; and Engels identifies two constant social types that emerged with the pairing marriage, the wife's attendant lover and the cuckold husband. Adultery became an unavoidable social institution, impossible to suppress.

Most disastrous for women, according to socialist theory, was the privatization of their work in the family setting. Once their work lost its public character, it no longer concerned society. The wife became the head servant, excluded from all participation in social production. Only with the coming of the industrial revolution was social production once again opened to women, but only to women of the proletariat. Moreover, the exigencies of capitalism put the working woman in an untenable bind. If she wanted to carry out her responsibilities as wife and mother in the private world of the family, she was excluded from the marketplace; if she wanted to engage in social production and gain independence, she was unable to undertake family responsibilities. To socialists the position of women illustrated that the modern individual family is founded on the open or concealed domestic slavery of the wife, "and modern society is a mass composed of these individual families as its molecules." In addition, the family reflected the property relations that existed in society. Within the family the husband, no matter to what class he belonged, represented the bourgeois, and the wife was the proletarian. The working man, however oppressed in his working life by his capitalist employer, enjoyed a position as property owner when he returned at the end of the day to his wife and family. This made working women the lowest class of all, the slave of slaves.

Once the problem was laid bare and analyzed, the solution was self-evident. The prerequisite for the liberation of women was to bring them back into public production. This desideratum, in turn, required the abolition, through revolution, of the monogamous family as the economic unit of society.

Engels waxed eloquent about the possibilities once the apocalypse was behind them. For the first time in history marriage could be based on love rather than on material considerations, the woman needing economic support and the man needing a guarantee for the perpetuation of his property. With both male and female part of the productive force—and therefore independent—mutual inclination would be the only motive for the choice of a mate. Sexual equality would result, since the superiority of the man in marriage was merely a function of his economic supremacy. Once housekeeping was socialized, the care and education of children too would become a public affair, and children would be entitled to care whether or not they were the products of a legal union. Once marriage became a matter of choice, prostitution, the issue that sounded such a profound note of discord among feminists, would disappear. In sum, the new age of social production, with all men and women participating, would have incalculable rewards. When the means of production were transformed into social property there would be no anxiety about bequeathing and inheriting, and therefore the family would cease to exist: "Monogamy will come into its own. For with the transformation of the means of production into social property there will disappear also wage-labor, . . . and therefore the necessity for a certain—statistically calculable—number of women to surrender themselves for money."

Despite the centrality of women's status to their theory and prospects, the Marxists did not believe that women were revolutionary material, and were unremittingly hostile to the struggle for women's rights because of its middle-class auspices. Sex war, according to the Marxists, would cease after the revolution, when the institutions which brought it into existence, marriage and the nuclear family, would be abolished. Until then there seemed to be little point in ameliorating women's oppression since this might serve to lull these victims of capitalism into a false sense of complacency. The position of women in the Marxist organizations was a subordinate one, and women taking matters into their own hands, as the suffragettes did, was totally anathema. H. M. Hyndman welcomed Emmeline Pankhurst's incarceration in 1913; he joined the masculinists who crowed that the suffragettes' militance showed women to be totally irrational and unfit for a political role.

The liberal tradition, which John Stuart Mill represented, had a linear theory of history which held that mankind had developed in stages from barbarism to civilization. Moreover, because the liberals believed in progress they saw history as a process whereby ever higher stages could be reached through the recognition of human rights and liberties and through individual effort. For liberal historians, women's rights was an issue whose time had come.

Thomas Henry Buckle (1811-1862) called himself an explorer of historical and social science, and identified as his purpose the recording of the history of human progress in England. Buckle's father was a Tory, but Buckle gave his allegiance to a Liberal, John Stuart Mill, and tried to fill the historical gap in Mill's philosophical empiricism. Buckle was a feminist who tried to show in his works that women's influence was necessary for future progress. The theme he chose for *The ABC History of England*, the first volume of which was published in 1857, was "As society advances the ecclesiastical spirit and the military spirit never failed to decline." Such sentiments precisely echoed those of the feminists, who believed that giving women their rights would at least accelerate the decline of the military spirit. Feminist freethinkers such as George Holyoake, Robert

Owen, and Bernard Shaw even hoped to wean women away from their religious allegiances.

Buckle's dedication to feminism was more precisely revealed in a paper entitled *The Influence of Women on the Progress of Knowledge*, which he delivered in 1858 before the National Association for the Promotion of Social Science. In it he propounded the thesis that the ancient civilizations fell because "society did not advance in all its parts but sacrificed some of its constituents in order to secure the progress of others." Specifically, he asserted that the Athenians and the Romans were unjust to women, and that in Sparta—a society not admired by nineteenth-century progressives, but which managed to defeat Athens during the Peloponnesian wars—women had some influence. The moral could not escape patriotic Englishmen, and Buckle went on to extol women's influence in the most explicit terms.

Buckle maintained that women's influence was justified because it had softened the violence of men; it had improved their manners; it had lessened their cruelty. He rejected the charge that women were less intellectual than men and that their putative emotionalism was a drawback to those who centered their hopes for progress on greater rationalism. Of the two kinds of knowledge—inductive and deductive—he considered that men, who had a propensity for going from facts to ideas, were adept at the former, while women, whose tendency was to reverse the process, excelled at the latter. Buckle clearly identified deductive knowledge as the ideal or highest type since it required intuition and imagination. "Women live in the world of the ideal," Buckle maintained, and they "think quicker than men." They had rendered an immense service to knowledge because through their influence science was more deductive than it might otherwise have been. Buckle gave Newton's theory of gravitation as an example of the deductive method, and implied it was feminine influence which made it possible. Buckle elaborated further: "The striking fact that most men of genius have had remarkable mothers and that they have gained from their mothers more than from their fathers, this singular and unquestionable fact can I think be best explained by the principles which I have laid down." Buckle, in fact, ascribed his own intellectual precociousness to his mother's encouragement, his father having had more practical ambitions for him. Buckle dedicated his essay to his mother, and concluded his case with an almost lyrical exposition of the virtues of women:

Their turn of thought, their habits of mind, their conversation; their influence . . . extending over the whole surface of society and frequently penetrating its intimate structure, have, more than all other things put together, tended to raise us into an ideal world, lift us from the dust in which we are so prone to grovel, and develop in us those germs of imagination which even the most sluggish and apathetic understandings in some degree possess. . . . Therefore it is that those who are most anxious that the boundaries of knowledge should be enlarged ought to be most eager that the influence of women should be increased in order that every resource of the human mind may at once and quickly be brought into play.[2]

The need to put the women's movement into a framework of evolutionary development; a desire to prove that women's influence had been beneficial and therefore could be trusted; a disposition to accord recognition to individual women who had emerged from their seclusion to struggle in the public domain; a conviction that the struggle for women's rights was the culmination of a reaction against oppression which inspired the French Revolution, and that its success would be the final step in making the humanitarian ideals of the revolution a reality—all were factors that called for the writing of women's history by the male feminists. In the early twentieth century, the publication of a spate of women's histories coincided with the intense campaign of the suffragettes. They were written by committed activists on behalf of women's rights, in part to answer masculinist charges that women were incapable of any but domestic functions, and to reaffirm the civilizing functions of women.

Joseph McCabe (1867-1955), author of *Women in Political Evolution* (1909), was a freethinker whose hero was George Jacob Holyoake, the self-designated father of feminism, whose philosophy and goals McCabe fully shared. Before he devoted himself full-time to the propagation of rational thought, McCabe was a Catholic priest, but he left the Church in 1896. He believed that women had to surrender their lamentable allegiance to religion if they were to continue their evolution. In *Women in Religion*, he adumbrated his historical study with the claim that women were better off in the ancient world than they were in the Christian era. He equated the decay of religion in the nineteenth century with the growth of justice and humanity, and considered the sedulous promotion of the rights of women by the feminist reformers to be one of the outgrowths of the rational spirit. Claiming that a restricted sphere for women was the ideal of the clergy, he proclaimed that "the days are gone when ascetic priests could exclude them [women] from the Sacrament as 'unclean' " and challenged women to "prove that they are not too docile to priestly dictation" and to rise to their new opportunities in the work of the world.[3]

Women in Political Evolution, an exhortation in a similar vein, was a response to masculinist attacks on women's suffrage. In the early twentieth century, with the centrifugal force of nationalism pulling at England's empire, the masculinist opposition to women's rights charged that female suffrage would sound the death knell of the British Empire, and argued that the subordination of women was the price of empire and, ultimately, of civilization. The masculinists brought their own historians into the fray, and the latter lent weight to the argument with the assertion that the Roman Empire started to crumble when women demanded their legal rights. McCabe was scornful of this allegation, and maintained that the advances women made in the Roman Empire were part of an evolutionary development toward the extension of human rights, the realization of which in the modern world would make men and women allies in a common struggle against age-old injustices.

Sensing that anthropological theories of a preliterate Golden Age played into the hands of masculinists, who asserted that the advent of civilization was made possible by masculine dominance, McCabe made a distinction between social equality—which, he maintained, existed in preliterate societies as well as in Egypt—and political equality. McCabe insisted that it was political equality, which he saw as evolving in fits and starts from classical times on, that was the significant factor in the progress of civilization. He firmly tied women's political evolution to the growth of secularism in a variety of ways.

As an atheist, McCabe tried to show that women's oppression was at its worst under Church domination during the medieval period. He characterized the Middle Ages, dominated as it was by religious influences, as akin to barbarism in their degradation of women. McCabe painted women's history in stark black and white contrasts, with misogynists such as St. Paul and St. Augustine and the popes who followed in their footsteps vitiating the tentative advances foreshadowed by Plato, Epicurus, and Zeno. McCabe cited a number of heroines whom he regarded as feminist prototypes. They included Hypatia, a Hellenistic academician murdered by zealous Christians; abbesses such as St. Brigid and St. Hildegard, who maintained the dignity of women during medieval times; Christine de Pisan, a fourteenth-century advocate of women's rights; and Mary Astell, whose plea for female education in the seventeenth century was considered a landmark by the feminist historians.

McCabe turned eloquent when dealing with the modern phase of women's liberation, which started in the nineteenth century. The achievements of Holyoake, Mill, and Elizabeth Cady Stanton were recorded, and McCabe affirmed his belief that their activities had advanced the prospects of the franchise to the point where the goal was within reach. In a final tilt at masculinists who would put new obstacles in the path of women's rights, he labelled the subordination of women as barbaric—"a phenomenon which is always challenged as culture increases."[4] For McCabe, women's rights had already been vindicated by the advances in education and legal rights of the previous fifty years, which had opened doors and made possible the discovery that women had aptitudes the existence of which men had never suspected. McCabe observed that "men are growing more feminine with every century" with unalloyed relish.

From 1837 to 1901, years which saw the women's movement burgeon, a woman sat on the throne of England. Queen Victoria was something of a burden for the feminists, since she was categorically antifeminist. Although it was not revealed till after her death, her comment on the suffrage activities of Lady Amberley stated her position in the most unequivocal terms. She wrote, "The Queen is most anxious to enlist everyone who can speak or write or join in checking this mad, wicked folly of 'Women's Rights' with all its attendant horrors, on which her poor feeble sex is bent, forgetting every sense of womanly feeling and propriety. Lady Amberley ought to get a good whipping."[5] It is very likely that Queen Victoria's example of solid domesticity made it harder for the nineteenth-century male feminists to enlist women in the cause of feminism since Victoria was a model they were taught to revere from childhood. The masculinists were hardly grateful to the queen for her support. She did, after all, discharge the functions of leadership for over fifty years, and raised suspicions that political activity was not beyond women's scope. When masculinists attempted to dismiss her and discredit her reign with a contemptuous "she was a nasty old woman," they were, in effect, impugning women's political potential.

In the task of redeeming women's past, Ford Madox Ford rose to the defense of England's sovereign queens, whose reputation the masculinists sought to tarnish as part of their concerted campaign against women's rights. Ford (1873-1939), a poet, novelist, and critic, was sometimes referred to as the last of the pre-Raphaelites because of his attachment to the past. He tended to steer clear of politics, considering it corrupting for the artist, but found the women's suffrage movement a cause he could support.[6] While Ford was not disposed to deny that Victoria had faults, he insisted that she was not, by far, as arrogant and overbearing as her male forebears. In her political dealings, Ford saw a tact totally absent from the behavior of her predecessors, and he doubted if the problems which had led to revolution on the Continent in 1848 would have been peacefully resolved in England without her. He suggested that the attributes of diplomacy which Victoria possessed were sorely needed in the troubled world of 1912.

Queen Elizabeth I could hardly be dispatched so easily by the masculinists, since her leadership qualities and political acumen were beyond dispute. "She ought to have been a man," was the plaint of the masculinists, and some zealots actually went so far as to suggest that she really was, or, what amounted to the same thing, that she was the puppet of her advisers. To counter this bald assertion that the combination of femininity and leadership was not only unnatural, but impossible, Ford retorted that if Elizabeth had been a man, England would not have had the peace and prosperity that were the hallmarks of her reign. England might well have ended up as a province of Spain, as the Netherlands was at the time. Moreover, Elizabeth's femininity was expressed in her policies, proving that womanly qualities were an asset in politics. Ford insisted that the long war Elizabeth carried on with Phillip II of Spain during her entire reign was, for the first thirty years, "purely feminine. In the first place she flirted; later she lied; and only in the last resort, and then with extreme economy did she resort to cannonballs." Ford listed the benefits to England of female rule, which included the extension of the empire, increased wealth, and the cultivation of the arts. He nailed down his case that female leadership is conducive to peace by saying:

Now it is a somewhat remarkable fact, it is surely something more than coincidence that if we take the three and a half centuries from the accession of Henry VII to the death of Queen Victoria, the two periods that have been times of peace, on the whole of internal tranquility and foreign respect that was at all lasting, . . . that these periods should have occurred when women sat upon the throne just as it is a little remarkable that what distinguished the early Tudor, the Jacobean and the Georgian periods was endless wrangling.[7]

The writing of women's history in the years of conflict that marked the suffragettes' entrance on the political stage was part and parcel of the campaign to publicize their ideals and justify their tactics to alarmed onlookers who saw their behavior as either irrational, and therefore feminine, or manly, and therefore unnatural. Masculinists believed that the "hysteria" women exhibited was proof that they were unfit for government; while nominal feminists such as Havelock Ellis thought their behavior "manly," and sought to turn them back in the direction of their domestic role. Their male supporters pointed out that, historically, no cause had triumphed without violent confrontation between the old values and the new. To give historical evidence for this assertion and to suggest that women's activities were part of the march of progress, W. Lyon Blease wrote *The Emancipation of the Englishwoman*. In 1909, the year before the book was published, the British government had started the forcible feeding of its female suffragette prisoners, a move which had profound significance for liberal supporters of the suffrage such as Blease (1884-1963), who made an unsuccessful run for Parliament in 1910 on the strength of his feminist convictions.

A thoroughgoing civil libertarian, Blease questioned the tactic of harassing public speakers, no matter what their opinions might be. Violence was abhorrent to Blease, but the actions of the government toward defenseless women struggling for legitimate rights—whose militant activities had produced no deaths, confined as they were at this stage to disrupting political meetings and demonstrating—reeked of a smug autocracy, determined to preserve masculinist principles. The formation of the antisuffrage organizations also suggested a concerted stop-the-suffragettes campaign which alarmed the male feminists with its overtones of a last ditch stand at the barricades of masculinity; and those who, like Blease, were proponents of nonviolence, were moved to rededicate themselves to the word as opposed to the sword. In the introduction to *Emancipation*, Blease stated, "I believe in the right of women to arrange their own lives and enjoy equal opportunities with men in all kinds of social activity, and it is in the hope of helping them to exercise that right that I have undertaken this work." He defined the feminist movement as "the slow and reluctant recognition by man of the fact that woman is not merely an appendage to him but a separate individual."[8]

Emancipation was a comprehensive response to the masculinst arguments against women's rights. One of the most formidable masculinists was A. V. Dicey, an erstwhile Mill Liberal and supporter of women's suffrage who had defected to the masculine cause. Once converted, Dicey, an Oxford don, became a zealous propagandist for antisuffragism; he also sought to undermine Mill's arguments by claiming that in *The Subjection of Women*, Mill was not his usual rational self, but showed "emotionalism"—a code word intended to convey the baneful influence of Harriet Taylor Mill.[9] Dicey articulated the physical force argument with telling effect, and in another of his forays into antifeminism argued that women cannot be freed, since they have never been, and were not at present, oppressed. Blease's response to Dicey's position is part of the rationale for his work. He chastised Dicey for deserting to the enemy camp, saying, "There is nothing more common or more melancholy in human experience than the slow decay of early ideals." As for Dicey's positive estimate of women's status:

Those who make this statement can have little knowledge of the facts of history. I shall show in these pages that, so far from having enjoyed freedom, women have for more than two hundred years been struggling against the egoism of the male sex; that the inferiority which want of physical strength has imposed upon them has been aggravated by religion, by law, and by custom; that they have to contend, always against the indifference, often against the active prejudice, contempt, and jealousy of men to obtain education, proprietary rights, opportunity to labour at any save inferior occupations, and the elementary rights of free persons in a modern State; and that this stupid and brutal repression. . .has been productive of disastrous moral, intellectual, and physical consequences.[10]

Intent on showing that the women's movement was related to modern concepts of progress, Blease limited himself to the modern period, starting with the Restoration of Charles II, a period in which, according to Blease, women's status was at its nadir, having precipitously deteriorated since the death of Elizabeth I. In this period, he maintained, the Anglican Church successfully worked hand in hand with the state to keep women in a condition of subjection. Women had no legal rights, and married women were even more egregiously oppressed, since marriage entailed the complete merging of the woman's personality and identity with the man's. In the vein of the feminist fathers Blease wrote: "Marriage at its worst was no better than slavery. At its best it was subjection tempered by generosity, the most degrading and precarious of all social situations." Without any rights, without any education, women were sex objects—"totally enveloped in an atmosphere of sex"—and earned little more than contempt from their masters, as the literature of the period indicated. Referring to the savage lampoons of women fashioned by Alexander Pope, Blease noted the sharp contrast with the impassioned love poetry of the Elizabethan age.

Blease stated an axiom adhered to by the male feminists: where women's status was low, the double standard of morality was both a cause and a major factor in keeping it low. In the early eighteenth century, women were advised that vice was natural in men and that they would be wise not to protest against it. Prostitution was hardly a new phenomenon in the early eighteenth century, but it was particularly rampant in that period, fostered by an unbridled male ego and by the masculinist attitude that the double standard "is not so much the reprobation of unchastity in women as the toleration of it in men." An improvement in the moral climate ensuing from the victory in the campaign to repeal the Contagious Diseases Acts was, for Blease, a reason in and of itself to applaud the feminist movement as a constructive force. Blease claimed that the majority of women in his own time no longer condoned vice in men, and the fact that they had forced a recalcitrant male power structure to pass laws raising the age of consent for girls was a measure of what could be achieved if women were unified and determined.

"No action was ever taken by the state so long as women were ill-educated." With this declaration, Blease made clear the importance of educating women, that they might attain knowledge of the world and of themselves. Lack of education, he insisted, perpetuated women's dependence on men and their sexual enslavement. That the majority of women accommodated themselves to this condition made the example of the few who did not all the more admirable; this was a partial explanation of the strong support given by the male feminists to the militant suffragettes, primarily in the struggle against their male opponents, but also against the women who opposed the suffrage. Blease noted that in the eighteenth century even society ladies could hardly write their names "and were as incapable of writing a letter as of leading an army into battle." Completely subjected to male needs and convinced that this was part of natural law, the typical women of the day were, according to Blease, hardly capable of inspiring admiration: "Their emotions ran riot; they had no sense of discipline. . . . After the fire of youth had departed every vice which want of education permits to flourish grew rank and luxuriant." Under such conditions Blease marvelled not that there were so many "stupid" women in England, but that there were any with sense.

The heroines of *Emancipation* are the women who transcended the roles they were expected to fulfill and who made efforts to overcome the handicaps imposed on their sex. Mary Astell and Mary Wortley Montagu won Blease's plaudits because they risked calumny and ridicule to realize their intellectual potential. Blease gave credit to the bluestockings, who cultivated learning for its own sake and helped to create a climate of tolerance for female education, but considered that even these noteworthy women tended too readily to accept the restrictions—mental as well as physical—imputed to their sex.

The stage was thus set for the entrance of Mary Wollstonecraft, who was duly enshrined by the male feminists as the mother of feminism. In the scenario of the male feminists, it was her ideals and hopes the suffragettes were on the verge of fulfilling. Blease described *The Vindication of the Rights of Women* as the landmark work which launched the women's movement, since it emphasized the individuality of every member of the female sex and asserted in the most unequivocal terms that no person, whether male or female, could be virtuous who was ignorant. About Wollstonecraft Blease stated, "She knew that every woman who found her beauty a sufficient compensation for strength of mind was thereby encouraged to neglect her higher faculties, and to make charm of face and figure an excuse for dishonesty of mind and heart." Blease transformed Wollstonecraft—who married William Godwin only after she became pregnant, and who continued to maintain her own establishment even after her marriage—into a model of rectitude and a proponent of the integrity of the family unit. Blease wrote of Wollstonecraft: "She pointed out that the stability of society depended on the family and there could be no security in a union when one of the parties had no attraction for the other but those which belonged to her sex." The fact that Mary Wollstonecraft's ideas were stimulated by the French Revolution was evidence that that event was crucial for the development of a new attitude toward the female sex. Blease considered the women's movement a symptom of the resurgence of the political idealism promoted by the French Revolution, and the triumph of equal rights for women as the culmination of a process that started with the demand for equal rights for all men.

After the French Revolution ended the political subjection of men, and the enthronement of reason raised inevitable questions about religious belief, Blease saw a new spirit of unity emerging among women as a class—a spirit "marked by the acceptance of independent work as an economic necessity and also as an end in itself to strengthen and develop character." The upward movement that Blease discerned in the nineteenth century was called the Great Revival, and was characterized by the influence women progressively sought to exert in politics. Stages in the Great Revival were the participation of women in the Anti-Corn Law League in the 1840s; the establishment of a forum for women with the founding of the National Association for the Promotion of Social Science in 1857; the publication of the first issue of *The Englishwoman's Journal* in 1858; and the legislation that enabled women to hold property, get divorced, and vote in municipal elections. After a bow in the direction of John Stuart Mill, whom he credited with buttressing the justice of the women's cause and with stressing the costs to society of the psychology induced by subjection, Blease was fervent in his insistence that women, and women alone, were responsible for the advances that had been made. In extrapolating women's contributions from the past, enlarging their roles, and projecting on to them characteristics of the new woman, Blease established the lines along which women's history has been written since. In a burst of hyperbole, he declared, "To claim any credit on behalf of men for the Married Women's Property Act is as absurd as to give credit to the House of Lords for the Reform Acts."

Any woman reading *Emancipation* might well be inspired, as Blease meant her to be, with the advances individual women had pioneered. Blease reported that their example had already produced a new woman, and that their determination held the promise for new opportunities for women including free choice on whether or not to marry and "greater frankness in the intercourse of the sexes." In this glowingly optimistic account women, who had to all intents and purposes been slaves in the late seventeenth century, stood poised on the verge of achieving their emancipation, which Blease defined as "their advance from sex subordination to sex friendship."

Blease regarded the militant struggle of the suffragettes, under way even as he was writing *Emancipation*, as a natural outcome of previous advances and as indicative of a new attitude among women, at least some of whom had ceased to regard themselves as men's inferiors, destined merely to follow men's dictates. Women's idealistic impulses—including their "purity of motive"—were put in sharp contrast to the materialism of the masculinists. Blease saw the masculine cause encompassed in the antisuffragists, whom he identified with the forces of despair because of their promotion and encouragement of the sex drive; their emphasis on brute force as the guiding principle in life; their distrust of the application of moral rules to public conduct; their "suspicion of the whole principle of representative government; and their dread of purposeful attempts to improve the conditions of society."

Blease was only twenty-six when he wrote *Emancipation*, and his hope "that by way of the sisterhood of women we may arrive more quickly at the brother-hood of man" is a pre-World War I testament of youth which equated feminism with idealism. He had unbounded confidence in the potential of the women's movement. He concluded his preface with these words:

To what changes in the social structure, in political institutions, and in family life the free expression of the opinions of women will ultimately lead us, I cannot tell. For the present I am content to work for the removal of all impediments which now prevent that free expression. As to what lies beyond, I have seen something of the new women, and I am not afraid.

The year 1913 saw two more assessments of the women's movement which put the ongoing suffrage struggle in a historical framework and provided a vision of a future in which men shared power with women to the benefit of both. They reflected the tensions and uncertainties of the pre-World War I years, when socialists and pacifists were trying to show the bankruptcy of the masculine cause and its promotion of physical force, the individual ego, and economic greed.

Henry Noel Brailsford saw feminism, pacifism, and socialism as inextricably intertwined, with each as necessary as the others for the future of civilization. *Shelley, Godwin, and Their Circle* affirmed that feminism was rooted in the same rational tradition as socialism and pacifism. The *Circle* included William Godwin, Mary Wollstonecraft, and Percy Bysshe Shelley; Brailsford saw it as the beginning of a new consciousness with feminist, socialist, and pacifist impulses. He focussed on this consciousness at a time when all three traditions were hanging in the balance.

Brailsford showed that Godwin and Wollstonecraft brought the radicalism of the Enlightenment to England with their belief in the perfectability of mankind through the use of reason. Godwin identified government as the source of all repression—which diminished the human spirit—and of war—which destroyed life. His idea was integral to socialism and pacifism. Since this theory had special import for women, whose freedoms had been totally eliminated by the man-made laws of governments hostile to their aspirations, Brailsford considered Wollstonecraft to be the heart and soul of the circle.

Brailsford saw Wollstonecraft's *Vindication of the Rights of Women* as an application of Enlightenment ideals to women. Wollstonecraft was, in fact, some-thing of a miracle for Brailsford, springing, as it were, full grown from the philosophes' heads, like Athene from the head of Zeus. She was an embodiment of reason, with no antecedents among her own sex and very few among males. Brailsford quite simply considered the *Vindication* the most original book of the eighteenth century, since in its pages a woman "was for the first time trying to use her own mind and coming to conclusions based on her own experiences rather than echoing ideas that males had stated more forcefully." He thought that, in stressing the importance of education for women, she brought home the essence of the Enlightenment, that reason acquired through education was the key to progress. According to Brailsford, there was little hope for women so long as the opinion prevailed that minds come into the world with their qualities innate and their limitations fixed by nature. Wollstonecraft not only disputed this point, but took on such bitter-enders in the masculine cause as Jean Jacques Rousseau to make her case that, if women were educated, they would show themselves the equals of males and would not remain the trivial, helpless creatures that they were expected to be. As an individual, Wollstonecraft was to Brailsford what all women who taste the heady brew of reason could become, a mover and shaker with enormous potential for the progress of civilization. Brailsford's evaluation of her was rhapsodic: "In asserting boldly and unequivocally that everything in women's future depended on changing men's attitudes toward women and women's attitudes toward themselves, she raised the banner of the revolution higher than the males who preceded her." In Brailsford's eyes she surpassed Godwin, since she was free of the "dogmatic individualism" which distorted his speculation and contradicted the socialism implicit in his thought.

When it came to stating the case for women's rights, no one could improve on Wollstonecraft as far as Brailsford was concerned, and it remained only for the latter-day feminists to realize the goals she had articulated. These he saw as coeducation, elimination of the double standard, equal employment opportunity, and the franchise. Lest the author of the women's Magna Carta emerge solely as a paragon of the intellect, Brailsford stressed that she was very much a woman and that her rationality did not detract from those feminine attributes that masculinists insisted women lost when they used their brains. Brailsford saw her as a romantic, who was "in love with love" and a "worshiper of domestic life" at the same time. Brailsford thus separated Wollstonecraft from the sex radicalism which Godwin personified, and asserted by implication women's moral and idealistic qualities. To read Brailsford is to become aware of the enormous task the male feminists were undertaking in justifying the women's movement as part of a historical process: giving positive support to those engaged in the ongoing struggle for equal rights; providing role models for women; and reassuring the large numbers of holdouts, both male and female, that equality was in their best interests.

It was an American, Floyd Dell, who went beyond Mary Wollstonecraft, and women's past, to examine contemporary prototypes of feminism as a means of assessing their future as world builders. Dell (1887-1969) was a novelist, poet, and critic whose feminism was born of a conviction that the United States was an ideological wasteland, and of a desire to change the materialistic value system of middle-class America. Toward this goal, he initiated a movement known as the New Renaissance, which flowered in pre-World War I Greenwich Village. It was intended to counter the distortions in class and sex relationships that were a by-product of the capitalist ethos through the healing and revitalizing effects of art. Born in Illinois, Dell came to New York via Iowa, where he grew up, and Chicago, where he did a stint as literary reviewer for the *Friday Literary Review*. In this capacity he championed Theodore Dreiser, Sherwood Anderson, and Sinclair Lewis, writers critical of middle-class values.

Dell's feminism had particular urgency, for he believed that the American middle class—hell-bent for profits—lacked any of the leavening sense of *noblesse oblige* that made the English aristocracy patrons of culture and devotees of philanthropic activities. His belief that capitalist exigencies made it impossible to develop any facet of the personality other than the materialistic one made him a socialist. He thought of socialism not just as a change in the economic and political structure, but as the best hope for that rebirth, that renaissance of culture which would enhance and give meaning to the stultified lives of Americans, whose world was bounded by the quest for material success. Dell was convinced that the emancipation of women was essential to his renaissance.

In *Women as World Builders* (1913), Dell explored the soul of modern feminism through a number of women whose energies had already wrought changes in old attitudes. He perceived that the women's movement was a creation of men who were rebelling against the dispiriting values of the patriarchal and capitalistic system and who wanted support from women, who, as their comrades-in-arms, would derive immediate benefits from their release from those twin oppressors of the human spirit. The women's movement was also by extension, a revolt against those women—"the courtesan type"—who defended the male power structure because of the indirect power they could gain by sexual seductiveness. "Men," Dell said, "are tired of the subservient woman—the pretty slave with all the slave's subtlety and cleverness." His own desire that women should become world builders gave him the credentials to evaluate the women's movement: "It is then as a phase of the great human renaissance inaugurated by men that the women's movement deserves to be considered...and what more fitting than that a man should sit in judgment upon the contemporary aspects of that movement, weighing out approval and disapproval." In his list of worthies Dell considered only those women who fitted his specifications for the new woman—"self-sufficient, able, broadly imaginative, and healthy-minded." He rejected those women whose concept of the feminine was focussed on their sexuality. Dell proclaimed his concern with woman as producer, not lover. He noted, "The woman who finds her work will find her love. But the woman who sets her love above everything else, I would gently dismiss from our present consideration as belonging to the courtesan type."[11]

Dell admired the Shavian who struggled against unwomanly women, patriarchical stereotypes and emerged to independent selfhood and equality with males. As a woman who challenged all the precepts of patriarchy, Charlotte Perkins Gilman enjoyed a premier place in Dell's gallery of contemporary feminist heroines. He identified her as the most intransigent feminist of them all, and categorically admired her for it. Dell regarded her as a poet, an idealist, "a lover of life who reveled in its beauty." He attributed her insistence that women must work outside the home and become part of the productive labor force to her understanding that women could not attain that creative outlook that Gilman had herself achieved while they were bound to "soul-deadening" tasks of housekeeping and child care. Gilman received Dell's heartfelt approval for being the enemy "of all base domesticity, of all degrading love. She gives her approval only to that work which has in it something high and free and that love which is the dalliance of the eagles." In the home, "this private food-preparing and baby-rearing establishment, she sees a machine which breaks down all that is good and noble in women,... which degrades and pettifies them." Dell credited Gilman with a sense of reality for perceiving that most male labor was no more edifying than women's domestic tasks; but, as a socialist, she hoped that a revolution in modern industry might make work more meaningful for both sexes. Without the opportunity for fulfillment outside the home, Dell declared, motherhood becomes "simply an inevitable perpetuation of the emptiness and boredom which characterizes the lives of most people." He chastised the majority of males, who were put off by Gilman's advocacy of cooperative kitchens and child care centers; as far as he was concerned the end of freedom from domestic drudgery was one "which all intelligent males must desire."

Dell considered Emmeline Pankhurst and Jane Addams in tandem in order to provide contrasts between them. While Dell was writing *World Builders*, Emmeline Pankhurst was defying all conventional precepts of femininity with her militant posture. He was not moved by the raging fears of the masculinists that militant women were showing themselves to be "deadlier than the male." He considered their militance all the more reason for giving women the vote so as to render them harmless. Dell clearly did not expect a great deal of change through the ballot, but believed that, if changes were possible through "this inordinately malfunctioning political system, women are the ones to accomplish them." He told dubious males that if women did transform politics "from a vicious end to an efficient means, from a cancer into an organ... we males who have so long played in our politics at innocent games of war, we shall have an opportunity to fight in earnest at the side of the Valkyries."

Jane Addams's methods were an obvious contrast to the militant ones of Emmeline Pankhurst. Dell saw Addams as conciliatory, never defiant, using the methods of the traditional woman in trying to ameliorate intolerable conditions. She acted in essence as a go-between among the male power centers of business and government. According to Dell, by playing the rules and not rocking the boat Addams had won respect, but little influence and even less power. Dell's conclusion from the two examples: "It is women's amazonian qualities, their uncompromising nature that will make the difference in their fortunes," rather than the patience and fortitude they are too ready to display.

Olive Schreiner and Isadora Duncan were also considered as a pair. They were compared rather than contrasted as they both represented a vital area of the female presence for Dell—the artistic world of truth and beauty. Dell saw their significance in their attempt to integrate body and mind, a goal of the New Renaissance. Duncan was a dancer who sought to demonstrate that the natural movements of the body contained the highest possibilities of choreographic beauty. Schreiner was a writer and an active feminist who believed that women should not be kept out of any area of work for which they had the capacity.

According to Dell, Duncan and Schreiner "have each shown the way to a new freedom of the body and the soul. . . . [They] are demanding everything as their sphere. . . . They will not exchange one place for another. . . but they will achieve all rights to which their bodies and brains give them explicit title."

Beatrice Webb and Emma Goldman were presented as another pair of opposites. The measure of the difference was that "Beatrice Webb had compiled statistics, and Emma Goldman had preached the gospel of freedom." Neither were areas in which women were able to function, let alone distinguish themselves, before an inward struggle provided the impetus for their pioneering work. Webb's affinity for facts contradicted a masculinist article of faith that insisted on the predominantly emotional makeup of women. Nor could any one think of researching statistics as romantic or sentimental. But it was Dell's point that the stereotype did not, and never had, reflected reality. He saw women as preeminently realists: "She deals when she is herself with the material facts of the life she knows. Her great talent is to confront facts starkly." Dell expected a future in which women were influential "to have more of the hard matter of fact quality, the splendid realism characteristic of women."

Emma Goldman was an anarchist. Dell noted that she entered the anarchist movement when it was shifting its tactics from violence to political methods, and believed that she influenced that change. For Dell, Goldman had a legitimate social function, "that of holding before our eyes the ideal of freedom. . . . She is licensed to taunt us with our moral cowardice, to plant in our souls the nettles of remorse at having acquiesced so tamely in the brutal artifice of present day society." In the last analysis, however, Dell admired the realism of Webb more than the revolutionary ardor of Goldman as he believed fact to have more revolutionary potential than feeling.

Ellen Key, the Swedish social reformer, was a contradiction to Dell. He regarded her as a mixture of science, sociology, and mysticism. In the name of a higher morality, she advocated bachelor motherhood for women who chose not to marry, and trial marriages for those who did. Dell viewed her emphasis on motherhood rather than on the legitimacy of the children, and her recommendation of trial marriages in order to preserve monogamy, as attempts to preserve what was most important in the Puritan tradition, the family. He viewed her as a conservative whose proposals had the best chance of eliminating prostitution, that perennial concern of the feminists. Dell considered it a supreme irony that to the "pervasive masculine world, women's acts of conservation will seem to the timid like the shattering of all values, the debacle of civilization, the Gotterdamerung."

THE POST-SUFFRAGE ERA

World War I cast a deep shadow over the women's movement, one that lengthened with the impact of Marxism and Freudianism in the postwar world. All the feminine values that the traitors to masculinity considered crucial to the humanization of society were called into question, and women's struggle to achieve equality with men was drastically undermined.

The male supporters of women's suffrage considered their feminism to be part and parcel of their commitment to democracy, pacifism, and in most cases, socialism. They thought of these ideologies as the political expression of "the women's point of view." World War I gave rise to questions on whether this triad had overriding significance for feminists. Emmeline and Christabel Pankhurst had jettisoned all three as part of the tactical twists and turns in their struggle to obtain the suffrage. The WSPU began as the women's branch of the Labour party, committed to democratic socialism. In 1907, the WSPU became an authoritarian organization exclusively controlled by Emmeline and Christabel Pankhurst. The expulsion of the Pethick-Lawrences in 1912 saw its remaining ties to socialism cut. In an ends-justify-the means strategy, the Pankhursts were even flirting with the Protestant rebels in Northern Ireland, who were threatening civil war to prevent Home Rule for Ireland. When World War I broke out, the Pankhursts showed that women could be as fiercely militaristic as any of the jingoists who had been in the forefront of the antisuffragist drives. The male supporters of the suffragettes tended to see the Pankhursts' authoritarianism as a military expedient, comparable to the action of a general commanding troops during battle. They saw the split with the Pethick-Lawrences simply as an elimination of male influence, and considered it as a legitimate part of the process by which women would adhere to their own principles and gain experience in public affairs. The Pankhursts' one-hundred-and-eighty-degree turn during World War I, during which they supported the war abroad on behalf of a government which had frequently reduced their legitimate demands to clubhouse ridicule, was less easy to explain. For Israel Zangwill, who had no problem supporting the Pankhursts' militancy on behalf of the suffrage, their militarism and affirmation of physical force were a distinct letdown. In his eyes, Christabel Pankhurst changed from a woman having "the spiritual assurance and practical genius of a St. Catherine of Siena" to a jingo "with whom not one of the demagogues who ship up the beast in man could vie."

The success of the Marxist revolutionaries in Russia in 1917 was another example of the triumph of the physical force theory that had been the stock-in-trade of masculinists in the prewar period. The male feminists derived their socialism from the democratic, "moral force" tradition of Robert Owen, and believed women's values were represented in their approach. Nevertheless, the heady victory of the Marxists won women converts in droves, even though the Marxists had never shown any sympathy for the feminists, and demanded loyal servitude of the women who joined rather than offering them the comradeship and equality which they nominally stood for.

These reverses did not deter Frederick Pethick-Lawrence or George Bernard Shaw, neither of whom could contemplate a future world that did not have women actively participating in public affairs. Pethick-Lawrence went into Labour politics after World War I. He did not find his wartime stand as a conscientious objector a political liability and was elected Labour M.P. for West Leicester in 1923, defeating Winston Churchill, who was the Liberal candidate. He saw his election as a victory for feminism as well as a vindication of his pacifism, and continued to work to bring women's point of view to bear in politics. His maiden speech in the Commons was made on behalf of pensions for widowed mothers. He refused to believe that the struggle for women's suffrage had been in vain because the women's movement was left ideologically bereft and without a program once the vote was won. The 1918 bill which gave women the suffrage had only enfranchised women over the age of twenty-eight. Pethick-Lawrence immediately began to work toward giving all women over twenty-one the vote. That goal was won in 1928. Pethick-Lawrence took the floor on that occasion to mark the importance of that day when "for the first time women were an equal sovereign with men."

Pethick-Lawrence believed the results of the suffrage fully justified the struggle. He noted, "We claimed it would give women higher status; alter the attitude of the sexes toward each other; end the subjection of women; ennoble them to obtain equality of opportunity; improve their economic position; procure reforms to benefit themselves, their children, and the community." He could see the psychological gain most readily when he looked at prewar pictures of working women, "old beyond their years, exhausted by the struggle of life. Let them look at women of all classes today. They cannot fail to note the difference."[12]

Pethick-Lawrence expanded on what was involved in the woman's point of view. He did not believe there were any differences in mental capacities between male and female but did feel that there were psychological differences. As Pethick-Lawrence put it:

Men tend to look upon life as an adventure to be lived at the time for its own sake, women tend to regard it as a means to an end which finds its highest expression in the concern for the future of the race....This inclines women to be more personal and subjective than men and to distrust the application of logic to individual life....It makes it more important that their viewpoint shall be represented equally with that of men in the counsels of the nation.

He refused to countenance any characterization of female traits which was used to put women at a disadvantage. Masculinists charged that since women were more "emotional" than men, they could not handle critical situations. Pethick-Lawrence saw only differences in emotional reaction: "It means simply that the emotion of the average woman gives a more sensitive response than those of the average man. The separate judgements of the two sexes are therefore a valuable check on one another."[13]

Pethick-Lawrence considered the goal of life to be the growth and the enlargement of the personality. He included in the process "the transcendence of the limits of sex, class, race, age, and creed." He tried to apply these criteria of personality growth in his own life and it may be surmised that he tried to express the woman's point of view in his own approach to public office. Pethick-Lawrence maintained his pacifism, but the feminist pacifists never believed in peace at any price. Surrender of basic principles was too high a price to pay for peace; therefore they supported the militant suffragettes in their stand against a government that sought to degrade them. Pethick-Lawrence was a pacifist before and during World War I because he thought a negotiated settlement was possible without either side having to compromise on basic principles. He did not think it was possible to accommodate Adolf Hitler without violating human dignity and self-respect. Thus, he thought it pointless to appease Hitler—"a kind of embodied Karma" —and fully supported the government in World War II.

Pethick-Lawrence was elevated to the peerage in 1945 and appointed secretary of state for India. In that capacity he undertook the monumental task of working out the plan for Indian independence, He saw the undertaking of building bridges among the Hindus and the Moslems over the Pakistan issue as a supreme test of his ability to "transcend the limits of race."

In 1949 when George Trevelyan questioned him about his role in the suffragette campaign of forty years past, Pethick-Lawrence was unapologetic and still working for greater involvement of women in public affairs. His affirmation that the women's struggle has been "of considerable historic importance" was based on his conviction that it was the women's suffrage issue which had discredited the Liberal party and which was a major factor in causing its ultimate demise. He justified the militance in which he and the suffragettes had engaged, stating that reason and argument were the preferred methods for an aggrieved group to win rights, but where these fail "it has no alternative but to use extraordinary and extra-legal methods unless it is prepared to acquiesce in its own subjection."[14] He noted that the Indians, whose independence he was instrumental in obtaining, had followed that course. Moreover, he believed that the suffragettes' tactics had been successful in rousing the sympathy of large numbers of women, in directing the attention of the general public to the question, and in making it a serious public issue rather than the club joke the masculinists thought it to be. Pethick-Lawrence was convinced that it was the suffragettes' activity which won women to vote. He thus took issue with the school of thought which held that the vote was given out of recognition for the wartime services of the Pankhursts and their followers.

In 1955, Pethick-Lawrence was still active in supporting women. In the general election of that year, he campaigned for Shirley Catlin, daughter of Vera Brittain and one of the youngest of the Labour party candidates. To him she typified the political young woman, whose viewpoint was essential in a polarized world, and for whose sake he had gone to prison years before she was born.[15] Shirley Catlin became Shirley Williams, a Labour cabinet minister and one of the founders, in 1981, of the Social Democratic party, an offshoot of the Labour party. She was the first of the Social Democrats to win election to Parliament.

George Bernard Shaw was convinced that the woman's point of view as well as her best interests should lead her in the direction of socialism. As a Fabian evolutionary socialist, he believed in the power of education for constructive change. Convinced that women were reasonable creatures who had the same intellectual capacities as men, he deliberately made his appeal to the intellectual, unwomanly woman he had drawn in his plays. Shaw's unwomanly women had an awareness of the world around them and took their social responsibilities seriously. The women to whom he addressed *The Intelligent Woman's Guide to Socialism* (1928) would not be able to gain gratification from owning diamonds while their poorer sisters had no clothes to wear.[16]

It was entirely consistent for the author of *Dear Dorothea* to advise the adult woman about her relations with the world, just as earlier he had advised the five-year-old about the perils of childhood so that she could protect herself against adult exploitation. *The Intelligent Woman's Guide* was written to explain to women how capitalism exploits them both in the marketplace and in the home. Shaw evidenced his respect for women's reasoning capacity, both in the thoroughness with which he undertook the task, going into every aspect of economic and political life from the intricacies of international finance to the mundane details of party organization, and in his attention to syntax, always using the pronoun *she* when giving examples.

A reading of *The Guide* is not just an education in the workings of capitalism; it is also an explanation of why the vote made no material difference, and would not, unless women began to express feminine ideology politically and to use their power in a concerted way. Shaw tirelessly reiterated that, under capitalism, exploitation was a woman's lot from childhood to the grave. As a girl her destiny was determined by lack of equal educational opportunity. Education, Shaw apprised the intelligent woman, was still class education, with rich boys going to the best schools, poor boys going to lesser institutions, and girls "usually having no opportunity to fulfill their natural abilities at all."

Even with the vote, Shaw made it clear that, under capitalism, marriage was a woman's only viable occupation, and once married, if she had to work or chose to work for wages, her oppression became even harsher. For crucial work she did in the home—that of bearing and rearing children and keeping house—she was never paid directly, "and so many foolish people came to forget that it was work at all and spoke of the man as the breadwinner." This was nonsense. From first to last the woman's work in the house was vitally necessary to the existence of society, whilst millions of men were engaged in wasteful or positively mischievous work, the only excuse for which was that it enabled them to support their useful and necessary wives."

Shaw explained that the women of the "idle rich" class fared no better than the poor in the marriage-go-round. This capitalist class of woman—the pervasive flappers of the 1920s—did not need to work for wages, and technological advances had reached the point where Shaw considered them "underworked" in the home despite the shortage of servants. Their only means of maintaining their leisured life was to marry a wealthy man. Shaw reminded such women that in order to obtain the all-important husband they often had to resort to "ruses." This was not good for their self-respect and did not lead to happy marriages, as men realized "they have been made a convenience of." Shaw considered it an "ironic vanity" for anyone—man or woman—to attempt to "secure happiness and freedom by having plenty of money and nothing to do."

Shaw put all of women's concerns in a socialist frame of reference. He insisted that marriage in a socialist system offered the possibility of independence, dignity, and self-respect. Since women would be able to get the education and skills to realize their talents, those who did not choose to marry need not do so. Happier marriages for those who did get married would be assured, since divorce would be both cheap and easy. No woman would need to worry about marriage becoming a permanent state of bondage because she had a large number of children which she was unable to support alone. A socialist regime would become involved in the population question, and the need to establish a balance between population and resources would inevitably benefit women, as their own desires to have fewer children would become the social norm.

Neither could women be good mothers under capitalism. The domestic feminists had promoted eugenics and professionalized motherhood as a means whereby women could gain power and status through adherence to their biological functions. The first step required that women use discrimination when selecting a mate. Under capitalism, the majority of poor women had little choice when selecting a mate. For poor women, marriage was a necessity, and they tended to marry without making any qualifications about the character or intelligence of the man. Those women who were in a position to marry for love, middle- and upper-class women, were guided by class interests above any other considerations. If redistribution of income were to take place—and that was how Shaw defined socialism—"a dustman's daughter could marry a duke's son and if the race did not improve under such circumstances it would be unimprovable."

As consumers women, who often had a difficult time making ends meet and who had to budget their various expenses to maintain the health and well-being of their families, were fighting a losing battle, according to Shaw. Capitalists were not above creating artificial shortages to drive up the price of necessities, thereby increasing their profits. For everything that she bought the consumer paid not only the labor cost of the article, which she justly should pay, but also the hidden costs that supported "the idlers" who made no contribution to the productive process.

Shaw warned women to avoid the Scylla and Charybdis of the extreme right and left—offered as solutions to the economic and social ills that ravaged the postwar world. He regarded the Bolshevik Revolution in Russia, "where it is now established that capital was made for man, and not man for capitalism, and where the children were being taught the Christian morality of Communism instead of the mammonist morality of Capitalism," as an improvement over the regime that preceded it; but he did not consider the Soviet system to be a socialist one, and thought the Russians had a long way to go to achieve economic equality. As early as 1927, Shaw saw fascism as a coup d'etat of the extreme right, whose purpose was to perpetuate the capitalist system. Shaw called it "the poor man's capitalism" and thought its appeal to ignorance; its romantic idealization of a leader; its assertion of all the brutal instincts; and its exhortation to excesses of patriotic fervor; to be the surest way to destroy civilization. His advice to the intelligent woman was, "You had better beware of it." Nor was Shaw impressed with the compromise agreements to maintain capitalism that were the rule in the United States. There, he felt, powerful corporate heads and ambitious union leaders were cooperating to perpetuate capitalism and thus defeat the ordinary people through the very democratic process that was supposed to enhance their lives.

Shaw attempted to instill his own commitment to democratic socialism in the intelligent women to whom he addressed *The Guide*. True to his Fabian heritage, he was convinced that socialism must be realized through the parliamentary process if its benefits were to be obtained. A revolution and the civil wars which follow in its wake would simply destroy the productive capacity of the society and render the economy a shambles, a situation from which it would be difficult to recover.

Shaw's appeal to women on behalf of democratic socialism testified to his belief that feminine values included a disposition to conserve what was good and useful while eliminating what was inefficient and wasteful. Although he did not think that the vote, manipulated as it was by power brokers, including politicians, businessmen, and labor leaders, could accomplish a great deal, he explained that it had a negative effect which could benefit women. The fact that one vote could turn the scale in close elections "secures you a consideration as long as inequality of income prevents you from being really represented by the members of the Government. Therefore cling to it tooth and nail."

While a vogue for force tended to undermine women's cultural values, the impact of Freudian psychology devastated them. The philosophical feminists believed equality between the sexes was possible if the aspirations and the intellectual capacities common to males and females were emphasized and if sex, which males and females approached from different perspectives and needs, was minimized. Although Sigmund Freud paid lip service to the nineteenth-century view of women as civilizers, his lasting contribution was the resexualization of women, which had been given forward momentum by Havelock Ellis.[17] Ellis and Freud had no differences about woman's sexual nature, her irrationality, and her proper role. Freud's influence, however, was more pervasive and his legacy more enduring because of the nature of the following he acquired. Ellis's constituency was the less educated lower class whom he reached through the mass media in both England and the United States, and he eventually suffered from over-exposure. Freud became the idol par excellence of the educated middle class primarily in the United States. So deeply was Freudianism imbedded in American middle-class culture that to "enter analysis" became a status symbol denoting both the monetary rewards of success and the guilt and conflicts engendered by the striving toward it. Freud's ideas were incorporated into the curricula of American colleges and universities, and the analysts who elaborated them in a doctor-patient relationship assumed the role of that elite of technocrats invoked by late nineteenth-century Progressives in order to maintain social control. In a setting putatively value-free, the Freudians disseminated the social philosophy of individualistic capitalism. They believed that the primary goal of the therapeutic process is individuation with any inclination to transcend the self regarded as a form of escape. The source of depressions and conflicts in the largely female clientele of Freudian practitioners is inevitably traced to destructive maternal influences; the patriarchal structure is the norm and adjustment to it a sign of maturity. The Freudians touted the doctrine of sexual rights and gave certified assurances as to the salubrious effects of sexual expression. In their view of society which supported the status quo and in their defense of male dominance and female subservience in society Freud and his followers differed on every fundamental from the male feminists in the philosophical tradition.

While the male feminists in the philosophical tradition regarded specifically female characteristics with great admiration and thought them capable of humanizing mankind, Freud put feminine traits in the general compartment of neuroses, or emotional maladaptation. The male ego, with which the traitors to the masculine cause had no patience and which they saw as the source of man's greed and destructiveness, was exalted by Freud. Equated with masculine pride, it was a thing to be nurtured and cultivated rather than questioned. An ideal that considered the development of the ego as the quintessential human aspiration fit in well in a society that fostered the individualism of laissez faire capitalism; it had no relevance to the social communitarian outlook that the male feminists valued in women.

The philosophical male feminists appreciated women on their own terms; Freud could not comprehend women without using the male as a reference point. As far as Freud was concerned, women were failed or incomplete men whose outlook was determined by their despair at finding themselves without a penis, the *sine qua non* of power, the focus of the male ego, and therefore the criterion of worth in the Freudian world. Moreover, the Freudians saw women brooding over the irrevocable fact of gender all their lives and trying frantically to compensate for their deficiency. The woman who chose to exercise her newly won political rights by entering public life or by pursuing a career—both highly desirable goals from the philosophical feminist standpoint—was, in the Freudian context, condemned as unnatural. She was viewed as trying to compensate for her unsatisfying biology by competing with men—a hopeless task on the face of it, and one which doomed her to bitterness and frustration. The old epithet of the masculinists—"unfeminine"—was reincarnated to describe these endeavors and was now given intellectual respectability, whereas previously such viewpoints were considered mere prejudices. Nor was the moral idealism which had solidified women in the nineteenth century considered a point in their favor. In the Freudian world view, the women who had been drawn into public life to campaign against the double standard and who had earned the respect and admiration of reformers in the process, were repressed hysterics who were venting their frustrations on men. Thus, all women's public activities were either attempts at compensation—if they entered male-dominated professions—or symptoms of repression—if they engaged in philanthropic work. In the male feminists' frame of reference, it was male activities that had a sexual base. Capitalism, with its demand for immediate gratification in profits; its disdain for the long-range consequences of the rapid depletion of natural resources; and its overproduction of progeny, was distinctively male.

If one believed in the biological determinism purveyed by the Freudians, a woman's place was once again in the private domain of the household. The extent to which a woman realized that her biological makeup made domesticity her ultimate destiny was considered an index to her emotional maturity and adjustment to reality. Male characteristics such as aggressiveness—frowned upon by the traitors to masculinity—were upgraded to the norm, and given a scientific imprimatur. Women's more pacific natures were considered as, at most, private virtues, which might arouse the male protective instinct and thereby gain them a husband, but which had no place in the real world. Freud was in basic agreement with those of his contemporaries who believed women's intellectual capacities were limited by their biology. Women's alleged difficulty in dealing with abstract concepts and their imputed failure to appreciate philosophical principles were further proof of an inferiority which was irremediable, since it was a function of women's sexual organs.

John Stuart Mill insisted that historically women had had no choice but to internalize male demands. He believed that women's real nature was unknowable as long as men defined it as they always had—to fit male needs. He stated, "It is a subject on which nothing final can be known, so long as those who alone can really know it, women themselves have given but little testimony, and that mostly suborned."[18] It was Mill who called for a science of psychology to examine women's nature in a spirit of objectivity. Freud, who had translated some of Mill's work into German, was probably aware of Mill's challenge, but it is unlikely that Freud's conclusions, based on a pastiche of clinical data, speculative constructs, and the cultural assumptions of *fin-de-siècle* Vienna, would have satisfied Mill's standards of truth. The search for a science of the mind was also hampered by Freud's personal style. Authoritarian to the core, he expected absolute fidelity not only from the women in his life but from his associates and colleagues as well. The regularity with which he pronounced anathema on dissenters gave to the psychology movement the aura of a religious cult rather than a scientific fraternity of equals.

In his approach, Freud was more the intellectual heir of Karl Pearson than of Mill. The stereotyping of females as inadequate to cope with the public world paralleled in many ways the stigmatizing of various ethnic groups as inferior, a cultural feature of the late nineteenth century. The Irish, the Jews, the blacks, and ethnic minorities in Eastern Europe were all endowed with unfavorable traits, always the opposite of those supposedly possessed by the dominant group.

Pseudoscientific theories evolved, maintaining that those negative characteristics, because they were genetic, were indelible. These theories served to give the dominant group a perpetual lease on their power over the "inferior" groups.

For the male feminists, some of Freud's philosophical constructs had valuable potential for shedding light on the troubled human condition. His theory of the unconscious as the repository of primitive forces in civilized mankind had significant implications for writers and artists trying to grapple with the conflicts in their internal and external worlds. However, Freud's emphasis on sexuality as the be all and end all of human possibilities led Israel Zangwill to say that "Freud had a good case which he ruined by obscene overstatement." He had no inclination to credit Freud with any scientific validity. As if to vindicate his father, Zangwill's son, who became a psychologist, wrote in the preface of a psychological work he authored that the "standard of evidence upon which principal theories of psychology is based cannot by any stretch of the imagination be held up to fulfill the requirements of scientific precision."[19]

It was in the spirit of the artist and social philosopher synthesizing his intellectual world that Floyd Dell made a noteworthy attempt to integrate Freudian psychology with feminism and socialism. His goal was to make men and women "modern-minded" and to enhance the possibility for psychic health, which he defined as the ability to love and work. In *Love in the Machine Age*, Dell thought that the patriarchal family, the *bête noir* of the traitors to the masculine cause, was in a stage of transition. The patriarchal family, which Freud had shored up with his masculinist bias, was described by Dell as the seedbed of the neuroses identified by Freud as obstacles in the path to adult maturity.

Using anthropological, sociological, historical and psychological sources, Dell updated Engels's *Origin of the Family* and traced the patriarchal family to nomadic origins. He thought of the family as an essentially military system, well adapted to a group on the march. It also served the purposes of foreign conquerers ruling over a settled agricultural population. From its historical beginnings, in Dell's view, the family was associated with ruling castes and with the institutions of slavery, serfdom, landed property, and the military state. Power necessities "were the sole influence in the workings of the patriarchal family, the position of wives and children being akin to slaves, serfs, and cattle."[20]

Dell enumerated the institutions characteristic of patriarchy as arranged marriage, homosexuality, prostitution, polite adultery, and sacred celibacy. Arranged marriage was intended to preserve landed property intact from one generation to the next, with the exercise of paternal authority over adult decisions such as marriage having the effect of stunting the emotional growth of children and keeping them permanently attached to parents. According to Dell, "A man who is not free to choose his own work or his own wife is still to that significant extent a child." Dell saw both homosexuality and prostitution as the sex-compromises that patriarchal authority was willing to offer the infantilized adult, who was willing to submit to the authority of another male if he could do so and still maintain his own self-respect. Homosexuality was a sexual outlet for males in a military society such as that of the ancient Greek city-state. Cut off in adolescence from any female society, the males had homosexual affairs with one another. According to Dell, this was socially approved because it encouraged rivalry in military prowess. Dell thought that both homosexuality and prostitution derived from a contempt for women, an attitude binding on all patriarchs. He stated, "The male homosexual contempt for women, and the corresponding emotional infantilism of women, furnished also the psychological basis of prostitution. Sexual attraction was here permitted free play—upon the customary understanding of the complete social irresponsibility of the male and the complete social helplessness of the female."

Polite adultery was an outgrowth of the arranged loveless marriage. Dell defined it as any extramarital sexual relationship which involves a tacit or express agreement that it is not to be taken seriously. Sacred celibacy grew out of the economic limitations of the patriarchal family. With land, the economic measure and the means of support, going to the eldest son, surplus sons and daughters were given over to sacred functions such as priestcraft. The male celibates achieved status by service to the state. The priesthood became one of the recognized roads to power and was regarded by Dell as a form of sublimitated patriarchy.

Dell described the maturity that individuals in a nonpatriarchal setting are capable of achieving in Freudian terms. He saw the individual developing in successive stages on the Freudian model, but dropped the sex stereotyping characteristic of Freud. Dell made no distinction between the development or the potential of males and females. Both aspired to a mature state where they could love and work, and in both sexes emotional health was described as the capacity for enjoyment of both functions. The growth from the narcissistic, totally dependent infant to the heterosexual adult capable of enjoying love and work was, in part, a biological function. Dell believed that both sexes had a mating instinct as well as a sexual instinct and that the two were united in both males and females. In previous feminist thought, the female's sexual instinct was considered to be part of her maternal needs, but the male's was not directed to any goal except satisfaction. In affirming the existence of a paternal instinct to complement the female's maternal instinct, Dell aligned himself with the moral impulses in which feminism was deeply rooted.

Dell believed that the patriarchal family was in a state of transition because of the middle-class revolution which had already eliminated arranged marriage and the power of the surrogate patriarchy—the church. Following the Marxist analysis, which gave tremendous importance to the introduction of capitalism by the middle class and its usurpation of aristocratic political power, Dell saw the middle class opening up new possibilities for work and giving a new value to work—an activity disdained by the aristocracy, whose power was based on landed wealth. Through the Protestant Reformation, the middle class broke the power of the patriarchal church as well. Dell believed that the abandonment of arranged marriage and the ideal of sacred celibacy weakened the patriarchal family and left it vulnerable to further attacks, such as those taking place as a result of the triumphs of socialism in the twentieth century. It was Dell's hope that the women whom he had earlier described as world builders would find their cause in completing the patriarchal downfall. But in postwar America, Dell had to come to grips with the fact that the women he had earlier dismissed as "courtesan types" had crowded out the resplendent world builders. They were part of the system and he referred to them as "patriarchal mothers."

Dell's premise was that individuals were still prevented from reaching the goal of psychic health because of obstacles imposed by the patriarchal family. According to Dell, "The force of the patriarchal tradition is in the tissue of ignorance, misery and failure in love that goes on from generation to generation." A mother raised in a patriarchal household, who sees marriage as her only opportunity, who does not love her husband, and who turns to her child for emotional satisfaction, is the source of the sexual or oedipal feelings that the child fixes on her. The oedipal complex, which Freud saw as universal and a major test for the child to surmount, could thus be avoided altogether if the mother was not oriented to patriarchal needs. As a result, Dell recommended early separation of mother and child, and while he recognized that in the transition era this might bring some penalties to children, he considered it more important to save them from "the concentrated maternal managerial attentions" indicative of patriarchy.

In dealing with still existing patriarchal institutions such as polite adultery, Dell spoke as much in the accents of the sexual conservative as any of his pre-Freudian forebears. He had little that was positive to say about the sexual revolution, free love, or erotic rights. Dell considered polite adultery as a continuation of the compromises that were made under patriarchy; viewed in a social context, it was a middle-class adaptation of the aristocratic code whereby unhappy marriage alliances were made on the assumption that the parties could find satisfactions elsewhere. He cited the casual sexual encounters which were being touted as an expression of sexual freedom as a "symptom of pre-adult sexuality" —cases of arrested development, the individuals involved never having achieved a heterosexually mature stage. Turning Freud topsy-turvy, Dell regarded the women engaging in meaningless sexual affairs as "patriarchal" and in competition with men. The women carving niches for themselves in public life—the world builders—were his feminine ideal.

Dell took a very dim view of the granting of sexual privileges to adolescents simply because they had sexual desires and the physical capacity to satisfy them. He saw behind the modern attitude to give these relationships social sanction "patriarchal-mindedness," and noted:

The patriarchal mind can be detected by its incapacity for realizing that heterosexuality is something which requires time and experience for its development to the point of sexual mating. The patriarchal mind used to put children to bed and call it marriage; now, trying its damndest to be modern, it proposes to put children to bed and call it "freedom."

Dell was in favor of birth control since it freed women from the dangers and cares of constant childbearing and enabled them to work outside the home; but he did not go along with the basic premise of the sexual revolution that the availability of contraceptive devices freed women to be as promiscuous as men and was thus a significant step in the direction of equality. Dell considered "sex as amusement" an old patriarchal safety valve for reconciling individuals to the loss of their "biological rights to make responsible choices and commitments." He concluded that the play view of sex was founded on "a quasi-infantile fantasy" that sex and childbirth had nothing to do with one another. It precluded meaningful love, and when handed to adolescents as a toy constituted an education in irresponsibility. For Dell the sex act was more than a biological release of pent up feelings. It was the ultimate act of love, which had both social and mystical overtones, containing components of tragedy and awareness of loss as well as mutual satisfaction and fulfillment.

Dell imputed the trivialization of sex, a concomitant of the sexual revolution, to Havelock Ellis, and was highly critical of him. While Dell favored tolerance and recognized the validity of investigating human behavior in all its forms, he complained that no one would know from a reading of Ellis's *Psychology of Sex* that some people had passed through the childhood blocs and fixations that Ellis described as "variations," were expressing their sexual impulses free from patriarchal encumbrances, and were deriving more than sensual thrills from the experience: "Hence it is that the accidental stopping places in this process of development have been given by the sage [Ellis] an importance which well-nigh if not altogether obliterates any view of the adult goal." Dell took into account that everyone harbors some remnant of a childish fantasy, some infantile longing never fulfilled and never resolved. He felt that feelings could be legitimately expressed through art, where they attain universal significance, and through which the individual could vicariously fulfill his early wishes. Thus, the New Renaissance to which Dell had devoted his early endeavors was linked to a nonpatriarchal society.

Dell's aversion to patriarchy was combined with a strong belief in the family as the only viable vehicle for finding love and rearing children; this contradiction left him in something of a dilemma in the America of the 1920s. He provided no means whereby the patriarchal family could complete the transition to its dialectical opposite as long as patriarchal economic forms were retained. It was only toward the end of *Love in the Machine Age* that he made the crucial point connecting patriarchy with capitalism:

The patriarchal father, having been cast out from other fields remains enthroned in economics in the form of the presumably all-wise and certainly all-powerful private owner of industry, and the workers are still supposed to content themselves with the role of obedient and loyal children. . . . The banishment of patriarchialism from industry will be required to complete the modernization of the world.

The banishment of capitalism called for either a revolutionary solution, as in Marxism, or an evolutionary solution, such as socialism through the vote. Dell had no faith that the vote could bring meaningful change in the American political system. His loss of faith in a revolutionary solution had personal roots. At the time of the Russian Revolution, Dell was editor of *The Masses*, a socialist journal. He witnessed at first hand the ruthless government repression of socialist and pacifist activists, and was himself indicted along with fellow feminist Max Eastman, on a charge of "conspiring to promote insubordination and mutiny in the military and naval forces of the United States, and to obstruct recruiting and enlistment to the injury of the service." The jury at the trial deadlocked, and he was freed; but the experience made him acutely aware to what lengths capitalism-patriarchy would go to maintain itself.[21]

Dell was left with the liberal's faith in reason and education as a force for change. He was very much the teacher as he discussed child rearing with parents and the goals of adulthood with adolescents.[22] Writing in the 1920s, Dell was in a position to see the results of the professional and concentrated mothering that domestic feminists and Freudians prescribed for women. He was not impressed, and characterized the advice that was being doled out by self-appointed child experts as "counter-revolutionary patriarchal propaganda." Dell had a profound faith in the maternal instincts which had served women for eons, and like other philosophical feminists wanted to see these instincts extended to society. He felt that they were being undermined in the name of a grandiloquent social order, over which the domestic feminists would preside, and he regarded the latter as little more than irredentist patriarchs.

Dell had a decided animus toward the John Watson school of behavioral psychology. Watson was a relentless critic of mothers who did not follow his particular regimen of child rearing.[23] Dell found Watson's inclination to blame mothers, rather than the patriarchal setting in which they functioned, for their alleged failures "reckless and not a little foolish."

Watson actually preferred institutional child rearing to "unscientific" mothering. A faith in the beneficence of social engineering, which was the basis of the modern liberal state being shaped by progressives in the United States, appalled Dell, who believed that, under the guise of benevolence, the bureaucratic state spread patriarchal values and subverted women's values. He gave as an example the property relations which the state fostered in the role of benign parent, saying:

The real aim of such pseudo-scientific pretenses that social coercion is necessary in the domestic realm is not to make parents love their children; it is to keep them from loving any but "legitimate" children—it is an attempt to preserve the institution of family property from the dangers of instinctive parental love.

It is apparent that, in Dell's view, domestic feminism was patriarchy's last stand, and his faith in the family was predicated on matriarchal values.

Dell was at odds with the trendy permissiveness in child rearing being dispensed as educational dogma. He thought that under the name of tolerance parents were simply evading their responsibilities for providing their children with a set of social and moral values. Social commitment being a desideratum along with psychic health, he maintained that tolerance is the method, not the goal. Tolerance toward poverty and disease was no virtue in Dell's eyes. Neither did he condone psychological theories that insisted that the child should be adjusted to the real world. Adjustment raised the age-old question: "To what shall we adjust? Shall we seek to have our children adjust themselves to our city streets, our exploited amusements, our industrial civilization, our weakened homes, mechanized schools, shallow moral standards?"

On the surface Dell was ebulliently optimistic in predicting that patriarchy was in its last stages. But he offered little evidence that this was the case and underneath there was a pessimism born of the realization that the female world builders, who were to bring their influence to bear and complete the destruction of patriarchy, had not materialized. Dell yearned for women like Charlotte Perkins Gilman, who would humanize the industrial process so that work outside the home would be meaningful, and like Ellen Key, who would transcend both radicalism and conservatism with her feminine perspective. But in the 1920s, the world builders Dell had glorified were no longer in the public eye. They had disappeared, to be replaced by the flappers who adapted completely to patriarchal modes. Dell was implicitly critical of the women's movement for accepting the advances that some had made on patriarchal terms, rather than striving to impose feminine values on what he perceived to be a faltering system. Dell saw sexual liberation, the banner unfurled by post-world War I feminism, as a surrender to patriarchal standards of sexual behavior that undermined the unity women had attained as moral idealists. He saw no advantage to women who behaved as sexual aggressors, seeing them as

confused and awkward in their role of overt huntresses; they [women] are instinctively geared to make a sexually correct choice only under conditions of male competition for them. Mutual female competition for the same man does not bring all their sexual instincts into play—it brings their egoistic impulses into play instead, with the result that they take incredible pains to capture a man whom they sexually do not want—

and who has been rendered childish as a result of excessive catering to his needs. According to Dell, "The situation is one in which their behavior is muddled and stupid."

Poorer women were still getting the worst of it in the patriarchal order, shaky though Dell thought it to be. They had no choice but to work outside the home. They worked under the lash of necessity, "not to keep their self-respect, not as a way of doing their duty to society, not as a way of keeping from stagnation and idleness." They might prefer the greater emotional excitement of family life, but could not maintain an exclusively domestic role. Stuck in meaningless jobs, Dell believed that they sought emotional satisfactions in sexual affairs, that they were doubly exploited as wage slaves and as sexual slaves serving the patriarchal need for prostitutes free of charge. Dell stated, "It needs to be said that useful wage labor enlivened by occasional secret sexual love affairs, probably punctuated at intervals by abortions...is not a glorious or even a satisfactory career for a young women." Dell characterized it as a continuation of "patriarchal harlotry."

Love in the Machine Age, the last concerted attack on patriarchal capitalism from a feminist point of view, was written in the 1920s and published in the depths of the Depression. That the matriarchal values Dell had documented and admired in *World Builders* were necessary to humanize mankind was taken for granted. Dell did not really succeed in showing that this process of humanization was proceeding despite his assertion that patriarchy was in a state of transition. Instead, he made it clear that patriarchy had found a way of perpetuating itself by offering a variety of spurious gratifications as bait. Sexual libertinism, once an aristocratic privilege, was democratically extended to all. Dell saw all the institutions of American life co-opted. The regal women whose infinite variety of strengths he had catalogued—these potential world builders had been cast aside in favor of patriarchal role models. He was left with a degree of faith in individuals whose maternal and paternal instincts had survived in a patriarchal environment and who might thus be able to realize the social implications of these instincts.

These individuals are much like Dell himself, and he is at his best when he personifies nonpatriarchal traits in the characters in his novels. *Moon-calf* (1920) is an autobiographical novel and describes his own painful road to the maturity which redefines freedom not as "the bent of one's will...but [as] a relationship of individuals whose honesty and integrity spring from a knowledge of reality."

In its depiction of sex role reversal, *An Unmarried Father* (1927) adumbrates contemporary experiments. In this book Norman Overbeck, a small town lawyer, discovers his paternal instincts after a casual sexual encounter makes him a father. Norman, who wants to keep his baby even though the mother, an aspiring artist, does not want to marry him, goes through all the torments a woman might under similar circumstances. Dell makes it clear that in small town America, where patriarchal roots run deep, a man can acquire a baby no more easily than a woman without attracting attention. Norman leaves his law practice and takes a clerk's job in Chicago so that he can look after his child. He becomes bitter toward the patriarchal values that equate children with property:

He was living in prosperous America where the legal family had property rights to be defended against the claims of bastards.... If men were permitted to do what he had done, what would become of the family in its legal, sacred, property-inheriting sense. It would mean red unions and the breakup of close corporation homes, to be sure.[24]

Norman's feelings toward the mother, Isabel Drury, are the test of his maturity. In her rejection of her child and the woman's traditional role, she both piques and angers Norman. Consulting a doctor about her perversity, he comes away with Freudian absolutes—that her denial of her true role is the result of an unresolved conflict with her father. Norman does not believe this. Conflicted she might be, but her need to be an artist is entirely valid on its own terms, and one that would be completely understood if a man in similar circumstances were to reject his child. The realization of this truth causes Norman to love Isabel more deeply than he loves the entirely decent woman to whom he was once engaged, and who is willing to marry him and care for his child.

Love Without Money (1931) is a fictionalized version of *The Outline of Marriage* (1927), in which Dell offered advice to young people on the pitfalls of love and marriage. Peter Carr, on the threshhold of life, has all the youthful exuberance of adolescence. His father is a socialist who tries to instill in Peter the values Dell himself held. He holds capitalism to blame for women prostituting themselves and for boys taking what they can get from women: "I think that under capitalism there's small blame to any of us if we behave badly and much credit to us that we behave as well as we do." The father is contemptuous of "hypocritical bourgeois morality," which encourages fornication in the manner of the "idle rich," but he realizes that Peter must learn these things for himself if he is to grow up. Peter meets Gretchen, one of the "idle rich" who is resigned to the role she must play in patriarchal society. Peter and Gretchen fall in love, and Gretchen frees herself from her predestined fate. She gets a job and gains self-respect. On their road to a marriage where both will have to work, they encounter other characters who reflect Dell's social imperatives. Peter has a friend who must free himself from a patriarchal mother, who does not care how many girls he has so long as he does not commit himself to any one of them, thus displacing her. The flaming youth of the twenties, whose social purpose was decidedly underdeveloped, receive short shrift from another character who firmly upholds her parents' moral values:

The flaming youth that I see is just plain dumb. When these kids aren't having illegitimate babies, they're having abortions, or getting venereal disease. They just have no sense. And I'd rather be mid-Victorian than be classed with the younger generation. The Victorians had their secrets. Only they kept them. They didn't parade them before the world.[25]

Dell's characters, who find within themselves the integrity to build their lives on values which are the antithesis of those of their patriarchal surroundings, are the heroes and heroines of the transition era.

An assessment of Floyd Dell some thirty years after his last novel was written in effect sums up a basic impulse of that philosophical male feminist tradition of which he was a part. It describes him as a "moralist, a believer in good and evil, in right and wrong, with a religious duty of serving righteousness and hating and fighting evil."[26] Dell's intellectual integrity did not permit him to follow any "party" line. His support of the family made him appear "bourgeois" to his one-time Marxist allies; the fact that he was upholding matriarchal values and maternal influence in the family made him antimodern to the burgeoning psychology movement which established its credentials by second-guessing mothers.

The precipitous decline of Floyd Dell who, during the 1920s and 1930s was regarded as a major influence in American literature, is perhaps the best evidence that the patriarchal culture to which he was a traitor was reasserting itself rather than passing away, as Dell believed. Dell's last works constitute a valiant rearguard action on behalf of philosophical feminism against a masculine cause which had won legions of new converts by waving the banners of science, modernism, and progressivism. In detailing women's accommodation to patriarchal values, Dell chronicled and explained the postsuffrage demise of the women's movement, to which he had given his wholehearted support. It is a period that contemporary feminists regard as merely a setback and a lull between the first women's movement and the second, which was called into being to redeem the promise of equality that had not been fulfilled.

NOTES

1. All quotes from Friedrich Engels, *The Origin of the Family, Private Property and the State* (Chicago: Charles H. Kerr & Co. Cooperative, 1902), ch. 2. First published 1887.

2. Thomas Henry Buckle, *The Influence of Women on the Progress of Knowledge* (1858; reprint ed., London: A.C. Fifield, 1912), pp. 24-28.

3. Joseph McCabe, *The Religion of Women: An Historical Study* (London: Watts and Co., 1908).

4. Joseph McCabe, *Women in Political Evolution*. (London: Watts and Co.), 1909.

5. Roger Fulford, *Votes for Women* (London: Faber and Faber, Ltd., 1947), p. 73.

6. See Ford Madox Ford, *Yesterday* (Liveright Paper edition, 1972).

7. Ford Madox Ford, *This Monstrous Regiment of Women* (Women's Franchise League, 1912).

8. All quotes from W. Lyon Blease, *The Emancipation of the Englishwoman* (London, 1910: reissued by Benjamin Blom, Inc., 1971), introd., chs. 1-4. See also W. Lyon Blease, *Votes for Women Against Prejudice*, 1912.

9. A. V. Dicey, *Letters From a Friend on Votes for Women* (London, 1909). In Museum of London.

10. All quotes from H. N. Brailsford, *Shelley, Godwin, and Their Circle* (New York: Holt and Co. 1913), p. 205 ff.

11. All quotes from Floyd Dell, *Women as World Builders* (Forbes and Co., 1913), introd., chs. 1-4.

12. Frederick Pethick-Lawrence, *Fate Has Been Kind*. (London: Hutchinson and Co., 1942), p. 107.

13. Ibid., p. 207.

14. Vera Brittain, *Pethick-Lawrence: A Portrait* (London: George Allen & Unwin, 1963), pp. 215-18.

15. Ibid., p. 201.

16. All quotes from George Bernard Shaw, *The Intelligent Woman's Guide to Socialism* (New York: Random House, 1928), pp. 166 ff., 59 ff., 199, 53, 379, 475, 454.

17. See Sigmund Freud, *Civilization and Its Discontents* (1929) for the view of women as civilizers. For Freud's version of the psychology of women see "Femininity" in James Strachey, trans. and ed., *Complete Introductory Lectures to Psychoanalysis* (New York: W. W. Norton & Co., 1966).

18. John Stuart Mill, *The Subjection of Women* (Philadelphia: J. B. Lippincott, 1869), p. 42.

19. Joseph Leftwich, *Israel Zangwill* (London: James Clarke & Co., Ltd., 1956), p. 12.

20. Floyd Dell, *Love in the Machine Age: A Psychological Study of the Transition from Patriarchal Society* (1930; reprint ed., New York: Farrar, Straus, and Giroux, 1973), pp. 17, 80, 30, 101, 403, 132, 206, 342.

21. See Floyd Dell, *Homecoming, An Autobiography* (1933; reprint ed., New York: Kennikat Press, 1969).

22. See Floyd Dell, *The Outline of Marriage* (London: Richard's Press, 1927).

23. Watson was suspicious of the mother's inclination to exhibit love for her sons, and recommended that all emotion between mother and son be removed lest boys become sissified. The mother who followed such advice quickly encountered another "expert" who attributed juvenile delinquency to lack of love. On the contradictory advice of the "experts," see Barbara Ehrenreich and Deirdre English, *For Her Own Good: 150 Years of the Experts Advice to Women* (New York: Anchor/Doubleday, 1979).

24. Floyd Dell, *An Unmarried Father* (New York: George H. Doran, 1927), p. 265.

25. Floyd Dell, *Love Without Money* (New York: Farrar & Rinehart, 1931), p. 235.

26. John Hart, "Floyd Dell: Intellectual Vagabond," *Western Humanities Review*, Winter 1962.

AFTERWORD

The second feminist wave of the post-World War II world was, in at least one significant respect, different from the first. It was masterminded and organized by women themselves. The latter-day feminists, largely middle-class, college educated women, were in a position, as their forebears were not, to arrive at their own awareness of the inequities that remained women's lot, and to establish the organizations and networks needed to put their case before the public.

After some fifteen years of concentrated effort, the results, at least in the United States, have been disappointing, as feminist leaders themselves admit. The power and influence commensurate with women's numbers in American society is sadly lacking. Moreover, a backlash, coming not only from men—which was to be expected—but also from women—which was not expected—has put in jeopardy the hard-won gains of the feminists. Using the frame of reference of the traitors to masculinity, some hypotheses can be advanced on why the high hopes with which the contemporary feminist wave began have been shattered.

The tradition of philosophical feminism was never as deep-rooted in the United States as it was in England. Philosophical feminists in the United States were, in the main, alienated from the power establishment in a way they were not in England. American feminists embraced as their mentors the social scientists who promoted the sexual revolution and who advanced domestic feminism as the solution to the woman's question. In doing so, they were preeminently ahistorical, and were caught in some fatal contradictions. There was little chance that a movement to unite women could have succeeded when it accepted such dogmas of popular Freudianism as: a female's rejection of her mother's values in favor of partriarchal principles is the hallmark of maturity; competition among women for men is normal feminine behavior; and close friendships between women who eschew the manhunt are suspect, if not pathological, that is, lesbian. The inclination of women to accept their gains on patriarchal terms, rather than imposing their own values on society, was early noted by Israel Zangwill, who maintained that the vote was not a victory for "womanliness," but was in all respects a triumph for "manliness."

Feminists accepted the premises of the sexual revolution, with its emphasis on female sexuality, while rejecting the idea of female intellectual inferiority explicit in a view that holds women to be primarily sexual creatures. They sought to escape the dilemma by proving themselves to be capable of marriage and motherhood as well as a career. The lives of these women, put forward as role models by the media, glorified the ethos of middle-class individualism and the goal of personal fulfillment. They had no relevance and held little inspiration for the great majority of poorer and ethnic women who were trying to survive in a patriarchal world where many had no choice about doing both socially productive labor and performing reproduction services. By contrast the British feminist movement is self-defined as working class and demonstrably anticapitalist.

American feminists acquired an abiding faith in the beneficence of patriarchal authority and in its modern manifestation, the bureaucratic, corporate state. They have maintained this trust even though the realities of American politics have shown that what the left hand gives the right hand in due time takes away. Rather than addressing themselves to issues of concern to poorer women, feminists have focussed on symbols such as the Equal Rights Amendment to advance unity. Many women have visceral doubts that ERA, the specifics of which will be interpreted by an almost totally male power structure, will, in fact, bring with it the much touted advantages claimed by the feminists. Under present circumstances, what Dell called "the patriarchal mind" can easily turn ERA to its own advantage. Indeed, a cursory review of recent litigation reveals that the "rights" men are most eager to grant women are the "right" to be drafted into the armed services; the "right" to support themselves if divorced; and sexual rights—all of which transfer additional burdens and responsibilities to women. It is noteworthy that the former two never appeared on the agenda of any nineteenth-century feminist, whether male or female. The third, it may be argued—and Floyd Dell did—was imposed on women less as a sexual revolution than as a patriarchal reaction. To reason, as some feminists do, that if women are drafted their rights will automatically advance is begging the feminist question. To argue that women are better at the menial and routine tasks that a peacetime army requires, and that they are just as good as men at pressing the buttons that future mechanized warfare will entail, is to abandon a feminist perspective altogether, and suggests that feminist leaders are serving, albeit unwittingly, the masculine cause. Such feminists as Frederick Pethick-Lawrence, when confronted by the physical force advocates, made it clear that women's equality did not hinge on their participation in military service. They maintained that (those) women who wanted to serve should be allowed to do so on a volunteer basis. But women as a class should have the same status as the numerous categories of males who never serve. The values women bring to society are other than military ones, but no less important on that account.

Pornography as a feminist issue has consistently been given short shrift by feminist spokespersons. Women who, like their nineteenth-century forebears, equate sex with violence, and who try to call attention to the one issue—sexual exploitation—that united women of all classes in the nineteenth century, are accused of fostering censorship and of being bent on destroying rights of free expression. The adoption by feminists of an interpretation of free expression that is nothing if not absolute, is all the more incomprehensible in view of the fact that John Stuart Mill, an ardent feminist and committed civil libertarian, stated in *On Liberty* that the welfare of the community—in which he wanted women to have a voice— superseded individual rights.

Fears have been voiced that, in advocating equality, feminists are urging women to march in lockstep toward a future where the sexes are interchangeable. It might be well to conclude by reiterating the belief of the traitors to masculinity that males and females are different in more than physiological characteristics. They posited a female culture and a male culture, each with its unique values. That women had different priorities, modes of thinking, and sexual needs did not render them in any way inferior. That biologists have discovered a substance, oxytocin, which women secrete when they hear a baby cry, is evidence for their theories. The conclusion of the sociobiologists that this relegates women to the domestic sphere would be regarded by the male feminists as simply another manifestation of the masculine cause. It was their firm conviction that women's traits—including a special sensitivity to those in pain or distress—were needed in public life. They considered women's values a vital counterweight to the excesses of the dominant male culture and essential to keep the delicate fabric of civilization from unravelling. They held that the extent to which a society incorporates female principles is a measure of how civilized it is.

BIBLIOGRAPHICAL NOTE

CHAPTER 1

The thought of the early nineteenth century fathers of feminism is intertwined with Utopian Socialism and with the Owenite movement, which is covered in all works on utopian thought. A very incisive discussion of Utopian Socialism, Owen, and the St. Simonians is found in Frank and Fritzie Manuel, *Utopian Thought in the Western World* (Cambridge, 1979). Owenism is an important theme in William Thompson, *The Making of the English Working Class* (New York, 1963), and in Dorothy Thompson, *The Early Chartists* (Columbia, S.C., 1971). Robert Owen's own works are the best source for his ideas; these are expressed in *A New View of Society* (1813) in Robert Owen, *A New View of Society and Other Writings* (New York and London, 1927). Thoughtful interpretations of Owen, his ideas and methods are in Sidney Pollard and John Salt, eds., *Robert Owen: Prophet of the Poor* (Lewisburg, Pa., 1971). A good exposition of Owen's views on marriage is "Robert Owen on the Family and the Marriage System of the Old Immoral World" by John Saville in Maurice Cornforth, ed., *Rebels and Their Causes* (Atlantic Highlands, N.J., 1978). In the numerous biographies of Robert Owen, his educational ideas receive a great deal of attention as do his communitarian experiments. A biography that elaborates on Owen's feminism is J.F.C. Harrison, *Quest for the New Moral World: Robert Owen and the Owenites* (New York, 1969).

Neither George Jacob Holyoake nor William Thompson receives attention in the works on the Utopian Socialists. Thompson is more deserving of such attention than Holyoake because he was a highly original thinker, as his works—*Inquiry into the Distribution of Wealth* (London, 1824), and *An Appeal of One-Half of the Human Race, Women, Against the Pretensions of the Other Half, Men...* (1825, reprint ed., New York, 1970)—reveal. The only biography of Thompson was written by Richard Pankhurst (grandson of Emmeline and Richard, of feminist fame): *William Thompson* (London, 1954). The work establishes Thompson's credentials as the founder of British social democracy and as a major influence on Robert Owen's cooperative phase.

The writings of George Jacob Holyoake illustrate that the male feminists were skillful propagandists in all the causes, feminism included, that they undertook. One need not mine unpublished material, as these men took great pains to put their message before the public. Holyoake advocated feminism, secularism, and cooperation through such journals as *The Reasoner* and *The Secularist*, and was also an inveterate writer of letters to newspapers. He commemorated Robert Owen, Richard Carlile, and Tom Paine in pamphlet form. *Bygones Worth Remembering* (London, 1906) contains occasional pieces and comments on specific issues in which he had an interest. His autobiography, *Sixty Years of An Agitator's Life* (London, 1893), is a very rich source of information on personalities and events of his long life and is a testimony to his commitment. The only biography of him, a hero-worshipping account, is by a fellow feminist and secularist, Joseph McCabe: *Life and Letters of George Jacob Holyoake* (New York, 1922).

There is no dearth of sources on John Stuart Mill. For an understanding of Mill, his *Autobiography* (London, 1873), published posthumously and edited by Helen Taylor, is still essential reading. *The Subjection of Women* (1869) is obtainable in a number of editions; the best is in *Essays on Sex Equality* (Chicago, 1970), edited and with an excellent introductory essay by Alice Rossi. The most detailed biography of Mill is *The Life of John Stuart Mill*, by Michael St. John Packe (New York, 1954). A work that sheds light on his relationship with Harriet Mill is *John Stuart Mill and Harriet Taylor* (London, 1951), by F. A. Hayek. Controversy persists on how germane feminism was to Mill's political and economic thought and on the derivation of his feminism. In *On Liberty and Liberalism: The Case of John Stuart Mill* (New York, 1974), Gertrude Himmelfarb argues that feminism is pervasive in Mill's work—specifically in his *On Liberty*— and she believes Harriet Taylor's influence to have been decisive. That there were "two Mills," and that the rationalist was in conflict with the emotional feminist in him, is the conservative position taken in the late nineteenth century by the antifeminist A. V. Dicey. The "two Mills" theory readily lends itself to psychobiography, and Bruce Mazlish has used this method in *James and John Stuart Mill* (New York, 1975). Mazlish's book also puts forward the theory that Harriet Taylor Mill's influence was the source of Mill's feminism.

CHAPTER 2

Vern Bullough, *Sexual Variance in Society and History* (New York, 1976) is important in documenting trends in sexual behavior. Useful works that shed light on the moral impulses of the Victorians are: David J. Pivar, *Purity Crusade* (Westport, Ct., 1973); Eric Trudgill, *Madonnas and Magdalens* (New York, 1976); Edward Bristow, *Vice and Vigilance: Purity Movements in Britain Since*

1700 (London, 1977); and Constance Rover, *Love, Morals, and the Feminists* (London, 1970).

Michel Foucault, *History of Sexuality* (New York, 1978), deals with efforts by scientific authorities to exercise social control through investigations into sexuality, and concentrates on the nineteenth century. In the same vein, emphasizing secular interest in sexual behavior, is Angus McLaren's "Some Secular Attitudes Toward Sexual Behavior in France, 1760-1860," in *French Historical Studies*, vol. 8, no. 4. The subject of scientists and physicians who serve the interests of patriarchal authority the way domestic feminists did is one that deserves further study. On woman's nature and how conceptions of it changed in the late eighteenth century, see H. C. Marlow and H. M. Davis, *The American Search for Woman* (Santa Barbara, Calif., 1976).

Recent articles have suggested some positive aspects of the Victorian sex code for women. Carol Smith Rosenberg, "The Female World of Love and Ritual," and Nancy Cott, "Passionlessness: An Interpretation of Victorian Sexual Ideology, 1790-1850," are prime examples. Both articles are in Nancy Cott and Elizabeth Pleck, eds., *A Heritage of Her Own* (New York, 1979).

The Contagious Diseases Acts have inspired two recent works: Judith Walkowitz, *Prostitution and Victorian Society: Women, Class and the State* (New York, 1980), focusses on the social implications and suggests the importance of involvement by males in financing and organizing the repeal groups: Paul McHugh, *Prostitution and Victorian Social Reform* (London, 1980), discusses the CD Acts from a political standpoint.

William Stead's writings are voluminous. As a newspaper editor, he had ample opportunity to express his feminism, and did so in such works as *The Life of Mrs. Booth* (London, 1900). Stead as a central figure in the development of popular journalism is treated in J. W. Robertson, *Life and Death of a Newspaper* (London, 1952). Frederic Whyte's *The Life of William Stead* (Boston, 1925) remains the only authoritative biography. Because of the diversity of Stead's acquaintances—from William Gladstone to the whole complement of feminist leaders—as well as wide involvement in reform movements, he deserves more attention from historians.

Several works examine the civil libertarian issues raised by the white slavery exposé. Among them are; Ann Stafford, *The Age of Consent* (London, 1963); Michael Pearson, *The Age of Consent: Victorian Prostitution and Its Enemies* (Newton Abbot, Eng., 1972); Alison Plowden, *The Case of Eliza Armstrong* (London, 1974).

CHAPTER 3

The secondary literature on birth control is extensive. An overall view is provided by Norman Hines, *Medical History of Contraception* (Baltimore, 1936, reprint ed., New York, 1970). Extremely informative is *The Birth Controllers*

(London, 1965), by Peter Fryer. More recent works have been inspired by the women's movement and examine birth control as a feminist issue. These include: J. A. and Olive Banks, *Feminism and Family Planning in Victorian England* (New York, 1964); Linda Gordon, *Women's Bodies, Women's Rights: A Social History of Birth Control in America* (New York, 1976); and Angus McLaren, *Birth Control in Nineteenth Century England* (New York, 1978). McLaren's work is especially important because it takes issue with the Banks, who deny the feminist roots of birth control. The Banks ignore the phenomenon of male feminism, while McLaren recognizes it in his study, and gives Francis Place and Richard Carlile credentials as feminist reformers. Rosanna Ledbetter, *A History of the Malthusian League, 1827-1927* (Columbus, Ohio, 1976) is, in essence, a history of the remarkable Drysdale family, and the best source for information on the three generations who devoted themselves to popularizing birth control. One would wish for a specialized study of George Drysdale because of the revolutionary aspects of *Elements of Social Science*. Biographies of Charles Bradlaugh stress the civil libertarian issue in his trial; for the feminist aspects of the Bradlaugh-Besant trial, works by and about Annie Besant are better sources. The most noteworthy of these is Arthur Nethercott, *The First Five Lives of Annie Besant* (Chicago, 1960).

CHAPTER 4

From the time Humphrey Noyes established Oneida in 1848, social reformers showed interest in the community, and it has not abated. Of special interest to feminists is Constance Noyes Robertson, *The Oneida Community: An Autobiography, 1851-1876* (Syracuse, N.Y., 1970). She elaborates on Noyes's proposal to socialize the motherhood instinct. A very incisive discussion of sex roles at Oneida is contained in Louis J. Kern, *Three Nineteenth Century Utopias: Oneida, the Mormons, and the Shakers* (Chapel Hill, N.C., 1980). Maren Lockwood Carden, *Oneida: Utopian Community to Modern Corporation* (New York, 1969) focusses on the decline of the communitarian ideal and the attempt to secularize Oneida. Robert A. Parker's *Yankee Saint* (New York, 1975) is a very good biography which places the man in his time. Robert David Thomas, *The Man Who Would Be Perfect: John Humphrey Noyes and the Utopian Impulse* (Philadelphia, Pa., 1977) is a psychological study of Noyes; but in dwelling on his aggressions and oedipal feelings, Thomas fails to come to grips with Noyes's charisma.

Karl Pearson's ideas on the woman's question are contained in *The Ethic of Freethought* (London, 1901). A critical biography of Pearson is sorely needed. Lacking one, biographies of Olive Schreiner and Havelock Ellis, close acquaintances, give some indication of the extent of Pearson's influence. A biography of Pearson would do much to illuminate the Social Darwinism, the racism, and the authoritarianism that infiltrated the thinking of the domestic feminists. Bernard

Semmel, *Imperialism and Social Reform* (New York, 1960), has a good discussion of these aspects of Pearson's thought.

Pearson's American counterpart, Edward Bellamy, has received a good deal of attention lately: William Leach, *True Love and Perfect Union: The Feminist Reform of Sex and Society* (New York, 1980), details the role feminists played in Bellamy's Nationalist Clubs. Arthur Lipow, *Authoritarian Socialism in America: Edward Bellamy and the Nationalist Movement* (Berkeley, Ca., 1982) explores the roots and legacies of America's national socialist movement.

Indications of Havelock Ellis's contributions to the sexual revolution are contained not only in major works such as *Studies in the Psychology of Sex* (New York, 1912), but in the numerous articles he wrote for popular journals in both England and America. His writings have been collected by Paul Robinson in *The Modernization of Sex* (New York, 1976). Edward Brecher, *The Sex Researchers* (Boston, 1969), is also helpful. Phyllis Grosskurth's biography, *Havelock Ellis* (New York, 1980), is very comprehensive and revealing.

CHAPTER 5

Some excellent guides to the shaping of the new woman as an intellectual are: Patricia Thomson, *The Victorian Heroine, A Changing Ideal, 1837-1873* (Westport, Ct., 1978); Gail Cunningham, *The New Woman and the Victorian Novel* (London, 1977); and Lloyd Fernando, *"New Women" in the Late Victorian Novel* (University Park, Pa., 1977).

Other works of Meredith, Hardy, and Shaw reveal their feminist concerns. Criticism of the male ego is inherent in Meredith's *Ordeal of Richard Feverel* (1859); *Beauchamp's Career* (1875); and *The Egoist* (1879). *One of Our Conquerors* (1891) and *Lord Ormont and His Aminta* (1894) are antimarriage novels. Hardy's *Tess of the D'Urbervilles* (1891) is a strong indictment of the double standard of sexual morality. Rodell Weintraub, ed., *Fabian Feminist* (University Park, Pa., 1977) contains a number of essays that analyze Shaw's feminism. Shaw's feminist leanings are very evident in such plays as *Getting Married* (1901); *Candida* (1904); *Misalliance* (1909); and *St. Joan* (1924). The plays and novels are available in many editions.

CHAPTERS 6 AND 7

The politics of the late nineteenth century have been very elaborately covered. But the capacity for the issue of women's suffrage to cause conflict in the Liberal party, and its significance in the formation of the Labor party, have been ignored. Important recent works that deal with the suffrage issue are Roger Fulford, *Votes for Women: The Story of a Struggle* (London, 1958); Constance Rover, *Women's Suffrage and Party Politics in Britain 1866-1914* (London, 1968);

David Morgan, *Suffragists and Liberals* (Oxford, 1975); and Brian Harrison, *Separate Spheres* (New York, 1978).

It has been possible to understate the importance of women's suffrage in English party politics because of the woeful neglect of such central figures as Jacob Bright, Richard Pankhurst, and Frederick Pethick-Lawrence. This is due in part to the activism of these men, which left them little time to pen the voluminous diaries and correspondence that are the historian's meat. Jacob Bright's speeches were published by women's suffrage societies, and evidence of his dedication to the suffrage movement can be gleaned from parliamentary records. Jacob Bright and his more famous brother, John Bright, might well provide a fruitful subject for someone interested in family history.

Richard Pankhurst has been thoroughly eclipsed by his flamboyant wife, Emmeline. His importance in the formation of the Labour party is brought out in the memoirs of Emmeline and Sylvia Pankhurst, and by writers such as David Mitchell, who recorded the family's deeds in *The Fighting Pankhursts* (New York, 1967). Richard Pankhurst's role is not covered in any of the histories of the Labour party. Similarly, the importance of feminism in the early days of the Labour party is ignored, although it is made explicit in the memoirs and biographies of Keir Hardie, Philip Snowden, and George Lansbury.

Frederick Pethick-Lawrence is a pivotal figure because he links socialism, feminism, and pacifism. The organ of the suffragettes, *Votes for Women*, which he edited, is an important primary source for information of these three movements. The only biography of him, Vera Brittain's *Pethick-Lawrence: A Portrait* (London, 1963), is entirely creditable, but written in the manner of a memorial. Pethick-Lawrence's memoirs, *Fate Has Been Kind* (London, 1942), and those of Emmeline Pethick-Lawrence, *My Part in a Changing World* (London, 1938), are extremely valuable.

The Proceedings of the women's rights conventions in the United States, starting in 1851 are a basic source on male participation in the American women's movement. Thomas Wentworth Higginson's contributions to feminism are substantial. They include *Women and Her Wishes* (Rochester, 1851) *The Women's Rights Almanac for 1858: Facts, Statistics, Records of, and Proofs of the Need for It* (Boston, 1857); *Ought Women to Learn the Alphabet* (Manchester, Eng., 1873); *Common Sense About Women* (London, 1891); *Women and Men* (New York, 1888). Higginson wrote biographies of prominent women such as *Margaret Fuller Ossoli* (Boston, 1884) and was a member of a collective which put together an encyclopedia, *Woman: Her Position, Influence and Achievement Throughout the Civilized World* (Springfield, Mass., 1901).

CHAPTER 8

Women's history written by men who tried to remove themselves from it should be of special interest to historiographers. The foregoing is with reference to W. Lyon Blease, *The Emancipation of the Englishwoman* (London, 1910) and H. N. Brailsford, *Shelley, Godwin and Their Circle* (New York, 1913). Of more than passing interest is Joseph McCabe, who carried the secular, socialist and feminist tradition of such feminist fathers as George Jacob Holyoake well into the twentieth century. McCabe's output of articles and books, on subjects ranging from evolution to the links between the Nazis and the Vatican, is staggering.

For the cultural influences on Sigmund Freud's thought, see Carl Schorske, *Fin-de-Siècle Vienna* (New York, 1980); and L. Toulmin and A. Janik, *Wittgenstein's Vienna* (New York, 1973). Both works place Freud in his increasingly antiliberal milieu. Freud has recently sustained a number of attacks. His publicity-mongering is exposed in Frank J. Sulloway, *Freud, Biologist of the Mind: Beyond the Psychoanalytic Legend* (New York, 1979). Freud's veracity has been questioned in Florence Rush, *The Best Kept Secret: Sexual Abuse of Children* (New York, 1981). In *Shrinking History* (New York, 1980) David Stannard has questioned whether Freudian assumptions have any validity or relevance for historians. A view of female psychology substantially in line with the thinking of the philosophical feminists is elaborated in Carol Gilligan, *In a Different Voice* (Cambridge, Mass., 1981).

Floyd Dell's wide-ranging mind makes his self-designation, "intellectual vagabond" a very apt one. His critiques of patriarchy, in *Love in the Machine Age* (New York, 1930), in his essays, and in his novels, are remarkably perspicacious, and have as much relevance after fifty years as they had in the late 1920s and early 1930s. A very affecting essay is *Were You Ever a Child?* (New York, 1919). Other novels that elaborate his ideas are *This Mad Ideal* (New York, 1925), *An Old Man's Folly* (New York, 1926), and *Souvenir* (New York, 1929).

INDEX

About the Author

SYLVIA STRAUSS is Associate Professor of History at Kean College in New Jersey. She has published articles on women's history in *The South Atlantic Quarterly Review*, *Papers in Women's Studies*, and *Memorandum*.

Recent Titles in
Contributions in Women's Studies